Disaster Law

This book looks at how legal frameworks can and do reduce risks arising out of disasters. The volume:

- analyses existing disaster laws and the challenges on the ground;
- brings together case studies from some of the most vulnerable regions; and
- proposes solutions to avert existing and possible future crises.

The book offers appropriate legal frameworks for disaster management which could not only offer sustainable institutional reforms towards community resilience and preparedness but also reduce risk within the frameworks of justice, equity and accountability. It examines the intricacies of governance within which governments function and discusses how recent trends in infrastructure development and engineering technology could be balanced within the legal principles of ethics, transparency and integrity. The chapters in the volume suggest that legal frameworks ought to resonate with new challenges of resource management and climate change. Further, these frameworks could help secure citizens' trust, institutional accountability and effective implementation through an unceasing partnership which keeps the community better prepared and more resilient.

This volume will be indispensable to scholars and researchers of disaster management, law, public policy, environment and development studies as well as policymakers and those in administrative, governmental, judicial and development sectors.

Amita Singh is Professor and Chairperson at the Centre for the Study of Law and Governance, Jawaharlal Nehru University (JNU), New Delhi, India.

'This book is a significant step toward a better understanding of how legal frameworks promote incentives for undertaking risk reduction activities, and how disaster risk reduction (DRR), in turn, helps advance legal reform, which includes migrating away from old ways and aligning laws so that they can deliver fresh results. It offers a timely antidote to the existing top–down pattern of DRR.'

– **Eduardo T. Gonzalez,** *Professor, Center for Integrative Development Studies, University of the Philippines*

Disaster Law
Emerging Thresholds

Edited by Amita Singh

Routledge
Taylor & Francis Group

First published 2018 by Routledge

2 Park Square, Milton Park, Abingdon, Oxfordshire OX14 4RN
52 Vanderbilt Avenue, New York, NY 10017

Routledge is an imprint of the Taylor & Francis Group, an informa business

First issued in paperback 2019

British Library Cataloguing-in-Publication Data
A catalogue record for this book is available from the British Library

Library of Congress Cataloging-in-Publication Data
A catalog record for this book has been requested

ISBN: 978-1-138-03643-7 (hbk)
ISBN: 978-0-367-27776-5 (pbk)

Typeset in Sabon
by Apex CoVantage, LLC

Contents

Illustrations

Figures

Tables

Contributors

Md Akbaruddin Ahmad is Director and Professor, Bircham International University, Spain; Vice Chancellor, Darul Ihsan University, Bangladesh; and Chairman of the leading civil society think tank, Policy Research Centre.bd (PRC-BD). He is also the Chairman (Administration) of the Network of Asia Pacific Schools and Institute of Public Administration and Governance (NAPSIPAG) at the University of Sri Jayewardenepura, Sri Lanka. He is the editor-in-chief of *Finance World Ltd*, a weekly tabloid.

Venkatachalam Anbumozhi is a senior economist at the Economic Research Institute for ASEAN and East Asia (ERIA), Indonesia, and has a doctorate from the University of Tokyo. Previously a Capacity Building Specialist and Senior Fellow at Asian Development Bank Institute, he was also Assistant Professor at the University of Tokyo. He has published several books, authored numerous research articles and project reports on natural resource management, climate-friendly infrastructure design and private sector participation in green growth. He was invited to the APEC Expert Panel on Green Climate Finance and the ASEAN Panel for promoting climate-resilient growth. He has taught Development Finance and co-areas at the University of Tokyo and has had speaking engagements at some of the leading international organizations.

Manjula Batra is Professor and former Dean of the Faculty of Law, Jamia Millia Islamia, New Delhi, India. She is also the Chairperson of the Ordinance Committee of Jamia Millia Islamia. She has previously served as Professor and Director at the School of Law, Vivekananda Institute of Professional Studies at the Guru Gobind Singh Indraprastha University, New Delhi. She has over 27 years of experience in teaching graduate and post-graduate students. She has also been a legal consultant to different organisations. She has authored several books and articles on matters relating to environmental and disaster law, and is a keen investigator of tort law, criminal justice administration, criminology and evidence law.

Rabindranath Bhattacharyya is Professor and Head of the Department of Political Science, University of Burdwan, West Bengal, India. He is a recipient of the Australian Government Endeavour Post-Doctoral Research Fellowship, 2009 and AIC Australian Studies (Senior) Visiting Fellowship 2007–2008. He was also appointed Australia Awards Ambassador by the Australian High Commissioner to India in 2014. He is the author of the books *Land, Leadership and Local Resource Management* (2016) and *Governance and Poverty Reduction: Beyond the Cage of Best Practices* (2009). He has also written several national and international papers and book chapters, in addition to his contribution to workshops and conferences. His research area focuses on democratic governance, including environmental governance, across countries with special focus on poverty alleviation programmes and the role of different groups.

P. K. Chaubey is Professor of Economics and Management at the University of Allahabad, Banaras Hindu University (BHU) and the Indian Institute of Public Administration, New Delhi, India. A specialist in training mid-career and senior civil servants in public policy and finance, he has published several books and research papers for the National Council for Educational Research and Training (NCERT), Indira Gandhi National Open University (IGNOU) and *Publius*. He is on the Editorial Board of several journals of economics, management and social sciences, and a recipient of several awards such as the Young Social Scientist Award, Dr Radhakrishnan Samman in Social Science, Dr DP Mukerji Fellowship, Schumpeter Distinguished Fellowship and UP Kautilya Award.

Yan Cui is Lecturer at the School of Law, Shandong University, Weihai, China. She is also Lecturer and International Program Coordinator, Faculty of Law, Shandong University, China.

Ramratan Dhumal is Assistant Professor at the Campus Law Centre, Department of Law, University of Delhi, India. He holds a Master of Philosophy and has submitted a doctoral thesis on 'Constitutionalism and Eminent Domain' at the Centre for the Study of Law and Governance, Jawaharlal Nehru University, New Delhi. His research interests include comparative constitutional law, criminology, human rights, governance and gender justice.

Mondira Dutta is Professor at the Centre for Inner Asian Studies, School of International Studies, Jawaharlal Nehru University, New Delhi, India. She has previously been a Chairperson and the Director of UGC Central Asia Area Studies Programme, Consultant to several national and international organizations such as the British Council, Ford Foundation, NOVIB (the Netherlands), the DFID, the World Bank, International Human Rights Commission (Geneva), Human Rights Commission (Maldives), UN Women (South Asia) and the Government of India as a Senior Advisor to the Ministry of Women and Child Development, Government of India in 2011. She has been a guest researcher at the Stockholm University, Sweden (2012). Currently she is engaged in driving the Disaster Research Programme anchored by the National Institute of Disaster Management and the Ministry of Home Affairs. Her research interests include gender and human security, violence against women, trafficking, child labour and disaster mitigation and community participation.

Gabrielle Emery is the Coordinator for the Disaster Law Programme at the International Red Cross and Red Crescent Societies (IFRC) Asia Pacific Regional Office based in Malaysia. She has a master's degree in International Human Rights Law and has graduated in Law and in Japanese. She has worked as Policy and Advocacy Manager for New Zealand Red Cross and was the Humanitarian and Development Adviser for New Zealand Ministry of Foreign Affairs and Trade at its Permanent Mission to the United Nations in New York. She has also worked with refugee and migrant organisations in the UK and Ireland.

Nivedita P. Haran is a civil servant with the Government of India in the state of Kerala. With a doctorate in Sociology and Public Administration from the Indian Institute of Technology Delhi, she has been a visionary strategist in not just being the first to initiate the State Disaster Management Authority under the Disaster Management Act 2005 in Kerala but also initiating the Young Administrators and Academia Forum within the Asia Pacific Governance Network (NAPSIPAG) to bridge the gap between policymakers and practitioners with academic researchers and training institutions. She was acknowledged for having participated in the UN peace-keeping mission in Kosovo to bring peace among warring ethnic groups. She is now a consultant with the Disaster Research Programme at Jawaharlal Nehru University, New Delhi, leads the Centre for Innovations in Public Systems, Hyderabad, and also heads the Ente Bhoomi Trust in Kerala.

Shibo Jiang is Professor and a master's instructor, School of Law, Shandong University at Weihai; Director of the Institute of International and Comparative Law; a member of the Academic Committee; and a member of the school teaching Steering Committee. She has been mainly engaged in teaching and research work in international economic law, private international law, international commercial law and the theory of international law. Her main area of research is international law and jurisprudence.

Stellina Jolly is Assistant Professor at the South Asian University (SAU), New Delhi, India. Her teaching interests include international environmental law, conflict of laws and bio-ethics, and she has published many articles in the field. She has worked with the Rajiv Gandhi Foundation, Delhi, on a research project to develop indicators for the 'Rule of Law' for various states in India. She is part of the Expert Group on National Consultation on Rule of Law project in the National Law University (NLU), Delhi. She has been part of the editorial board of peer-reviewed journals, including the *Indian Journal of Human Rights*, the *International Journal of Bioethics*, the *NUJS International Journal of Legal Studies and Research* and the *Kuwaiti Journal of Health Care Management*. She has been a visiting professor at the Indian Institute of Public Administration (IIPA), the Indian Society of International Law (ISIL) and the National Law University Delhi.

Manika Kamthan is a lawyer and completed her BA, LLB and LLM from Aligarh Muslim University, India. Her master's thesis is on 'Women in Prisons' from the Centre for the Study of Law & Governance (CSLG), Jawaharlal Nehru University, and is thereafter working on 'Women in Agriculture in India' for her doctoral thesis. She has published many research papers in reputed journals and has presented papers in conferences. Her interest areas include gender, politics of identity, constitutional law and environment studies.

Sumaiya Khair is Professor at the Department of Law, University of Dhaka, Bangladesh, where she served as Head of the Department of Law from 2009 to 2011. She has been serving at Transparency International Bangladesh (TIB) as its Deputy Executive Director since July 2013. She finished her doctorate from the UK where she studied as a Commonwealth Post-Doctoral Academic Fellow. Her areas of interest and research include human rights, child rights, legal empowerment, refugee and migration, governance, labour standards and gender issues. She consults for UN agencies and international development partners on rights and governance issues and serves as a resource person in her areas of expertise in national, regional and international forums. She is part of governing boards of several rights-based development sector organisations.

Binod Kumar is a doctoral candidate at the Centre for the Study of the Law and Governance, Jawaharlal Nehru University (JNU), New Delhi, India. He specializes in disaster law and community resilience. He is a lawyer by training with an additional training in socio-legal studies from Tata Institute of Social Sciences, Mumbai. He has a multi-disciplinary background and holds a special interest in ecology, disaster and law.

Himanshu Shekhar Mishra is a journalist and Editor (Government Affairs) at NDTV, a major TV news channel in India. He has a master's degree in Philosophy from the School of International Studies, Jawaharlal Nehru University, New Delhi, India. He has been part of several prestigious assignments, including the Prime Minister's official entourage to the UN Annual Summit held in New York in September 2003; Indo-Turkish Summit, Ankara, September 2003; SAARC Summit Islamabad in January 2004; and Prime Minister Manmohan Singh's first official visit to Afghanistan, Kabul, in August 2005. His exemplary journalistic skills and stifling helplessness during the devastating floods in Jammu and Kashmir (2014) brought out the researcher in him as he started investigating the governance failures during disasters and presenting his studies at the Disaster Research Programme of Jawaharlal Nehru University; UN World Conference on Disaster Risk Reduction in Sendai, Japan (2015); and AUN/SEED-Net Regional Conferences on Natural Disaster, Manila (2015) and Kuala Lumpur (2016).

Ved Mittal is a visiting faculty member in Urban Planning, School of Planning and Architecture (SPA), New Delhi, India, and a short-term consultant at the World Bank Mission. He has worked as chief architect and town planner with various development authorities in Uttar Pradesh. He planned the first World Bank–aided urban development project in Kanpur, Uttar Pradesh, and worked with the US National Park Service Team for planning of the Taj National Park. After his retirement, he has worked as Consultant UNDP on Techno-Legal Regime for Safety against Natural Hazards with the objective to suggest amendments in town and country planning acts, land use zoning regulations, development controls and building by-laws of the states and UTs in India.

Sanghamitra Nath is a doctoral researcher at the Centre for the Study of Law and Governance in Jawaharlal Nehru University (JNU), New Delhi, India. She is part of the research group of Disaster Research Programme, JNU. She was awarded the Junior Research Fellowship by the University Grants Commission in 2012. She worked as a resource person for IGNOU Public Administration for Right to Information (PG Diploma) modules and was invited as chair and discussant to many international conferences (USA, Germany, Turkey). Her research interests include disaster management, sustainable development, climate change, poverty, gender and international politics.

Padmini Nayagam is Officer for the Disaster Law Programme at the International Red Cross and Red Crescent Societies (IFRC) Asia Pacific Regional Office based in Malaysia. The disaster law programme seeks to provide support through Red Cross and Red Crescent National Societies to governments to strengthen their disaster-related legal frameworks in order to regulate the flow of international assistance into a country during a disaster, and also with regard to disaster risk reduction legislation and policy. Previously she has worked as Legal Editor for LexisNexis Malaysia and at a law firm in Kuala Lumpur, Malaysia.

Sunita Reddy is Associate Professor at the Center of Social Medicine and Community Health, School of Social Sciences, Jawaharlal Nehru University, New Delhi, India. She is an anthropologist, specializes in medical anthropology and has worked on various issues of women and child health, childbirth, child-rearing practices and tribal health. She has researched on disaster issues from a social science perspective and published the book *Clash of Waves: Post-Tsunami Relief and Rehabilitation in Andaman and Nicobar Islands* (2013). She has also co-edited *Marginalization in Globalizing Delhi: Issues of Land, Livelihood and Health* (2016). Her current areas of research are public–private partnership in medical care, medical tourism and surrogacy issues. She is a founder member of Anthropos India Foundation, a trust that promotes visual and action anthropology.

Renu K. Sharma is UGC Post-Doctoral Fellow at Special Centre for Sanskrit Studies, Jawaharlal Nehru University, New Delhi, India. She has written a book and more than 20 research papers.

Amita Singh is Professor and Chairperson at the Centre for the Study of Law and Governance, Jawaharlal Nehru University (JNU), New

Delhi, India and the longest-serving Secretary General of the Network of Asia Pacific Schools and Institutes of Public Administration and Governance (NAPSIPAG), located in Colombo, Sri Lanka. She leads the Disaster Research Programme and the Institutional Ethics Review Board at JNU. As a scholar of administrative reforms and policy implementation, she has served in many national and international boards and committees on adopting new and innovative administrative practices which are sustainable as well as just. She has received several awards and worked closely with many government and academic institutions including the Government Innovators Network at the John F. Kennedy School of Government at Harvard University, Australia India Council Fellowship of 2006 and collaborated extensively with other universities in the UK, Nepal, Pakistan, Sri Lanka, China and Bangladesh. She has edited six and authored four books. Her recent writings include 'Coastal Ballads and Conservation Ironic: Understanding Implementation Slippages' in the *Economic and Political Weekly* (2016); 'Disaster Law and Community Resilience', *Delhi Law Review* (2016); 'Disaster Law: The Rubric of Institutional Preparedness in Disaster Risk Reduction', Middle East Institute, www.mei.edu/content/disaster-law-rubric-institutional-preparedness-disaster-risk-reduction (2016); 'Culling Animals: A Myopic View', *India Legal Magazine* (July 2016); and 'A Myopic View', *Power Politics* (September 2016).

Subhalakshmi Sircar is Assistant Professor of Economics at the Management Development Institute, Gurgaon, India. Her consultancies at the Planning Commission, New Delhi, and contribution to the Eleventh Five Year Plan document have been specially acknowledged. She specializes in the training of executives from leading private and public sector companies such as ONGC, IOCL and BHEL, as well as senior defence personnel. She is an institutional economist for ecosystem sensitive ergonomics, and her research interests are in macroeconomic theory, monetary economics, international macroeconomics and finance.

Deepa Sonpal is Programme Coordinator with the NGO Unnati Organisation for Development Education based in Ahmedabad, Gujarat, India. She completed her master's degree in Social Work from the Tata Institute of Social Sciences, Mumbai. For the past 25 years, she has engaged as a development educator in promoting participatory development, and gender and disability rights. Her specific interest lies in exploring the potential for inclusion of the marginalized and vulnerable communities – specifically persons with disabilities, especially women – in the mainstream development process, researching, engaging in policy advocacy and law-making processes.

Shiranee Tilakawardane has the distinction of being appointed as the first female State Counsel in Sri Lanka in 1978, the first female judge of the High Court, the first woman Admiralty Court Judge, the first woman Justice of the Court of Appeal and the first woman President of the Court of Appeal. Her research interests include equality, gender and child rights, and she holds honorary doctorates in Law from Smith College and William's College, USA. She has helped draft the SAARC protocol on trafficking of men, women and children and the initial guidelines for child witness testimony for adoption in the ICC. She was awarded a fellowship in 'Human Rights, International Law and Intervention' from Brandeis University, USA, and has received accolades including the Sakshi of India Award and the International Zonta Award for contributions to Law, as well as awards from Canada and the USA.

Md Akmal Wasim has extensive experience in legal practice. He is an Advocate of the Supreme Court of Pakistan. After spending 20 years as a litigator, he opted for legal academics and was affiliated to the Faculty of Law, Hamdard University as Associate Professor for 14 years. He was also associated with the Committee for the Welfare of Prisoners in the Province of Sindh, where he worked as Head of Litigation & Research, for providing *pro bono* legal services to under-trial prisoners. He has served as Assistant Advocate General, Government of Sindh, and later as Advisor, Federal Ministry of Human Rights, Member of the International Law Organizations as World Jurists Association, Law Asia and American Bar Association. He has also drafted legislations such as the (Model) Sindh Police Act, 2014, and is currently involved in the study of Pakistan's Criminal Justice System.

Abha Yadav is a legal officer at Jawaharlal Nehru University (JNU), New Delhi, India. She has previously been a faculty member at the University of Delhi and is currently Central Public Information Officer at JNU under the Right to Information Act 2005. She is the recipient of the prestigious Fox International Fellowship from Yale University, USA, and has studied Intellectual Property Management from the Indian Institute of Technology Delhi. She has conducted training sessions for senior managers in various prestigious institutions and has worked closely with NGOs for social causes and to spread awareness about women-centric themes and Right to Information. She has also presented papers in national and international conferences and seminars.

Shishir Kumar Yadav is a research scholar at the Centre of Social Medicine and Community Health (CSMCH) in Jawaharlal Nehru University, New Delhi, India. He is an anthropologist by training, and his doctorate work explores livelihood issues in relation to recurrent floods. He has a master's in Anthropology from Allahabad University and a diploma in Hindi Journalism from the Indian Institute of Mass Communication (IIMC), New Delhi. A recipient of Senior Research Fellowship by the University Grants Commission, his papers and presentations have been included in several conferences. His interest areas include disaster studies, international humanitarian relief and rescue policies.

Preface

This dialogue on disaster law was ignited as the negligent, unreliable and inexplicable institutional behaviour and brazen governance got exposed during the 2013 Uttarakhand cloudburst. As bodies of humans and animals were flowing down the sacred Ganges, people unleashed violence and hatred against administrative and political decision makers in Rishikesh and Dehradun. The Asia Pacific Governance Network (NAPSIPAG) held night-long discussions at MC Mehta's 'Eco Ashram' in Dehradun valley on 20 June 2013 immediately after the devastating Uttarakhand cloudburst and floods. When the academia critiqued the framework of development, much responsibility was found to be that of government and non-government local institutions and insulated scientific discoveries. Every city created a disaster by ignoring the norms of nature and the limits of human greed. These scholars found great similarity in the manner that disasters were dealt with across different regions of the world. From Louisiana in USA to Uttarakhand in India, preparedness was missing in the disaster management vocabulary of administrative institutions, highlighting more than ever before that disasters were an outcome of bad governance against which 'law' is the only messiah.

Social scientists realized that the new challenge was to collaborate and strengthen partnerships between scientists and administrators. In an activist-driven seminar at the Centre for the Study of Law and Governance, many sociologists, including Susan Vishvanathan from JNU, indicated that the blocking of Neela Hauz water body in Delhi was a disaster in the making as much as the *tongas* (horse carts) being driven out of the old city areas. The government and the scientists had no clue to link such unrelated factors as emerging causes of disasters. If trawlers improved fish business in coastal areas and mechanized boats improved livelihood in backwater lakes, why would it become a cause for disasters? If farmers decide to grow rice instead of wheat, on what rationale would the government regulate their freedom of choice? Poverty, unemployment, labour welfare and low per capita income had become the sacred shrines of governance, and anything in their favour was justified. Such anthropological, sociological and critical governance perspectives challenged the ongoing disaster management strategies.

More research was needed from communities and isolated administrative initiatives on these new emerging but overlapping domains of societies. Faculty from seven centres in JNU came together: Prof. Mondira Dutta, Dr Sunita Reddy, Prof. Bupinder Zutshi, Prof. GVC Naidu, Prof. Milap Punia, Mr Sanjeev Kumar and Prof. Vaishna Narang constituted the initial team. Realizing the phenomenal dependence of disaster management research on geo-spatial, GIS, plate tectonic, remote sensing and satellite imagery, the DRP team broadened to include some teachers from the sciences. The need for developing a cognitive domain of administration and communities in the context of compliance and acceptability of disaster law led to DRP's research linkages with the youth in Delhi university colleges through 'Neighbourhood Mapping Programme' of looking into their local disaster management institutions and community vulnerability to earthquakes and urban floods. As young boys and girls moved through the clustered hotspots of disasters within the city, it became more and more evident that disasters were being created and nurtured between the information deficit of people and the absence of administrative accountability in sustaining that. As young students from Miranda House, Lady Shri Ram College and Kamala Nehru College (they are partners in the DRP) started visiting these city hotspots of disasters in the Lal Dora (community land out of municipal boundaries) land areas, they discovered the 'total regime of irresponsibility' despite the warnings of science and law. In nurturing this regime, the administrator was not alone to be blamed as the role played by the community institutions such as the Resident Welfare Institutions, Market Associations, local caste panchayats, community realtors, religious community groups, Waqf Board and cultural and festivity forums were all at par in weakening the city master plans which itself winked on enforcement.

The emergence of DRP fulfils a long-awaited requirement of international specialized agencies of the United Nations (Economic and Social Council Resolution 1999/63 and in General Assembly Resolutions 56/195, 58/214, and 58/215) to create 'National Platforms' for coordinating and providing policy guidance on disaster risk reduction in a multi-sectoral and inter-disciplinary manner which could involve public, private and civil society participation, including all country-specific

United Nations agencies. These 'National Platforms' were expected to represent the national mechanism for the International Strategy for Disaster Reduction, which in the 2014–2015 multi-year programme of the Commission on Sustainable Development selected the theme of 'vulnerability, risk reduction and disaster management'. This provided the best opportunity for interdisciplinary social sciences research to take a leap into transformations awaited and ignored in public institutions. This was laced with vivid and long discussions with the brilliant Joint Secretary Mrs Neelkamal Sinha Darbari at the National Disaster Management Authority and the consultant Ms Naghma Firdaus. We were also fortunate to interact with an exceptionally efficient and enlightened team of officers such as Mr Keshav Kumar Pathak (IAS), Mr Vikas Anand (IAS) and Mr Sonam Gechen Agola (addl. personal secretary to the minister) who have made a lasting contribution by supporting academic research in the social sciences perspectives of disaster management. Inadvertently, this team of officers has ignited a critical pedagogy in the discipline which would in times to come put JNU at a dominant position of T6 in the Asia-Pacific.

The turning point came when the DRP finally got an appointment with the new Minister of State for Home Affairs Hon'ble Mr Kiren Rijiju before whom the case for the phenomenal presence of social sciences was spread out. The need for taking disaster management out of engineering approaches to sociological approaches was well appreciated by the minister who also encouraged the much-required institutional synergy in the context of the Hyogo and Sendai framework, especially the common concerns on vulnerable communities inhabiting remote regions of the country and those institutions which stand to address these concerns. The most appropriate place for locating this new research area could be none other than JNU which had a truly well-represented national character and people from all geographical regions and social segments of class, caste, culture and religions.

On 6 August 2015, an MoU was signed between JNU and the National Institute of Disaster Management for setting up a 'Centre for Excellence in Disaster Research'. The Disaster Management Act 2005 looked forward to relevance and applicability in a diverse set-up of India. It had definitely launched Hyogo's changing dimensions in managing disasters, yet institutions were slow and also clueless to address a responsibility which was onerous and bigger than what administrative agencies were equipped to handle. The epistemology of disaster research was changing, and we felt proud to see this happening at JNU in a historic collaboration with leading administrative agencies.

Within JNU we acknowledge our gratitude towards the former vice chancellor Prof. S. K. Sopory who shared his passion and understanding of transdisciplinarity. We also express our thanks to Prof. Prasenjit Sen, Rector II at the university who as the coordinator for TRC at JNU held assessment meetings for our proposal at many stages before forwarding and recommending it to the NDMA for a research grant. In May 2015, the TRC Standing Committee acknowledged that DRP was out of its incubation period and can be taken to the academic council for a separate status of a programme for research.

We would also place on record the support we have got from the university library. The chief librarian Dr Ramesh Chandra Gaur always found ways to help through the scarcity of available literature on disaster law. A few of the rare international volumes DRP suggested now adorn the library and are made available for more than 20 social science research students working on disasters in JNU.

The United Nations Development Programme (UNDP) is always remembered as DRP's first mentor. Under the exemplary leadership of Ms Lise Grande, UN resident coordinator and resident representative, we could share her international experience as a soldier of United Nations in Somalia and a passion for building community resilience. Mr G. Padmanabhan, the head of disaster management in UNDP, has always shared his unmatched experience for expanding this area of research. We also acknowledge the intellectual support and the philosophical clarity of approach we received from Prof. Santosh Kumar, the director general of the SAARC Disaster Management Authority and director of the National Institute of Disaster Management.

An unparalled and radiantly committed group of scholars from the NAPSIPAG (Network of Asia Pacific Schools and Institutes of Public Administration and Governance) which had been located at the Centre for the Study of Law and Governance at JNU until December 2015, have put their trust and conviction in DRP activities. Prof. Lalitha Fernando and Justice (Rtd) Shiranee Tilakawardane from Colombo, Dr Huong Ha from Singapore, Prof. Md. Akbaruddin Ahmad, Prof. Sumaiya Khair and Prof. Shahnaz Huda from Dhaka, Justice (Rtd.) Md. Nasir Aslam Zahid, Dr Shandana Khan, Prof. Md. Akmal Wasim and Mr Raza Ahmad from Pakistan, Dr Erna Erawati from Djakarta, Dr Clarisa Sia, Dr Mervin Gascon, Prof. Isaias S. Sealza and Dr Emilia Pedrosa-Pacoy from Philippines, Prof. Shri Krishna Shrestha, Prof. Tek Nath Dhakal, Prof. Govind Dhakal and Prof. Laxmi Kant from Nepal, Prof. Rumki Basu, Dr Suman Sharma, Dr Vinay Sharma, Prof. Rabindranath Bhattacharyya, Prof. Neena Joseph, Prof. Furqan Ahmad and Prof. Sanjeev Mahajan have nurtured the NAPSIPAG. Besides this academic team there have been many administrators heading the disaster management and city municipal departments of their respective governments who decided to participate in our regular brainstorming sessions. To name a few from Sri Lanka we had Mrs S. M. Mohamed, Dr K. D. Chitrapala, Ms Wasantha Samaraweera, Ms Subhashinie Dayananda. From Indonesia Mr Stuarto Mochtar, from Afghanistan Dr Mohammad Daim Kakar and from India the brainstorming was led by Hon'ble Justice Gita Mittal, Dr Nivedita Haran (IAS) and the environmental lawyer Mr M. C. Mehta. I also deeply acknowledge and appreciate the short interaction but striking scholarship experienced from Dr P. Puneeth and Dr Thongkholal Haokip who shared serious observations on the role of public law, analysis of the concept of space, geographically marginalized communities and most important of all the enormous role of justice to make meaning out of the distorted skeleton of disaster law.

Much of this work could be possible because my office was most efficiently taken care of by Mr A. N. Aggarwal, Ms Anju Gupta, Mr Mohanlal Meena (CSLG) and Ms Darakshan (IERB). The research team of students Ms Manika Kamthan, Mr Binod Kumar, Mr Shishir Yadav, Ms Malini Pravah Sethi, Mr Devinder Jindolia was available to organize events, collect data from the field and also design sessions for an effective brainstorming. Later this team became larger with the addition of brilliant and perceptive Dr Aashita Dawar, Dr Priyaanka Jha, Ms Homolata Borah and Ms Sukhreet Bajwa. Yet this whole office and research team could not have advanced much if the office attendant Mr Jhuman Yadav was not coordinating the inter-office exchanges and bridging the communication gaps which multi-disciplinary offices generally stumble upon.

In the end, I do wish to say that the ground of JNU provides the right atmosphere for critical thinking especially around the meandering subjects which are yet to emerge. The transdisciplinary team of scholars in the Disaster Research Programme is hopeful that its timely and appropriate research interventions in law and governance can bring greater clarity in formulating and enforcing disaster law through state and community institutions.

Abbreviations

ACWF	All-China Women's Federation (ACWF)
ADB	Asian Development Bank
AMS	Asian member states
ASEAN	Association of South East Asian Nations
BGMEA	Bangladesh Garment Manufacturers and Exports Association
CAREC	Central Asia Regional Economic Cooperation
CBM	community-based approach (NGO on disability)
CCA	climate change adaptation
CEDAW	Convention on the Elimination of All Forms of Discrimination against Women
CHS	Core Humanitarian Standard on Quality and Accountability
CRED	Centre for Research on the Epidemiology of Disasters
Cr.PC	criminal penal code
CRF	calamity relief fund
DiDRRN	Disability-inclusive DRR Network for Asia and the Pacific
DM	disaster management
DMA	Disaster Management Act
DRP	Disaster Research Programme
EM_DAT	Emergency Events Database
ERRA	Earthquake Reconstruction and Rehabilitation Authority
FATA	Federally Administered Tribal Areas
GAR/DRR	Global Assessment Report on Disaster Risk Reduction
GDP	gross domestic product

GFDRR	Global Facility for Disaster Risk Reduction and Recovery
GSDRC	Governance and Social Development Resource Centre
HDI	Human Development Index
HFA	Hyogo Framework for Action
IAP	International Strategy for Disaster Reduction-Asia Partnership
IASC	Inter-Agency Standing Committee of the UN
ICF	International Classification of Functioning, Disability and Health
ICG	International Crisis Group
ICT	information and communication technology
IDRL	International Disaster Relief and Initial Recovery Assistance (also known as the IDRL Guidelines)
IDRL	International Disaster Response Law
IERU	Inclusive Emergency Response Unit
IFRC	The International Federation of Red Cross and Red Crescent Societies
ILC	International Law Commission
IOM	International Organization on Migration
IPC	Indian Penal Code
IPCC	Inter-Governmental Panel on Climate Change
MCA	Ministry of Civil Affairs
MIC	methyl isocyanate
MOFTEC	Ministry of Foreign Trade and Economic Cooperation
MPS	Ministry of Public Security
NAPSIPAG	Network of Asia Pacific Schools and Institutes of Public Administration and Governance
NCCD	National Calamity Contingency Duty
NCCF	National Calamity Contingency Fund
NDMA	National Disaster Management Authority
NDRF	National Disaster Response Force
NGO	non-government organization
NGT	National Green Tribunal
NIDM	National Institute of Disaster Management
OCHA	Office for the Coordination of Humanitarian Affairs
ODI	Overseas Development Institute
OECD	Organisation for Economic Co-operation and Development

OFDA/CRED	Office of Foreign Disaster Assistance/Centre for Research on the Epidemiology of Disasters
PETS	Pet Evacuation and Transportation Standards Act
RCSC	Red Cross Society of China
RRM	Risk Reduction, Resilience Building and Mitigation
SAARC	South Asian Association for Regional Cooperation
SAARD	Agreement on Rapid Response to Natural Disasters
SDG	sustainable development goals
SDRF	State Disaster Response Force
SOD	Standing Orders on Disasters
TAHA	The Asian Health Agency
TI	Transparency International
TRC	Transdisciplinary Research Clusters (at JNU)
UNCRPD	United Nations Convention on the Rights of Persons with Disabilities
UNCTAD	United Nations Council for Trade and Development
UNDP	United Nations Development Programme
UNDRO	United Nations Disaster Relief Office
UNESCO	United Nations Educational, Scientific and Cultural Organization
UNFCCC	United Nations Framework Convention on Climate Change
UNGIFT	United Nations Global Initiative to Fight Human Trafficking
UNICEF	United Nations Children's Fund (formerly United Nations International Children's Emergency Fund)
UNIDO	United Nations Industrial Development Organization
UNISDR	United Nations International Strategy for Disaster Risk Reduction
UNODC	United Nations Organizations like the United Nations Office on Drugs and Crimes
UNTOC	United Nations Convention against Transnational Organized Crime
USD ($)	US dollars
WATSAN	water and sanitation
WHO	World Health Organization

Introduction

Amita Singh

There are many reasons to edit a book on disaster law. The disaster management studies have an overload of scientific findings which have continued to languish in some kind of a disjunction with realities of policy implementation. Science as such has no meaning to citizens if it fails to provide understandable and enforceable solutions. Scientists have studied glaciers, rainfall, geo-spatial warnings, tides, fish catching, drought and meteorological changes in nature and have been the first entrants to courses on disaster management. They understand nature and its behaviour better than anyone else, nevertheless let alone their discoveries appear like sermons of a Sanskritized monk who refuses to be distracted in the lowly problems of everyday miseries. Undoubtedly, an understanding of the community and its political parameters becomes important to safeguard people against disasters. Social sciences provide a crucible within which all boundaries of knowledge melt to synergize action for human security. Law is the greatest tool to provide safeguards against disasters not only at the level of preparedness and resilience building of citizens but also in rescue, relief and international humanitarian assistance.

Evolving disaster law

The role of legal frameworks in disaster risk reduction emerged with the Hyogo Framework for Action (HFA), Building the Resilience of Nations and Communities to Disasters 2005–2015. It recognized the need for good legislation. This was further strengthened in the Sendai Framework for Disaster Risk Reduction 2015–2030 which set its top priority to 'strengthening disaster risk governance' and 'legal frameworks'. The Asian tsunami created an urgency for mitigation and also a legal framework for each country, which they quickly followed by bringing about a Disaster Management Act. The IFRC and the United Nations Development Programme (UNDP) started a major study to examine 31 countries. In 2015 they launched a new tool, 'A Checklist on Law and Disaster Risk Reduction', and its accompanying guide, 'The Handbook on Law and Disaster Risk Reduction', to clarify the parameters of what could effectively be called 'disaster law'.[1]

This checklist enumerated ten concerns of law for disaster mitigation and community resilience building. These may be summarized in brief as follows:

1 The law for the country which established clear roles and responsibilities for DRR for all levels of institutions from national to local. This should also have sectoral laws to address current and future risks. Knowledge of these laws should be disseminated through education, research, training and awareness raising at the remotest and most vulnerable regions of the country.
2 A budgetary grant and resources for DRR.
3 Laws should establish clear procedures, responsibilities and accountability system for ensuring appropriate risk assessment at every stage of developmental processes.
4 Full community participation which addresses considerations of age, culture and also concerns of vulnerable and marginalized groups and communities.

The World Conference on Disaster Reduction was convened by decision of the General Assembly, with five specific gaps and challenges being identified in the following five main areas:

(a) Governance: organizational, legal and policy frameworks;
(b) Risk identification, assessment, monitoring and early warning;
(c) Knowledge management and education;
(d) Reducing underlying risk factors;
(e) Preparedness for effective response and recovery.

These became the key areas for developing a relevant framework for action for the decade 2005–2015.[2] As per the General Assembly Resolution 58/214 of 23rd December 2003 there has been a consistent and sustained effort towards strengthening institutions, institutional and legal mechanisms and capacities at all levels, in particular at the community level, that can systematically contribute to preparedness and risk reduction. It is in this direction that scholars from around the Asian region have together and, building upon the experience from their respective countries, have made a strong case for 'disaster law' as an indispensable requirement for 'disaster mitigation'.

Addressing the changing pedagogy of disaster management

The most important reason to bring out this book is the need to initiate a discourse on law within the programmes of disaster management which as of now are far away from Sendai's pedagogy of 'preparedness' and 'resilience building'. The tsunami led most Asian nations to formulate a legal structure in the form of disaster management acts. Most of these acts continue to strengthen the past by having little to strengthen and clarify law on administrative accountability, non-enforcement and also to link damages to culpability. Issues of public liability, insurance and compensation are still enforced without a reasonable understanding of these issues beyond the post-disaster rescue and rehabilitation. It has been a long and protracted discussion on why the hard-worked models in geospatial research, space and meteorological sciences have not been able to influence administrative decision making on mitigating and preventing disasters. The scientist is unaccountable for the relevance of his or her experimental findings, and likewise it works better for the administrator not to take note of them in planning. It is here that a potentially powerful role of social sciences has emerged which can re-design a framework through which a holistic and inclusive 'institutional ecosystem'[3] of disaster management could emerge. Law and the law makers had themselves not realized that this is a new species of legal jurisprudence for a world threatened by the devastating impact of changes in the global climate. The spate of an ever-increasing injuriousness of natural calamities upon development and human life could not simply be an 'act of god', but an outcome of human recklessness and insatiable desire of decision makers to bypass prudent messages on carrying capacity brought out within laboratories is the concern that drives the idea that environmental law supports but never completes the cycle of disaster preparedness. It is time that relevant strands from environmental, administrative and constitutional law are weaved to prepare a framework of 'disaster law' as a tool of governance to mitigate disasters.

Global ramifications of disaster law

Disaster law has local to global ramifications. It is a design for sustainable human security which indicates that human beings are under greater threat from natural disasters than by wars. Yet collaborations on war are much simpler than collaborations for human security from disaster management. Ironically, the world is spending more on preventing wars than on preventing disasters,[4] yet the legal frameworks are low on constitutional and administrative accountability. War losses are much less than the losses accrued due to disasters, yet the global annual military expenditure stands at over $1.7 trillion at current prices for 2012.[5] In stark contrast a Global Humanitarian Assistance Report[6] suggests that the world spending on preventing the over-encompassing spectre of destruction is less than 1 per cent ($3.7 billion) of annual GDP. The IFRC warns, 'If current trends continue, natural disasters could have a global cost of more than USD 300 billion a year by 2050.' This would undo all efforts towards development and achieving a high Human Development Index (HDI). Many studies have repeatedly emphasized that disaster risk reduction (DRR) is highly cost-effective, unlike war prevention efforts. It is well established that 'a dollar invested in DRR can save two to ten dollars in disaster response and recovery costs'.[7] Another study by Godschalk[8] *et al.* (2009) suggests that each dollar spent on mitigation grants saves society an average of $4 in real resource costs.

Yet countries are too slow to act on preventing the heavy cost of inaction. Then how could one achieve the DRR objectives which have to pass through many obstructions such as the availability of accurate information and its dissemination, planning and collaboration, compliance framework, quick response administration, national emergency response system, responsibility and culpability framework. An appropriate framework of disaster law addresses all this and much more.

Law to address the economics of disasters

Disasters have damaged more than wars, but while effort is generated to prevent the latter, the former continues to be treated as an act of God. The *Annual Disaster Statistical Review 2014: The Numbers and Trends*[9] has revealed that despite the fact that the year 2014 had the lowest number of triggered disasters to 324 (in contrast to 384 annual average between 2004 and 2013) and the lowest number of fatalities to 7,823 (in contrast to 99,820 annual average between 2004 and 2013), the economic damages amounted to $99.2 billion out of a Gross World Product of $77,868 billion.[10] Asia was worst hit with 44.4 per cent disasters. The poorest regions suffered the most as the Asian disasters cost its economy 64.6 per cent of the total world disaster losses. The fact that governance matters in DRR was well exposed in the Jammu and Kashmir floods in India which turned out to be the costliest natural disaster in 2014 amounting to $16 billion.

However, mitigation is quite possible, yet it is never attempted with a similarly required discipline as in preventing wars. A World Bank report[11] found that the most cost-effective forms of DRR investment are through non-structural approaches such as 'land use planning, warning systems and household-level changes', and they all are part of legal frameworks which constitute disaster law. The structural approaches are deeply embedded in these non-structural approaches, and this recognition should be clear to a DRR policymaker. This holistic approach is possible only through a framework of disaster law which brings the administration close to the problem and its victims.

It is generally believed and also proven by research that the main reason why DRR savings are not always enacted is because political capital is rarely gained from cost-effective DRR measures (ibid., p. 3). The post-disaster rescue and relief is media-projected administrative chivalry which can spin into immediate electoral votes in contrast to the long-term land, water and soil conservation measures. Disaster law would nail down this post-disaster political dramatics and retrofitting by questioning the issues of responsibility and accountability. Law to prevent disasters may also take into account its linkage to climate change which otherwise is treated in closed insulated compartments by two separate departments. Investments in DRR could overlap with investments in climate change and may double the impact of its outcome. However, such studies are yet to take a more boisterous acceptance in DRR. Developing disaster law would not only make DRR cost-effective but also improve and sensitize governance to the needs of mitigation over and above the desired political capital.

The thematic structure of the book

The book has been divided into five thematic parts. Part I titled 'Disaster law: content and correlations' explains and clarifies the location of this new socio-legal and cultural terrain of disaster management studies within the intersection of administrative and natural sciences. The debate is ignited by Amita Singh in chapter 1 'Disaster law and the post-Hyogo pedagogical change in the framework of governance'. In this chapter, Singh captures the changing pedagogy of disaster management after Hyogo Declaration changed the course of disaster management from 'rescue, relief and rehabilitation' to 'resilience building, risk reduction and mitigation' (RRM in place of DRR) in which the author prioritizes resilience building in DRR. This creates wider space for 'law' to influence risk reduction by reducing vulnerability and improving governance. Disaster law is a way of strengthening communities and identifying culpability, accountability and penalty for inaction. This chapter is followed by Gabrielle Emery and Padmini Nayagam on the multidimensionality and as a bridge between the global and national concerns. The third chapter in this part by Renu K. Sharma highlights the cultural context from some of the oldest cultural manuscripts in the world to show disaster law as a prerequisite of good and ethical governance. In 'Disaster laws: saving lives, reducing risk in the Asia Pacific' Emery and Nayagam place disaster law at the core of action against embedded inequities and poverty. Evidence shows that the largest price is consistently borne by the poor and the vulnerable, both in wealthy and in developing countries. The disaster not only affects individuals and communities but also impacts on state and business infrastructure and can reverse long-term developmental gains of countries. Over the past 20 years, natural disasters have caused $2 trillion in economic losses globally.[12] The term disaster risk reduction in its broadest sense means 'making choices to reduce the human impact of natural hazards'. It is evident therefore that laws, policies and regulatory frameworks can and should play a critical role in ensuring both risk reduction and that they are legally prepared in the event of a large-scale disaster response. Globally, domestic institutions and local organizations have significant and increasing capacities to manage the risk and impact of humanitarian crises in their countries. This is elucidated in the UN General Assembly resolution[13] that underpins the current international humanitarian architecture, providing the basis for principled humanitarian action. The third chapter by Sharma, on 'Disasters: a ubiquitous legal framework in ancient BC literature', emphasizes that a true understanding of law comes from its historical and cultural location. The author explores the term 'disaster' from some of the oldest Asian literature which describes the survival of races, history of migration and trade links among kingdoms to understand how people during those eras perceived disasters and found ways to address their impact either through preparedness or through framing policies of public accountability of administrators or prohibiting certain practices which brought disasters. It was a time when kingdoms were demarcated with rivers and mountains as boundaries, but sufficient historical proof exists to suggest that at the time of Vedas,[14] the region what we now refer to as India extended to the Samarkand in Uzbekistan, Kandahar or Qandahar and Kabul in Afghanistan, Gandhara in Peshawar beyond the Indus River, towards the Pamirs, the Hindu Kush and the Central Asian steppes. It is most likely that this phenomenal spread into varieties of cultures that 'disasters' have been addressed more holistically than the pre-Hyogo perceptions. Therefore, disasters are found to be the fallout of irresponsible governance, bad environmental management and lawlessness.

After a general understanding about the location and link to governance, the book explores the country-specific understanding of disaster law to highlight comparability and prospects for replication of initiatives. Part II deals with Country-Specific Disaster Laws. Md. Akmal Wasim in chapter 4, 'The landscape of disaster management in Pakistan: gaps in the legal framework', brings out the experience of Pakistan, while Md. Akbaruddin Ahmad writes on the state capacity to manage disasters in Bangladesh in chapter 6. Yan Cui and Shibo Jiang discuss the manner in which China handles such emergencies in chapter 7. Binod Kumar and Ramratan Dhumal highlight the India experience and how the legislative structure formulates law. The purpose of the chapter by Wasim is to identify the existing gaps in the governance of disasters and in the process of legislation. Pakistan has definitely come a long way in developing and strategizing a proactive disaster management system besides a relatively better sensitized judiciary. The other but foremost is the connection of law with society in the absence of which the survivors of calamities are far more vulnerable and open to exploitation. Pakistan has gradually developed a sensitized legal mechanism in the form of National Disaster Management Act, 2010. No law can be said to be perfect but can have the right intentions if it has an inbuilt impetus to evolve. It is only through trials that the laws evolve and attain sustainability. It can safely be said that Pakistan is now in a position to address disaster situations, yet it is rather too early to admit that gaps have been identified. The next chapter titled 'Disaster law and community resilience in Bangladesh' explains that human, animals and other living creatures face such calamities with varying degree of intensity and damage to life and property. Nations facing such disasters may or may not be equipped to handle such emergency situation on their own. Therefore, in such case institutional relief and assistance may be sought from other countries, international aid agencies, Red Cross and Red Crescent Societies, the UN agencies, donors and NGOs. Enactment of laws to monitor the movement of relief food, machinery, equipment affected people. The author compares the post-disaster relief and rebuilding in Hurricane Katrina in New Orleans in USA, tsunami in Bali, Indonesia, and Rana Plaza building collapse in Bangladesh. The chapter concludes that these man-made disasters could have been prevented if simple laws on building construction, safety regulations on fire management and escape route laws had been implemented. Cui and Shibo Jiang in chapter 6 'International disaster response law in China: a study on strengthening national disaster response legislation' approaches the lacuna addressing comprehensively on international disaster response law in China. The authors look at the law from its growth and development, reflect current deficiencies and suggest solutions by developing and facilitating China's national disaster response legislation to keep pace with recent development in international community. In order to strengthen the legal and policy framework for international disaster response in China, the authors make several proposals for improvement of disaster response legislation in China to be consistent with international norms and practice. Kumar in his chapter 'Interrogating disaster law in India' believes that the disaster law is a collection of legal rules of various kinds which comes into play before, during and after the disaster. The portfolio of disaster law includes law relating to mitigation, emergency response, compensation, insurance and strategies which largely deal with catastrophic risk. The author delves deeper into the disaster law, skimming through human rights jurisprudence and constitutional imperatives. Uncovering the new vistas, the chapter tries to give a holistic review of Disaster Management Act, 2005, through case laws. Not much different is the next chapter by Dhumal, 'Interrogating the trajectory of disaster laws in India' which addresses legal enforcement of policy implementation for disaster mitigation. Quoting Roscoe Pound's 'Sociological Engineering Theory' the chapter considers law as a tool that overcomes problems in the society. However, what matters is the genuine construction of law that addresses social vulnerability and accommodates all sections of the society to ensure social resilience. This chapter critically reviews the post-tsunami legislation such as the Disaster Management Act, 2005, in India to assess if it has actually achieved the fundamental rights of the victims of disaster as cherished in the Indian Constitution.

Part III, 'International legal framework of disaster management' recognizes the rationale for collaboration and joint action. In chapter 9, 'Overcoming the patriarchal insulation of international legal framework' written by Shiranee Tilakawardane, disasters observe no boundaries and most of the hotspots of disasters are generally at the international boundaries of hills, mountains, rivers and oceans which remain neglected for lack of civil governance. Added to it is an absence a legal framework for cooperation, relief sharing and international obligations. This part is therefore a critical survey of the International Legal Framework for Disaster Management. The authors Shiranee Tilakawardane, Stellina Jolly, Sanghamitra Nath and Venkatachalam Anbumozhi bring out a critical comparative framework of vulnerability and how law can help to overcome it. These chapters suggest a gender-specific framework of law, a standard relief framework in governance, an ICT framework and the ADB strategy, respectively. Tilakawardane who as a judge in the Supreme Court of Sri Lanka is committed to overcome the patriarchal insulation of international legal framework. Undertaking a critical comparative framework of vulnerability during many international disasters, that is, the 2004 earthquake and subsequently the tsunami in the Indian Ocean, the 2010 earthquake in Haiti, the 2011 Tohuku earthquake and the tsunami in Japan and the 2015 Nepal earthquake, the author suggests that such catastrophes demand gender-sensitive risk assessment and gender-responsive recovery and rehabilitation as integral components of disaster management law. From the available data on tsunami in Sri Lanka, a very large majority of those who died were women as they did not have many skills such as climbing trees, swimming and understanding or deciphering information. Besides social prejudices reduce survivability of women through disasters. In an overall accounting carried out by the World Health Organization more than 75 per cent of displaced persons were women. Post-disaster trauma, psychological sickness and mental problems affect women in a big way. In the next chapter, 'Interrogating the pedagogy of state responsibility and individual rights in disaster law', Jolly attempts to analyse the application of R2P (relief to people) in the context of some case studies from Haiti earthquake, Asian tsunami, Myanmar Nargis Cyclone and Pakistan floods to come out with certain suggestions for an effective disaster management relief mechanism. The author emphasizes that the recommendations given by the United Nations had been one of the revolutionary concepts (R2P) at the World Summit in 2005 yet unachievable so far. Nath in 'Disaster law, ICT and performance through "standard setting" in disaster law' highlights the grim lapses in administrative and technological matters in disaster preparedness. An important lesson from the Uttarakhand tragedy and CAG report is the need for a criterion to evaluate standards of performance and instill deeper accountability. This is possible only if certain standards are set to identify and evaluate performance through the glaring loopholes in emergency governance. Standard-setting helps as legal parameters of performance and can become an indispensable tool to bring greater clarity and serious implementation of disaster laws. Disaster laws should adopt and enact such legal parameters which will, in turn, make enforcement compelling at three levels of disaster management. In chapter 12, 'Building national resilience through international law' Venkatachalam, from his experience in the Asian Development Bank, unfolds a very wide monitoring and evaluation framework for disaster laws. The year 2015 ushered in global conversations that impact national and regional initiatives in disaster management and, conversely, provide opportunities for the regional institutions like ASEAN to influence regional dialogues on legal concerns like the Hyogo Framework for Action, the review and subsequent development of the post-2015 sustainable development goals, the Nansen Initiative on disaster-induced cross-border displacement and the potential occurrence of natural disasters in conflict areas. The necessity of enhancing and strengthening synergy and cooperation between and among various stakeholders across multiple sectors and to maintain the ASEAN Agreement on Disaster Management Emergency Response was established. This chapter identifies key thematic areas arising from the ongoing and emerging regional and global discussions on disaster risk reduction, climate change adaptation, development of the post-2015 sustainable development goals and then recommends five critical steps viz., strengthening legal framework, implementing integrated risk management, establishing a monitoring and evaluation framework, capitalizing private finance and capacity development as key components for formulating the post-2015 disaster management blueprint.

Part IV exposes the informed ignorance aptly referred to as 'The wide-eyed slippages of disaster law'. There are many areas which the government is well aware of as the causes and consequences of disasters, yet it prefers to push it under the carpet due to the fear of public scrutiny. Sumaiya Khair demands an end to corruption in DM, while Manjula Batra shares the shocking neglect to deal with trafficking. Deepa Sonpal highlights the major gap in the DMA 2005 on its failure to incorporate Convention on the Rights of Persons with Disabilities. Subhalaxmi Sircar exposes the neglect towards non-human species in all disaster management acts and the economic linkages of these losses to development. While Mondira Dutta and Manika Kamthan complete the debate on trafficking by demonstrating its absence in laws on DM, Ved Mittal clarifies the government's patience and neglect towards the non-enforceability of techno-legal regime in city governance. Sunita Reddy and Shishir Yadav, on the other hand, bring out medical issues and emergencies of community health as being repeatedly ignored despite the district authorities being well aware of them. Khair in 'Corruption in humanitarian assistance: challenges and opportunities' laments that there is very little scholarship on corruption and irregularities in humanitarian aid and assistance in South Asia. Apart from a few standard practices the issue has not been sufficiently researched, nor has it generated any significant discussion from a policy perspective. While corruption in the public sector and now increasingly in the private sector occupies a central position in the corruption discourse prevailing in the South Asian countries, there has virtually been no focus on real and potential governance deficits in humanitarian action in emergency situations, whether natural or man-made. Recognizing the significance of addressing corruption for ensuring quality, accountability and sound management in humanitarian operations, this gap has been filled to a certain degree by the contribution of several NGOs led by Transparency International in the assessment of corruption risks and in the development of social accountability tools to monitor aid disbursement processes. The author demands an end to corruption through stringent legal framework in disaster management as a sin qua non of sustainable DRR. Batra writes in 'A legal framework to prevent trafficking of women and young girls during disasters in India', that it is ironical that the missing girls and women during disasters are nowhere accounted in much of the government data. Around 225,000 women and children are trafficked from the Southeast Asian countries every year, accounting for approximately one-third of the global human flesh trade. India has served as a destination and transit point of trafficking victims from Bangladesh, Nepal and Bhutan. Trafficking of vulnerable persons, especially women and young girls, is directly proportional to the disasters. Taking note of the inadequacy of the laws to deal with the various forms of human trafficking that take place during disasters, the Indian Disasters Management Act, 2005, along with certain provisions of the constitution of India and the role played by the Supreme Court of India in addressing issues of sexual exploitations of women, can show the way towards combating human trafficking of women and young girls in the context of disasters. The present chapter focuses on the issue of human trafficking in women and young girls, which takes place rampantly during disasters. The public authorities also fret at the data on disability. Sonpal in 'Disability, disaster and the law: developing a mandate for disability inclusive law making process for disaster risk reduction' attends to the fact that the Convention on the Rights of Persons with Disabilities, and now with the publication of the World Report on Disability, this century can frame disaster mitigation plans and the laws for an inclusive framework of disasters. The Disaster Management Act 2005 is nowhere close to making the community resilience plans inclusive. In the next chapter the debate on making disaster laws inclusive reaches out to the most voiceless victims of disasters, 'the animals or the non-human species'. Sircar in 'Anthropogenic disaster economics and the non-human species' makes a brilliant case for the need of an animal-friendly disaster management act. The author argues that there are no specific guidelines either in Disaster Management Act of 2005 or the

National Plan of 2009 for preparedness, rescue and rehabilitation of animals after any disaster. The chapter reviews the disaster management in India in terms of an inclusive institutional framework, available database and budgetary allocations for disaster response and mitigation to find out how far disaster management plans accommodate the non-humans like domesticated, wild and homeless stray animals despite a constitutional responsibility under Article 48A and Article 51A of the constitution. While just two Congressmen in the US could bring about the Pet Evacuation and Transportation Standards Act (PETS) in 2005, the gigantic Indian parliament with world's largest animal population facing disasters and world's strongest religion to vouch for their rights is yet to initiate minimal preliminary steps towards even recognizing its need with equanimity and ecological justice. Dutta and Kamthan focus upon 'gender and trafficking'. The world today is a witness to the mass exodus of people migrating from one place to another due to conflict, war, natural calamities, ethnic cleansing, terrorism and insurgency or simply in search of livelihood options. There seems to be a thin line between migration, human smuggling, human trafficking and other related issues. South Asia happens to be a home to the second-largest number of internationally trafficked persons, estimated to be around 150,000 persons annually.[15] India, Bangladesh and Nepal have been identified as the major source countries for women and children being trafficked for the purposes of sexual exploitation, involuntary domestic servitude and bondage of debt. Disaster only doubles the hardships faced in such areas. There are a slender collection of laws which are difficult to implement across the countries and international borders thus being unable to protect the cross-border victims. The next author Mittal in 'Techno-legal regime for safety against natural hazards' points out at urban policy slippages which make the city habitat a hotspot of disaster. The author highlights that the Yokohama Strategy for Safer World in 1994, the Ministry of Home Affairs, Government of India, constituted an expert committee to prepare model amendments required in Town & Country Planning Legislations of various states and also to suggest regulations for land use zoning and provisions in development control and bye-laws, pertaining to safety in natural hazard prone areas throughout the country. This chapter is the excerpt from the recommendations of the experts committee with the objective to disseminate the information to a very large number of professional town planners working in various states in different capacity, so that the town planner would take a step to get the amendments in Town & Country Planning Legislations and DCR/bye-laws, as well as to take care of vulnerable areas while preparing settlement plans for safer India. Another area which demands much attention of state authorities is well argued by Reddy and Yadav in 'Post-disaster medical services: can law ensure services?' The authors point out that the state of medical emergency response in India, especially during disasters, is yet to evolve. Given the weak structure of health service systems in the country, it is pertinent to focus on medical emergencies in a disaster scenario, especially during the relief period and long-term rehabilitation stage. There is no dearth of laws in India, but the implementation is always a challenge. India has Disaster Management Act, 2005, which is quite comprehensive; however, the rules for each component neither demand mandatory compliance nor provide teeth for implementation. From the past experiences of Bhopal gas disaster and the lessons learnt from other major disasters, there is an ardent need to look into the medical emergency plans, especially in disasters where lives are lost due to the lack of medical preparedness and emergency response. There is need for developing an area for disaster medicine like the sport's medicine and bring to effect through legal sanctions which fix accountability and ensure service delivery to affected people.

Part V of the book takes up well-researched case-specific studies which explain the challenges and potential need for legal enforcement and preparedness policy. The first study by Himanshu Shekhar Mishra surveys the case study of Kashmir floods. Abha Yadav finds the case study of RTI and disasters, which brings out many hidden realities of state structures. Rabindranath Bhattacharyya sought to learn lessons from the Mandarmani Sea Beach in West Bengal. For P. K. Chaubey city management itself becomes a case study of government apathy towards a just approach to city management in the context of disasters. Mishra's chapter titled 'Interrogating right to compensation in disaster laws: a case study of Jammu and Kashmir floods' explains his vivid experience as a journalist sent to cover the beautiful terrain submerged under floods. The Jammu and Kashmir in September 2014 marked a watershed in the history of disaster management in India. It exposed the fault lines in this strategically important border state's disaster relief and response mechanism and also highlighted the weaknesses inherent in India's disaster management strategy at the larger level. The scale at which the relief and rescue operations were launched marked a paradigm shift in Indian state's response mechanism to a natural disaster. It received unprecedented attention from the central government and the media which relayed images of devastation caused by the floods for many weeks. Unfortunately, the weaknesses in the reconstruction and rehabilitation measures initiated in the aftermath of these floods have not received the requisite attention it deserved. Also the struggle of these flood victims to seek compensation from the state leads us to an important question: should there be a rights-based paradigm to address the issue of relief and compensation to disaster victims? The next chapter analyses the use of the Right to Information Act during disasters. Yadav in 'Unanswered questions in disaster preparedness and the Right to Information' says that the Right to Information is a tool for resilience building of vulnerable communities. Making this the central argument for this chapter, the connection between resilience building and information as a plea for empowered community has been established. Some selected cases have been looked into in which the RTI has helped to expose corruption mismanagement and flawed decision making and protected natural resources from harm and destruction. The RTI has also brought to surface land records, which has enabled post-disaster compensation task much simpler and just. The RTI has also helped improve hospital conditions in vulnerable regions. The crux of the problem which would be taken up in the conclusion is that despite huge funding to climate change adaptation measures and disaster relief there is no other way but through the RTI that resilience of communities could be obtained and strengthened. Bhattacharyya in 'Can laws ensure disaster risk reduction? a study of Mandarmani Sea Beach in West Bengal', argues the implementation of an all-embracing law, namely, Environment Protection Act 1986, which exists till today in an inverse correlation between myopic profit-making governance and sustainable development. This chapter attempts to focus on the lack of coordination, communication and accountability among different government departments and other authorities in West Bengal that resulted in the increase in all sorts of environmental hazards that becomes evident from the study of Mandarmani, a village on the sea coast of East Midnapore in West Bengal. Chaubey in his study on 'DRR and city governance' focused on disaster management policies which were once considered merely a post-disaster management activity such as taking care of post-disaster problems and conducting operations which were better known as relief operations. Taking cognizance of rapidly rising human toll and economic losses due to natural disasters the High Powered Committee in India shifted hereafter from rescue and relief to preparedness and mitigation. By 2005, in World Conference on Disaster Reduction (held in Kobe, Hyogo, Japan), a detailed framework of strategic goals, priority areas for action and tasks for stakeholders at operational levels was evolved. A few years after, United Nations International Strategy for Disaster Reduction announced two years of 2010 and 2011 to be devoted to safer cities. The author argues that there are a number of areas which are yet to be attended to despite a plethora of laws around them.

Part VI, 'Epilogue' by Nivedita P. Haran, presents a workable and optimistic scenario of disaster laws in India. The author in 'Disaster laws in India: the way forward' highlights that the Disaster Management Act of December 2005, which came around the same time as in other neighbouring countries except in Pakistan where it came up as late as 2010, Afghanistan in 2012 and in Bhutan much later in 2013, indicates that the consciousness graph is rising in this region. The acts in India, Sri Lanka and Bangladesh immediately established the Disaster Management Authority at the apex level, which is responsible for all policy formulation on disaster-related issues. The framing of institutional building processes are under way. So a lot of progress has taken place over the past nine years. The SAARC centre for Disaster Management was also set up during this decade. But is it enough? Could more have been done? Is the act adequate? Have the states moved in unison? Is the international community ready to shed their political insecurities and collaborate on preparedness and mitigation as enshrined in the Sendai Declaration: 'The realization of the new framework depends on unceasing and tireless collective efforts'. Disaster management is a field-specific subject and if changes and improvements do not take place on the ground, the act and the rules would remain impotent. In this chapter which focuses on the findings from India, an attempt has been made to seek replies to the questions raised above and to chalk out the way forward.

In conclusion the book indicates three major findings: first, that disaster management is currently at the core of law and governance; second, disaster law would strengthen a non-hierarchical collaboration towards a holistic and inclusive approach to DM; and third, that disaster law ensures transparency by taking a balanced view of damages and culpability. Disaster law would be a flywheel of disaster management in the coming decades of accelerated action on disaster management and climate change.

Notes

1 See more at: www.ifrc.org/en/what-we-do/disaster-law/about-disaster-law/legislation-for-disaster-risk-reduction/#sthash.9SylLbpb.dpuf
2 Review of the Yokohama Strategy and Plan of Action for a Safer World (A/CONF.206/L.1). Retrieved from www.unisdr.org/2005/wcdr/intergover/official-doc/L-docs/Yokohama-Strategy-English.pdf
3 All institutions which are directed to achieve a particular end, that is, poverty reduction need to work in tandem since they have overlapping

domains. They can decide not to stay together only at the cost of harming their institutional objective. It is an ecosystem of institutions. If disasters create poverty by destroying humans, animals and the developmental infrastructure, then NDMA should have close linkages with the institutions of urban and rural planning, development and livelihood regeneration. In reality NDMA's and SDMA's work in perceived independence or isolation promoted by their cautious exclusion from urban and local bodies, planning and management. It is ironic that SDMAs have no role when the District Town and Country Planning, State Industrial Development Corporations, Urban Development Authorities and departments decide upon the change of land use demands on reports obtained from the forest department, tehsildar and Patwari (local governance land assesse officers).

4 In the past decade alone there have been 75,000 deaths, 200 million people affected each year and an average of 162.2 billion annual GDP losses (International Federation of Red Cross and Red Crescent Societies, *World Disasters Report* [2015], Annex Disaster Data, 216–218). Colin Schultz (Human Security Report 2013, smithsonian.com) writes 'Globally, deaths from war and murder are in the decline. The world is getting safer, even if it doesn't necessarily feel like it'. It shows, for example, that the number of international wars has fallen hard since the 1950s (from more than six a year, to less than one a year now). Likewise, the number of war deaths has also plummeted. In the 1950s, there were almost 250 deaths caused by war per million people. Now, there are less than 10 per million. 'There have been some pretty extraordinary changes and they haven't been recognized', Mack says. Military leaders, for example, say we live in the 'most dangerous time ever'. And yet, in statistical terms at least, this isn't remotely true (Watson Institute of International and Public Affairs, Brown University).

5 www.globalhumanitarianassistance.org/wp-content/uploads/2012/03/GHA-Disaster-Risk-Report.pdf

6 In March 2012, the Global Humanitarian Assistance (GHA) programme published 'Disaster risk reduction: Spending where it should count', which examined the levels of donor investment in DRR. The report found that despite the rhetoric, just 1 per cent (US$3.7 billion) of total ODA had been spent on DRR in 40 of the world's poorest and most disaster-affected countries. (www.globalhumanitarianassistance.org/wp-content/uploads/2012/10/Aid-investments-in-disaster-risk-reduction-rhetoric-to-action-Dan-Sparks1.pdf)

7 Global Alliance for Disaster Risk Reduction. Retrieved from www.ifrc.org/Global/global-alliance-reduction.pdf

8 D. R. Godschalk, A. Rose, E. Mittler, K. Porter and C. T. West (2009). 'Estimating the Value of Foresight: Aggregate Analysis of Natural Hazard Mitigation Benefits and Costs'. *Journal of Environmental Planning and Management*, vol. 52, no. 6, pp. 739–756.

9 Debarati Guha-Sapir, Philippe Hoyois and Regina Below (2015). *Annual Disaster Statistical Review 2014: The Numbers and Trends*, Université catholique de Louvain – Brussels, Belgium: Centre for Research on the Epidemiology of Disasters (CRED) Institute of Health and Society (IRSS). Available at www.cred.be/sites/default/files/ADSR_2014.pdf

10 'Gross Domestic Product 2014' (PDF). The World Bank DataBank. 2015. Retrieved 24 June 2016.
11 Ilan Kelman (2014). 'The World Bank Report', '*Disaster Mitigation Is Cost Effective*' CICERO: Norway. This document is a briefing on cost-benefit analyses (CBA) for disaster risk reduction (DRR) based on studies documented at www.ilankelman.org/miscellany/MitigationSaves.rtf
12 EM-DAT database maintained by the Centre for Research on the Epidemiology of Disasters at www.cred.be/projects/EM-DAT
13 General Assembly Resolution 58/214 of 23rd December 2003.
14 World's oldest manuscript written sometimes between the 3000 and 5000 BC.
15 UNFPA, 2006, State of the World Population Report, UNFPA, 2006, p. 45. The highest numbers are estimated to come from South East Asia, estimated to be 225,000.

Part I

Disaster law

Content and correlations

1 Disaster law and the post-Hyogo pedagogical change in the framework of governance

Amita Singh

How disaster law addresses risk: resilience: mitigation (RRM)?

The World Conference on Disaster Reduction was held between 18 and 22 January 2005 in Kobe, Hyogo, Japan, and adopted the present Framework for Action 2005–2015: Building the Resilience of Nations and Communities to Disasters (hereafter referred to as the 'Framework for Action'). Prior to this, the Yokohama Strategy for a Safer World: Guidelines for Natural Disaster Prevention, Preparedness and Mitigation and Its Plan of Action ('Yokohama Strategy'), adopted in 1994, had highlighted the grave consequences for the survival, dignity and livelihood of individuals, particularly the poor, and hard-won developmental gains. Disaster risk is increasingly a global concern compounded by increasing vulnerabilities to environmental degradation, climate variability, geological hazards and health-related epidemics. Disasters increasingly threaten the world's economy and its prosperity. In the past two decades, on average more than 200 million people have been affected every year by disasters. The focus on 'law for managing disasters' is likely to be the driving force of governance in the context of the four priority areas of Sendai Declaration,[1] namely, understanding disaster risk, strengthening disaster risk governance to manage disaster risk, investing in disaster risk reduction for resilience and enhancing disaster preparedness for effective response and to 'Build Back Better' in recovery, rehabilitation and reconstruction

This chapter argues on the relationship of disasters to bad governance and law as an important tool to bring about a more holistic and inclusive system of power sharing within which resilient communities survive.

In this discourse on disaster mitigation, the more commonly used term 'disaster risk reduction' (DRR) is replaced by a more appropriate term 'resilience building, risk reduction and mitigation' (RRM). The term DRR appears to be rooted in the old engineering approaches in which the model or a solution is woven around 'risk'. The normative edge is missing in it as much as the aspect of the role of intangibles and intuitive elements which do not form part of the measurable, definable and calculable aspect of 'risk reduction'. Communities may perceive of a hazard as 'no risk' as they have been used to acclimatized to this hazard for ages. However, the engineer may perceive this differently and may recommend an enormous investment in a DRR programme even though a minor but focused investment could strengthen community resilience. RRM is the process of perceiving 'risk' through the eyes of a community, and this holistic process takes into account the whole ecology, ecosystems within it and the bonds of relationships between the human, non-human, the flora and fauna inhabiting the region since prehistoric times.

History of human progress is an unbridled advance against the weaker and differently looking species. Extinction is even legally accepted for human survival and comfort. This process is considered as an outcome of policy prudence and practical reasoning, notwithstanding its fundamental ethical deficits and moral problems and the degree of criminal liability attached to killing. 'Killing' in hunting becomes a sport, in the rural habitats at the forest rims it is justified for resource protection, in euthanasia it's a choice, at the guillotine as much as in wars it's the larger social and national good which can justify and legitimize killing. What about killing by negligence? Since most disasters are man-made due to oversights in planning and management which can be considered 'negligence', should it not entail criminal liability? In defining a law around 'negligence', there are soft penalties fixed for infractions such as negligent driving or building additional floors not permitted under building bye-laws. Therefore, 'negligence' does not bring dire penalties as it is neither considered to be morally as bad as deliberate nor direct as the intention to kill as in a 'murder'. Thus there is a need to redefine law from the perspective of disasters as 'the non-criminal and less morally bad, nature of imprudence in normal life has carried over to disaster planning' (Zack, 2012, 821).

In a sheer lack of ethical research in law on human progress, governments are confused and fail to turn back, take a breath, pause a while to think 'where have we gone wrong?'. The United Nations acting as a lighthouse has set some speed breakers in the form of new indices of Human Development, Ecosystem Services, Millennium Development Goals and the Sustainable Development Goals on a common minimum denominator to facilitate inclusive governance. This has always been the core concern of United Nations on how to make governance more inclusive of the voices of the marginalized. The creation of UNCTAD in 1964 and the debates centring around Raul Prebisch's[2] (Love, 1980) theory of trade relations, unequal exchange and centre-periphery approach had shown that the UN has been open to the rationale of bridging the gap that exists between the industrial centre and the agrarian periphery or between the developed and the developing countries as much as between affluence and scarcity. However, in doing so the agrarian periphery has now been carved out as islands of insulated market-oriented agriculturist communities distanced from their ecosystem of forest, grazing grounds, community lands and wild life. This has only thrown them into greater vulnerability and insecurity, but most of all it has trapped them into a vicious cycle of markets and production with no pre-existing indigenous buffer to fall back upon. Law needs to address the processes in which a non-habitant decides for a habitat and generates avoidable vulnerability.

Underneath the silent neglect by governments is the brewing fury of nature which erupts as disasters. Neither the government nor the pace of the development is able to withstand the prowess of destruction. If only they (government and communities) work together in advance and share information, experience, planning and preparedness, the spectre of death and devastation can be averted. Disaster law brings the two together with a common aim of deciphering the pre-warning messages of earth sciences with regard to carrying capacity, scarcity and the pattern of climatic changes in the region so that the administrative and individual conduct could be synchronized to achieve RRM. Disaster law strengthens the understanding that certain types of human conduct cannot be ignored as optional but should be treated as obligatory. It is an indispensable regulatory mechanism like a gauntlet around an ambitious and fast-track developers who discount life to things. It is a developing discourse and is not much encouraged by governments, administrators and private developers since it produces the future before the present and, then on that basis, demands policy restraints. Therefore it empowers communities against administrative and political recklessness, abuse of authority to inflict an irretrievable injury to natural habitats and living creatures. Resilience against disasters can be effectively built by empowering communities rather than just empowering administrative departments. RRM efforts are more sustainable through bottom-up approaches in contrast to the top-down government relief activity. Nations inadvertently create obstacles to RRM efforts in their inability to address legal gaps and promote collaboration to strengthen resilience of communities to disasters. At the same time it is also seen that the failure to build appropriate legal instruments in advance to address community responses, collaboration and emergency management can push administration into an overwhelming inflow of philanthropy and relief operations as a result of which specific vital aid can be delayed or even lost to affected communities. Disaster law relates to participation, damage control and local habitat management as mandatory conditions of governance besides fixing criminal liability of public administrators for being negligent towards this planning process or in its enforcement. The disaster law inadvertently sets a sustainable, reliable and cost-effective model of addressing disasters.

Formulating and identifying laws which prevent disasters and empower communities to participate and lead efforts in disaster management from cradle to grave is one of the strongest ways to build their resilience and reduce risk of disasters. Law helps in preventing, healing and in compensating the wrongdoings perpetrated by governance driven by consumerism and commodification over the habitat of clueless communities to disrupt their relationship with nature. It reinstates 'communities' as the sultans of local ecology and local administration as the beacon of disaster management.

Law a pivot for the post-Hyogo pedagogy of DM

It is important to understand the Hyogo Framework to analyse the pedagogies of disaster policies. This framework was a break from the past in converting a neutral and isolated science and technology-based learning to the one embedded in political, social and cultural categories or what one may like to address as 'critical pedagogy'. It reaffirmed the connection of RRM policies to a process of accompanying learners (administrators, scientists and communities) to discover ways to care for rather than impose drill learning in human lives. RRM is not just about knowing but also about changing ourselves and the world we live in. Hyogo changed the whole perception of looking at disasters from the erstwhile 'knowledge banks of science' which treated people as objects to be acted upon during crisis but as a relationship which generates compassion, peace, togetherness and sustainability. Ironically, this has neither been able to influence nor change the manner in which disaster management institutions have been functioning even though we are standing over the Hyogo deadline of 2015. Even though some individuals seem to have enjoyed the benefits of progress, institutions follow the old bureaucratic paradigm.

Introduction of 'resilience' in DRR indicated a need for institutional transformation, a refreshing institutional pedagogy of understanding the factors through which people return to normalcy after absorbing the trauma and shocks or surviving through devastating infrastructural, physical and emotional trauma striking them down and pushing them several years behind or even leaving them standing all alone in a rubble of human settlements. The whole new meaning brings the state in a new garb of decentralized constellation of community institutions being coordinated by enlightened and knowledge-based professional district-level bodies. Knowledge sharing would entail substantial commitment from governance to maintain a database of pre-existing community and household vulnerabilities such as disability, gender, age and education. These disabilities which prevent them from deciphering warnings prior to disasters and even if they did their inability to protect themselves or be rescued the way those who could shout, run and find their way to safety are crucial in the planning and design for preparedness. What is institutional preparedness to address trafficking and poaching of young girls, women and children during disasters? Several thousand women and children were trafficked during the June 2013 Uttarakhand disaster alone, but policies are still not open to anything beyond property and cash loot which are dealt with under IPC and CrPC sections through a fairly outdated set of dismissive police personnel. National Disaster Management Authority (NDMA) has to explore its new proactive leadership role in the midst of clueless and untrained local governance institutions.

Three words given here define the landscape of disaster management and now require a redefinition in the light of the changed pedagogy from 'rescue' to 'preparedness'. The whole epistemology changes from the first to the second approach. The three words used as pillars to plan and implement DRR may now be looked into through their new adopted pedagogies:

1 Vulnerability
2 Resilience
3 Risk

(1) *Vulnerability* means 'wounds' from the Latin *vulnerabilis* (Coppola, 2007). The literature on the definition of vulnerability has spread across disciplines from a 'physical exposure to extreme events' in engineering and sciences to 'a lack of power or access to information' in the social sciences literature. The two are closely linked to a pedagogical understanding of a

disaster. If one even starts from a seismologist's description, 'Earthquakes do not kill but bad buildings do'(Walsh, 2010), every disaster would simply become an 'act of human frailty' rather than 'an act of God', thereby entailing moral, administrative, constitutional and legal measures to prevent such frailties. It then becomes a problem of governance but a problem so immense that it can only be handled by communities and local institutions through decentralization of information, planning and finances. The problem is on how far the conventionally governed centralized systems are ready to share power with the local communities and how far the insulated structures of engineering and science would allow this to happen. This will be, in coming times, the key to preparedness. Therefore public law of accountability and constitutional responsibility of government may have to be brought in to invoke a meaningful understanding and a working structure to preparedness.

(2) *Resilience* is no more a biophysical attribute of bouncing back but the capacity of life to withstand and insulate suffering resulted from the nature and human frailties. It's an attribute of self-confidence coming from the knowledge of the system and the degree of bonding prevailing within the system. It's also a characteristic in which communities realize the benefits of collaboration in place of divisiveness in terms of caste, class, gender, language, wealth and positions. One may also realize the need for entrepreneurship so strongly emphasized by governance experts Osborne and Gaebler (1994) whose writings generated justifications for responsible citizenry by downsizing bureaucracy and generating a cost-effective governance. RRM can boast of resilience only if it brings in decentralization and entrepreneurship, but this would in turn need as much action at the community level as it would be at the district level. The district level may have to open gates for investing meaningfully in skill building, training, information dissemination, compulsory school education, implementing stringent programmes pertaining to primary health services directed at reducing infant mortality and maternal mortality, vocational and extra-curricular participation in all forms of local needs-based conservation, use and marketing of local products. Self-help groups, marketing cooperatives and usufruct sharing local groups are the pillars of resilience. There is also an immense need to prevent migration of outsiders in a community habitat since migrants are not bonded to local

ecosystem care and conservation. Therefore, resilience building efforts invoke relationships, interdependence and trust which is partly an outcome of shared local history and partly a product of social engineering through self-help groups, microcredit and reviving conventional agrarian and folk activities. Simple solutions such as a raised platform in a low-lying grassland habitat or a dyke construction in flood-prone regions or a small dam and sluice gates under the management of local villagers indicate that resilience is basically a two-pronged solution in RRM. The first solution is embedded within the policy maker's realization of local capacities, and second solution lies within the district administration's ability to explore locally available, time-tested, simple indigenous practices before implanting a mega-project in RRM. Such big solutions may not be sustainable as sooner or later they tend to become cash guzzlers for their dependence upon skills, expertise and equipment which can only be imported from outside.

(3) *Risk* is the third potentially used term in RRM, and this would be revisited here to highlight a substantially increased role of law in the usage of this term. Risk is commonly defined as the probability of a hazard multiplied with the frequency of its recurrence.

R (Risk) = Probability of hazard (PH) × Frequency of recurrence (FR) × Estimated losses

This is close to one of the older definitions given by Lawrance (1976, 8): 'Risk is a measure of probability and severity of harm', taking into account the magnitude of losses and severity of impact on lives and property. Looking at any hazard one need not jump to a conclusion that disasters are inevitable since every hazard is not really a disaster. Lack of law, weak governance and non-participative community converts a hazard to a disaster. An alert government would not take a backseat and discount scientific evidence. It is here that the technological perceptions of risks stand face to face with the social and political perceptions of these risks notwithstanding their different and crosscutting routes of understanding a risk. Thus many scholars have converted the risk formula by taking into account the social perceptions. Whyte (1982) suggests perceptions of probability and the magnitude which go beyond science and may come from local history and narratives of previous disasters:

$$R = \text{Probability of occurrence of an extreme event} \times (\text{Magnitude})^n$$

Here, n represents those social values which carry exclusive perceptions on a risk. In all fairness the local communities which include both human and non-humans are sensors to local risks, and ignoring this conveniently available inexpensive local wisdom for the mega-science of experts would only increase the severity of exposure and enhanced vulnerability of communities to disasters. Some social scientists have brought an assessment of risk closer to culture and administrative practices in a given terrain (Singh, 2005).

How would RRM look at community spaces?

The critical pedagogy of RRM suggests that whenever a state bypasses community cultural norms prevailing within a given space, it generates a form of anxiety (Giddens's 'existentialist anxiety' 1991, 187–201) which may more appropriately be addressed as termed by Lefebvre (1991, 281) and Giles (2006) as 'spaces created by violence'[3] which 'subordinates and totalizes the various aspects of social practices – legislation, culture, knowledge education – within a determinate space; namely the space of the ruling class's hegemony over its people and over the nationhood that it has arrogated'(Lefebvre, 1991, 281). The community spaces are likely to get traversed by what the state believes to be 'resilience building' which in reality may be working against it. Lefebvre indicates that it is the mass culture of disaster management that would also define resilience, consequently turning community effort on resilience building as more interfering and authoritarian. He writes, 'It (violence) manifests itself from the moment any action introduces the rational into the real from outside by means of tools which strike, slice and cut and keep doing so until the purpose of their aggression is achieved' (p. 289). The disaster law is expected to demand and make sure that it is not just the nuts-and-bolts understanding of resilience building but the cultural, anthropological and ecological understanding of resilience which can bring some meaning to RRM.

The whole of the RRM activity could look like a monolithic giant machine rolling over these community spaces of vibrant autonomy called areas, regions, localities and nations. If disaster management is taken up as an engineering and instrumental approach, it may definitely turn into such a money guzzler Leviathan which would attract foreign experts, NGOs and private companies trying to demonstrate their corporate social responsibility records. A new form of commodification would usurp knowledge and information embedded in local communities, which would easily fall prey once again to the mass culture of disaster management. Interestingly experts currently working on disaster management have missed this point that new forms of commodification can entrench themselves, from where they replaced the previous form. Shane Gunster in *Capitalizing on Culture* (2004, 26) expands this phenomenon further as a type of 'Culture Industry' where commodification of culture becomes a major concern. This critical pedagogy of disasters suggests that the three terms, that is, vulnerability, resilience and risk, which are characterized by measures such as standardization, interchangeability, repetition and pseudo-individuation to achieve some form of a cultural or existential shift are determined by 'capital' (Gunster, 2004, 41). Therefore, resilience building perceptions hinge on cash economy or commoditization of environmental and ecosystem services without bringing any respite from recurrent disasters. The process gets distanced from its objective in creating a dangerous epistemological divide between RRM activities and occurrence of disasters. Most recent disasters like the one in Uttarakhand, Chennai and even the earlier one in Louisiana (USA) are examples of such unbridled commodification.

Eric Fromm[4] indicates how individual identity (or community identity as in DRR) gets easily compromised with the mass culture. The technological firms gasping to sell their products may create a mass culture of technology-driven early warning systems at a place where the howling of a dog or a shrieking bird can prevent the community from a disaster. Eric Fromm writes, 'The individual ceases to be himself; – he therefore becomes exactly as all others are and as they expect him to be'. Justifications are enormous to accept these technologies, but what is the community relationship to these adopted technologies? In a developing country that has a starving, below-poverty population, the huge allocation of funds to states for RRM should be used discerningly so that what is adopted should also be functional rather than be adopted simply because of the mass culture of adoption. The Gadgil and Kasturirangan report on the Western Ghats has demonstrated how individuals start cockatooing the majority's stronger voice, and DRR gets diluted to fulfil the demands of the stronger, better-mobilized technocratic interests. This is very well manifested in a scenario of human insecurity, environmental risk and extinction of species which the global leaders continue to treat as part of national politics rather than a survival issue for the whole universe.

Shane Gunster (2004) successfully attempts through anthropological studies a non-reductive theory of human experience that attends to the opportunities and dangers arising from the confluence of culture and economics.

Singh (2005) explains how quantum mechanics offers a method to understand the structures of society and about the ecological bonds which are epistemic bonds (EB), bringing people together and sustaining them within a common mode of beliefs, values and culture or more appropriately in an ecosystem. Thus EB is a 'strong attractive force' composed of a set of relationships between the resources and the resource-dependent community (Singh, 2005, 68). This fostered a sense of security by evolving a social order which took care of contingencies and corrosiveness of change and could be referred to as the community's 'Ontological Security' (Giddens, 1991, 35). This ontological security is the key to facilitate and promote with ease activities on community resilience building. Disaster law would be rooted within this ontological security of community systems and local governance.

Strengthening resilience through dispensation of justice

Hart writes, 'We talk of justice "according to law" and yet also of the justice or injustice of the laws' (2002, 7). To understand this paradox one needs to understand the nature of the best and the most comprehensive legislation which may fall short of justice as much as the fact that even the best law has a fair amount of moral rules derived from natural law and yet may have left out much of morality and natural justice. Thus as Hart emphasizes (ibid., 14), there is much about law and its relations to other things that not every lawyer can explain or understand. This is exactly what the disaster law is challenged with and is likely to be used to serve the interests of the more consolidated commercial interests. The critical legal scholars would argue that the idea of RRM is a safe rationalization of a hidden social reality[5] of unequal power relations. The need for a legal philosophy arises for undertaking conceptual analysis which leads to sustainability rather than a repeat of the failed policies. Thus RRM may not be a completely neutral policy, whereas the disaster management experts may continue to believe in this.

Therefore, disaster law demands much more than what the judiciary has been giving or is able to give to disaster prevention, mitigation and risk reduction. This law works at the junction of administrative negligence, environmental harm and human rights. Taken alone the three situations mentioned earlier are most likely to become the captives of the letter of law, and justice may slip away in favour of stronger interests. That the 'law has been followed' would provide an ethical veil over the ghastly foundations which the nexus of administrator-commercial interests-governments lay for the eruption of disasters.

Under this highly volatile environment, what could be the role of disaster law?

If administration fails to dispense justice, then the courts have to take a proactive stand to prevent the large number of fragile zones in Asia affected by man-made disasters. Unbridled and unchecked chemical effluents and toxic discharges from industries have polluted groundwater, eroded coastline and generated a large number of diseases in the region. A large number of ecological refugees migrate to safer zones. For example, in the 1984 Bhopal gas tragedy, the leakage of an unprecedented storage of a highly toxic methyl isocyanate gas in the densest part of city area had resulted in more than 4,000 deaths, almost the same number as being disabled and more than 500,000 partially maimed. Administrative negligence, unaccountable extraction, unregulated industries, greedy extraction are all situations that cause catastrophic events and thus grievous injury and setback to communities and developmental process.

The courts have risen up to address these forms of administrative lapses and political corruption while dealing with environment including the life and health of people. The suo motu provisions within which courts have the discretionary powers to prevent such action in achieving sustainable development have increased. Khurram Hashmi[6] observes that India has the most active suo motu jurisdiction as compared to judiciaries in neighbouring countries. Pakistan apex judiciary has invoked Article 184(3) of the constitution along with the high courts, under Article 199 of the Constitution to dispense justice suo motu[7] under the currently functional 1973 Constitution. The scope of Article 184(3) was expanded by Justice Md. Haleem by including Public Interest Litigation (PIL) in the original jurisdiction under the said article. Justice (Rtd.) Nasir Aslam Zahid[8] describes Justice Saleem Akhtar as the green judge who woke up one morning to find that the coastline of Balochistan which was inhabited by extremely poor people was being dumped with chemical waste. He immediately convinced his other colleagues and took a suo motu action forbidding the disposal of chemical waste off the coast of Balochistan. This was considered as the human rights case[9] as it invoked Article (9) 'the right to life' under the 1973 Pakistan Constitution. However, it also prevented the coastline from being eroded and thus protected the coastline from such arbitrary misuse forever. In *Lahore Conservation Society v. Government of Punjab*,[10] the Chief Justice Chaudhry prohibited the felling of trees and prevented the construction of roads through a green area. The famous case of *Shehla Zia v. WAPDA*[11] applied the 'precautionary principle' and also expanded the scope of Article (9) 'Right to

Life' by adding 'healthy and safe environment' into it. The concept of sustainable development was also invoked by referring to the need for balancing economic progress and prosperity with a healthy and safe environment. The chief justice of Pakistan has taken suo motu action in a number of other cases such as the New Murre Project[12] and the Islamabad Chalet Case & Pir Sohawa Valley Villas[13] to prevent action which caused immense environmental harm and also human distress.

In Bangladesh suo motu action by courts has been slow, but Justice M. M. Hoque in the Dhaka High Court[14] passed rule *nisi*[15] in order to free Nazrul Islam who was illegally detained and was languishing for 12 years in jail for a petty offence he committed when he was nine years old. This led to a more proactive suo motu action from the judiciary[16] when many other undertrial children were released from many jails of Bangladesh.

The Indian Constitution has many provisions through which courts can legitimately impart justice to the victims. Disaster law would preferably stand up to Article 48A, which states 'the state shall endeavor to protect and improve the environment and to safeguard the forests and wildlife of the country', and Article 51A (g), which states that 'it shall be the duty of every citizen of India to protect and improve the natural environment including forests, lakes, rivers and wildlife and to have compassion for all living creatures', to suggest as in the case of *N. R. Nair and Ors., etc. v. Union of India and Ors*[17] (6 June 2000) that no trade or business or any activity commercial or otherwise could be permitted under Article 19(1) (g) if it inflicts unnecessary pain or suffering on animals. These directive principles of state policy cannot be ignored while considering the reasonableness of restrictions as was ruled by the Supreme Court in *MRF Ltd. v. Inspector, Kerala Government*[18] (1998).

Many provisions are part of the discretionary jurisdiction of the courts and are more often invoked to protect the rights and entitlements of suffering individuals or communities. Articles 32, 136, 142 and 226 allow courts to take suo motu cognizance of a situation and deliver justice to the victims. Article 136 enables the Supreme Court to grant a special leave to appeal against any judgement, decree, determination, sentence or order of a court. It vests the Supreme Court with extraordinary powers; for example, in *Tirupati Balaji Developers (P) Ltd. & Ors. v. State of Bihar & Ors*[19], the judgement highlighted that 'it is an extraordinary jurisdiction vested by the Constitution in the Court with implicit trust and faith and extraordinary care and caution has to be observed in the exercise of this jurisdiction'. Article 142 further observes that the Supreme Court in the exercise of its jurisdiction may pass such decree or make such order as is necessary for doing *complete justice* in any case or matter pending before it. These articles confirm that the constitution makers perceived of this Apex Court as a provider of justice and an eradicator of injustices within the whole trajectory of justice dispensation in the country, or the expression under Article 142, 'complete justice' wouldn't have been mentioned. Article 142 has been a much-contested section of the powers of the Supreme Court. While in *E. K. Chandrasenan v. State of Kerala*[20] this article was held to empower the Supreme Court to deliver complete justice and initiate suo motu proceedings, it was also considered to be used with caution yet should not be controlled by any statutory provisions or enactments in delivering justice.[21]

Article 226 vests the High Court with suo motu jurisdiction for the protection of rights as enshrined in Chapter III and for imparting justice to the affected party. High Court shall have powers, throughout the territories in relation to which it exercises jurisdiction, to issue to any person or authority, including in appropriate cases, any government, within those territories, directions, orders or writs, including writs in the nature of habeas corpus, mandamus, prohibitions, quo warranto and certiorari, or any of them, for the enforcement of any of the rights conferred by Part III. There have been a large number of suo motu decisions taken by the Supreme Court as well as the High Court in case of Coastal Zone Regulation (CRZ) violations and against the construction of apartments and hotels within the prohibited zone in Kochi, Ernakulam and Vembanad. One could link the development of law, which in this case is about the CRZ laws in relationship to fishing communities, which could have high potential for enhancing resilience levels of local communities to coastal disasters.[22]

With this jurisdictional freedom to judges through the use of suo motu provisions of the constitution, they are in a position to address community concerns of public-spirited individuals and issue injunctions or stay on activities which bear a substantial influence on resilience building activities in fragile and vulnerable regions. This has, however, brought criticism from ambitious developers and states hungry for foreign economic investments.

Strengthening green institutions such as the National Green Tribunal

The concern for environmental justice has come a long way. The 1972 Conference on Human Environment at Stockholm and the 1992 World Commission on Environment and Development (WCED) at Rio de

Janeiro and the frequent exercise of the constitutional right to life conferred under Article 21 suggest that environmental rights and human rights cannot be separated. This has also enabled the institutionalization of justice dispensation structures like the National Green Tribunal (NGT) through the Parliamentary Act 2010. The Tribunal functions to protect and promote (1) 'sustainable development', (2) 'polluter pay principle' and the (3) 'precautionary doctrine'. The Tribunal has been given wide powers to look into and watch the functioning of various acts for groundwater, water bodies, air, rivers, sea and coastal regions, mountains. Under its Chapter III, Section 19, (1–3) the Tribunal is not being bound by the procedure laid down by the Code of Civil Procedure but shall be guided by the principles of natural justice. It has also been authorized to regulate its own procedure and to try cases suo motu to prevent harm to environment and human life. The Tribunal has also not been bound by the Indian Evidence Act 1872 despite the fact that for the purpose of discharging its functions, it would be vested with the same powers as are vested in a civil court under the Code of Civil Procedure 1908. The NGT is expected to implement the decisions taken at various UN Conferences on environment protection. In the past one year the suo motu proceedings of the NGT have been recognized as a valuable contribution to environmental protection following which the government has increased its budgetary grant by four times from a meagre Rs 8 crore in the past to Rs 32 crore.

The NGT is currently the strongest protector against environmental hazards which are surreptitiously turning into disasters. The Tribunal has been moving forward and has attempted to steer through despite the stringent criticism coming from the pro-profit-alone forces. The NGT has taken action against mining[23] work in the Mandla district in the state of Madhya Pradesh on the plea that mining industries which lie in the midst of two prominent national parks, Kanha National Park and Bandhavgarh National Park, would do irreparable harm to the wildlife habitat. The Tribunal also highlighted the 'irresponsible attitude' of miners in bypassing the approved production capacity by the competent administrative authority. Close to Delhi, the capital city, NGT has initiated proceedings against the Delhi government for constructing roads in Asola Wildlife Sanctuary. In a major battle to protect the Mangar Bani forests in the Aravallis ranges over which Delhi, Haryana and parts of Uttar Pradesh and Rajasthan are dependent upon as the only remaining rechargeshed for water and green corridor for wild life in the midst of Seismic Zone IV, it has also been classified as a natural conservation zone in the draft regional plan 2021. The massive media coverage led by the *Hindustan Times* reporter Snehil

Sinha and the environmental group led by Chetan Agarwal and Jamia Millia Islamia University's media department strengthened the movement to 'Save Mangar Bani Forest' from the real estate developers.

The task of bringing resilience is fraught with political contestations as well as acrimonious legal battles not just between communities, private players and the government but also among government organizations. NGT[24] faced the ire of the Kerala government when it was addressing concerns in an appeal by two Thiruvananthapuram-based environmental activists, Wilfred J. and V. Marydasan, seeking the NGT's intervention to direct that coastal areas throughout the country to be protected under the 1991 CRZ notification and specifically to save the Vizhinjam coast of 'outstanding natural beauty' and those around which were 'likely to be inundated due to rise in sea level consequent upon global warming'. Jogy Scaria, the counsel for the Kerala government, questioned the suo motu powers of NGT to intervene in the CRZ notifications and environmental clearances already given to the Rs 5,000 crore Vizhinjam Sea Project in Kerala by the Ministry of Environment, Forest and Climate Change (MOEFCC) in January 2014. The NGT took cognizance of the fisherfolk communities as well as the fragility of ecosystems which were both to be protected.

The NGT was again questioned when its southern zone headed by Justice M. Chockalingam and the expert member Prof. Dr R. Nagendran issued notices suo motu[25] to the commissioner of Chennai Corporation for the closure of 869 companies of Packaged Drinking Water Manufacturer's Association in Chennai. This action was taken after a newspaper report on concerns regarding groundwater and pollution control measures in Chennai. The reaction to prevent a proactive NGT position came in the form of questioning[26] the very grounds of its suo motu jurisdictional powers under the NGT Act of 2010. A few months later we saw the blatant exposure of this government organization in its helplessness in preventing floods by blaming the incessant rains. Floods only exposed the environmental neglect emerging out of lethargic, corrupt and irresponsible governance alliances which these public organizations develop to give a scintillating modern look to the city. The environmental neglect was exposed on many fronts (reduced level in groundwater, loss of water bodies, blocked drainage, illegal constructions, concretization of green spaces), and the Chennai Corporation did push the whole city to a kind of disaster, death and displacement never experienced before by its inhabitants. NGT could play a powerful role in resilience building in urban and rural terrains. Disaster law is well positioned to fix accountability of disasters as it is a recordkeeper of performance and decision making despite the long gestation period within which a disaster gradually builds up to surface. Therefore it is also a tool to interrogate mega-structures of globalization which are built within the neo-liberal rhizome[27] state structures.

The MOEFCC accused NGT for causing major embarrassment to the government. However, NGT quickly snapped back to clarify that the MOEFCC is merely an administrative body to sanction funds for the NGT to function and beyond that it cannot have any controls. It also explained that the language of the provisions of the NGT Act is such that notwithstanding the power of judicial review under Article 226 and Article 32 for the High Courts and the Supreme Court, respectively, it is by necessary implication given the power of judicial review under Section 19(1–3) as well. To deny this would be a 'Travesty of Justice'. The government later withdrew its affidavit.

The trajectory of NGT itself suggests that mitigation and risk reduction will not occur unless the justice dispensation institutions are strengthened and are made autonomous bodies.

Disaster laws have a clear thematic focus

(i) Land use and land conservation policy, water conservation laws, river bed protection laws, coastal regulatory zones and natural resource protection laws: Implementation of these laws would need enormous sensitivity in generating a region-specific 'building laws and by-laws' so that any acquisition of agricultural and forest land does not ignore natural waterways, aquifers, natural watersheds and water bodies which are reachargesheds for ground water and aquifers. The government should encourage sustainable land use and carrying capacity–based management of ecosystems to reduce risk and vulnerabilities. In achieving this task, courts have to largely depend upon GIS and digitized mapping in resolving local conflicts and standardize justice dispensation. Many state forest departments are currently relying on digitized maps of the area to identify the notified forest lands but a lot needs to be done here before communities could actually become resilient on local issues.

(ii) *Legal framework for 'convergence planning' at all levels of governance*: National institutional and legislative frameworks which reduce the risk of disasters build community resilience and decrease human, non-human and ecosystem vulnerabilities. This should integrate disaster risk reduction planning into the health sector; promote the goal of 'hospitals safe from disaster', reinforce existing healthcare facilities, particularly those providing primary health care.

(iii) Ensuring a design of governance based on the link between administrative responsibility and culpability as grounds of public accountability: This would suggest that communities have rights to decide on their planning and processes of resource sharing and management while administrators would act as information disseminators on hazards and their mitigation or resilience against disasters. This encourages a trans-disciplinary approach to governance which has a knowledge-based access to situational as well as sustainable planning mechanisms.

(iv) *Reducing Vulnerabilities*: Incorporate RRM measures into post-disaster recovery and rehabilitation processes, social safety nets, insurance sector and use opportunities during the recovery phase to develop capacities through the sharing of expertise, knowledge and lessons learned. Engage fully in supporting and implementing the International Strategy for Disaster Reduction, and cooperate with local community groups and experts to advance humanitarian and sustainable development fields as set out in this framework for action.

(v) *Non-human species and ecosystem protection laws*: Implement integrated environmental and natural resource management approaches that incorporate safety and food arrangements for the domestic, pet and wild animals. Communities in flood- and drought-affected regions lose their animals in large numbers, which causes not just an immense economic loss but also deep psychological trauma because most of these animals lost are like family members to them. There is no other country in the world where the Parliament has risen with such great sensitivity through the experience of disasters like the US Congress which passed the Public Law 109–308 (HR3858) on the Pet Evacuation and Transportation Standards Act (PETS).[28] In India the state and central governments have shown great complacency to repeated disasters in the Northeastern states and in Bihar.

(vi) *Emergency governance:* This would mean a functional network of administrative agencies like the National Disaster Response Force, well coordinated and skilled to handle multidimensional aspects of emergencies beyond specialized territories. On one hand, this needs inter-agency coordination and on the other a training of personnel in domestic facilitation and regulation of International Disaster Relief and Initial Recovery Assistance (also known as the IDRL Guidelines). The firefighting department in a city is a part of emergency governance.

Conclusion

Disaster law is a tool to regulate governance, ethics and decisions to the demands of sustainable, inclusive and healthy planet. Disaster law brings the communities close to governance and reactivates them to decide for their safety while generating accountable governance. Disaster law may also push the need for preparedness in terms of deciphering the pre-warning messages of earth sciences with regard to carrying capacity, scarcity and the pattern of climatic changes in the region so that the administrative and individual conduct could be synchronized to achieve RRM. Disaster law strengthens the understanding that certain types of human conduct cannot be ignored as optional but be treated as obligatory. It is a developing discourse and is not much encouraged by governments, administrators and private developers since it produces the future before the present and then on that basis demands policy restraints. However, strengthening green tribunals, local governance and community self-help groups may facilitate a lasting resilience building (RRM) in an area.

Notes

1 The Sendai Framework for Disaster Risk Reduction 2015–2030 was adopted at the Third UN World Conference on Disaster Risk Reduction in Sendai, Japan, on 18 March 2015.
2 Raul Prebisch was the founder of UNCTAD in 1964 within United Nations and emphasized equal trade relations between the developed and the developing states.
3 Henri Lefebvre (1991) links the desire to create a space with the violence of excluding others through a powerful control.
4 Eric Fromm in *The Fear of Freedom* (p. 160) indicates a phenomenon of 'authoritarian conformity' or how people acquire the face of what everyone wishes to see.
5 For further reading, Jeffrie G. Murphy and Jules L. Coleman (1997). *Philosophy of Law: An Introduction to Jurisprudence*, Delhi: Oxford University Press.
6 Khurram Hashmi (2012). The Power of Suo Motu, *The Express Tribune*, Opinion page, 1 May.
7 See Dominic Nardi (2010). Pakistan Judiciary: Suo Motu Tango. Retrieved from http//www.comparative constitutions.org/2010/05/dominic-nardi-on-pakistan-judiciary.html (Accessed 15 December 2015).
8 Singh and Zahid (2008). *Strengthening Governance through Access to Justice*, Delhi: PHI Learning, p. 146.
9 PLD 1994 SC. 102.
10 CP No.16/2006.
11 1994, PLD, SC 693.

12 2005, PLD, SC 10.
13 2005, PLD, SC 13.
14 State v. Deputy Commissioner, Satkhira (1993) 43, DLR (HLD) 643.
15 *Nisi* is a Latin phrase where the ruling of a court becomes final unless one or both parties show cause for it not to be.
16 Editor, *The Daily Protham Alo v. Bangladesh* (2003)11 BLT (HLD) 281 and *Labu Mia v. State* (2001) 53 DLR (HLD) 218.
17 AIR 2000, Kerala 340.
18 AIR 1999 SC 188.
19 AIR 2004 SC 2351.
20 AIR 1995 SC 1066.
21 Laxmidas Morarji v. Behrose Darab Madan (2009) 10 SCC 425.
22 See S. Rodrigues, G. Balasubramaniam, S. M. Peter, M. Duraiswamy and P. Jaiprakash (2008). Community perceptions of resources, policy and development, post-tsunami interventions and community institutions in Tamil Nadu, India, Chennai & Banglore, India: UNDP/UNTRS & ATREE.
23 Judgement of the National Green Tribunal (Central Zonal Bench, Bhopal) Suo Motu Vs Ministry of Environment Others dated 04/04/2014 regarding Dolomite mines in Mandla District of Madhya Pradesh and being a threat to Tiger corridor in Kanha. Original Source: www.greentribunal.gov.in/judgment/16_2013(App)(CZ)_4Apr2014_final_order.pdf
24 *Wilfred J., Marydasan v. Ministry of Environment and Forest, State of Kerala, Vizhingjan International Seaport Ltd.* (a State government undertaking) Original Jurisdiction appl. no.(74), Appeal no.(14) of 2014. Justice Swatantra Kumar took note of fisherfolk communities and the ecosystem losses in the judgement.
25 In Application No. 40 of 2013 (SZ) (Suo motu v. The Commissioner, Corporation of Chennai and others), Application No. 181 of 2013 (SZ) (Suo motu v. Union of India and others), and Application No. 299 of 2013 (SZ) (Suo motu v. Additional Chief Secretary to Government, Environment and Forest Department) and Application No. 294 of 2013 (SZ) (Suo motu v. Union of India and others).
26 Chief Justice Sanjay Kishan Kaul and Justice T. S. Sivagnanam on hearing the writ petition of *Sundararajan v. The Deputy Registrar NGT Southern Zone* (No.35098, 2013) prevented the NGT (SZ) from using suo motu powers in this case.
27 'Rhizome' state structure is a philosophical concept developed by Deleuze and Guattari in their book *Capitalisme et Schizophrénie* (1972) which was translated in English by Brian Massumi in 1987 as *A Thousand Plateaus*. Rhizome as an underground subterranean plant has a root-like stem and leafy apex which defies organizational structure and planning. It is unplanned, can connect to anything non-hierarchical and can ceaselessly establish connections between semiotic chains, organizations of power and circumstances related to arts, science and social struggles. This model of culture is being used in this chapter to describe a neoliberal opportunistic connections which defy a regular planning mechanism and chronological order of decision making.
28 Amita Singh (2015). 'Disaster Management Is Not Only about Humans', 25 July, 02:29 IST.

References

Coppola, D. P. (2007). *Introduction to International Disaster Management*. Amsterdam: Elsevier.

Fromm, E. (1960). *The Fear of Freedom*. London: Routledge, p. 160.

Giddens, A. (1991). *Modernity and Self-Identity: Self and Society in the Late Modern Age*. Stanford, CA: Stanford University Press.

Giles, J. R. (2006). *The Spaces of Violence*. Alabama, USA: University of Alabama Press.

Gunster, S. (2004). *Capitalizing on Culture: Critical Theory for Cultural Studies*. Toronto: University of Toronto Press.

Hart, H. L. A. (2002). *The Concept of Law*. New Delhi: Oxford University Press, 2nd ed.

Hashmi, K. (2012). The Power of Suo Motu. *The Express Tribune*, Opinion page, 1 May.

Lawrance, D. M. (1976). *Of Acceptable Risk: Science and the Determination of Safety*. Los Altos, CA: William Kauffmann.

Lefebvre, H. (1991). *The Production of Space*. Oxford: Cambridge, MA: Blackwell.

Love, J. L. (1980). Raul Prebisch and the Origins of the Doctrine of Unequal Exchange. *Latin American Research Review*, *15*(3), 45–72.

Murphy, J. G. & Coleman, J. L. (1997). *Philosophy of Law, An Introduction to Jurisprudence*. Delhi: Oxford University Press.

Nardi, D. (2010). *Pakistan Judiciary: Suo Motu Tango*. Retrieved December 15, 2015 from http//www.comparative constitutions.org/2010/05/dominic-nardi-on-pakistan-judiciary.html

Osborne, David. & Gaebler, Ted. (1992). *Reinventing Government*. Boston: Addison-Wesley Publishing Co.

Rodrigues, S., Balasubramaniam, G., Peter, S. M., Duraiswamy, M. & Jaiprakash, P. (2008). Community Perceptions of Resources, Policy and Development, Post-Tsunami Interventions and Community Institutions in Tamil Nadu, India, UNDP/UNTRS Chennai & ATREE Bangalore, India.

Singh, A. (March, 2005). Indian Administrative Theory, Context and Epistemology. *Administrative Theory & Praxis*, 27(1), 51–80.

Singh, A. (2015). *Disaster Management Is Not Only about Humans. Hindustan Times*, 25 July.

Singh, A. & Zahid, Nasir Aslam. (2008). *Strengthening Governance through Access to Justice*. Delhi: PHI Learning.

Walsh, B. (2010). After the Destruction: What Will It Take to Rebuild Haiti? www.com/time/special/packages/printout/0,29,239,_1953494_1954338.00.html#

Whyte, A. V. (1982). Probabilities, Consequences, and Values in the Perception of Risk. *In Risk Assessment and Perception Symposium*. Toronto: Royal Society of Canada. (as given in Paul, Bimal Kanti. (2011). *Environmental Hazards and Disasters, Contexts, Perspectives and Management*. Oxford: Wiley-Blackwell).

Zack, N. (2012). 'Disaster Relief' in Ruth Chadwick (ed.) *Encyclopedia of Applied Ethics*. Amsterdam: Elsevier, Academic Press, p. 821.

2 Disaster laws

Saving lives, reducing risk in the Asia Pacific

Gabrielle Emery and Padmini Nayagam

It is common knowledge that the Asia Pacific is the most disaster-prone region in the world – it is where 40 per cent of the world's natural hazards occur, where 60 per cent of all deaths due to natural hazards happen and where 80 per cent of people affected by natural hazards live. Such extreme events show no sign of abating, and due largely to the effects of climate change, the number and destructiveness of disasters are on the rise.[1]

Recent years have unfortunately continued to bring massive disasters overstepping previous records of misery and destruction. During 2016–2016, Nepal suffered a series of earthquakes affecting over 8 million people – a third of its population – and Cyclone Pam, one of the worst storms in Pacific history, affected more than half of the population of Vanuatu. Western Africa is just emerging from the world's largest outbreak of Ebola haemorrhagic fever, killing more than 11,000 people.

These disasters are not impartial in the way they spread their impact. Evidence shows that the largest human price is consistently borne by the poor and the vulnerable, both in wealthy and in developing countries. They affect not only individuals and communities but also state and business infrastructure and can reverse long-term development gains of countries. Over the past 20 years, natural disasters have caused $2 trillion in economic losses globally.[2]

It is also well accepted that the actions and decisions of individuals, communities and nations make a significant difference as to whether a natural hazard turns into a disaster. The term 'disaster risk reduction' in its broadest sense means 'making decisions to reduce the human impact of natural hazards'. It is evident therefore that laws, policies and regulatory frameworks can and should play a critical role in ensuring both risk reduction and that they are legally prepared in the event of a large-scale disaster response.

Globally, national-level institutions and local organisations have significant and increasing capacities to manage the risk and impact of humanitarian crises in their countries. The primacy of national-led approaches and the right and responsibility of each state to take care of the victims of natural disasters and other emergencies occurring on its territory has long been recognized under international law. This is elucidated in the UN General Assembly resolution[3] that underpins the current international humanitarian architecture, providing the basis for principled humanitarian action.

Since this time, there is evidence of increasingly professional disaster management institutions and frameworks in place which allow governments to provide assistance through specialized agencies, line ministries, military and civil defence units and other public organs. This range of tools and the sheer size and geographical coverage of government institutions in many countries mean that they are potentially able to deliver timely, large-scale disaster response informed by an understanding of local cultures and languages.

Such trends are also evident in South Asia. The experiences of many South Asia states affected by tsunami in the Indian Ocean triggered progress in the region to develop and strengthen laws and policies related to disaster risk management. This has been carried out with varying levels of success across in the individual countries. There have also been initiatives to strengthen regional collaboration and coordination on disaster risk management. This is illustrated by the 2011 South Asian Association for Regional Cooperation (SAARC) Agreement on Rapid Response to Natural Disasters (SAARD) which, among other things, demonstrates South Asian Member States' commitment to being legally prepared to facilitate and regulate international disaster assistance to the needy. Although this agreement is not yet in force, it reflects the desired direction of governments in the region.

In the same year that South Asian governments came to this regional agreement, a resolution was adopted at the 31st International Conference of the Red Cross Red Crescent[4] which called upon all state parties to the Geneva Conventions (including South Asian states) to strengthen their legal, policy and institutional frameworks for disaster mitigation, response and recovery. It also encouraged them to work in partnership with their National Red Cross and Red Crescent Societies and other external partners in doing so.

For over a decade, the International Federation of Red Cross and Red Crescent Societies (IFRC) has been conducting research and undertaking advocacy on legal issues that arise in international disaster response operations, and more recently on risk reduction and the law.

International assistance can sometimes mean the difference between life and death in disasters like these, and very frequently mean the difference between a quick and a protracted shift towards recovery. Yet, while there has, unfortunately, been a great deal of practice with international response operations, they have become increasingly complex to manage, as the numbers and variety of international responders have grown over time.

In 2001, the IFRC commenced a dedicated project of research and consultations related to how international response operations are facilitated and regulated. In 2003, the 28th International Conference of the Red Cross and Red Crescent[5] welcomed this initiative and invited the IFRC to extend its research and to consider the 'development of models, tools and guidelines for practical use in international disaster response activities'.

Over the course of the next six years of extensive research and consultations,[6] including conducting case studies in several dozen countries, the IFRC found a common set of regulatory problems plaguing response operations. These included both excessive bureaucracy in some areas and insufficient oversight in others. Seemingly simple issues, such as obtaining visas for relief personnel, customs clearance and tax exemptions for relief goods and equipment, or permissions to operate in affected areas, have often snarled operations. At the same time, oversight gaps allowed for the arrival of inappropriate or unnecessary relief items, uncoordinated and unprincipled aid activities and other quality issues in some international efforts. As a result, aid was slower, more expensive, less effective and much less supportive of domestic efforts than it should have been.

The IFRC's research found that the major reason for these problems was the widespread lack of specific rules related to international disaster relief. Very few states had comprehensive domestic rules on this topic and thus find themselves improvising once a disaster strikes. While a great deal of rule-making has occurred on these issues at the regional and global levels, the resulting instruments remain rather scattered and incomplete, with little implementation in practice.

In 2007, Resolution 4[7] of the 30th International Conference adopted the 'Guidelines for the Domestic Facilitation and Regulation of International Disaster Relief and Initial Recovery Assistance' (also known as the 'IDRL Guidelines'[8]). The IDRL Guidelines were drawn from existing laws and norms at the international and regional levels and negotiated over a two-year period after wide-ranging consultations with disaster management officials and experts. The IDRL Guidelines insist that responders should be expected to abide by minimum standards in delivering their relief efforts, in particular the principles of humanity, neutrality and impartiality. In 2011, Resolution 7[9] of the 31st International Conference reiterated the determination of conference members to make use of the guidelines as well as the 'urgency' for states to strengthen their legal preparedness. Over the course of this period, National Red Cross and Red Crescent Societies, with the support of the IFRC, have assisted their governments in using the IDRL Guidelines to examine existing laws and procedures in many countries around the world, including through formal technical assistance projects in some 46 countries. As of today 21 countries have changed their laws or procedures drawing in part on the IDRL Guidelines, and draft bills, policies or regulations are pending in a further 16.[10]

Nevertheless, the overwhelming majority of states still lack comprehensive rules for managing international disaster assistance, and existing regional and global frameworks remain scattered and of highly variable application. There is little disagreement with the notion that better legal preparedness would be helpful, but developing the political capital to actually adopt new rules has been a slow process in many countries. Moreover, a number of countries that have adopted new legislative language have preferred to leave key details to subsequent regulations or procedures that have yet to be completed.

Meanwhile, regulatory problems remain a major concern in operations. A 2014 survey[11] commissioned by the IFRC of 15 major international operations since 2007 has found persistent and generalized lack of clarity around roles and responsibilities among domestic agencies for managing international relief, inconsistent approaches (often dependent on personal relationships) related to the clearance of imported goods and equipment and issuance of visas, complicated registration rules and major coordination gaps. Likewise a forthcoming report jointly commissioned by IFRC and WHO focuses specifically on the management of foreign medical teams in 14 recent global operations and has found that many governments have struggled with the selection, coordination, tasking and oversight of such teams, in the absence of previously developed procedures. As a result, many teams have lacked capacity, materials and competence in areas actually needed. Concerns about these issues have also regularly surfaced in the many regional consultations that have been held in connection with the upcoming World Humanitarian Summit.[12]

Another significant development in this space in recent years has been the International Law Commission's (ILC) nearly completed work on its 'draft articles on the protection of persons in the event of a disaster',[13] which it is likely to present to states in the form of a draft global treaty. The ILC adopted a first reading of its draft articles in 2014 and requested written comments from states and certain agencies as of January 2016. This process is still under way. However, outside the specialized context of the United Nations' Sixth Committee, there has been little awareness of the initiative or discussion (in particular among disaster management officials) about the merits of the ILC's text and whether a treaty would add value.

In terms of South Asia, agreements like the SAARD lay the foundation for South Asian states to improve their legal preparedness for disaster response and regional cooperation and a basis on which to take forward IDRL issues regionally. Despite the known issues surrounding multilateral work on trans-boundary issues in South Asia, there continues to remain a considerable level of expectation for a regional disaster risk management approach. Although the SAARD goes someway to address the legal framework for regional cooperation for disaster management, the agreement is not yet enforceable and lacks binding force on member states.[14]

Even without the implementation of a regional framework, it remains a concern that few South Asian states have robust domestic procedures or mechanisms to manage and regulate international disaster assistance in their laws or policies. Recent events such as the Nepal earthquakes and reoccurring flood situations throughout the region should serve as a wake-up call for all countries in South Asia to review their laws and policies to continue to develop, update and implement strong disaster laws and policies. It is these laws that form the foundation for the actions, roles and responsibilities that can – and do – save lives.

Strong and inclusive legal frameworks are necessary not only to better guide response operations in the event of 'mega disasters' but also to ensure better preparedness in the face of a disaster or to reduce the risk of a natural hazard turning into a 'disaster' in the first place. In fact, law presents one of the most powerful tools at states' disposal for reducing disaster risks. In Vietnam, for example, legal and policy frameworks concerning structural works such as dykes, drainage and safe shelters, together with non-structural measures such as DRR awareness and education, timely evacuations and relocations based on risk assessments, have tangibly resulted in saving lives. Over the 10 years that these measures were implemented, the number of deaths from floods dropped from 600 down to 60 in the Mekong Delta region.

In 2005, the Hyogo Framework for Action identified legislation as a key means to ensure that disaster risk reduction is a national and a local priority with a strong institutional basis for implementation. Earlier in

2014 the stakes were raised yet further with the Sendai Framework for Disaster Risk Reduction, which set 'strengthening disaster risk governance to manage disaster risk' as one of the international community's top priorities.

What does good law look like? IFRC and other relevant organizations, such as the United Nations Development Programme (UNDP), have been leading a multi-country research project in order to provide further evidence of best practice and common gaps in domestic law for DRR. This project analysed laws in 31 countries, with in-depth case studies conducted in 14 of these countries to assess impact and implementation challenges. This is the largest comparative study on this topic undertaken to date. The results were summarized in a synthesis report launched in June 2014, entitled 'Effective law and regulation for disaster risk reduction: A multi-country report'.[15]

The report found that there has been a significant global progress in updating and adopting national disaster management laws to include more focus on DRR, and these efforts have helped to generate much more national attention to the issue of DRR. At the same time, the report also found that there are reoccurring gaps and challenges in the implementation of legal frameworks common to many countries. These include gaps with respect to the allocation of significant legal mandates or DRR responsibilities to local authorities without the necessary funding or capacity, missed opportunities to ensure the engagement of communities and civil societies in decision-making processes and a lack of consideration given to the risk of natural hazards in rules and regulations concerning development and the environment, in particular those related to land use, building permits, environment protection and natural resource management. The report further found significant challenges in the implementation of existing laws and few formal mechanisms available to ensure accountability and compliance.

Concurrent with the research project, the IFRC and UNDP led consultations to develop a 'Checklist on law and disaster risk reduction'.[16] The concept of the Checklist stemmed from the recognition of the need to condense the findings of the multi-country report into a practical tool that could be used by different domestic stakeholders. The Checklist provides a prioritized and succinct list of 10 key questions that lawmakers, implementing officials and those supporting can consider to ensure that their laws provide the best support for disaster risk reduction. It addresses not only national disaster risk management laws but also other sectoral laws and regulations that are critical for building safety and resilience, as well as the environment, land and natural resource management.

The Checklist is designed to serve as an assessment tool to guide a review process of national and local level laws and regulations that can enhance DRR and provide guidance on how to bring national legal frameworks in line with existing international standards, in particular, the Sendai Framework for Disaster Risk Reduction. It also aims to foster a more integrated approach to disaster risk reduction by taking into account climate change and sustainable development considerations within the review of legislation, and it is hoped that national and local authorities, including in the South Asia, will utilize such tools to take affirmative action to strengthen their frameworks and ensure that laws are conducive to providing an enabling environment for disaster risk reduction.

Conclusion

Disasters are not inevitable. Much can be done to reduce risks posed by natural hazards and, even more importantly, stop new risks from arising as a result of development. To build any collective resilience to natural hazards though, we need wide-reaching, inclusive and robust legal frameworks. Legal frameworks do not stop at disaster management laws, and a greater focus needs to be placed on the implementation of laws and regulations related to development planning and the environment, including building codes, land use planning and management and climate change laws. Strong laws will be key to the future safety of the millions of people still facing preventable risks in South Asia.

Notes

1 Asian Development Bank website: www.adb.org/.
2 EM-DAT database, maintained by CRED, see www.em-dat.net/.
3 A/RES/46/182.
4 Ever since 1867, the components of the Red Cross and Red Crescent Movement have met every four years with the state parties to the Geneva Conventions at the 'International Conference of the Red Cross and Red Crescent' in order to examine and decide upon humanitarian matters of common interest.
5 IFRC website: www.ifrc.org/en/what-we-do/disaster-law/research-tools-and-publications/key-resolutions/red-cross-and-red-crescent-resolutions-on-disaster-law/.
6 Law and Legal Issues in International Disaster Response: A Desk Study which compiled the insights gained by the International Federation's IDRL programme through its legal research, case studies, consultations and a global survey on existing regulatory frameworks and remaining problem

areas. Available at the IFRC website: www.ifrc.org/en/what-we-do/idrl/research-tools-and-publications/publications/.

7 IFRC website: www.ifrc.org/en/what-we-do/disaster-law/research-tools-and-publications/key-resolutions/red-cross-and-red-crescent-resolutions-on-disaster-law/.

8 IFRC website: www.ifrc.org/en/what-we-do/disaster-law/.

9 IFRC website: www.ifrc.org/en/what-we-do/disaster-law/research-tools-and-publications/key-resolutions/red-cross-and-red-crescent-resolutions-on-disaster-law/.

10 IFRC website: www.ifrc.org/en/what-we-do/disaster-law/.

11 The Impact of Regulatory Problems and the Gains from Legal Preparedness in recent Response Operations. Available at the IFRC website: www.ifrc.org/PageFiles/195860/IDRL%20Impact%20Study%20Draft%20for%20Expert%20Meeting_270215.pdf.

12 World Humanitarian Summit website: www.worldhumanitariansummit.org/.

13 IFRC website: www.ifrc.org/what-we-do/disaster-law/research-tools-and-publications/the-ilc-and-disasters/.

14 The 'SAARC Agreement on Rapid Response to Natural Disasters' was signed at the Seventeenth Summit (Maldives, 10–11 November 2011) and will come into force once all member states complete the ratification process, which has been completed by five countries till date (November 2014). South Asian Association for Regional Cooperation website: http://saarc-sec.org/.)

15 Available at www.drr-law.org/.

16 IFRC website: www.ifrc.org/PageFiles/115542/The-checklist-on-law-and-drr.pdf

3 Disasters

A ubiquitous legal framework in ancient BC literature

Renu K. Sharma

In the history of mankind disasters have been affecting life, devastating development and increasing human miseries. The scope of this chapter is limited to the study of disasters and their management in ancient literature which is considered to be some of the earliest piece of information in the subcontinent.

The four Vedas,[1] *Ṛigveda*, *Yajurveda*, *Sāmaveda* and *Atharvaveda,* are full of hymns which clearly advocate the sovereignty of different natural powers. *Ṛgveda* presents hymns of many gods and goddesses and are personified with natural entities like *Agni*[2] (fire), *Āpaḥ*[3] (water), *Prithivī*[4] (earth), *Parjanya*[5] (clouds), *Sūrya*[6] (sun). In the present scenario solar energy has been declared to be the most important mode of energy through which flow of different types of energy can be regulated, and in this way the eco system of the earth can be controlled, as it is already illustrated in our ancient texts.

Disaster can be explained as a sudden great loss related to not just human being but also with every animate creature living in the society.

As regards, *Encyclopedia of Disaster Management* (2007) defines the disaster as 'anything that befalls of ruinous or distressing nature; a sudden or great misfortune, mishap or misadventure; a calamity'.[7] Thus, disaster is basically a serious disturbance of the active life causing extensive human, economic or environmental losses. India is among the world's disaster-prone areas, and a large part is out to such natural disasters, which often causes disruption of socio-economic life that leads to loss of life and poverty.

In Sanskrit literature mainly three terms have been elucidated for disasters:

(i) *mahābhaya*
(ii) *ītī*[8]
(iii) *vyasana*

In Kauṭilya's *Arthaśāstra* eight *mahābhaya*-s (disasters) and six types of *īti*-s (calamities) and *vyasana*-s have been mentioned. All *mahābhaya, īti* and *vyasana* can be understood as disasters.

A terse sign of earthquake (*bhūkampa*) has also been indicated in *Kāṭhaka Gṛhyasūtra* (ca. 600 BC–300 BC) of *Yajurveda* in the section of 'prohibited situations for the study' (*anadhyāya*) in the explanations of the *sūtras*[9]:

> '*bhūkampacandrārkoparaganṛpatimahāpuruṣapramayaprabhṛtayā anumantavyāḥ*'. [one should not study during earthquakes, moon and solar eclipses also at the prohibition of kings and scholars]

Kālidāsa (first century BC) also mentioned *ītis* in his epic *Raghuvaṁśa* in the conversation of Guru Vaśiṣṭha and King Dilīpa. The king mentions both natural and man-made disasters and *ītis* as other calamities like drought, rats and enemies.[10]

In *Mahābhārata* (500 BC) also, word *īti* is described as one of the causes of suffering of human beings:

> Ītayo vyādhayastandrā doṣā *krodhādayastathā*.
> Upadravāśca vartante ādhayaḥ kṣudrabhayam tathā.[11]

That is, calamities (*īti*-s), diseases (*vyādhi*), idleness (*standrā)*, anger (*krodhā*), starvation and thirst.

(a) **Disasters in Arthaśāstra of Kauṭilya** (300 BC–AD 100)[12]: In Kauṭilya's *Arthaśāstra 'mahābhayam'* is elucidated as disasters; those are as follows:

> Devānyaṣṭau *mahābhayāni*. Agnirudakam vyādhirdurbhikṣam mūṣikā vyālāḥ sarpaḥ rakṣānsiti:[13]

> that is, fire (*agni*), water (*udaka*), diseases (*vyādhi*), famine (*durbhikṣa*), rats (*mūṣikā*), beasts (*vyāla*), snakes (*sarpa*), demons (*rakṣānsi*).

(b) **Calamities in *Nītisāra* of Kāmandaka** (400 BC–AD 600): A brief account of disasters has been mentioned in *Nītisāra*. In chapter 13, disasters have been pointed out through the term *vyasana*.[14] The term *vyasana* can be understood as the elements which are repulsive and also destroy (the good or the progress and prosperity of a kingdom.) It is explicated both as disasters and vices of human beings. Accordingly, five forms of calamities are fire, floods, famine, diseases and plague.

(i) *Hutāśuno jalaṁ vyādhirdurbhikṣo marakastathā.*
iti pañcavidhaṁ daivaṁ vyasanaṁ mānuṣaṁ paraṁ.[15]

That is, fires, floods, famine, prevalence of diseases and plague or pestilence five kinds of *vyasanas* (calamities) that proceed from fate; the rest comes from human sources.[16]

In the same chapter at another place some more calamities also have been examined such as rain, drought and locusts. These are considered as *vyasana*-s (calamities) of a kingdom:

(ii) *Ativṛṣṭiranāvṛṣṭiḥ śalabhā mūṣikā śukāḥ.*
asatkaśca daṅḍaśca paracakrāṇi taskarāḥ.
rājānīkapriyotsargo marakavyādhipīḍnaṁ.
paśūnāṁ maraṇaṁ rogo rāṣṭravyasanamucyate.[17]

That is, excessive rain, want of rain (drought), locusts, rats, mice and parrots (and other such corn-destroying agents), unjust taxation, confiscation of the properties of the people, foreign invasion and depredation and thieves and robbers.

Now comes the passage for the king how to protect the kingdom from such disasters by taking up prudent policies:

Daivaṁ puruṣakāreṇa śāntyā ca praśamanyet.
utthāyitvena nītyā ca mānuṣaṁ kāryatattvavit.[18]

That is, the evils proceeding from fate should be averted by means of human efforts and the celebration of propitiatory rites: and a king knowing what should be done should remove the evils coming from human sources by his energetic behaviour and adoption of wise measures of policy.[19]

In the following verse it is also stated that protection of the kingdom from these disasters is also an important responsibility of king's minister.[20]

(c) **Disasters in *Vṛhatsaṁhitā*** (AD 505–AD 587): In *Vṛhatsaṁhitā* of Varāmihira we find signs of earthquakes as natural disaster.[21] In the chapter titled '*Bhūkampalakṣaṇādhyāyaḥ*', causes of earthquakes, in particular *nakṣatra*-s, what are the exact forecast signs of earthquakes and others, have been mentioned explicitly. A brief description of drought is also depicted in the chapter titled '*Indrāyudhalakṣaṇādhyāyaḥ*' (signs of rainbows).[22]

In Kauṭilya *Arthaśāstra* eight types of major disasters have been mentioned. The scope of the present chapter is centred to mainly fire, water, disease, drought and rats. Description of disasters in *Arthaśāstra* is as follows:

As we know many of the disasters occur due to lack of management.

1 **Fire** (*agni*): In *Arthaśāstra* fire is listed as first and the foremost disaster which occurs due to geological and biological conditions and also due to human negligence. Kauṭilya mentioned preventive methods already in the 'rules of the city' before the description of fire as disaster. It seems as if according to him 'prevention is better than cure'.

Preventive methods:

- In summer cooking should not done inside the house especially during four middle parts of a day. This instruction is basically for those houses which are made of grass: *Agnipratikāram ca grīṣme madhyamayorahvaścaturbhāgayoḥ.*[23] Fire work should be done outside the house or the roofs should be removed: *Bahiradhiśrayaṇam vā kuryuḥ*[24] and *Tṛṇakaṭchannānyapanayet.*[25]
- The people engaged in fire profession should stay at one place: *Agnijīvina ekasthān vāsayet.*[26]
- At night, house owners should stay near the main doors of the house rather gathering at one place of all family members: *Svagṛhapradāreṣu gṛhasvāminovaseyurasaṁpātino rātrau.*[27]
- Thousands of water-filled jars should be kept on roads, in main gates of the city and also at royal offices: *Rathyāsu kaṭvajrāḥ sahasratiṣṭheyuḥ. Catuṣpathadvārarājaparigraheṣu ca.*[28]

Penalties on negligence:

- The one who does not follow the preventive methods should be charged eight *paṇa* (a kind of currency which was used in that particular period) as a fine: *Aṣṭabhago'gnidaṇḍaḥ.*[29]
- If the owner of house does not try to save the house on fire, the fine for this negligence is 12 *paṇas,* and if the tenant also does the same, then he should be charged six *paṇas: Pradīptamanabhidhāvato gṛhasvāmino dvādaśapaṇo daṇḍaḥ.*[30]
- If fire is caused because of negligence, house owner should be fined 54 *paṇas*: *Pramādādīpteṣu catuṣpañcāśatpaṇo daṇḍaḥ.*[31]
- If a careless person whose carelessness is the reason for fire is caught red-handed, then he should be put to death by fire: *Prādīpiko'gninā vadhyaḥ.*[32]

- If a person does fire work even in the prohibited period of the day and also has not arranged big jars filled with water, a ladder, iron hook and skin bag, then he should be fined with a quarter of *paṇa*: *Pādaḥ pañcaghaṭīnām, kumbhadroṇīniśreṇīparaśuśrpāṅkuśkacagr ahaṇīdṛtīnām cākaraṇe.*[33]

2 **Water** (*udaka*): In Kauṭilya's *Arthaśāstra,* the importance of the disasters depends on the loss caused by them. According to Kauṭilya, the water disaster is more harmful than fire, because fire may destroy half or one village, but water or flood can affect many villages at a time: *Agnirgrāmamardhagrāmam vā dahati. Udakavegastu grāmaśatapravāhīti.*[34]

Water disaster can be mainly of two types: *Ativṛṣṭi* (great deal of rain) which causes floods and *Anāvṛṣṭi* (drought).

In *Ṛgveda*, ṛṣi prays to protect from *Ativṛṣṭi*:

> *Avarṣīrvarṣamudu ṣū gṛbhāyākadhanvānyatyatavāu.*
> *aījana oṣadhīrbhojanāya kamuta prajābhyovido manīṣām.*[35]

That is, O Lord! You have poured down sufficiently; now withhold the rain. You have made the deserts very much fed for utilization. You have given birth to plants for man's nourishments. Verily you have obtained laudation from all living creatures.

The losses of *ativṛṣṭi* are:

> *Vi vṛksān hanyuta rakṣaso viśvaṁ vibhāya bhuvanam mahāvvadhāt.*
> *Utā nāgā īṣte vṛṣṇyāvato yatparjanyaḥ stanayan hanti duṣkṛutaḥ.*[36]

That is, he strikes down the trees, he destroys the wicked, he terrifies the whole world, by his mighty weapon. Even the tender-hearted innocent shudders at the appearance of the thundering cloud, smiting the wicked.

Preventive methods:

- At the nights in rainy weather, those stay at the banks of the rivers should stay away from there:

  Varṣārātramangrāmā pravelāmutsṛujya vaseyuḥ.[37]

- They should always maintain some wooden boats and some other instruments as supportive source of swimming:

  Kāṣṭhaveṇunāvaścāpagṛhṇīyuḥ.[38]

- People should try their best to rescue a drowning person with the help of tree stems, boats and so on:

  Uhyamānamalābudṛtiplavagāṇḍikāveṇikābhistārayeyuḥ.[39]

Penalties on negligence:

- People who do not rescue someone should be fined 12 *paṇas*. If they don't have any supportive instrument to swim, then they are not guilty:

  Anabhisaratām dvādaśapaṇo daṇḍaḥ. Anyatra plavahīnebhyaḥ.[40]

3 Disease (***vyādhi***): According to Kauṭilya drought is more harmful than diseases, because diseases harm only the people of a particular place but drought harms the whole country. With the help of medicines the effect of diseases can be cured but not the effect of drought:

Ekadeśapīḍano vyādhiḥ śakyapratīkārśca. Sarvadeśapīḍanam durbhikṣam prāṇināmajīvānāyeti.[41]

Preventive methods:

- When ill one should take medicines from a physician and should also worship for good health:

  Auṣadhaiścikitsakāḥ śāntiprāyāścittairvā siddhatāpamāḥ.[42]

4 Famine (*durbhikṣa*): In *durbhikṣa, a king* should provide already-stored seeds and food to his subjects:

Durbhikṣe rājā bījabhaktopagraham kṛtvānugraham kuryāt.[43]

Vṛhatsaṁhitā also states about *anāvṛṣṭi* (drought) as per the position of the planets:

Raviravisutaketupīḍite bhe kṣitijanayatrividhādbhutāhate ca.
Bhavati can a śivam na cāpi vṛṣṭi. . . . . .[44]

That is, if an asterism is affiliated with the Sun, Saturn or *Ketu*, or hurt by Mars, or by the threefold portent, there will be no prosperity to mankind, nor will there be any rain, but if the asterism is unhurt and conjoined with benefices, beneficial results will accrue.

In *Chāndogyopaniṣad*, it is clearly mentioned that if there was ample rain, then all the creatures would suffer badly:

Suvṛṣṭirna bhavati vyādhīyante prāṇāḥ.[45]

Ṛgveda prescribes that cutting trees is a chief cause of drought and emphasizes to grow trees:

Vanaspatim vana āsthāpayadhvam.[46]

In *Arthaśāstra,* drought is another major cause of suffering for living beings:

Sarvadā pīḍanam durbhikṣaṁ prāṇināmajīvanāya.[47]

In ancient Indian *yajñā* is described as a source of rain

Yajñādbhavati parjanyaḥ.[48]

Same statement echoes in *Manusmṛti* (200 BC–AD 200); in addition, the *havi* offered in the fire goes to the *ādityamaṇḍala,* then it rains and rain results in a good harvest of crops, which brings happiness:

Agnau dattāhutisamyak ādityamupatiṣṭhate.
ādityājjāyate vṛṣṭiḥ vṛṣṭerannam tataḥ prajāḥ.[49]

That is, an oblation duly offered in the fire reaches the Sun; from the Sun comes rain, from rain food and from food the living creature derives life.

Kālidāsa in his well-known epic *Raghuvaṁśam* mentions about the importance of *yajña*:

Havirārjitam hotaḥ tvayā vidhidagniṣu.
vṛṣṭirbhavati sasyānāṁ avagraha viśoṣiṇām.[50]

In this way it is firmly accepted in ancient literature that for creating the balance on earth for the welfare of the creatures, *yaj(a* is an essential part of life.

5 **Rats** (*mūṣikā*): Kauṭilya was conscious about the problem of rats; therefore he added them as a natural calamity.

Preventive methods:

- When a disease (disaster) breaks out because of rats, cats and mongoose should be used to kill the rats so that they may not be able to spread an epidemic-like plague:

  Mūṣikābhaye mārjārānakulotsargaḥ.[51]

- Medicated food grains should be spread to catch the rats:

  Dhānyāni visṛujedupanipadyogayuktāni vā mūṣikakaram vā prayuñjīta.[52]

Penalties on negligence

The people who try to catch the cats and mongoose should be fined 12 *paṇas:*

> *Teṣām grahaṇahiṅsāyām dvādaśapaṇo daṇḍaḥ.*[53]

In *Vṛhatsaṁhitā* of Varāmihira we find signs of earthquakes as a natural disaster.[54]

Description of earthquakes:

> *Kṣitikampamāhureke bṛhadantarjalanivāsisattvakṛtam.*
> *bhūbhārakhinnadiggajaviśrāmasamudbhavam cānye.*[55]

That is, some hold that that an earthquake is caused by huge animals living in the midst of the ocean, while others opine that it is the result of the rest that is availed of by the elephants of the quarters tired by the weight of the earth.

> *Anilo'nilena nihataḥ kṣitau patan sasvanam karotyanye.*
> *kecittvadṛuṣṭakāritamidamanye prāhurācāryāḥ.*[56]

That is, yet, there are others who hold that earthquake is caused by the atmospheric wind colliding with another and falling to the earth with a booming sound.

> *Giribhiḥ purā sapakṣairvasudhā prapatadbhirutpatadbhiśca.*
> *ākampitā pitāmahamāhāmarasadasi savrīḍam.*
> *Bhagvannama mamaitattvayā kṛtam yadacaleti tanna tathā.*
> *kriyate'calaiścaladbhiḥ śktāham nāsya khedasya.*
> *tasyāḥ sagadgadgiram kiñcitsphuritādharam vinatamīṣat.*
> *sāśruvilocanamānanamālokya pitāmahaḥ prāha.*
> *manyum harendra dhātryāḥ kṣipa kuliśam śailapakṣabhaṅgā.*
> *śakraḥ kṛutamityuktvā mā bhairiti vasumatīmāha.*
> *kintvaniladahanasurapativaruṇāḥ sadasatphalāvabodhārtham.*
> *prāgdvitricaturbhāgeṣu dinaniśoḥ kampayiṣyanti.*[57]

That is, in days of yore, the earth being shaken severely by the winged mountains which flew up and down spoke bashfully to the creator in the assembly of the God: 'My lord, the name that has been given to me by you-namely-*Acalā* (immoveable) is not quite right; for it is falsified by the flying mountains and I am unable to put up with this misery.'

Hearing these words of mother earth who was choked with the tears, whose lower lip quivered slightly, and observing her face hanging down with tears trickling down from her eyes, the Creator thus says, 'Indra, remove this humiliation by mother earth, throw your thunderbolt and chop off the wings of the mountains.' At this, Indra says 'so be it', comforted her with the word 'Don't you fear; but wind, fire, myself (Indra) and Varuṇa will shake you in the four parts of the day and night put together respectively in order to reveal the good and bad effects of the world.'

In *Vṛhatsaṁhitā* (*Bhūkampalakṣaṇādhyāyaḥ*), the leading reasons of earthquakes are atmospheric wind, fire, *Indra* and *Varuṇa* circles. Explanations of the particular circles are as follows:

> *Rūpāyudhamṛdvaidyāstrīkavigāndharvapaṇyaśilpijanāḥ.*
> *pīḍyante saurāṣṭrākakurumagadhadaśārṇamatsyāśca.*[58]

That is, the circle presided over by the wind god consists of the seven asterisms, viz., Uttarā, Hasta, Chitra, Svāti, Punarvasu, Mṛgaśirā and Aśvini (that is whenever an earthquake occurs in any of these stars, it has to be construed that it is due to the wind circle). The following symptoms of this circle will be revealed a week in advance: the quarters are covered with smoke, a wind blows lashing with the dust of the earth and breaking trees, and the Sun does not cast bright rays. During an earthquake of the wind circle the decay of crops, water, forest and herbs, the outbreak of swellings, asthma, madness, fever and trouble to the trading community will ensue. Concubines, warriors, physicians, women, poets, singers, traders, artists, the Saurāṣṭra, kurus, Magadha, Daśārṇas and Matsyās will suffer.

Just like wind circle, fire, *Varuṇa* and *Indra* circles in different *nakṣatras* cause various diseases and different levels of damages.[59]

An earthquake has limits to its impact which is prescribed by its occurrence in a particular circle of wind, fire, *Varuna* and *Indra*:

> *Calayati pavanaḥ śatadvayam śatamanalo daśayojanānvitam.*
> *salilapatiraśītisaṁyutam kuliśadharo'bhyadhikam ca ṣaṣṭitaḥ.*[60]

That is, the earthquake of the 'wind' circle shakes the earth to an extent of 200 *yojanas*, one of 'fire' circle 110 *yojanas*, one of '*Vruṇa*'s' 180 *yojanas* and one of *Indra*'s 160 *yojanas*.

In this way a complete account of earthquake ranging from its signs and influence in various directions to its extensions has been enunciated clearly in *Bhūkampalakṣaṇādhyāyaḥ* of *Vṛhatsaṁhitā*.

Illustrations of drought

In *Vṛhatsaṁhitā* in the 35th chapter '*Indrāyudhalakṣaṇādhyāyaḥ*' (signs of rainbows) through the sight of rainbows in different situations forecast of drought has been pointed out:

> *Jalamadhye'nāvṛṣṭirbhuvi sasyavadhastarau sthite vyādhiḥ.*
> *Vālmīke śastrabhayaṁ niśi sacivavadhāya dhanauraindram.*[61]

That is, a rainbow seen in the middle of water causes drought; on land, destruction of crops; on a tree, disease; on an anthill, danger from weapons; and in night, the death of a minister.

And also a rainbow seen in east brings rain, but a rainbow in west is a sign of no rain:

> *Vṛṣṭim karotyavṛṣṭyāṁ vṛṣṭim vṛṣṭyāṁ nivārayatyaindyām.*
> *paṅcātsadaiva vṛṣṭim kuliśabhṛtaścāpamācaṣṭe.*[62]

Different colours of rainbows create different situations:

> *Pāṭalapītakanīlaiḥ śastrāgnikṣutkṛtā doṣāḥ.*[63]

That is, one (rainbow) that is pink, yellow and blue produces evils from war, fire and famine, respectively.

Ancient Indian literature is rich in all respects, and it touches almost every sphere of our life. Disasters can be controlled to some extent by balancing our nature. Some of the ideas in ancient texts to control disasters are as follows:

(i) Vedic *yajñās* prescribes to purify the environment by putting *havi* in the *yajñā*:

    Ā juhotā haviṣā marjayadhvam.[64]

(ii) Save nature through plantation. Greenery not only purifies the air but also protects us from disasters like *ativṛṣṭi*. As Vedas assert for plantation:

    Vanaspatim vana āsthāpayadhvam.[65]

(iii) *Yajurveda* prescribes that water and plants are friendly to us:

    Sumitriyā na āpaḥ auṣadhayaḥ santu.[66]

(iv) A prayer is always powerful. Vedas are a complete compendium of prayers. At a place, a prayer to protect from snakes and scorpions is in *Athrvaveda*:

yas te sarpo vṛścikastṛṣṭadaṃśmā hemantajabdho bhṛmalo guhā śaye. Krimir jinvat pṛthivī. Yadyad ejati prāvṛṣi tan naḥ sarpan mopa sṛpad yacchivaṃ tena no mṛḍa.[67]

That is, the serpent, the scorpion with thirsty fangs, that hibernating torpidly lies upon thee; the worm, and whatever living thing, O earth, moves in the rainy season, shall, when it creeps, not creep upon us: with what is auspicious (on thee) be gracious to us!

Thus we can say that ancient Indians were very much aware about the ecology and sustainability. It helps in solving specific environmental problems, and the modern principles of sustainability were adopted at that time. But unfortunately we have forgotten those golden principles laid up by them.

To sum up, there are many other ways in ancient literature through which we can balance our eco system at a certain level. But first of all it should be the duty of everyone to protect the environment so that any disaster may not occur due to the negligence of human being. And people should be penalized for negligence or carelessness, as Kauṭilya mentioned in *Arthaśāstra*.

According to Kauṭilya, punishment is extremely important because a person who committed a crime but was not punished is similar to a big fish that eats a tiny one, and powerful people will start hurting weak people. Punishment provides strength to the weak people.[68]

King should protect the country from the disasters.[69] Disasters take place not just naturally but they are also man-made. All precautions and preventions should be followed strictly so that at least man-made disaster may not come about.

Notes

1 As there is no unanimity about Vedic period, according to *Orion*, the Vedic period arrives at about 4000 BC–6000 BC – Bal Gangadhar Tilak, *The Orion*, pp. 207, 220.
2 *Ṛgveda*, 1/1, 1/89, 3/62, 10/4, 10/16.
3 Ibid., 7/49, 10/9.
4 *Atharvaveda*, 12/1.
5 *Ṛgveda*, 5/83, 7/101–102.
6 Ibid., 7/63, 7/66.

7 Encyclopedia of Disaster Management Introduction to Disaster Management, Deep and Deep Publications, 2006, Chapter 1, p. 1.
8 *Ativṛṣṭiranāvṛṣṭiḥ śalabhā mūṣikā khagāḥ.*
Pratyāsannāśca rājānaḥ ṣaḍetā ītayaḥ smṛtāḥ.- Dev, Raja Radhakant, *Śabdakalpadruma*, Vol. 1, p. 216
9 Kāṭhaka Gṛhyasūtra, 1/9/8.
10 *Daivīnāṁ mānuṣīṇāṁ ca pratihartā tvamāpadāṁ.*- 1/60
and
Puruṣāyuṣajīvinyo nirātaṇkā nirītayaḥ- Raghuvaṁśa of Kālidāsa, 1/64.
11 *Mahābhārata*, Vana Parva, 149/35.
12 P. V. Kane (1941). *History of Dharmaśāstra*, Vol. 2, Part. 2, Poona: Bhandarkar Oriental Research Institute.
13 *Arthaśāstra*, 3/78.
14 Williams Monier, *A Sanskrit-English Dictionary*, Oxford: Oxford University Press, p. 1035.
15 *The Nītisāra* or *The Elements of Polity* by Kamandaki, 13/20.
16 Kamandakiya *Nītisāra* or *The Elements of Polity* (Eng. Trans.), (ed.) Manmatha Natha, English translation on 13/20.
17 *The Nītisāra* or *The Elements of Polity* by Kamandaki, 13/63–64.
18 Ibid., 13/21.
19 Kamandakiya *Nītisāra* or *The Elements of Polity* (Eng. Trans.), (ed.) Manmatha Natha, English translation on 13/21.
20 *The Nītisāra* or *The Elements of Polity* by Kamandaki, 13/24.
21 *Vṛhatsaṁhitā*, Varāmihir (Eng. Trans.). Subrahmanya Sastri, V.B. Soobbiah & Sons, Bangalore, 1946, Chapter 32 (*Bhūkampalakṣaṇādhyāyaḥ*).
22 *Sūryasya vividhavarṇā pavanena vighaṭṭitāḥ karāḥ sābhre.*
viyati dhanuḥsaṅsthānā ye d'śyante tadindradhanuḥ.
i.e., the rays of the Sun which have various colours, being thrown back by the wind in a cloudy sky, are seen in the form of a bow which is called the rainbow. Ibid., 35/1.
23 *Arthaśāstra*, 2/36/17.
24 Ibid., 2/36/19.
25 Ibid., 2/36/21.
26 Ibid., 2/36/22.
27 Ibid., 2/36/23.
28 Ibid., 2/36/24–25.
29 Ibid., 2/36/18.
30 Ibid., 2/36/26.
31 Ibid., 2/36/28.
32 Ibid., 2/36/29.
33 Ibid., 2/36/20.
34 Ibid., 4/8/5–6.
35 *Ṛgveda*, 5/83/10.
36 Ibid., 5/83/2.
37 *Arthaśāstra*, 4/3/9.
38 Ibid., 4/3/10.
39 Ibid., 4/3/11.
40 Ibid., 4/3/12–13.
41 Ibid., 8/4/10–11.
42 Ibid., 4/3/18.

43 Ibid., 4/3/18.
44 *Vṛhatsaṁhitā*, 23/10.
45 *Chāndogyopaniṣad*, 7/10.
46 *Ṛgveda*, 10/101/11.
47 *Arthaśāstra*, 8/4/132–6.
48 *Bhagavadgītā*, 3/14.
49 *Manusmṛti*, 3/76.
50 *Raghuvaṁśa*, 1/62.
51 *Arthaśāstra*, 4/3/30.
52 Ibid., 4/3/34.
53 Ibid., 4/3/31.
54 *Vṛhatsaṁhitā* Chapter 32 (*Bhūkampalakṣaṇādhyāyaḥ*).
55 Ibid., 32/1.
56 Ibid., 32/2.
57 Ibid., 32/3–7.
58 *Vṛhatsaṁhitā*, 32/11.
59 Ibid., 32/12–30.
60 Ibid., 32/31.
61 Ibid., 35/5.
62 Ibid., 35/6.
63 Ibid., 35/4.
64 *Sāmaveda*, 1/1/2/63.
65 *Ṛgveda*, 10/101/11.
66 *Yajuveda*, 36/23.
67 *Atharvaveda*, English translation of Holy Vedas by Maurice Bloomfield, p. 159. http://www.sacred-texts.com/hin/av.htm.
68 *Arthaśāstra*- (*Vinayādhikaraṇa*).
69 *Tebhyo janapadam rakṣet*. Ibid., 2/3/3.

References

Atharvaveda with English (Trans.), S. P. S. Svami & V. V. Udaya, New Delhi: Veda Pratishthana, Arya Samaj Mandir Marg, 1996.

Encyclopedia of Disaster Management, Introduction to Disaster Management, Delhi: Deep and Deep Publishers, 2007.

History of Dharmaśāstra (Vol. 2, Part. 2), by P. V. Kane, Poona: Bhandarkar Oriental Research Institute, 1941.

Kamandakiya *Nītisāra* or *The Elements of Polity* (Eng. Trans.), M. Natha (ed.), Calcutta: Elysium Press, 1896.

Kāṭhaka Gṛhyasūtra (ed.), W. Calend, Lahore: Vidya Prakash Press (V. Samvat), 1981.

The Manusmṛti, S. Kumar (ed.), Delhi: Arsh Sahhitya Prachar Trust, 2000.

Monier, Williams, *A Sanskrit-English Dictionary*, Delhi: Sharda Publishing House, 2005.

The Nītisāra or *The Elements of Polity* by Kamandaki R. L. Mitra (ed.), Calcutta: Bibliotheca Indica: A collection of Oriental Works, Asiatic Society of Bengal, Nos.19 &179 &, Baptist Mission Press, 1861.

The Orion or Researches in to the Antiquity of the Vedas by B. G. Tilak (ed.), Bombay: Radhabai Atmaram Sagoon Bookseller & Publishers, 1893.

Raja Radhakant Dev, *(abdakalpadruma*, Vol. 1), New Delhi: Rashtriya Sanskrit Sansthan, 2006 (Reprint).

Ṛgveda with English (Trans.), S. P. S. Svami & S. Vidyalankara, New Delhi: Veda Pratishthana, Arya Samaj Mandir Marg, 1996.

Vṛhatsaṁhitā, Varāmihir with English (Trans.), S. Sastri (ed.), Bangalore: V.B. Soobbiah & Sons, 1946.

Part II

Country-specific disaster laws

4 The landscape of disaster management in Pakistan

Gaps in the legal framework

Md Akmal Wasim

The rudimentary principles underlying the policies, management and administrative reforms undertaken in historically rich countries appear to either ignore or get swept in the international standards, mechanisms and modules rubric designed in the established governance systems. In the International Conference on Corruption 2012 jointly hosted by the Legal Aid Office, Pakistan and NAPSIPAG in Karachi, Prof. N. Bhaskar[1] and the author on the question of Perception Indices critically took up their reservation, on *apriori* or *a posteriori* approach to the problems besetting Pakistan, India and Bangladesh (including Nepal and Sri Lanka). The criticism was based on the viewpoint that in any analysis involving these countries their unique history and socio-cultural anthropology must never be disregarded. In the given scenario the analysis will always remain incomplete and undervalued. South Asia holistically embodies the subcontinent, whose history and culture is traceable up to 4000 years BC. Politics, economics and religion playing the dominant roles in the development of the governance systems have in the natural course twisted and understandably convoluted the primary tiers causing the iniquities witnessed today. From *Sarasvati* to the modern *Indus*, the subcontinental governance ethos has suffered limitless erosions and recoveries in its socio-cultural and political arrangements.

Subcontinent is a land of pronounced topographic and climatic contrasts. The topography varies between sea coastal ranges and sandy deserts, to high mountains and snow-covered peaks. After 1947 Pakistan inherited much of the varied topology and became a constitutional federal state comprising four main provinces: Punjab, Sindh, Khyber Pakhtunkhwa and Baluchistan. Other regions include the Federally Administered Tribal Areas (FATA) and Gilgit Baltistan. Later Gilgit Baltistan acquired a provincial status. The country is divided into three geographic areas: the northern highlands, the Indus river plains (with two major subdivisions corresponding roughly to the provinces of Punjab and Sindh) and the Baluchistan plateau.[2]

Pakistan has felt the effects of severe natural disasters as well as conflict and threats to its security. Tensions in the north of the country in 2009 saw the biggest displacement crisis in Pakistan since its partition from India in 1947, with over two million people internally displaced. While still coping with the effects of this crisis, Pakistan was hit by the most severe floods it has seen to date. The heavy monsoonal rains which occurred in July 2010 created floods affecting over 20 million people, more than that of the 2004 Indian Ocean Tsunami, the 2005 South Asia Earthquake and the 2010 Haiti Earthquake combined. The scale of destruction was unprecedented, and the country is still suffering the effects of this natural disaster.[3]

Pakistan's population in mid-2011 was estimated at approximately 177.1 million, and is expected to reach 210 million by 2020. Due to its troubled political and economic history, Pakistan remains one of the poorest countries in the world, with approximately 62 million people (or 39 per cent of the population) living below the national poverty line.[4]

Pakistan has always been a disaster-prone country, and the timeline of recent history provides sufficient evidence for this conclusion. At a quick glance the top-four devastating disasters which shook Pakistan's infrastructure are:

2005 Kashmir quake: A 7.6-Richter scale quake struck the Kashmir region on the India-Pakistan border and parts of north-western Pakistan on 8 October 2005. According to official figures, at least 73,000 people were killed and more than 3.3 million made homeless. The worst-affected areas included Neelum Valley and Bagh District in Pakistan-administered Kashmir and Mansehra Division. A massive international relief effort was launched. Work continues today to rebuild damaged infrastructure.[5]

2007 Cyclone Yemyin: At least 380 people were killed in Baluchistan, 250 in Sindh and 100 in NWFP as a result of flash floods triggered by Cyclone Yemyin, which struck coastal areas in early July 2007. Some 350,000 people were displaced, 1.5 million affected and more than 2 million livestock perished.[6]

2010 Hunza Lake disaster: A landslide in January 2010 in Attabad village in Hunza-Nagar District in the far north of the country killed 20 people and led to around 40 houses sliding into the Hunza River. Debris from the landslide caused the river to dam, leading to the formation of a large lake which threatened to flood downstream areas. Some 20,000 were forced to leave their homes by June.[7]

2010 floods: The toll so far: 1,600 deaths; over six million affected. Pakistan has sought international help to cope with the catastrophe. Despite mass evacuations, fears of increase in the death toll rose as flooding reached the southern province of Sindh and the risk of water-borne disease outbreaks increased in many areas.[8]

As noted earlier Pakistan is known to be vulnerable to a wide array of natural and man-made disasters.[9] The human impact of natural disasters in Pakistan can be judged by the fact that 6,037 people were killed and 8,989,631 affected in the period from 1993 to 2002 (World Disasters Report 2003).[10] A major factor generally ignored is the fact Pakistan lies in a seismic belt and therefore suffers from frequent earthquakes of small magnitudes. Earthquakes normally occur along the Himalayas, Karakoram and partly Hindu Kush ranges in the north, Koh-e-Sulaiman range in the west with Chaman fault line along Quetta, and Mekran fault line along the sea coast. Their occurrence is normally associated with the dynamics associated with the Indian plate exerting continuous pressure on the Eurasian land mass. This plate incidentally lies only 62 nautical miles from the megacity of Pakistan, that is, Karachi, a city of 250 million people.

Floods, excessive rainfall, cyclones, drought are also the major hazards confronting Pakistan. These have seen a sharp increase in recent years generally attributed as an impact of El Nino factor.

The wake-up call

The paradigm shift finally came about with the massive earthquake hitting the entire northern Pakistan including the Pakistan-administered Kashmir in 2005. The earthquake severely affected over 30,000 square kilometres of nine districts of Khyber Pakhtunkhwa, Punjab and Pakistan-administered Jammu and Kashmir.[11]

Legal framework up to 2005

Pakistan continued to be governed by procedural laws distinctly distinguishable from substantive legal framework, enacted as early as 1950s, to address natural calamities. This imperfection was, however, not limited to Pakistan alone. For example, the Federal Civil Defense Act of 1950 is the foundational document for the United States Federal

Emergency Management Agency. In some of the developing countries, disaster management systems were drastically restructured as a consequence of the apparent inability to handle a major disaster in the country, as was the case of the National Disaster Management Agency in Pakistan that was developed after the devastating earthquake of 2005.[12]

The first ever law to be passed in Pakistan to address disasters was the National Calamities (Prevention and Relief) Act, 1951. This was later adopted for the state of Khairpur (Sindh) in 1954 as the Khairpur Natural Calamities (Prevention and Relief) Act, 1954. On the dissolution of provinces and the establishment of one unit system in 1956, the West Pakistan Natural Calamities (Prevention and Relief) Ordinance, 1956 came into effect.

A more substantial and effective legislation, Natural Calamities (Prevention and Relief) Act (hereinafter referred to as the NCA) was passed in 1958. This law continued to be the primary legislation on natural calamities (disasters) till the enactment of National Disaster Management Act, 2010 (hereinafter referred to as the Act). Noticeably, the Act was enforced retrospectively from 17 August 2007.

Before entering the post-2005 earthquake disaster developments, a closer inspection of the NCA will provide an opportunity to appreciate the innovations in the development of law as the regulatory agency in disaster management.

Section 3 of the NCA read as follows:

> 3 Declaration of calamity affected area. – Whenever the Province or any part thereof is affected or threatened by flood, famine, locust or any other pest, hailstorm, fire, epidemic or any other calamity which, in the opinion of Government warrants action under this Act, Government may, by notification, declare the whole or any part of the Province, as the case may be, as calamity-affected area.

The language of the section reflects the understanding of the term 'calamity' used in the title and elsewhere in the NCA contents. Applying the rule of 'ejusdum generis',[13] it legally remained an open question, as to what other catastrophes could be attached to the description of 'calamity'. The latter word itself has its own connotation as the same is not legally defined, and the term as borrowed from English must be given its linguistic meaning as found in the dictionary. No interpretation by the courts is found for the term 'calamity' in the context of the NCA statute. By general comparison, another statute dating back to 1867 can be cited to exhibit the profundity required in legislative drafting, so to cover the many undiscovered dimensions of attraction, which *in futuro* may attract the concerned law. Exactly 10 years after the mutiny of 1857, a law by the name of 'Murderous Outrages Act' was passed in 1867. The word used for the offender in the said law was 'fanatic', and the law was specifically enacted to discourage the use of blasphemy attacks by the Hindu and Muslim communities against each other, and to protect the British from both communities. Almost 200 years later, fanatic has lost it meaning to the words as 'extremist' and 'radical' more finely tuned and specific to the purpose and object of combatting terrorism and radicalization. Incidentally, the statute is still a law, even if redundant, in Pakistan's Corpus Juris.

The NCA contained another provision, that is, section 4. It was this provision that made the NCA a sustainable law, which in the given comprehension at large of a disaster, provided impetus to NCA:

4 Prevention and relief. – (1) Subject to the other provisions of this Act and of the rules made thereunder, the Relief Commissioner shall, with respect to the calamity-affected area, take such steps as he may deem necessary in order to maintain order, prevent, check or control the calamity or reduce the extent and severity thereof, or to provide immediate relief to the victims of the calamity in the calamity-affected area.

(2) In particular and without prejudice to the generality of the powers conferred by the preceding sub-section the Relief Commissioner shall have power [10][* * *] –

(a) to evacuate or segregate population;
(b) to requisition bulldozers, tractors, motor vehicles, carts, carriages, boats and other means of transport by air, land or water, and beasts of burden;
(c) to require the residents to declare surplus stocks of food, fodder, fire-wood, clothing and beddings and to requisition all or any of these articles;
(d) to requisition building materials;
(e) to requisition any building or land;
(f) to demolish any building or other structure;
(g) to conscript labour;
(h) to direct any person to abstain from a certain act or to take certain order with regard to certain property in his possession or under his management; and after approval of the Government –

(i) to acquire any land; or
(j) to remit in whole or part any Government dues payable by any person or in respect of any property affected by the calamity:

Provided that with respect to the powers conferred by clauses (b), (c), (d), (e), (f), (g), (h) and (i), of this sub-section the person owning the articles, beasts of burden, building or land which is requisitioned or acquired, or the building or other structure which is demolished, or the person directed to abstain from any act or to take any order with regard to any property, and the persons conscripted to work as labourers shall be entitled to reasonable compensation as may be claimable under any law for the time being in force, or if no such law exists as is applicable to the case, then as prescribed by rules under this Act, and such compensation shall be paid within one year from the day it falls due [11][:]

In 2006, a stark cleft in NCA was formally pronounced by the Lahore High Court in one of its judgement based on sections 3 and 4 of the NCA. In a case involving compensation and deferment of the recovery of agricultural loan, on the ground of Tehsil Ferozewala, Punjab was officially declared calamity-hit area due to floods in 1988, by a formal notification to this effect issued on 29 October 1988. The High Court concluded that a bare reading of the notification does not cover a Federal Government Institution, and as such would not apply to House Building Finance Corporation but will apply to Agricultural Development Bank of Pakistan, as the former did not fall in the purview of the notification which was issued under Section 3 of the Punjab Natural Calamity (Prevention & Relief) Act, 1958.[14] The judgement puts the spotlight on the humanitarian issues of concern arising in a calamity or disaster-affected areas, which are not encompassed in the prevention and relief systems in disaster-affected situations.

The legal regimes most often do not consider the ancillary legal logistics, while dealing with the emerging post-disaster conditions.

As a case study let us again revert to the earlier-cited judgement. Rasheed Ahmed, the appellant in the instant case, had obtained a loan/investment from the House Building Finance Corporation to the tune of Rs 5,200,000 vide Deed of Assignment and

> Partnership dated 3 January 1984 for construction of house. The defendant/appellant could not keep the repayment schedule and thus committed breach of the terms and conditions of the aforementioned Assignment and Partnership Deed. The plaintiff/respondent, Corporation, made an application on 12 December 1995 to the learned District Judge Sheikhupura under section 30 of the House Building Finance Corporation Act, 1952, for delivery of the vacant possession or sale of the building which was already mortgaged and assigned to the Corporation. The application was resisted alleging that the suit house had collapsed in 1988 due to the flood and some cracks also occurred in the walls and the floor of the house. In the circumstances it was not fit for habitation. The defendant/appellant requested the Corporation to re-evaluate the house, but the request was declined. The First Regular Appeal filed by Rasheed Ahmed was also dismissed.
>
> Besides the immediate problem faced on account of the floods, *the parallel accruing setback facing the appellant in the case had no remedy in law.* This is the area which the legal experts' policy-makers and legislators must attend to while designing any disaster-related system.

When disasters strike, they adversely impact every facet of human life, disrupting the social system as well besides causing the physical damage. From the questions of missing persons and adoption procedures to property matters, while the standard legal systems are capacitated to deal these in normal times, no exceptions are found in the statutory laws; for that matter the emergency devised mechanisms also do not consider these human issues. Stress is laid on the physical aspects of the disasters for which not only the requisite modules are in place but also supported by massive financial resources, domestically and by foreign aid donors.

The immediate need to adopt a comprehensive policy on the matters to be dealt with in hazardous conditions continues to rise with the steep upsurge in disasters.

Pakistan evidence law (Qanun-e-Shahadat Order, 1984) contemplates Article 124 of the Order as under:

> **124. Burden of proving that person is alive who has not been heard of for seven years**
>
> When the question is whether a man is alive or dead, and it is proved that he has not been heard of for seven years by those who

would naturally have heard of him if he had been alive, the burden of proving that he is alive is shifted to the person who affirms it.

Section 2 of the Dissolution of Muslim Marriages Act, 1939, assumes in Subsection (i) that the whereabouts of the husband not known for a period of four years is a ground for dissolution of marriage. In the second proviso to section 2 clause (b) states that a decree passed on ground (i) shall not take effect for a period of six months from the date of such decree, and if the husband appears either in person or through an authorized agent within that period and satisfied the Court that he is prepared to perform his conjugal duties, the Court shall set aside the said decree.

A distinct disparity appears the relevant provisions of the Qanun-e-Shahadat Order 1984 and Dissolution of Muslim Marriages Act, 1939.

Keeping the canvas of a post-disaster situation, the position for the women becomes more precarious. These provisions should be amended, or a new law catering for such emergencies ought to be passed, which would apply in disaster-like conditions.

There is no statutory law specifically enacted for adoption of children.

However, a procedure does exist in Pakistan catering to adoption. Eligibility requirements for Pakistani adoption are noted here:[15]

- The adoptive parents have to be Muslim (unless the agencies know they are placing a Christian Child, they would not place a child with Christian family);
- At least one of the parents must be of Pakistani origin and be eligible for a NICOP or CNIC;
- Couples must be married for at least three years;
- For a single man/woman, although the law does not prohibit adoption, it is not very common and may be more difficult; and
- At least one of the prospective adoptive parents must be a citizen of the country of residence (i.e. America, Canada, UK, etc.).

Finally an application lies before the family court for adoption.

The procedure with the heavy workload in the courts is cumbersome even in routine matters. This certainly creates myriad of problems than providing any solace either to the surviving or traumatized children victims of hazardous conditions but also discouraging the aspirant foster parents. For securing the future of the adopted children, recourse may be taken through the process of appointment of the foster parents as *guardian ad litem* by the courts. This process definitely cannot succeed in emergencies. The earthquake of 2005 provides frightening facts on the missing children.

Another dimension to the procedure is the addition of human trafficking. While adoption is formally part of the Guardian & Wards Act, 1890, the statute itself requires major amendments in face of the present conditions, the lack of which makes this and other archaic statutes act as facilitators of crime.

Property issues during natural calamities create additional bottlenecks for the already-overburdened archaic legal system. From ownership rights as in joint properties, tenancies and license, all rights and interests therein come under cloud. Special laws have to be in place to address these valuable rights inherent in property disputes arising as natural consequence of disasters and the consequential deaths and the unfortunate disappearances of the persons residing in the calamity-affected areas.

The Illegal Dispossession Act, 2006, is one law which has all the potential for abuse in unnatural emergencies. Citing this example of one law recommends that the vast annals of laws must be amended and new laws must be enacted to meet the circumstances. Needless to mention that most of the statutes have lost their relevancy but continue to occupy the Corpus Juris.

A deeper scrutiny of the post-2005 disaster becomes necessary as noted earlier in this chapter. Reverting to the disaster management after a cursory glance on the obvious gaps prevalent in the system becomes more important from the lessons learnt.

The Government of Pakistan established the Earthquake Reconstruction and Rehabilitation Authority (ERRA) on 24 October 2005 to take up the mammoth task of rebuilding nine earthquake-affected districts of AJ&K and KP spread over 30,000 square kilometres. ERRA is a hybrid organization comprising civil servants, technocrats, armed forces personnel and contractual employees. ERRA's mission is to 'convert adversity into opportunity' by reconstructing lost and destroyed facilities, while following highest standards of reconstruction and rehabilitation with an obligation to 'build back better'.[16]

ERRA was created to bring all efforts and activities pertaining to post-disaster damage assessment, reconstruction and rehabilitation in the affected areas under one umbrella, with a view to providing fast-track and seismically safe reconstruction solutions. The authority is responsible for macro-planning, strategy formulation, financing, project approval and monitoring and evaluation. Additionally, it ensures required coordination and provides facilitation to implementing partners, leaving physical implementation of projects to respective governments. ERRA seeks to achieve disaster reduction through sustainable development by raising resilient socio-economic infrastructure and promoting a culture of preparedness among vulnerable populations.[17]

Through its reconstruction portfolio ERRA has intervened in 12 different sectors (housing, livelihood, social protection, health, education, water and sanitation, governance, power generation, telecommunication, transportation, environment and tourism), implemented 3 cross-cutting themes (DRR, gender mainstreaming and environmental safeguards) and is required to reconstruct over 13,000 projects (at a cost of over US$5 billion).[18]

ERRA is in the process of developing alternate legal mechanism relating to property disputes in post-disaster situations. The questions posed earlier in this chapter were found to be in the addressing stage at ERRA.

To a query on what will happen when there is an ownership or inheritance dispute involved in compensation matters?, the answer provided by ERRA was for the just and equitable disbursement of funds and to ensure that the money goes to the rightful owner of the property, it is very important that the title and the ownership of the house are not ignored as determining the correct title of the property has become difficult due to the destruction of the legal documents during the earthquake. Assessing the ownership of the property will be the responsibility of the assessment and inspection team (AI) who will do it by resorting to legal document wherever possible and in case the legal documents have been destroyed, the title will be established through developing alternate mechanism as well as verification with the local community.[19]

To another query again touching on legal issues such as how should landlord and tenant disputes be dealt with?, the answer given was to the effect: For the grant of compensation to tenant living in the house owned by another person, the tenant should get the first installment because as per government notification No. 99405/Relief/EQ/05, the first installment of Rs 25,000 will be paid to the tenant in possession. As of now the policy of the government is that the owner will get the subsidy for one house in which he or she is residing. Subsidy for the other houses will be given to the tenants subject to the provision of NOC from the owner.[20]

So far as the legal landscape in the disaster-prone regions in Pakistan is concerned, positive and healthy developments are under way.

The other side of the evolving NDM Act 2010 when critically analysed shows gaps as ActionAid[21] report offers:

- The work ability and effectiveness of the legal framework is impeded by overlapping laws and institutional jurisdictions. NDM Act 2010 itself prescribes no special measures for addressing the issues of establishing linkages and incorporating overlapping provisions. These include West Pakistan National Calamities (Prevention and Relief Act l 958), The Civil Defence Act 1952 (as amended in 1993), Local Government Ordinance 2001 and Punjab Emergency Service Act 2006.[22]
- Generally, most of the disaster-related laws when drafted were never aimed at addressing the issue of disaster in a holistic manner and were responsive to specific needs arising out of necessity, for example, West Pakistan National Calamities Act 1958, Civil Defence Act 1952 and Local Government Ordinance 2001.
- The disaster-related laws do not cross-refer or attempt to relate or incorporate the provisions of existing laws. A succinct comparison with Punjab National Calamities (Prevention & Relief) Act, 1958, and Punjab Emergency Service Act 2006 can elicit this.
- The major criticism on NDM Act 2010 comes out on the constitutional plane. Disaster management is a subject under the exclusive jurisdiction of provinces as it is neither included in the Federal Legislative List nor the defunct Concurrent List as enumerated in the fourth schedule of the constitution [Fourth Schedule, Article 70 (4)]. Besides, Article 142 (c) of the constitution clearly states that Parliament shall have no powers to make laws with respect to any matter not enumerated in either the Federal Legislative List or the Concurrent Legislative List.
- The National Disaster Management Ordinance 2006/National Disaster Management Act 2010 was enacted by invoking the powers given to the Federal Legislature under Article 144 (Part V, Chapter 1), which confers the power upon Federal Legislature to legislate for two or more provinces, if two or more provincial legislatures pass resolutions to the effect that the Parliament may by law regulate any matter not enumerated in either legislative list in the fourth schedule of the constitution. Therefore National Disaster Management Law was promulgated after the Parliament was empowered by four provincial assemblies through their resolutions.
- The NDM Act 2010 envisages working in nine priority areas, enshrined in Hyogo Framework for Action (HFA) 2005. The act

provides for administratively autonomous institutional arrangements at all tiers of governance: federal, provincial and district levels. Their integration to the mainstream legislation becomes a complex problem.

- The definition of disaster as given in National Disaster Management Act 2010 is limiting and fails to qualify an event demanding a high quantum response. Moreover, in regards to man-made causes, a disaster could be a result of disregard and neglect of what one was supposed to do. Therefore it is important to incorporate negligence in the definition.
- The definition of 'disaster management' in NDM Act 2010 does not include two key ingredients of disaster risk management, namely, mitigation and capacity building. The definition needs to be broadened to make it inclusive of all steps, procedures and arrangements to ensure DRM.
- Another obvious deficiency in NDM Act 2010 is its failure to define 'declaration of disaster', and to outline the procedures and processes for declaration of a disaster at national, provincial or local levels.
- Minimum standards of relief as provided by NDM Act 2010 need further elaboration. This is, particularly, important in the context of compensation to be provided to the disaster-hit areas and people.
- Disaster management at district level is of vital importance and serves as the lynchpin of the whole framework, yet the law does not provide for a mandatory (legally enforceable) mechanism for functionalizing District Disaster Management Authorities (DDMAs).

Other legislative initiatives in disaster management

- The West Pakistan National Calamities (Prevention and Relief) Act 1958 provides for the maintenance and restoration of order in areas affected by certain calamities and for the prevention and control of and relief against such calamities, or any other calamity which, in the opinion of the government, warrants action under this act. The act was being adopted as mirror legislation in all the four provinces.
- The Civil Defence Act 1952/Civil Defence (Amendment) Act 1993 originally mandated the envisaged civil defence department to 'take measures not amounting to actual combat, for affording defence against any form of hostile attack by a foreign power or for depriving any form of hostile attack by a foreign power of its

effect, wholly or in part, whether such measures are taken before, during or after the time of the attack'. In 1993 its mandate was expanded to peace-time activities, and it also included remedial measures against natural or man-made disasters, for example, rescue, evacuation and relief measures; supplemented anti-flood equipment for army; and provided personnel for flood training in rescue and relief work.

- Local Government Ordinance 2001 (LGO2001) devolved the subject of disaster management to district level. It provides for context-specific disaster management at district, tehsil, and union council and village council levels.
- Punjab Emergency Service Act 2006 was created in October 2004 (Rescue 1122), and the governing legislation was passed in June 2006. The service is mandated to and provide for time-sensitive emergency.
- The defunct Local Government Ordinance (LGO) 2001 provided disaster management services at district, tehsil, union council and village council levels; however these institutions and processes were not aligned with the existing national disaster framework. Any future legislation on the subject needs to take account of this shortcoming.

Thus the ActionAid offers a remarkable critical analysis of NDM Act 2010 and thus highlights the areas that need attention.

While ActionAid has analysed, the positive aspects must not be allowed to be undermined by the critical approach. For the first time the legislation acknowledges 'vulnerable groups' in Section 11 of the NDM Act. It also envisages special provisions in the law to secure these groups.

Pakistan in 68 years has come a long way in governance areas. The year 2005 was the watershed as far disaster management is concerned. As in all other legislations NDM Act is undergoing the tests, the mechanism placed by the law is developing and recent events in disaster scenario are meeting the litmus tests.

The problems underlying any disaster creep up in the post-disaster situations. Unfortunately, majority of the disaster management systems do not survey the post-hoc events; the fallout is at the individual and subjective levels which require a micro-management system. This has yet to be built. The first step in mitigating the problem lies in revisiting the laws. This can act as the harbinger of a real transformation in further developments in disaster management.

Conclusion

With the introduction of NDM Act 2010 and ERRA, Pakistan has entered in the circle of proactive countries. Notwithstanding the criticisms which are certainly requiring attention from the Government of Pakistan there is no doubt that post-2005 disaster, the federal government has taken up strategic steps in developing a formidable disaster management system at all tiers from the national level to the district level. Pakistan certainly has come a long way from its formative phase of limited legislations to challenge the natural calamities through a tiered strategy.

The problem recognized in the legal framework is the dichotomy of positive law and the absence of normative law. Hence, the humanitarian problems shown in this chapter are afoot to sensitize law in Pakistan, even though this is a long and gradual process.

So far as the NDM Act 2010 is concerned it is encouraging to note that it takes into account of this ambiguity and clarifies the government position on vulnerable classes and ameliorates their problems distinctly.

Equally important is the fact that for the first time policy, planning and legislation is closely linked. The linkage is also clear on tier system from the national level to the district level. Administrative machinery has been harnessed to their potential levels. However, transparency and accountability is necessary. ERRA has been sufficiently made accountable, and it is expected that the governance system of NDM will develop its own accountability intrinsically.

Today Pakistan is far better equipped to face natural calamities than it ever was before 2005.

Notes

1 Professor N. Bhaskar Rao; Chairman, CMS; RESEARCH HOUSE, Community Centre, Saket, New Delhi-110 017, India. Ph. 26851660, 26864020; F. 91–11–26968282; E. info@cmsindia.org; Web: www.cmsindia.org
2 International Disaster Response Law (IDRL) in Pakistan: A desk review of the legal framework for facilitating and regulating international disaster assistance; International Federation of Red Cross and Red Crescent Societies.
3 Ibid.
4 Ibid.; also see R. Chandio (2015). 62 Million People Fall below Poverty Line. *The Nation*. [online] Retrieved from http://nation.com.pk/Business/31-Oct-2009/62-million-people-fall-below-poverty-line (Accessed 16 October 2015).
5 Ibid.

6 Ibid.
7 Ibid.
8 Ibid.
9 H. Khan and A. Khan (2015). *Natural Hazards and Disaster Management in Pakistan*. [online] Munich University. Retrieved from https://mpra.ub.uni-muenchen.de/11052/1/MPRA_paper_11052.pdf (Accessed 15 October 2015).
10 Ibid.
11 M. Adnan (2015). 'Pakistan's Crisis Management: Examining Proactive and Reactive Strategies'. *Journal of Political Studies*, vol. 21, no. 1, pp. 161, 177.
12 Naval Postgraduate School, Monterey, California, (2014). *Comparative Analysis of Immediate Response by National Disaster Management Systems of the U.S., Pakistan, and Turkey*. Monterey, CA: Naval Postgraduate School, p. 105.
13 Latin for 'of the same kind', used to interpret loosely written statutes. Where a law lists specific classes of persons or things and then refers to them in general, the general statements only apply to the same kind of persons or things specifically listed. Example: if a law refers to automobiles, trucks, tractors, motorcycles and other motor-powered vehicles, 'vehicles' would not include airplanes, since the list was of land-based transportation.
14 Rasheed Ahmed v House Building Finance Corporation through its district manager; Regular First Appeal 443 of 1998 heard on 23 October 2003; 2006 YLR 751 [Lahore].
15 M. Associates (2015). Divorce Papers, Divorce Lawyer, Best Law Firm, Court, Karachi, Lahore Pakistan. [online] Ma-law.org.pk. Retrieved from www.ma-law.org.pk/adoption+Pakistan-%20child_%20adoption+adopt%20-child_%20adoption-of-children-adoption-process-international-adoption%20-%20what-is-international-%20adoption-services+adoption+lawyer+law+firm+karachi+lahore+Islamabad.html (Accessed 27 October 2015).
16 Preventionweb.net (2015). Earthquake Reconstruction and Rehabilitation Authority (ERRA) | PreventionWeb.net. [online]. Retrieved from www.preventionweb.net/organizations/3586 (Accessed 26 October 2015).
17 Ibid.
18 Ibid.
19 Ibid.
20 Ibid.
21 ActionAid (2015). Governance Issues in Disaster Risk Management. [online]. Retrieved from www.actionaid.org/sites/files/actionaid/policy_brief-governance_issues_in_drm.pdf (Accessed 14 November 2015).
22 Ibid.

5 Disaster law and community resilience in Bangladesh

Md Akbaruddin Ahmad

The rising scale and number of disasters and their impacts on human life have impelled the need for an international disaster response laws (IDRL) of the International Federation of Red Cross and Red Crescent (IFRC) studies and legal issues related to disaster response with particular emphasis on international humanitarian assistance. The IDRL programme seeks to promote the use of the IDRL Guidelines and support national Red Cross societies in improving legal preparedness for natural disasters in order to reduce human vulnerability. Three areas of disaster law demand exceptional and deep attention:

- Settlements
- International custom
- UN resolutions (soft law)

Recent developments in IDRL

IDRL is still in a nascent stage. It has gaps that remain in its outline where development has been made. The adoption of the 'Guidelines for the Domestic Facilitation and Regulation of International Disaster Relief and Initial Recovery Assistance' (IDRL Guidelines) by the International Federation of Red Cross and Red Crescent Societies in 2007 is considered to be a significant development. Although these guidelines are non-binding, they are comprehensive in geographic scope, relevant for all sectors and for all types of disasters, and address both state and non-state actors. They aim to foster international agreement on how to address key issues specific to disaster settings. They define the responsibilities of affected states (reinforcing that primary responsibility lies with affected states) and offer a set of recommendations to governments for preparing their domestic laws and systems to manage international assistance during relief efforts. This includes encouraging legal facilities for operation, such as visa, customs and transport facilitation; tax exemptions; and a simplified process for acquiring temporary shelter on foreign soil with a legal status of a refugee or citizens under care. These facilities are provided on condition to humanitarian actors to adhere to core humanitarian principles and minimum standards drawn from widely recognized sources, such as the Code of Conduct.

The substance of the guidelines is drawn primarily from international laws, rules, norms and principles, and from lessons and best practices used in the field. The guidelines have gained broad international support. State parties to the Geneva Conventions adopted these guidelines at the International Conference of the Red Cross and Red Crescent in 2007. Moreover, several countries have already adopted new regulations or administrative rules based on or inspired by the guidelines. The International Law Commission (ILC), an expert body of the UN charged with codifying customary international law, has also been engaging in advancing the framework for disaster response. Its 'Protection of Persons in the Event of Disasters' programme is aimed at developing a legally binding framework at the global level. Draft articles include attention to humanitarian principles; the duty of states to seek assistance when their national response capacity is exceeded; the duty not to arbitrarily withhold consent to external assistance; and the right of the international community to offer assistance.

A comprehensive disaster policy in Bangladesh

Bangladesh has a long historic and successful experience of handling both natural and man-made disasters such as floods, cyclones, droughts, tidal surges, tornadoes, river erosion, high arsenic contents in ground water, water logging, soil salinity, fire and collapse of building. Recently, the country has found an increase in the intensity and magnitude of disasters in both forms – natural and man-made – due to climate change and vicious industrial practice. Bangladesh has experienced disasters for a long time. The civil society organizations and 'think tanks' have been demanding a comprehensive disaster risk management policy and act since the early 1990s. It took over 20 years to pass the Disaster Management Act in 2012. This chapter highlights the indispensable nature of legal framework or legislation for the disaster readiness in Bangladesh to obtain development with sustainability.

(1) Geographic vulnerability: Bangladesh is a natural disaster-prone country of an area about 147,570 square kilometres with a

population over 160 million (Bangladesh Bureau of Statistics, 2015). Bangladesh is affected by multifarious natural disasters due to its geographic and geologic settings (Carter, 1991). Bangladesh's geo-physical location makes it prone to various natural hazards, for example, flood, cyclone, drought, earthquake and landslide and man-made disasters such as fire and building collapse (Nasreen, 2004). From time immemorial, the geographical location, land characteristics, multiplicity of rivers, monsoon climate and coastal morphology of Bangladesh have been a mixed blessing (Sabur, 2012). Bangladesh also lacks the essential pre-, during- and post-disaster management operations that lag the mitigation procedures. Disaster management in Bangladesh is mainly concerned with disaster mitigation and preparedness (Kafiluddin, 1991). Both natural and man-made disasters cause immense losses of lives and damage to properties and economic infrastructure. The country faces at least one major disaster a year on average; it has lost on average 3.02 per cent of its GDP every year during the past 10 years and holds the highest disaster mortality rate in the world (UNDP, 2004). Conversely, Bangladesh is one of the most densely populated countries of the world with 1,125.5 people per square kilometre (July 2015) with the population growth 1.57 per cent. The population of Bangladesh is estimated to increase by 2,538,131 people and reach 164,615,491 in the beginning of 2016. The natural increase is expected to be positive, as the number of births will exceed the number of deaths by 2,792,593 people. If external migration will remain on the previous year level, the population will decline by 254,461 people due to the migration.

(2) Economic vulnerability: With the per capita income $1,314, Bangladesh experiences a very high physical and social vulnerability. One would find a strong correlation between disasters and poverty. The three main rivers, Ganges, Brahmaputra and Meghna, have a catchments area of about 1.7 million square kilometres, of which 92.5 per cent is located outside the country. The disasters often befall due to the climate change, for example, rain, flood, heat wave and the rising sea level. For past couple of decades, the total number of the disasters is about twice in the previous decades. Most of the districts with the highest percentage of poor people are also the most disaster-prone areas within Bangladesh. Climate changes have added a new dimension to community risks and vulnerabilities and according to German watch (2009), Bangladesh is at the top of a global climate risk index.

(3) International borders and cooperation: Due to its location in the delta of major river systems, Bangladesh depends on maintaining good relationship with its neighbouring countries, especially India. In case of any devastating natural disaster, collaboration of government agencies with non-government agencies, international and UN agencies plays a crucial role in providing immediate response and relief efforts and subsequent rehabilitation of the affected people (Khan, 2000). The adverse impacts of all the natural hazards affecting socio-economic condition need to be reduced for sustainable development (Pande, 1992). Disaster management requires effective communication, collaboration between different departments and NGOs which can reduce and minimize the loss of lives and properties (Shafiq and Ahsan, 2013).

(4) Technological vulnerability: The disasters of Bangladesh are complex and diverse, which demands an elaborate system giving warning well ahead of time. The complexity of the problems makes it very difficult to predict the impending danger, and the socio-economic conditions and the logistic support facilities make it more difficult to take appropriate actions (Rahman, 1991). To mitigate and manage disasters a policy assessment was carried out by Khan and Rahman in Bangladesh (2007). It was found that for a long time disaster management suffered from the disaster readiness plans, communication, bureaucratic hassle, confusion about legal framework and the collaboration between national- and local-level organizations.

However, existing policies, laws and acts related to addressing disaster readiness due to natural and man-made disasters provide the basis to establish a legal and institutional framework to deal with loss and damage in Bangladesh. Mandatory obligation and liability of different ministries and committees and ensuring the integrity and accountability in the overall disaster management system have now been established.

Risk profile of Bangladesh

As mentioned earlier, Bangladesh is a disaster-prone country, which is disproportionately affected by disasters because of its limited resource, weak infrastructure and lack of disaster preparedness plan (Watson *et al.*, 2007). For example, cyclone on 29 April 1991 is the most devastating one in its history (Haen and Hemrick, 2006). Both losses of life and property are unbearable, and the direct impact of this type of disastrous event on social and economic life of Bangladeshi people is overstraining

(Sabur, 2012). Bangladesh exposed its coping deficiencies so many times against violent natural disaster events. In a disaster situation, early response is very much important to minimize the casualties and the damages to human lives (Chandio *et al.*, 2006).

Analysing the cyclonic storm 'Mahasen'

A depression formed over southeast Bay of Bengal at 14:30 hrs IST on 10 May 2013 near latitude 5.00N and longitude 92.00E. It moved northwestwards and intensified into a deep depression in the evening of the same day. Continuing its northwestward movement, it further intensified into a cyclonic storm, Mahasen, in the morning of 11 May 2013 with a sustained maximum wind speed of about 85–95 kilometres per hour.

How was the Cyclone Mahasen governed?

Monitoring and community interaction

The cyclonic storm Mahasen was monitored mainly with satellite supported by meteorological buoys, coastal and island observations. It was monitored by Doppler Weather Radar (DWR). According to the Bangladesh Meteorological Department, cyclonic storm Mahasen was positioned over west central Bay and adjoining east central Bay on 15 May 2013 and moved slightly north-northeastwards. By then

Table 5.1 Record of loss and damage

Loss or damage	*Amount/number*	*Costs/specification*
Total number of people affected	1,285,508	
Dead	13	
Total number of districts affected	10	
Worse-affected districts	3	Patuakhali, Bhola and Barguna
Total number of people evacuated to cyclone shelters	1.1 million	
Total number of houses completely destroyed	49,178	
Total number of houses partially destroyed	45,825	
Estimated total economic loss	US$5.14 million	

Source: Red Cross and Government of Bangladesh.

the maritime ports of Chittagong and Cox's Bazar had been advised to lower local warning signal number four and instead hoisted danger signal number seven, and for Mongla, signal number five had been hoisted. Earlier in the week, a total of 49,365 Cyclone Preparedness Programme of Bangladesh (CPP) volunteers had been mobilized in the 13 coastal districts. The CPP volunteers disseminated alert messages to coastal communities to prepare them for safe evacuation and advised fishermen not to sail too far off the coast until noon on 17 May and then proceed with caution until further notice. About 1.1 million people were evacuated to safer places like cyclone shelters. Air traffic in Chittagong and Cox's Bazar port was suspended on 15 May. Government of Bangladesh and different organization jointly conducted search and rescue operations, giving first aid and distributing food and clean water to the affected population, especially in the remote islands of Patuakhali, Bhola and Barguna districts.

Post-disaster management and community participation

The Government of Bangladesh (GoB) sanctioned the distribution of food (of about 3,501 metric tonnes of rice) and cash amounting to BDT 12 million (approximately CHF 146,323) in the cyclone-affected districts. The prime minister's cabinet authorized the District Disaster Management Committees (DDMCs) to treat all public buildings, and some private buildings such as hotels, as safer shelters. Around 100 water treatment plants were mobilized to serve the cyclone-affected population. The armed forces, under the prime minister's office order, established an information hub to coordinate food distribution.

Despite the huge impact of the cyclone, many lives were saved due to the existing early warning system in place and close monitoring of the cyclone by the local authorities and other humanitarian organizations. Thousands of volunteers were mobilized to take part in the evacuation of vulnerable communities in Bangladesh. Early warning messages were also disseminated through radio and loudspeakers. The damage of Cyclone Mahasen was drastically reduced in comparison with Cyclone Bhola in 1970 in which over 400,000 people were killed and Cyclone Sidr in 2007 in which nearly 4,000 were killed. The progress is mainly due to the increased capacity of communities after disaster risk reduction and preparedness activities.

Since Cyclone Mahasen hit Bangladesh after the passage of the Disaster Management Act 2012, the scale of loss was minimal when compared to previous cyclones.

Rana Plaza disaster

The 2013 Savar building collapse or Rana Plaza collapse was a structural failure that occurred on 24 April 2013 in the Savar Upazila of Dhaka, Bangladesh, where an eight-story commercial building named Rana Plaza collapsed. The search for the dead ended on 13 May 2013 with a death toll of 1,129. Approximately 2,515 injured people were rescued alive from the building. It is considered the deadliest garment-factory accident in history, as well as the deadliest accidental structural failure in modern human history. The building contained clothing factories, a bank, apartments and several other shops. The shops and the bank on the lower floors immediately closed after cracks were discovered in the building. Warnings to avoid going to the building after cracks appeared the day before had been ignored. Garment workers were ordered to return the following day, and the building collapsed during the morning rush hour. The total economic losses were around $40 million.

Guidelines expected in disaster management

Prediction

On 23 April 2013 people in the Rana Plaza were evacuated due to the cracks founds on the building. The adjacent shops and bank were also closed. But the next day the owner of the Plaza, Mr Rana, a local leader and politician of the ruling party, declared the building safe without any proper investigation. This raises many questions for reform in disaster law.

Causes

Shortly after the collapse, the Bangladeshi government organized and directed a high-level committee to investigate the disaster site and determine the causes of the failure. Through their investigation, they discovered several contributing causes, many developing from the initial phases of its construction. These causes were:

- Unsuitable land for multi-story construction
- Use of poor quality construction materials
- According to the architect, the building was designed for the shops and offices not for the factory.
- Loads that were placed on the building were not within design criteria.

- Poor regulation and enforcement of building codes.
- Huge crowd in garment shops.

Search and rescue operation

Immediately following the collapse, police and fire brigade were dispatched to Rana Plaza, but they did not arrive for 10 to 15 minutes. The first responders to the scene were several hundred local residents who had heard the collapse or heard of the collapse and came to assist those trapped inside the rubble. Many people voluntarily entered the debris field, risking their own lives, in order to save as many of the victims as possible. They also brought supplies such as water, medicine, and bandages to help anyone in need. If they were running low on any valuable materials, they utilized social media to communicate with each other and ask for additional supplies.

Medical emergencies

Emergency personnel arrived and rescue efforts intensified, and body parts of some survivors had to be physically cut from the rubble they were trapped under. In many unfortunate instances, they had to be amputated in the field in order to be safely freed. From the plaza, the wounded were transported to Enam Medical College & Hospital, located less than a mile away. Though the hospital could treat only 750 patients, makeshift beds were set up to treat more patients and the first-year medical students were called in to assist the staff of the hospital. Nearby medical facilities sent supplies to restock the hospital's reserves as they were depleted to treat all of the wounded. Rescuers worked quickly against the clock. Trapped victims faced death from dehydration, exposure to high temperatures, oxygen depletion and their injuries. On 13 May, after 20 days, rescue efforts were concluded with over 2,500 survivors saved from the debris. The government had been ill-prepared to deal with the scope of the disaster, and it was primarily the heroic efforts of the local residents who saved the lives of so many people.

Lessons from disasters

These disasters in Bangladesh have awakened its construction industry. International organizations, foreign allies, local institutions and large retailers have been strong promoters of improving the working conditions for garment factory workers. In addition, the Bangladesh public has been in outrage since the disaster and has prominently voiced their desire to bring about changes to the garment industry and its working conditions. The catalyst of this movement comes from the collapse of Rana Plaza. In the weeks following the tragedy, public protests of the garment industry were commonplace. On 1 May, one of the largest protests occurred with several thousand workers marching through Dhaka to protest poor working conditions. In 2013 the police used tear gas and batons to diffuse a belligerent mobilization of workers at the site of the Plaza. The unrest continued as workers demanded an increase in minimum wage from $37 per month to $104 per month. Facing pressure from upset workers and the government, in November 2013, the Bangladesh Garment Manufacturers and Exports Association (BGMEA) raised the minimum wage to $68 per month, a huge victory for the workers.

The compensation of $40 million was delivered to the victims and their family. Although there was some compensation from the factories, the loss of the life is irrecoverable. Negligence and corruption should be taken up as causes of disasters to locate culpability of administration. The present case can be investigated as follows to suggest culpability of administration:

- The land was not suitable for constructing more than four stories but the owner constructed eight stories out of it.
- The design was for the shops and offices not for the factories.
- The owner fixed heavy machineries and generators which pressurized the building with tremendous load.
- The materials and rods used for the construction were not up to the mark.
- Inspection and regulation system failed to check the building standards during construction.
- The local and relevant authorities were unable to cease while building was constructed.
- The plaza owner acquired illegal permits and ignored professional opinion, leading to immoral decisions that put thousands in harm's way.
- The building failed to meet the safety standards.
- The owner illegally used political power to do all these without any monitoring.

The government found the ineffective and dismissive implementing of the Disaster Management Act after its approval by the parliament in the case of Rana Plaza tragedy.

Recommendations for reform

As it has been strongly demanded, the implementation of the Disaster Management Act is important since Bangladesh is mostly a disaster-prone county. The skullduggery of some powerful people and the negligence of the concern authorities make the demand of a formal framework more acute in operation. The long-cherished Disaster Management Act of September 2012 has placed mandatory obligations and responsibilities on ministries and committees, and ensures transparency and accountability in the overall disaster management system. The prime objectives of the noble act are:

- to substantially reduce the overall risks of disasters to an acceptable level with appropriate risk reduction interventions,
- to provide effective post-disaster emergency response, rehabilitation and recovery measures,
- to ensure the provision of emergency humanitarian assistance to the most vulnerable community people,
- to ensure the strongest institutional capacity for effective coordination of disaster management involving government and non-government organizations and other international aid organizations,
- to establish a multidimensional disaster management system capable of dealing with all hazards of the country,
- to help in promoting a comprehensive disaster management programme to respond to the all hazards, both natural and man-made, and
- to prepare all-hazard and all-systems approach where risk reduction as a core element of disaster management has equal emphasis with emergency response management with greater focus on equitable and sustainable development.

Before the passage of the DMA 2012, the draft Standing Orders on Disaster (SOD) was first issued in 1997 and the draft SOD were approved in 2010 policy, which did not have much legal value in the absence of a Disaster Management Act.

Immediately after the approval, it was found that some visible institutional reforms brought significant progress in Bangladesh disaster management. The Ministry of Disaster Management and Relief is one of the outcomes of institutional reforms. On account of the more comprehensive disaster management, the Directorate of Relief and Rehabilitation has been transformed into the Department of Disaster

Management. The newly formed ministry was dedicated to make the disaster management system more sturdy and multidimensional. All level responsibilities of the policies for the disaster management fall upon the ministry. For the disaster risk reduction and emergency management with the strategic framework and the national disaster management principles the draft National Disaster Management Policy has been formulated after the act and it is yet to be approved by the parliament.

Notwithstanding the onerous achievements in the legislation and the institutional framework, several immediate actions need to be functional at the national and local levels of disaster management because we believe the activities are so far so good so further enhancement is needed to make the act actually functioning. To achieve the ultimate goal the Ministry of Disaster Management and Relief and the act need to do the following:

- To make the act effective, dissemination of the information is most important through proper training and orientation to both national- and local-level organizations.
- Orientation for the different level disaster management committee to make them more informative and ensure the strength.
- Since the National Disaster Management Plan was approved long before the approval of the DMA, the plan demands revision and redesigning based on the DMA to ensure the overall guideline for the relevant systems and disaster management committees at all levels to prepare and implement their roles according to specific plans.
- Proper guidelines for government, NGOs, disaster management committees and the civil societies need to be in place to aid the Ministry of Disaster Management and Relief.
- A national-level research institute with other significant branches to the disaster-prone areas needs to be functional to handle the different natural disasters along with strengthening the national disaster management system.
- To exchange information and to use space-based technologies government can sign the MOU with the expert foreign country or agencies to make the research effective.
- Establishing national volunteer unit and enhancing the capacities of the existing volunteer community is needed to make the preparation phase smooth and also the search and rescue operation effective.

- Merging the urban volunteer units and the Department Fire Service and Civil Defense is needed in order to make rapid response in all levels of disaster management.
- A charitable disaster management fund needs to be formulated with a proper legislation to raise the fund legally from both home and abroad.
- The charitable fund rising, especially from the abroad, needs to be freer while releasing.
- The funds need to be disseminated to all levels, including upazila levels.
- Since the specified guideline for the emergency management is present in the act, now it needs to be disseminated to the local level.
- Local disaster management committees have been given the provision of requesting the deputy commissioner to declare emergency for a particular disaster-affected area.
- Under the DMA,there is provision of rewarding individuals and organizations which come forward to help in emergency management and also disseminate information and warnings through the media.
- A strong rule needs to be formulated to define the process of requesting the aid services, vehicles, building and any other emergency demands.
- Rules and monitoring must be in place to regulate or control specified vicious practices, such as:

    - Creation of problems in delivering services in disaster management system.
    - Violation of government orders and laws relevant to media and coordination groups.
    - Making inappropriate and lame statements and claims.
    - Misappropriation of resources.
    - Intentional price hike of necessary commodities in the disaster-affected zones.
    - Obstructing water flow for personal benefit – such as creating salinity and flood and making illegal holes in the embankments.
    - Skullduggery in emergency directives to the mass media and others.
    - Failure of government staff to discharge their duty; misuse of position and power.

Conclusion

Bangladesh attained the lower–middle-income status in 2015 through United Nations. The very high level of resilience shown by the Bangladesh population against natural and man-made disasters is treated as role models in the entire world. This has resulted in fast recovery process. In many cases the astonishing recovery within three months' time when people returned to their usual activity of agricultural work. The annual flood is a form of enriching the soil that helps in bumper harvest of crops. With the high-yielding variety of food grains and short-term food crops, the Monga region, which is drought-stricken for several months in a year, now turns green, producing paddy for the people of that region. This is a classic case of government and people efforts to withstand all forms of shock on account of natural and man-made disaster and its successful mitigation. The DMA 2012 in Bangladesh is a landmark achievement which can be made stronger through the inclusion of assistive legal requirements suggested earlier in this chapter. The DMA will help in promoting a comprehensive disaster management programme to respond to all hazards, both natural and man-made.

References

Akter, T. (2009). *Climate Change and Flow of Environment Displacement in Bangladesh*. Dhaka: Unnayyan onneshan.

Arafin, K. S. (2013). *The Daily Star, Man-Made Disaster: Policy and Practice,* retrieved at 12:46 AM, May 18, 2013.

Bangladesh Bureau of Statistics (BBS). (2015). Retrieved 3 June 2015, from www.bbs.gov.bd/home.aspx

Bannon, V. (2008). International Disaster Response Law and the Commonwealth: Answering the Call to Action. *Commonwealth Law Bulletin*, 34, 843–857. http://dx.doi.org/10.1080/03050710802521622

Carter, W. N. (1991). *Disaster Management: A Disaster Management Hand Book*. Manila: ADB.

Chandio, A. F., Shu, L. Y., Memon, N. M. & Khawaja, A. (2006). GIS Based Route Guiding System for Optical Path Planning in Disaster Management. *IEEE International*, 2996–2999.

Chowdhury, A. M. (1978). Rose Petals for Tropical Cyclones. *Nuclear Science and Applied*, *11*(B), 1–7.

Clean Cloths Campaign. (2014). 'Survivors Rana Plaza Collapse Start Claiming Compensation' Mirjam van Heugten, published online https://cleanclothes.org/news/press-releases/2014/03/24/survivors-rana-plaza-collapse-start-claiming-compensation,15:19, retrieved 12-12-2016.

Das, K. M. (1997). *Disaster Management with Particular Reference to* Bangladesh. Dhaka: DMB.

de Urioste, A. (2006–7). When Will Help Be on the Way: The Status of International Disaster Response Law. *Tulane Journal of International and Comparative Law*, 15, 181–206. http://heinonline.org/HOL/Page?handle=hein.journals/tulicl15&div=10&g_sent=1&collection=journals

ERMA, Enterprise Risk Management Authority, Bangladesh and Reasons Buildings Collapse. http://erm-academy.org/publication/risk-management-article/bangladesh-and- reasons-buildings-collapse

Fisher, D. (2010). The Right to Humanitarian Assistance. *Studies in Transnational Legal Policy*, 47, 41–128. http://heinonline.org/HOL/Page?handle=hein.journals/stdtlp41&div=9&g_sent=1&collection=journals

Government of Bangladesh (GoB). (2010). Standing Order on Disaster, Disaster Management Bureau, Ministry of Food and Disaster Management. Retrieved 3 June 2012, from www.dmb.gov.bd/reports/sod_final.pdf

Government of India, Ministry of Earth Sciences, India Meteorology Department. (2013). A Preliminary Report on Cyclonic Storm, Mahasenover Bay of Bengal.

Government of the People's Republic of Bangladesh. (2012). Disaster Management Act.

GSDRC. (2013). *International Legal Frameworks for Humanitarian Action: Topic Guide*. Birmingham, UK: GSDRC, University of Birmingham. www.gsdrc.org/go/topic-guides/international-legal-frameworks-for-humanitarian-action/challenges/-traps-and-debates/the-emergence-of-international-disaster-response-laws-rules-and-principles

Haen, H. & Hemrick, G. (2006). The Economics of Natural Disasters – Implications and Challenges for Food Security presented 26th conference of International Association of Agricultural Economics, Bridgetown, Australia, 12–18 August 2006.

Haris, M. (1999). Country Report: Bangladesh, IDNDR-ESCAP Regional Meeting for Asia was held during 23–26 February, Bangkok, Thailand.

IRIN, Humanitarian News and Analysis. (2012). BANGLADESH: Where Landslides Are Becoming a Man-Made Disaster. Retrieved from www.irinnews.org/report/96614/bangladesh-where-landslides-are-becoming-a-man-made-disaster

Islam, A. R. M. T., Tasnza, A., Islam, M. T. & Haque, R. M. (2014). Management Approach to Disaster Scenario in Bangladesh: An Overview. *International Journal of Scientific and Research Publications*, 4(3), ISSN 2250–3153.

Kafiluddin, A. K. M. (1991). *Disaster Preparedness for Bangladesh Flood and Other Natural Calamities*. Dhaka: Padma Printers & Color Limited.

Khan, M. N. U. (2000). *Disaster Management System in Bangladesh*. Dhaka: Bangladesh Army Journal.

Khan, M. R. & Rahman, M. A. (2007). Partnership Approach to Disaster Management in Bangladesh: A Critical Policy Assessment. *Natural Hazards*, 41(2).

Nasreen, M. (2004). Disaster Research: Exploring Sociological Approach to Disaster in Bangladesh. *Bangladesh e-Journal of Sociology*, 1(2), 1–8.

The New York Times. (2013). Report on Deadly Factory Collapse in Bangladesh Finds Widespread Blame.

Pande, M. (1992). Disaster Relief. *Trisul Journal*, III (2).

Rahman, M. M. M. (1991). *Training the Armed Forces for Disaster Operation*. Dhaka: Bangladesh Army Journal.

Sabur, A. K. M. A. (2012). Disaster Management System in Bangladesh: An Overview. *India Quarterly: A Journal of International Affairs*, 68 (1), 29–47.

Shafiq, F. & Ahsan, K. (2013). Knowledge Management for Disaster Scenario: An Exploratory Study. *Research Journal of Recent Science*, 2(10), 61–66.

Todres, J. (2011). Mainstreaming Children's Rights in Post-Disaster Settings. *Emory International Law Review*, 25, 1233–1262. www.law.emory.edu/fileadmin/journals/eilr/25/25.3/Todres.pdf

UNDP. (2004). *Human Development Report: 2004. United States Development Program (UNDP)*. Oxford University Press, New York.

Watson, J. T., Gayer, M. & Connolly, M. A. (2007). Epidemics after Natural Disaster. *Emerging Infectious Diseases*, 13(1), 1–5.

6 International disaster response law in China

A study on strengthening national disaster response legislation

Yan Cui and Shibo Jiang

Introduction

The growing number of natural disasters and their humanitarian impacts prompted the need for legal regulation. China as one of the world's most disaster-prone countries is still at a comparable lower stage on national legislation of international disaster law.[1] Although it is well accepted that international humanitarian assistance is provided by the United Nations and other agencies irrespective of borders, China's attitude towards international humanitarian assistance has experienced rejection to gradually acceptance period since the 1980s. The regulation on the ground developed from the promulgation of policy to rule of law.

This chapter approaches the lacuna addressing comprehensively on international disaster response law in China. The authors look at the law from its growth and development, reflect current deficiencies and suggest solutions by developing and facilitating its national disaster response legislation to keep pace with recent development in international community. This chapter consists of five sections: this section is the introduction to of the chapter, which outlines the main aim and content of this chapter; the second section reviews the development on international disaster assistance policy in China, by reflecting the gradual changing attitude of Chinese government towards international humanitarian assistance; the third section examines loopholes exiting in China's current international disaster response law compared with international legislation; the fourth section provides corresponding resolutions and proposals with the legal coordination from the perspective of international and domestic levels. The final section is the conclusion, which generalizes the main theme of the chapter, which appraises the shortcoming of current legal framework in China's international disaster law and proposes further resolutions to develop its domestic law through learning from international practice.

Development of international disaster response law in China

The development of international disaster response law in China experienced five stages, respectively:

Phase one (1949–1979): from non-acceptance to acceptance of foreign assistance

After the People's Republic of China (PRC) was established in 1949, new China had pursued the low-risk and non-adventurous policy to refuse foreign disaster assistance in the next 30 years. In the 1950s, the U.S. secretary of state Dean Acheson expressed willingness to provide food aid to China while China suffered severe floods. But the offer was turned down by the former vice president Liu Shaoqi, who made the following remarks: 'The purpose of the so-called relief is to carry out sabotage activities in uncovered U.S. own will. Chinese people welcome foreign assistance from who are indeed in good faith, but we should refuse "the sugar-coated bullets of imperialism", which we have experienced too much in the past years.'[2] Some changes were done in foreign policy attitude under the guidance of premier of the State Council Zhou Enlai, who once made the following remarks: 'We welcome any real and friendly assistance from international friends in principle. We believe China has ability to overcome famine by material transfers between different provinces and areas based on its vast territory and abundant resources.'[3] From then on, China began to accept international assistance with great caution in the next 30 years.

Phase two (1980–1986): passively and limited acceptance of international humanitarian assistance

The shift on Chinese government attitude towards international relief from rejection in the past 30 years to partial acceptance is of historical significance. China suffered severe floods and droughts in the summer of 1980. For the first time, China was willing to accept international relief. The Ministry of Foreign Economic Liaison,[4] Ministry of Civil Affairs and Ministry of Foreign Affairs (hereinafter referred to as 'the Three Ministries') jointly proposed the consultation bill to the State Council seeking the assistance acceptance order from the United Nations Disaster Relief Office (UNDRO). The consultation bill was approved by the State Council with following guidelines: 'It is approved that China could duly and timely seek the assistance from the United Nations Disaster Relief Office (UNDRO) to cope with the disaster. China should provide timely report on national disaster and seek assistance from UNDRO under serious conditions.' The new principle on international disaster relief assistance was established to usher in a new era thereafter. It is positively commented by the international community that the shift on attitude of Chinese government in the past 30 years is of historical significance. In March 1981, the delegation of the UNDRO investigated in Hubei and Hebei Provinces and found the actual disaster situation was even more serious than what the Chinese government reported. They called for international assistance and received disaster relief materials worth more than $20 million from more than 20 countries and international organizations. This was the first time that Chinese government accepted foreign assistance after its founding. China dramatically changed international disaster relief policy when the upper reaches of the Yangtze River suffered floods in the fall of 1981. The new policy encouraged China to overcome hardship of disaster relief with the power of self-dependence. Relief should only be provided in the form of relief materials and funds. The request of sending volunteers and individuals to disaster areas by foreign governments and international organizations should be strictly controlled. During the time period of 1981–1986, China's foreign aid was standstill under the guidance of the changed policy.

Phase three (1987–1999): open for international disaster assistance

The 1987 Daxinganling Fire became a landmark event on China's policy of international assistance. The fire continued for a month, causing huge losses and aroused the widespread concern of the international community. Facing with the catastrophic disaster, Chinese government accepted relief assistance from foreign countries, international organizations and individual donators. The Three Ministries once again jointly submitted proposal for the change of international relief policy which was set out as follows:

Disaster information release

The Three Ministries submitted a consultation proposal which was approved by the State Council in June 1987. The proposal stated 'information on the extent of disaster and the updated relief work should be timely released to international community; information should be timely provided when it is inquired by international organizations, news agencies or foreign embassies; domestic news agencies may appropriately coordinate with them on information report; disaster information will be published abroad unless under the consideration of abnormal death and other non-normal conditions (such as flee from famine, begging or flee abroad)'.

The basic guideline to accept international disaster assistance

The new policy 'Amendment on Policy Guidelines for International Disaster Relief' was approved by the State Council thereafter. In case of serious disasters, disaster relief should call for international community assistance through the UNDRO. In case of minor disasters, assistance will be accepted only if international organizations and foreign countries make offers of disaster relief to affected areas. Donations from international non-governmental organizations (*NGOs*) as well as countries and patriotic overseas Chinese will normally be accepted. However, donations from religious or sectarian organizations may be politely refused or accepted in only exceptional cases. Reviews may be made based on a case-by-case basis.

The responsible coordination authorities

The responsible coordination authorities of international disaster assistance are suggested and approved by the Three Ministries:

i) The Ministry of Foreign Trade and Economic Cooperation (MOFTEC) is responsible for communication and coordination with assistance offered by the UN as well as other international organizations and governments. The Ministry of Civil Affairs (MCA) is responsible for sharing disaster information on time, organization of media coverage as well as relief supplies and distribution;
ii) The Chinese government was advised to set up China Anti-Disaster and Relief Association as a national society handling international relief from non-government sources such as the International Federation of Red Cross and Red Crescent Societies (IFRC). It was further suggested that the Red Cross Society of China (RCSC) and All-China Women's Federation (ACWF) will be responsible for handling international reliefs from corresponding international NGOs. However, the consultation paper was not approved by the State Council. Instead of establishing China Anti-Disaster and Relief Association, the State Council prescribed that the Ministry

of Civil Affairs (MCA) be in charge of all international disaster relief affairs. The State Commodity Inspection Bureau, Ministry of Health, General Administration of Customs and other ministries also have the right to issue regulations on international relief;

iii) The Ministry of Civil Affairs (MCA) will formulate appropriate measures through diplomatic channels and cooperate closely with various NGOs and private donors;

iv) Chinese State Council in collaboration with the Three Ministries will handle international disaster reliefs in special circumstances (such as the Daxinganling Fire case). General affairs on disaster information release shall be handled by the Ministry of Civil Affairs (MCA) directly.

China had made substantial progress in domestic facilitation and regulation of international disaster relief under the guidance of policies mentioned earlier. For instance, severe floods washed out Jianyang in Fujian Province in May 1988. The Three Ministries on behalf of the Chinese government declared to the international community that Chinese government was ready to accept emergency assistance from foreign governments and international organizations. A list of varieties of required items was provided to international community as well. Another example was when flood disasters occurred in the vast areas of East China in 1991. Chinese government under the name of 'China Committee for the International Decade on Natural Disaster Reduction' appealed to the international community to provide international humanitarian relief for emergency needs. This was the first time China made an official appeal to the international community for international relief since it was established. Later, China gradually formed an integrated systematic international relief policy to keep up with international regulations on international relief. The 1996 Lijiang earthquake, the 1998 Yangtze River floods and the 2003 SARS outbreak witnessed the great practice on international humanitarian assistance of Chinese government in collaboration with the Red Cross Society of China (RCSC) and other organizations. China's foreign aid thus entered a new stage through regulation reforms in this period.

Phase four (since 1999): transition from policy to rule of law

China's policy on international assistance in disaster relief had entered into the orbit of the rule of law when the law of the People's Republic of China on Donations for Public Welfare was adopted on 10th session of the Standing Committee of the Ninth National People's Congress on 28 June 1999. Article III of the law clearly stipulated that 'disaster relief' belongs to the category of 'public welfare' on which the law will apply. For the purpose of regulating the administration of donated money or goods for disaster relief, the Interim Measures for the Administration of Donations for Disaster Relief (Order No. 22 of the Ministry of Civil Affairs) was promulgated by the Ministry of Civil Affairs (MCA). Regulations on foreign disaster relief donations were set out in Chapter III, in which a hierarchical administration system was set up: In the upper level of the hierarchy, the MCA was responsible for releasing disaster information, appealing to international community for international relief and accepting donations on behalf of the central government. In the lower level of the hierarchy, the civil affairs department of local government at or above the county level was responsible to accept foreign relief donations on behalf of the local government. The identified public welfare associations can accept overseas donations for disaster relief and should report to the MCA for the record. The donation should respect the dignity and will of the donor to foster transparency. Freight for transportation of goods and other fees during the journey shall be borne by the recipient or by the nominating government.

In the 21st century, China constantly promulgated a series of regulations and rules governing the initiation, access and response of international relief confronted with a drastic increase in the scope and frequency of natural disasters, such as the National Emergency Response Plan for the Relief of Natural Disaster (hereinafter referred to as 'Emergency Response Plan', which was promulgated in 2005), Emergency Response Law of the People's Republic of China (hereinafter referred to as 'Emergency Response Law', which was promulgated in 2007), which deals with issues related to receiving international disaster assistance. It is stimulated in the emergency response plan that on the occasion of nature disasters, the emergency response and disaster relief headquarters established by the MCA should appeal to the international community for disaster assistance. The headquarters should publicly announce the donation recipient unit list, set up disaster donation hotlines, take initiatives to accept the donation from international community, release disaster information and post-disaster demand on a daily basis, allocate donated funding and materials to the needy on time, periodically publish the funds received and spent on relief efforts to the public. Article III of the Emergency Response Law situates that sudden onset of disasters includes natural disasters, accidents, public health incidents and social safety events which suddenly occur and may cause serious harm to the society and thus there is a need to take emergency measures in dealing with disasters. Article IV prescribed that Chinese government will cooperate with foreign governments and international organizations in emergency prevention, monitoring and early warning, response to emergencies, rescue, recovery and reconstruction system. As noted earlier, the overview on the development of China's acceptance of international disaster assistance illustrates that whether the international relief was accepted depends upon China's political attitude to donor countries.

Analysis on loopholes in China's current international disaster response law

China faces increasing challenges together with opportunities brought with the increasing number of international disaster assistance in China. Such scenario calls for China to take a forward-looking vision and further amend the legal framework on international disaster. Good legal framework and updated laws are essential to the smooth running of international relief framework, how we reduce disaster risks and how we prepare and improve resilience when responding to disasters.

In an effort to promote better preparedness for disaster relief globally and properly solve the problem, the International Federation of Red Cross and Red Crescent Societies (IFRC) developed and released 'Guidelines for the Domestic Facilitation and Regulation of International Disaster Relief and Initial Recovery Assistance' (also known as 'the IDRL Guidelines') as well as the 'Model Act for the Facilitation and Regulation of International Disaster Assistance' (also known as 'the Model Act on IDRL') to support national governments in improving their domestic legal framework for disaster preparedness and response. The laws are soft law as legal instruments with non-binding characters. They were drawn from many existing international instruments, including United Nations General Assembly Resolutions 46/182 of 1991 and 57/150 of 2002, the Measures to Expedite International Relief of 1977 and the Hyogo Framework for Action of 2005. The former drew on a wealth of existing treaties, resolutions, guidelines and codes that have been agreed on by the international community.[5] The latter intended to provide references for domestic lawmaking and improvement.

It has been observed by the authors that China's current regulatory framework in light of the IDRL Guidelines and international instruments has following deficiencies:

Lack of comprehensive legal framework

Current legislation concerning international disaster response is fragmented across various legal instruments from the perspective of legislative form.

First, numerous legal provisions involving international disaster relief scattered in a series of branches of laws, such as Customs Law of the PRC., China's Exit-Entry Administration Law, Laws and Regulations of China Entry-Exit Inspection and Quarantine, Foreign Exchange Control Regulations of the PRC., People's Republic of China Public Welfare Donation Law. There is a lack of comprehensive domestic legal framework currently to keep up with uniform international norms and practice in international disaster assistance.

Second, there is no generally accepted definition of 'disaster' or uniform approach to it. A uniform definition of 'disaster' should encompass both society and natural hazards; however, current legislation mostly focuses on the latter. In the Emergency Response Law of PRC., the concept of 'disaster' is quite inclusive and is defined as the 'abrupt incidents' that cover four accidents. However, it seems such definition missed the group of 'slow-onset disasters' (e.g. drought) in Chinese disaster law. For instance, it may take consecutive months or even years for drought to become famine. Besides, climate change, environmental degradation and desertification are very slow onset events, but can and should be considered as disasters in terms of the damage and disruption to lives.[6] The key distinction was made between slow (climate change, environmental degradation and desertification) and rapid (earthquakes, cyclones, hurricanes and typhoons) onset events by OCHA (Office for the Coordination of Humanitarian Affairs). The main reason for OCHA and humanitarian actors to distinguish is that slowly unfolding emergencies can be mitigated by early response. If preparedness, early warning and early response systems are fully functioning, coordinated and integrated, the longer lead time means the humanitarian community can step in early enough to reduce human suffering and help prevent the downward spiral of increased vulnerability to future hazards.[7] We may note that the term 'incident' (except the term 'natural disasters') was used in several older studies in place of disasters.

Lack of protection of rescue personnel and organizations

As far as the entry permit of international disaster assistance is concerned, current legislation in China ignores protection of rescue personnel and organizations. Thus, legislation should be developed to smooth the path of rescue services, humanitarian aid and recovery help.

For example, Article I of the Rules Governing the Implementation of the Law of the PRC on the Entry and Exit of Aliens illustrates ten cases of foreigners who needed to travel to China and did not have enough time to apply for visas. Foreigners may apply visas from port visa agencies authorized by the Ministry of Public Security (MPS), yet international relief personnel are not included. In addition, there are no provisions for the entry of rescue dogs in the Law on the Entry and Exit Animal and Plant Quarantine or its Regulation on Implementation of People's Republic of China. For instance, there is a lack of provision regarding whether rescue dogs are allowed to be carried by rescue teams on the same flight and facilitation provision on their quarantine. The deficiency in legal framework would inevitably create many problems in practice.

Take the Wenchuan Earthquake for instance. When the earthquake occurred on 12 May 2008, the Chinese government for the first time allowed rescue team from six countries, including Japan and Korea, to enter into disaster areas. This was a historic breakthrough of the past decade in the history of international disaster assistance. However, problems in disaster assistance and rescue cropped up. According to international norms and practices, the rescue time should be deployed within 72 hours after the disaster strikes. But after the earthquake, though the 20-people rescue team of Japan fire department was ready for rescue work, Chinese government didn't officially issue invitation to Japanese government to dispatch international rescue team until the morning of 15 May due to various reasons. There was a lack of understanding of disaster situation and role of international rescue team in the case.

New problems on the scope of rescue activities and whether the rescue aircraft can enter the airspace over China to rescue arise in practice. Thus, there is an urgent need for China to enact new laws and develop legal framework being compatible with the needs of international disaster practice. Strengthening of the coordination of humanitarian and disaster relief assistance has become a subject of growing concern of the United Nations (UN), the International Federation of Red Cross and Red Crescent Societies (IFRC) and other world and regional organizations.

The brinkmanship with non-governmental organizations (NGOs)

In international disaster practice, the Chinese government usually attaches importance to the role played by international organizations (e.g. the United Nations) and inter-governmental organizations (IGOs) and multinational corporations but snubs the role played by non-government organizations (NGOs). The Red Cross Society of China (RCSC) is a vice-ministerial level unit directly under the government of State Council, widespread from central government to country and township level. Its status is regarded by China in corresponding laws as quasi-governmental association which is different from the independent charitable organization role of the International Federation of Red Cross and Red Crescent Societies (IFRC).

As a case in point, the proposal for establishing China Anti-Disaster and Relief Association as a national society handling international relief from non-government sources was not approved by the State Council on 8 September 1988. Another example is the Regulations for the Management of Foundations issued in 2004. According to Article II of the regulation, foundation refers to a non-profit legal entity established in accordance with regulations that employ assets donated by persons, legal entities or other organizations for the purpose of engaging in public benefit enterprise. The regulation only covers and handles foundations registered and qualified as legal entities, but sets aside large-scale private donation entities who are not legal persons.

Poor coordination with neighbouring countries

Recent years have seen the increasing diversification of humanitarian assistance to disasters – natural and man-made disasters and other various disasters. The issues and problems associated with disasters have become globalized, which calls for bilateral and regional cooperation between neighbouring countries in international disaster relief. Many cooperative and efficient disaster response cases already happened in the past century.

For instance, the United States entered into the international relief agreement with Haiti in 1956 to provide food assistance to alleviate food shortages caused by continuous drought in Haiti. The agreement set out the amount of money to be provided and responsibilities of Haiti on relaxing port charges, in-land transportation, free distribution, information release and observation in international relief.[8] Another case is an agreement signed between the United Kingdom of

Great Brain and India in 1964 regarding the policy of duty-free entry of food relief to India.[9]

The study by IFRC found a second and third wave of bilateral treaties starting in the 1970s and the 1990s, respectively. Some were exclusively concerned with technical assistance (e.g. with regard to training or capacity building). A more substantial proportion of treaties were mutual assistance agreements, particularly between European states, such as the agreement between Sweden and Norway concerning the Improvement of Rescue Services in Frontier Areas in 1974 and the agreement between Austria and the Czech Republic on Mutual Assistance in the Event of Disasters or Serious Accidents in 1998. Like those of the first wave, there were also some assistance agreements crossing regional boundaries, such as the memorandum of understanding between the Government of the United States of America and the Government of Ukraine on cooperation in natural and man-made technological emergency prevention and response in 2000 and the Swiss Federal Council and the Government of the Republic of the Philippines on cooperation in the event of natural disaster or major emergencies in 2001.[10]

However, China has not yet established cross-border, regional or international cooperation disaster relief assistance programmes with neighbouring countries. Two key reasons for lack of coordination with neighbouring countries should be considered. The first main reason is there had not been any disasters wiped out between China and neighbouring countries before, and thus cross-border coordination assistance was not needed. The second important reason is China tends to employ diplomatic and legal manners on handling international affairs in practice.[11] However, in recent years some disasters have triggered neighbouring countries to engage in a bilateral or multilateral agreement with China.

Proposals for improvement

A comprehensive legal framework on international relief should be brought into the legislative agenda

The authors would like to suggest that a comprehensive legal framework on international disaster relief should be brought into the legislative agenda. Whereas current legislation on international disaster relief is scattered among general laws of China, there is a lack of a well-structured and comprehensive international relief act in place.

Thus, the authors suggest to develop a unified law, that is, the International Disaster Assistance Act (or the Ordinance) of the People's Republic of China (hereafter 'the Act') following the 'IDRL Guidelines' and 'the Model Act', which are useful reference tools to build domestic legal framework in the field. The Model Act was drafted by IFRC in cooperation with the United Nations Office of the Coordination of Humanitarian Affairs and the Inter-Parliamentary Union. Since the IDRL Guidelines were adopted in the 30th International Conference of the Red Cross and Red Crescent in November 2007, the past few years had witnessed tangible progress made in several dozen countries, nine of which had already adopted new laws, regulations and procedures consistent with recommendations of the IDRL Guidelines. Moreover, a number of global forums and research institutes mainstreamed the guidelines into their work, taking efforts to develop the field by study or practice.

The authors would also like to suggest the coming Act in China should cover two aspects on both foreign humanitarian disaster relief and reception of disaster aid, which include provisions on principles of disaster assistance, coordination bodies and mechanisms, initiation and termination procedures, customs facilitation measures for goods, special equipment, search and rescue dogs, certification and working permit of volunteers, security measures, simplified visa procedures, recognition on relief organizations, rights and obligations of rescue personnel (including volunteers), management of disaster relief account, tax relief policy on supplies, transportation, distribution, international cooperation and legal responsibility during relief.

Full and effective protection of victims' rights needed

China made clear that the state respects and safeguards human rights and enshrined the principle in China's top legislature the Amendments to the Constitution in 2003. This is the first time the human rights spirit and principle was written into the constitution.

Undoubtedly, disaster victims were the most vulnerable groups whose fundamental human rights should have been fully protected. The victims of disaster are entitled to the right of life protection, right on security, right on human dignity, rights related to basic necessities of life, right of education, right on property, right to insure security of housing and livelihood, right of documentation, freedom of movement, right to return to family life, right of expression, assembly and association, right of religion, right of election. Powerful earthquakes, hurricanes and tsunamis hit areas of Asia Pacific and the United States during

2004–2005. The disaster events highlighted the need on human rights protection on victims affected.

The Inter-Agency Standing Committee (IASC) of the UN codified an Operational Guidelines on Human Rights and Natural Disasters in June 2006. The International Law Commission included the topic 'Protection of Persons in the Event of Disasters' in its programme of work in Resolution 62/66 at its 59th session on 6 December 2007. The Commission drafted 12 clauses in the following sessions, which provided guiding principle on human rights protection of disaster victims. It is promulgated that an affected state, by virtue of its sovereignty, has the duty to ensure the protection of disaster-affected persons and provide disaster relief and assistance on its territory (see Draft Article IX). The affected state has the duty to seek assistance, as appropriate, from other states, the United Nations, other competent IGOs and NGOs if the disaster exceeds its national response capacity (see Draft Article X). Article VIII of the Draft provides provisions that the affected state is primarily responsible for protecting persons and providing humanitarian assistance on its territory and retains the right under its national law to direct, control, coordinate and supervise such assistance within its territory. Furthermore, any external assistance may be provided only with the consent of the affected state. Article XI also provides that consent to external assistance shall not be withheld arbitrarily if the affected state is unable or unwilling to provide the assistance required. These provisions illustrate that a state should receive external humanitarian assistances only if it cannot handle the disaster with its national response capacity.

The authors suggest further that China should change its negative, alert and vigilant attitude towards foreign aid. Every country is safe and is entitled the right to refuse conditional humanitarian assistance. Developed countries that suffer from catastrophic events and are unable to cope are entitled to call for international assistance. The United States' response to Hurricane Katrina is a good case. China as a disaster-prone country is suggested to develop international network and to be open to international humanitarian disaster assistance.

NGOs should be granted legal status on international relief by legislation

China's attitude towards foreign aid has gone half a century's discourse evolution as illustrated in the second section of the chapter. The evolution of International Disaster Response Law (IDRL) in China experienced a shift from complete refusal of external disaster assistance to selectively acceptance of limited assistant since the 1980s. China initially accepted foreign assistance from the United Nations (UN) and other international organizations and later from foreign governments. However, China is cautious when accepting assistance from NGOs (the case of IFRC is an exception).

As mentioned earlier, the Three Ministries explicitly closed the door on accepting assistance from foreign religious organizations in 1988. The action and response was very inappropriate. On the one hand, the policy discriminates foreign organizations on the basis of religion, which was exploited to provide foreign assistance enjoyed by domestic religious organizations. On the other hand, this discrimination does not conform to the constitution of China on the notion of freedom of religion. The authors suggest that China should accept disaster relief from foreign religious organizations as long as the aid meets the criteria of humanitarian assistance and does not damage its sovereignty and national interest.

Thus, NGOs are recommended to be granted the same legal status and rights that are conferred to foreign governments and international organizations by legislation on international disaster relief in China.

Strengthening disaster relief coordination with other countries

Industrialization leads to an increase in trans-boundary disasters, such as trans-boundary pollution, nuclear leak, typhoon and large-scale epidemic spread of infectious diseases. As the world's third-largest country sharing land borders with 14 countries, China is suggested to cooperate with neighbouring countries on disaster relief by signing mutual assistance agreements or establishing regional relief organizations so as to provide assistance and relief efforts on time to rescue disaster victims, to get an opportunity to know expertise, strategies and experience of neighbouring countries on disaster prevention, mitigation, preparedness and thus to reduce disaster losses to a minimum.

The Association of Southeast Asian Nations (ASEAN) is a case in point. ASEAN signed the ASEAN Agreement on Disaster Management and Emergency Response (AADMER, hereinafter referred to as 'the ASEAN Agreement') in July 2005. Six overarching principles have been set out in the ASEAN Agreement, namely (1) respect for national sovereignty, (2) overall direction, control and supervision of relief by the affected state, (3) strengthening regional cooperation, (4) giving priority to prevention and mitigation disasters, (5) mainstreaming disaster risk reduction efforts into sustainable development policies and programming and (6) involving all stakeholders including local communities, NGOs and private enterprises utilizing disaster preparedness and early response approaches. In addition to provisions concerning cooperation in disaster risk reduction and early warning systems, the ASEAN Agreement has set out a number of specific measures to smooth barriers on international response, including the establishment of an emergency fund and a new ASEAN Coordinating Centre for Humanitarian Assistance on Disaster Management, the first institution authorized to coordinate relief efforts.

In case of China, two events may trigger China's greater concern on international cooperation in international disaster relief. One is the Songhua River major water pollution incident which occurred in 2005, and the other is the 2008 Japan nuclear leak event. The former event represents devastating disaster impact over China and the vice versa. The two cases demonstrate the great necessities of cooperation in international disaster relief between countries by sharing updated disaster information, initiating co-relief measures and so on.

Therefore, China should learn from the aforementioned European model and enter into bilateral agreement with Japan, Korea, Russia and other neighbouring countries to coordinate on cross-border international disasters relief. Furthermore, China is advised to learn from the ASEAN Agreement and conclude regional cooperation agreements with Asia-Pacific Economic Cooperation (APEC) members.

Conclusion

China's attitude towards international humanitarian assistance experienced gradual changes in the past century. One reason may be due to the fact that the modern China was bullied by Western powers for a long time, and thus China had been maintaining vigilance to foreign assistance from Western countries. Another reason may be Western countries pursued blockade and hostile policy against China after it was established, which resulted in the negative attitude China took towards foreign aid. Following the resumption of China's lawful seat in the United Nations at the 26th Session of UN General Assembly in 1971 and gradual improvement on foreign relations with Western countries, especially after China's reform and opening up to the world since 1978, China started to receive disaster relief from Western countries, even though it accepted aid selectively and cautiously. As far as the development of awareness on the value and nature of international humanitarian assistance, China changed its attitude and actively participated into international relief and assistance. China's promulgation in international relief gradually changed from a knee-jerk policy to a rule of law since the 1980s. The disaster events that occurred in the past 30 years have made a strong case for developing new legislations in compliance with international disaster norms and practice.

China's most current laws in international disaster assistance still have many loopholes, such as the legislations are too scattered among general laws, lack of a unified and comprehensive act and an oversight of the assistance provided by NGOs and individuals in disaster relief. The legal status of NGOs and other civil society groups, especially religious groups in the assistance, are not highly valued. Moreover, scenarios such as selective release of disaster information, remaining hostile and distrustful towards foreign relief organizations and insufficient collaboration with neighbouring countries should be changed.

As China progresses on its environmental protection and conservation chart, it would be pertinent to look into the pervasive vulnerability of many regions in China to disasters, displacement and deaths. That would complete the cycle of legislation towards a more robust and sustainable disaster law in the world's most populated country.

Notes

1 See *International Federation of Red Cross and Red Crescent Societies on Disaster Law Program*, Retrieved from www.ifrc.org/en/what-we-do/idrl/about-idrl/ (Accessed 25 August 2015).
2 See Liu Shaoqi (2005). *Collectanea by Liu Shaoqi since the Founding of PRC*, Vol. 2, Beijing: Central Literature Publishing House, p. 105.
3 See Sun Shaocheng (2004). *Chinese Disaster Response Law*, Shanghai: The Commercial Press, p. 140.
4 The Ministry of Foreign Economic Liaison was developed into Ministry of Foreign Trade and Economic Cooperation after merging with other ministries in May 1982.
5 The International Federation of Red Cross and Red Crescent Societies, Annotations to the Draft Guidelines for the Domestic Facilitation and Regulation of International Disaster Relief and Initial Recovery Assistance, Version of 26 October 2007, p. 4.
6 Develop Workshop, Slow & Rapid Onset Disasters, see www.dwf.org/en/content/slow-rapid-onset-disasters (Accessed 17 May 2012).
7 OCHA Occasional Policy Briefing Series Brief No. 6: OCHA and slow-onset emergencies. Available at http://ochanet.unocha.org/p/Documents/OCHA_OPB_SlowOnsetEmergencies190411.pdf, p. 4. (Accessed 25 August 2015).
8 See Exchange of Notes Constituting an Agreement between the United States of America and Haiti Relating to Emergency Relief Assistance, 28 December 1956, 279 U.N.T.S. 107.
9 See Agreement between the Government of the United Kingdom of Great Britain and Northern Ireland and the Government of India for the

Duty-Free Entry of Relief Supplies and Packages, 20 October 1964, 534 U.N.T.S. 78.

10 See International Federation of Red Cross and Red Crescent Societies, Law and Legal Issues in International Disaster Response: A Desk Study, 2007, p. 80.

11 See Su Xiaoxong (2003). 'Why Does the Great Power Not Like International Justice'. *Legal Science*, vol. 11.

7 Interrogating disaster law in India

Binod Kumar

Introduction

'Disaster' has different meanings for different sets of people. At the household level, disaster could be a major illness, death or a substantive economic loss. At the community level, it could be an earthquake, flood, fire or tsunami.[1] Present meaning of disaster has been shaped by different set of realities and is context-specific. Much of the mitigation and preventive efforts in disaster policy is woven around the specific meaning given to 'disasters' in a country.

Differences on perspectives as to what constitutes disasters are dependent on a sense of loss which varies from one person to other. Altering status of disaster can also be the result of politics, humanitarian aid (Middleton & O'Keefe, 2001), state ideology and reporting/under-reporting by media. However, broadly there is consensus that disaster includes disruption beyond people's capacity to cope and this definition has been accepted by International Federation of Red Cross and Red Crescent Societies (IFRC), the United Nations International Strategy for Disaster Reduction (UNISDR), United Nations Development Programme (UNDP) and United Nations Environment Programme (UNEP).

With the passage of time, the concept of disaster has undergone immense changes. In the 1970s people talked about 'disaster prevention', whereas in the 1980s and 1990s this term was superseded by disaster mitigation which in turn was replaced by the term 'disaster risk reduction' which considers development in mitigating disasters. In the present context, it is important that disaster is not to be looked upon as a natural phenomenon but as a function of development. Sometimes the disaster is caused by insufficient development of means to avoid crisis, and sometimes the aspect of development itself becomes the reason for crisis and thus ultimately leads to disaster. Against this backdrop, law comes into picture to adjudge the veracity of decisions taken by the executive and to foster the interest of the community at large. Disasters are no longer a phenomenon beyond our capacity as communities or, in legal terms, force majeure or acts of God per se. Contrary to the principle of act of God or nature, the modern conception of disasters allows us to attribute blame to the unknown. Thus, disasters are increasingly juridified, as they are being dealt with the same yardstick as other social phenomena.

Disaster and Indian Constitution

Legislative competence of Parliament and state legislature to legislate on the matter of disaster is highly ambiguous. The scheme of legislative competence under Indian Constitution provides three lists under the seventh schedule. Union and state lists provide exclusive jurisdiction to the Parliament and state legislature, respectively, whereas concurrent list provides common jurisdiction to centre and state. 'Disaster' as a subject matter of legislation is not directly mentioned in the constitution; hence power to legislate on the same has been derived from other subject matters of the list. Where centre derives its power from entry 23: 'Social Security and Social Insurance; Employment and Unemployment' of union list, the states invoke entry 14: 'agriculture including pest and plant diseases' and entry 17: 'water including water supply, drainage and embankments' of state list (Mishra, 2013, p. 12). To remove this ambiguity, High Powered Committee (HPC) on disaster management and 2nd Administrative Reform Committee felt the need for the specific entry of subject 'disaster' under seventh schedule of Indian Constitution (ibid.).

Under the scheme of disaster law, the legislative branch takes decision and enacts law regarding mitigation, preparedness and recovery in normal times, but the executive branch assumes the greatest degree of discretionary authority during disaster response. Of late, judiciary has started taking urgent and time-bound cognizance of disasters as has been the case of Gujarat earthquakes and Kashmir floods.

Constitutional law takes a particular interest in disasters whether it is natural or man-made as it impacts society at large, particularly, the loss of human being and property (McEvoy, 2013, p. 296). Constitutional scheme of India accords justice to all sections of society in all situations whether it is disaster or normal times. The fundamental rights under constitution work round the clock, and disaster is no exception. The case of people's relief and rehabilitation during disaster falls under Article 21 of Indian Constitution which talks about protection of life and personal liberty. Especially, after the *Maneka Gandhi v. Union of India*[2] case, Supreme Court has expanded the scope of life and personal liberty. A logical and liberal interpretation of this judgement will lead to the conclusion that the right to rescue, relief and rehabilitation is a right guaranteed under Article 21 of Indian Constitution.

Although disaster relief in India is not a constitutionally mandated right that is justifiable in the court of law, the Disaster Management Act (DMA), 2005, put duty upon the state to provide relief notwithstanding the absence of the 'right to receive relief' by the victim. In making claims of relief after the disaster, the recipients take recourse of moral stance of victimhood rather than justifiable rights. In the absence of a rights-based legal framework of disaster risk management, the state and individuals are locked in a relationship where they connect only after the occurrence of a disaster when relief is sought (Chhotray, 2014). The intent of the state in framing disaster relief as a moral obligation rather than a legal entitlement has a bearing of colonial legacy.

Financial assistance given by government in the wake of natural disasters is towards relief not towards compensation of loss. The objective behind giving relief is to assist the affected persons to return to normal life and restart the economic activities (Chhotray, 2014) and it has a moral sanction attached to it. Whereas compensation is the part of contractual agreement, relief given by the state completely depends on vagaries of the state. Other form of instrument to compensate in case of natural disaster is insurance which establishes legal obligation on the part of insurance companies.

Evolution of disaster law

International level

Disaster law has been developed as a branch of the international humanitarian law. It received special attention in post–World War II period. Various international agreements and soft law instruments contain a wide range of regulations which are relevant during and after a disaster. Although people who migrate from their home country due to disaster are not covered under 1951 Conventions on Status of Refugees, provisions related to disasters can be found in various international documents like International Covenants on Civil and Political Rights, 1966; International Covenants on Economic, Social and Cultural Rights, 1966; Convention on Elimination of All Forms of Discrimination against Women, 1979; and Convention on the Right of the

Child, 1989. The International Convention on Protection of the Rights of All Migrant Workers and Members of Their Families, 1990, covers climate-related migrants who work abroad, although fewer states have ratified this agreement (Haumer, 2014).

In the year 1994, there was a paradigm shift when Yokohama Strategy and Action Plan for Safer World was adopted at First World Conference on Natural Disaster. In the year 1999, United Nations General Assembly adopted a resolution for International Strategy for Disaster Reduction (ISDR) and created a secretariat for the ISDR to ensure its implementation. The review of achievement of Yokohama Strategy and Action Plan for Safer World led to the conception *of* Hyogo Framework for Action 2005–15: Building the Resilience of Nations and Communities to Disasters (HFA) which was adopted at Second World Conference on Disaster Reduction held in 2005 and subsequently endorsed by UN General Assembly. The Inter-Agency Standing Committee's Operational Guidelines of 2011 on the protections of persons in situations of natural disaster aim to complement existing guidelines in the context of natural hazards (Haumer, 2014). Recently, Third United Nations Conference on Disaster Risk Reduction was held in Sendai in Japan between 14 and18 March 2015, which underscores the achievement of previous frameworks and sets the agenda for future targets. Unlike its predecessor, Sendai Framework for Disaster Risk Reduction 2015–30 includes seven targets to protect people and assets from natural and man-made hazards.

National level

National regime on disaster law dates back to the colonial period with the appointment of Famine Commission in 1878 which produced first Famine Code of India. Prior to that there had been *ad hoc* approach to deal with the crisis with few laws related to hoarding and crime. In independent India, the same code was adapted by various state governments with some modifications though the essence of code was same. The code does not qualify to be a law; hence it cannot be enforced by the court of law. However, it provides formal basis for relief work in the time of disaster. Merit of code lies in the fact of its suitability for relief and rehabilitation, but it hardly talks about risk reduction.

The current regime of national-level legal framework owes its origin from recurrent big disasters like Orissa Super Cyclone in 1999, Bhuj, Gujarat earthquake in 2001 and Indian Ocean tsunami in 2004. These three natural disasters shook the conscience of the nation, and it resulted in a national-level legal framework to deal with future disasters which culminated in the form of National Disaster Management Act (DMA), 2005. The act mandates disaster management as an all-time activity rather than merely relief and rehabilitation during and after crisis. In the wake of loss in the event of disasters, Government of India constituted a High Powered Committee (HPC) on disaster. HPC submitted its report in 2001 and recommended the government to enact law to tackle disasters at national and state levels. However, central government held the view that 'disaster' as a subject matter of legislation is not directly mentioned in any of three lists under Seventh Schedule of India's Constitution and hence states should be encouraged to enact law. In the meantime, Gujarat, Bihar, Uttar Pradesh and Uttarakhand enacted law on disaster management through their respective state legislature. However, the central government changed its stance after seeing the interstate nature of tsunami in 2004 and subsequently enacted the DMA.

Scarcity Relief Division, created under Ministry of Agriculture, Government of India, deals with natural disasters in the post-independence period. Nomenclature of this unit was changed to Natural Disaster Management Division. And Ministry of Agriculture became the nodal ministry for coordinating disasters in India. However, by amending the Government of India (Allocation of Business) Rules, 1961, all work related to disaster management (excluding drought, epidemic and emergencies and disasters specifically allocated to other ministries) was transferred to Ministry of Home Affairs, citing the reason for better coordination (Mishra, 2013). In the absence of any strict guideline, disaster administration at the state level had been part of Revenue Department traditionally. However, its role was limited to relief and rehabilitation. Of late, some states have created Department of Relief and Rehabilitation, whereas others have named it as Department of Disaster Management.

Navigating jurisprudence of disasters

Law plays a central role in successful disaster management. Jurisprudence is theoretical part of law as discipline. As has been the case with many other disciplines, law also varies as per time, place and tradition. The current trend of increasing disaster events worldwide has necessitated the need of disaster law. However, law has to be based on logic and reasoning which is supplied in the form of jurisprudence of disaster. Although, the role of law in tackling disaster has been highly recognized, it is not the sole tool. Disaster as a subject matter of study is highly interdisciplinary as have been responses to a disaster situation.

As a matter of fact, jurisprudence of disaster has been drawn from a range of legal philosophies ranging from human rights, environmental to constitutional jurisprudence.

One of the leading disaster researchers, the American sociologist Charles Perrow says: 'The regulatory potential for avoiding disaster and reducing their consequences is obvious' (Perrow, 2007, p. 295). Of late, law has become one of the main apparatuses to create disaster resilient societies. Besides this proactive role, law also creates new rights and obligations not only for individual but also for the state. In that spirit, Lauta (2015) termed *modern disasters as potential injustices*. He further goes on to emphasize the role of law and the state and says that while hazards might be unpredictable and uncontrollable, the government efforts, the building standards and the social inequality that led to the devastating results are not (Lauta, 2015).

The right of a person during a disaster is also protected under the doctrine of *parens patriae*, meaning 'parent of the country'. The concept is explained as 'right of the sovereign, in public interest, to protect persons under disability who have no rightful protector'. The doctrine developed under common law system of royal prerogative in England (Hawkes, 1988, p. 186). The doctrine of *parens patriae* provides ample power and authority to a legislature to provide persons' life and property. The doctrine of *parens patriae* was applied originally to the king and is used to designate the state referring to the sovereign power of guardianship over persons with disability. The English law required following four elements to apply *parens patriae* to a sovereign state: '(i) party is legally incapable of securing his rights; (ii) the sovereign or his alternative is the only alternative; (iii) the sovereign has duty to protect the subject's welfare; (iv) the sovereign has no personal interest and acts on someone else's behalf' (Hawkes, 1988, p. 186). The doctrine was invoked by the Indian government to pursue cases of Bhopal gas tragedy in foreign court. The doctrine has now become a tool to protect the citizens. The courts in India have applied this doctrine in several other cases too. Therefore, under the doctrine of *parens patriae*, the state is obliged to render adequate relief and rehabilitation to the victims of disaster (Alex, 2006, p. 6).

Judicial response

In *Vasundhara Pathak Masoodi v. Union of India*,[3] Supreme Court asked union government to explain the measures taken by the government to provide relief and rehabilitation to victims of floods in Jammu and Kashmir in 2014. Court opined that life of the people affected by the disaster have to be saved and issued guidelines for relief work.

In *Kranti v. Union of India*,[4] Supreme Court acted proactively and directed the government to facilitate the rehabilitation of tsunami victims on high priority.

In the leading case of *Bin K Kuriokose and Others v. The Commissioner Municipal Corporation and Others*,[5] the petitioner filed a writ petition under Article 226 of Indian Constitution. Petitioner questioned the validity of the notice issued by Assistant Commissioner K West ward in the context of disputed structure by invoking provision of Section 2, 14 (1), 25 (1), (2), (4) and Section 34 of DMA, 2005. Petitioner contended that notice issued by the commissioner is *ultra vires* according to Section 34 of said act, as it mandates that only district authority has power to issue such notice. Court held that the notice issued by the assistant commissioner cannot be sustained in the eye of law notwithstanding respondent is at liberty to take appropriate action mandated under the DMA, 2005.

In the case of *Shruti Singh v. National Disaster Management Authority and Others*,[6] Patna High Court abstained to intervene for want of substantive evidence. The case involved problem of recurrent flood in the state of Bihar. The Patna High Court contended that court should direct Bihar State Disaster Management Authority, National Disaster Management Authority and Ministry of External Affairs to protect the breaches both upstream and downstream in order to check further widening. It involved Ministry of External Affairs, too, as the river involved runs through international boundaries. The case also contended that relief and rehabilitation to the flood victims should be given on par with tsunami victims. The Patna High Court opined that 'any intervention by the court on scanty pleading without any material may act counterproductive for whatever actions and reliefs being provided by the statutory authorities. It is true that the disasters like this have brought miseries to the life of lakhs of people and their property but there is nothing to assume that adequate and proper steps are not being taken by the Central Government and the State Government' (MANU/BH/0882/2008).

An overview of the Disaster Management Act (DMA), 2005

The present section glances through various provisions of the Disaster Management Act (DMA), 2005, and tries to highlight the functional incapability to disaster risk management law in India. The DMA over past decade has yielded desired results and has identified several glitches which need to be removed.

Section 12(ii) of the DMA mentions special provision for widows and orphans, but people with disability and marginalized people have been ignored which need to be explicitly mentioned in the act. Ironically, there is no provision for handling, protecting and rescuing non-humans and biodiversity in the disaster-affected regions, which indicates that DMA suffers from an intense influence of divisiveness and speciesism.

Further, Section 13 reads, 'The National Authority may, in cases of disasters of severe magnitude, recommend relief in repayment of loans or for grant of fresh loans to the persons affected by disaster on such concessional terms as may be appropriate.' As provision goes, it has no preferential policy regarding disbursement of loan and relief in the wake of disaster to weaker sections. Recognizing the fact that disaster affects different people differently, legal provision ought to be incorporated to prioritize the weaker section.

Coordination of relief and rehabilitation is a big problem in the time of crisis. Sometimes various agencies do the work which overlaps, and without coordination work itself becomes redundant and goes waste. Provision under Section 24(J) and 34(l) of the DMA, 2005, mandates the state and district executive committee to 'ensure that non-governmental organizations carry out their activities in an equitable and non-discriminatory manner'. But in the absence of a robust framework of rules to coordinate with NGOs during disaster, coordination becomes impossible.

Ironically, the DMA stipulates punishment of maximum two years' term and a fine for false claim under Section 52 which discourages the victims in the absence of sufficient documents and convincing power to claim compensation.

Furthermore, the act specifies in Section 71 that action of national, state and district authorities as well as central and state government under DMA, 2005 cannot be challenged except in Supreme Court and High Court (Sarkar & Sarma, 2006). It places restriction on poor and marginalized people, as they are not able to access High Court and Supreme Court. In the absence of grievance redressal system, Section 71 of the DMA poses severe restriction on the victims. Besides, good faith clause in Section 73 grants high level of immunity to the officials which may encourage them to involve in the activities that go against vision of the act.

Additionally, the DMA should be amended to accommodate the provision of social audit of relief and rehabilitation work to ensure the participation of affected population. Besides, it also does not delineate the provision related to entry of citizens for relief work in restricted areas (reserve, biosphere, etc.); specific rules should be made to facilitate the relief work in restricted areas. With the number of disasters and actors increasing, in the event of disaster there is a huge flow of relief material not only from foreign countries but also from within the country. Against this backdrop, it is important to have an inventory system and supply chain system to supply aid materials in the disaster-stricken areas. Sadly, the current legal provisions are highly insufficient to handle outpouring aid materials during relief work.

Conclusion

Addressing the concern 'why and 'how' law has an important role in disaster risk management, the chapter questions the 'all-hazard approach' of disaster risk management. While responses to man-made and natural disaster are the same, ways to prevent and mitigate the risks have huge differences. So, law has to be crafted in such a way that it handles disasters of all types and considers all the cycles of disaster. Disaster law is important not only to execute mitigation, relief and rehabilitation work but also to abstain authorities and institutions from functioning arbitrarily. Law related to disaster establishes a sustainable mechanism and makes the disaster reduction and mitigation an all-season affair rather than an *ad hoc* one. In this way, sound legal framework of disaster is a premise on which risk reduction, mitigation and relief are based on.

Notes

1 www.jhsph.edu/research/centers-and-institutes/center-for-refugee-and-disaster-response/publications_tools/publications/_CRDR_ICRC_Public_Health_Guide_Book/Chapter_1_Disaster_Definitions.pdf (Accessed 21–22 December 2015).
2 1978 AIR SC 597. The said case is related to the right to go abroad. The question before the court was to assess that whether right to go abroad is part of personal liberty. It was held violative of Article 21 of Indian Constitution, since it does not affirm the word 'procedure' as mentioned in the clause.
3 Writ Petition (Civil) No. 826/2014.
4 Civil Appeal No(s). 2681 of 2007.
5 MANU/MH/0628/2010.
6 MANU/BH/0882/2008.

References

Alex, J.P.(ed) (2006), Disaster Management: Towards a Legal Framework. New Delhi: Indian Institute of Public Administration, UNDP. 6.
Chhotray, V. (2014). Disaster Relief and the Indian State: Lessons for just Citizenship. *Geoforum*, *54*, 217–225.

Haumer, S. (2014). Disaster Law. *Forced Migration Review*, 45, 72–74.
Hawkes, Lisa Moscati. (1988). Parens Patriae and the Union Carbide Case: The Disaster at Bhopal Continues. *Cornell International Law Journal*, 21(1), 181–200. http://scholarship.law.cornell.edu/cilj/vol21/iss1/5
Lauta, K. C. (2015). *Disaster Law.* New York: Routledge.
McEvoy, A. F. (2013). The Role of Law in Engineering 'Natural' Disasters. *Onati Socio-Legal Series in Disasters and Sociological Studies*, [online], 3 (2), 293–311.
Middleton, Neil., & O'Keefe, Phil., (2001) Redefining Sustainable Development, London: Pluto Press.
Mishra, D. P. (2013). *Report of the Task Force.* New Delhi: Government of India.
Perrow, C. (2007). *The Next Catastrophe.* Princeton: Princeton University Press.
Sarkar, S. & Sarma, A. (2006). Disaster Management Act, 2005: A Disaster in Waiting? *Economic and Political Weekly*, 41(35), 3760–3763.

8 Interrogating the trajectory of disaster laws in India

Ramratan Dhumal

India is vulnerable to natural and man-made disasters.[1] According to the World Risk Report 2014, India is vulnerable to the disasters with 58.91 per cent risk.[2] This vulnerability was explicitly witnessed, in recent times, in Indian Ocean tsunami in 2004,[3] in Uttarakhand floods in 2013,[4] in Hudhud Cyclone in Andhra Pradesh in 2014[5] among others that resulted in immeasurable loss of life and property.[6] Severe disasters like Uttarakhand floods and tsunami have been considered to be caused due to human negligence.[7] Man-made disasters such as Bhopal gas leakage[8] in 1984 killed thousands and, even after 30 years, it still poses threats to the people.[9] So, in order to overcome loss of life and property from disasters, the government enacted the Disaster Management Act in 2005, an outcome of the 'High Powered Committee on Disaster Management in 2001' that provided an outline for disaster-free India with the prime concern on preparedness, quick response, strategic thinking and prevention.[10] The paramount object of the Act (hereinafter referred to as 'the Act') is to provide 'effective management of disasters'.

The chapter undertakes critical review of the Act in ensuring disaster justice. It evaluates the Act within the contours of social vulnerability and social resilience as outlined in the constitution of India. Finally, the chapter argues that the Act has to adopt holistic approach towards the vulnerable sections of the society with comprehensive rehabilitation policy in order to seek effective management.

Disaster, social vulnerability and Indian Constitution

Disaster causes immense loss to the life and property. Robert Verchick refers disasters as 'socialized catastrophes' that involve social features of 'policy choices, economics, and cultural behavior'.[11] Disaster produces community hazards. Community hazard is an amalgamation of physical vulnerability and social vulnerability.[12] Physical vulnerability includes geophysical characteristics and built infrastructure that highlights community's physical exposure to an area-based risk like flood or earthquake. Whereas social vulnerability is a complex term that refers to the susceptibility of social groups to the impacts of award and includes subjects such as health care, social capital among others.[13] Among the two, social vulnerability is significant as it relates with the ability of the community to withstand or ability to hold out against the immediate harm.[14] Any loss resulting from disaster will be severe if the society is deeply divided. Inequality in the society produces social vulnerability.[15] Social vulnerability has received enormous consideration in the Western literature.[16] The presence of social vulnerability causes grave injustice to the socio-economically vulnerable sections. And the best remedy besides creating good engineering is not mere resilience but a 'social resilience'. Social resilience stands for an ability of the community to recover or rebound against the immediate harm.[17] A social resilience, as Robert explains, is 'more than refusing to intentionally discriminate against a disfavored group, or promising not to make social inequality any worse than it is today. It requires identifying the places where social vulnerability exists and improving the real-life capabilities of all people living there'.[18] It suggests the identification of the vulnerable categories and to provide them mitigation and to enhance capability of each community depending on their social-economic position, rather than adopting a broad-brush or one-size-fits-all approach.

Now, in the Indian context, the concept of social vulnerability is not unique or unknown. It has received significant recognition from the constitution of India. It is not merely a document that incorporates a scheme of fundamental rights and administration of state. Rather, it outlaws social evils like caste discrimination and discrimination on the ground of religion, race, sex or place of birth. Further, it recognizes social and educationally disadvantageous groups and ensures special protection to them.[19] Therefore, eminent constitutional scholar Upendra Baxi terms Indian Constitution as 'transformative constitution'[20] for the obvious reason that the constitution on the normative point directly addressed millennial wrongs such as untouchability and rural serfdom.[21] Additionally, Baxi points out six features, namely, legitimation of state power, the radical evils in the Indian and civil society, innovation of participatory rights of lower classes (SC, ST and OBC), innovation of the international regime of human rights, particularly of minority rights, people friendly regime of representation and the vibrant Supreme Court.[22] Another eminent scholar Granville Austin describes Indian Constitution as a fundamental law that breaks the shackles of traditional social hierarchies like caste and strives for social justice.[23] Overall, the constitution recognizes social vulnerabilities in the form of 'exploitation' in the social, economic, political life, and attempts to resolve it with constitutional safeguards of special treatment to the schedule castes, schedule tribes, other backward classes, women, children and people with disability.[24] Constitutional recognition and the allocation of special safeguards to the aforementioned disprivileged sections is to assimilate such sections into the mainstream society and to create social resilience and maintain a vibrant social democracy, as the constitution's ultimate aim is not merely to achieve political democracy but to attain social democracy, which stands for individual respect and value.[25] Hence, adequate recognition of underprivileged and fragile sections and the allocation of resources to overcome such discrimination equally resembles with the identification of social vulnerability and social resilience. After the exposition of constitution, the vital question arises is that 'whether the Disaster Management Act 2005 addresses the constitutional mechanism of social vulnerability and social resilience?'

Overview of the Disaster Management Act, 2005

The DMA provides for effective management of disasters. As a result, it lays down mechanism for funding disaster relief and response. The Act broadly defines 'disaster' that includes both man-made and natural disasters. Section 2(d) defines disaster as a 'catastrophe, mishap, calamity or grave occurrence in any area, arising from natural or man-made causes, or by accident or negligence which results in substantial loss of life or human suffering or damage to, and destruction of, property, or damage to, or degradation of, environment, and is of such a nature or magnitude as to be beyond the coping capacity of the community of the affected area'. Disaster management is defined as 'a continuous and integrated process of planning, organising, coordinating and implementing measures which are necessary or expedient for – prevention, mitigation or reduction, capacity-building, preparedness, prompt response, assessing, evacuation, rescue and relief, rehabilitation and reconstruction of the disasters' (Section 2[e]). Additionally, the Act incorporates provisions related to administrative machinery and independent agencies, financial funds, penal provisions among others.

Administrative machinery and independent agencies

Beginning with the administrative machinery, the Act has established three-tier, top-down administrative hierarchies, namely the National Disaster Management Authority (NDMA), State Disaster Management

Authorities (SDMA) and District Disaster Management Authority (DDMA). The NDMA, established by the central government, is a body of nine members with the prime minister as its ex-officio chairperson. Its function is to lay down policies, plans and guidelines for disaster management for ensuring timely and effective response to disaster. NDMA acts as the policy-framing apex body. It approves the plan, issues guidelines, recommends funds, issues measures for prevention, mitigation, preparedness and capacity building. In order to assist the NDMA, the Act constitutes National Executive Council (NEC). Under Section 10, the NEC discharges the functions of the NDMA. Among other functions, it prepares the National Disaster Plan under Section 11.

At the state level, the state government establishes the State Disaster Management Authorities (SDMA). The chief minister of the respective state acts as the chairperson of the SDMA. Its composition is limited to nine members. The SDMA has the responsibility under Section 18 to lay down policies and plans for disaster management in the states. Moreover, it frames state disaster management policy, approves state plan as per the guidelines of NDMA, issues guidelines to the state departments, coordinates the state plan, recommends funds for mitigation and preparedness, reviews the development plans of prevention and mitigation and other measures. Further, the state government constitutes State Executive Council (SEC) to assist the SDMA. It consists of the administrative officers, particularly the secretaries. Its main function is to implement the national plan and state plan, maintain coordination and monitor the management of disaster in the state. The important function of the SEC is to approve the State Disaster Management Plan. At the district level, the state government establishes the District Disaster Management Authority (DDMA). It consists of seven members and a chairperson. Collector/district magistrate/deputy commissioner acts as the *ex-officio* chairperson. The DDMA works as a district planning, coordinating and implementing body for disaster management and follows the guidelines laid down by the NDMA and the SDMA. DDMA prepares the district plan for every district after consultation with the local authorities and in compliance to the National and the State Plans (Section 31). Additionally, the Act under Section 34 authorizes DDMA with certain powers in the event of any threatening disaster situation or disaster.

The three authorities, namely, NDMA, SDMA and DDMA prepare national, state, and district disaster plans, respectively. National plan includes measures related to prevention, mitigation, preparedness, capacity building to respond to disasters, and roles and responsibilities of different ministries or departments (Section 11). The state plan under Section 23 comprises the aforementioned measures, and additionally it has to specify vulnerability towards different forms of disasters. The district plan under Section 31, other than the said functions, specifies the response plans and procedures including prompt response, procurement of resources, establishment of communication skills and dissemination of information to the public.

The Act has established the National Institute of Disaster Management (NIDM) under Section 42 with the objective (1) to provide planning and promoting training and research in the area of disaster management and (2) document and develop national-level information base related to disaster management policies, prevention mechanisms and mitigation measures. Besides general functions, detailed functions are laid down in Section 42(9). The Act has also envisaged the creation of National Disaster Response Force (NDRF) with personnel from the para-military forces, which under the supervision of director general provides specialist response to a threatening disaster situation or disaster (Section 45).

Financial and penal provisions

The Act for effective disaster management constitutes two funds, namely, (1) National Disaster Response Fund (NDRF) and (2) National Disaster Mitigation Fund (NDMF). NDRF's main purpose is to meet the expenses for emergency response, relief and rehabilitation in accordance with the guidelines of central government in consultation with the NDMA (Section 46). The NDMF was formed basically for projects exclusively for the purpose of mitigation and the fund established in accordance with the law made by the Parliament. Since there was a difference in the constitution of funds, the NDRF was proposed by this Act; however, for NDMF a separate legislation was proposed. Similarly, the State Disaster Response Fund (SDRF) and State Disaster Mitigation Fund (SDMF) and District Disaster Response Fund (DDRF) and District Disaster Mitigation Fund (DDMF) have been established at the state and district levels, respectively (Section 48).

Some other provisions include the participation of media for communication of warnings (Section 67), every ministry of central and state governments; non-governmental organizations, voluntary social-welfare institutions at the grassroots level; coordination with United Nation Agencies (Section 35). In terms of accountability, the Act proposes annual review of the disaster plans. Moreover, chapter X specifically deals with the offences and penalties. It punishes acts such as obstruction to any officer; making false claims towards relief, assistance, repair, reconstruction or other benefits consequent to disaster; misappropriation of money or materials; making or spreading false warning leading to panic; failure of officer in duty or his connivance against the Act. It also incorporates provisions against the company's director, manager, secretary or other officer for the negligence or consent or connivance of the said acts. The maximum punishment under this Act is imprisonment for two years.

Analysis and conclusion

After an overview of the Act, let us revisit the question, 'whether the Disaster Management Act 2005 addresses the constitutional mechanism of social vulnerability and social resilience?' It appears that the Act merely focuses on the creation of institutional framework without substantially identifying the vulnerable sections: schedule castes, schedule tribes, women, children and persons with disability who are socially vulnerable.[26] Although the Act under Section 61 has incorporated anti-discriminatory provision which states that 'while providing compensation and relief to the victims of disaster, there shall be no discrimination on the ground of sex, caste, community, descent or religion', this provision appears inadequate on two grounds. First, it merely relates with relief and compensation; the vulnerable sections deserve more than the general distribution, that is, a preferential treatment, not only in compensation and relief but also in rehabilitation, reconstruction, assistance, repair or other benefits. Second, the provision fails to fix the accountability in the event of any discrimination on the ground of sex, caste, community, descent or religion.

There is enough evidence to substantiate these arguments. Disaster results in long-term significant social impacts such as migration among others.[27] According to the 'United Nations Development Programme on the Migration and Human Development in India' the disadvantaged or socially vulnerable communities such as scheduled castes, scheduled tribes and the other backward classes heavily migrate due to inferior social and political status.[28] As one of the studies on the draughts in Bolangir District of Odisha observed, nearly 60,000 people, socially vulnerable sections, migrated to Andhra Pradesh in search of food and work.[29] Besides migration, another study pointed caste discrimination in the distribution of relief. A study on the politics of tsunami response stated that 'in the case of India, where the government also declined offers of a coordinated international humanitarian emergency response, there is evidence of discriminatory practices by local officials and populations alike against dalits (still commonly referred to as "untouchables") in tsunami-affected areas. Trapped within a social structure of caste-based hierarchy and domination, dalit survivors were reportedly only reluctantly received in many temporary shelters and camps housing (higher caste) IDPs from coastal fishing communities; some dalits were driven away. There is also evidence of other IDPs preventing government officials, NGO staff and other civil society groups from distributing emergency relief to dalits'.[30] Additionally, another report titled 'Equality in Aid', funded by the European Commission Humanitarian Aid and Civil Protection Office (ECHO), explicitly traces the caste discrimination in aid and compensation distribution.[31]

Overall, these studies clearly suggest that, due to the presence of social vulnerability and absence of comprehensive and targeted policy in establishing social resilience in pre- and post-disaster situation, the objective of effective disaster management under the 2005 Act remains unfulfilled. Moreover, the structural framework under the Act gives little space to the vulnerable communities to interact with the administrators; as a result the objective of building social resilience appears prescriptive. At the same time, the Act in fixing the accountability of various bureaucratic machineries such as NDMA, SDMA, DDMA appears liberal. It involves too much regimentation with more bureaucratic control, lack of committed leadership and less involvement of local groups. In order to make the Act effective, the government should adopt a holistic approach by undertaking the concern of every member of the society without any discrimination. Moreover, a comprehensive rehabilitation policy in the post-disaster would render the true effective management that is enshrined in the spirit of the Indian Constitution. At the same time, the legislature should establish social vulnerability index on the basis of United States Model to ensure speedy justice and social resilience to overcome social vulnerability.

Notes

1 The National Policy on Disaster Management 2009 Extensively Describes the Vulnerability of India towards Various Forms of Disasters. Retrieved from www.ndma.gov.in/images/guidelines/national-dm-policy2009.pdf
2 World Risk Report 2014. Retrieved from http://ehs.unu.edu/news/news/world-risk-report-2014.html#info
3 'Tsunami Kills Thousands across Nations'. *The Hindu*, 27 December 2004. Retrieved from www.thehindu.com/2004/12/27/stories/2004122707470100.htm

4 Aarti Dhar. Uttarakhand a Man-Made Disaster. Retrieved from www.thehindu.com/todays-paper/tp-national/uttarakhand-floods-a-manmade-disaster/article4835692.ece
5 'Cyclone Hudhud Caused Rs 21,908 Crore Loss, Agriculture Sector Worst Hit: Andhra Government'. *DNA Analysis*, 19 December 2014. Retrieved from www.dnaindia.com/india/report-cyclone-hudhud-caused-rs-21908-crore-loss-agriculture-sector-worst-hit-andhra-government-2045435
6 Tsunami: 10 Years Later, 26 December 2014. Retrieved from www.thehindu.com/news/national/tsunami-10-years-later/article6724667.ece; Government of India, Ministry of Home Affairs Report on Tsunami. Retrieved from www.ndmindia.nic.in/Tsunami2004/Sitrep20.htm
7 Utkarsh Anand (2014). Govt Admits Hydropower Projects Aggravated 2013 Uttarakhand Floods, 9 December. Retrieved from http://indianexpress.com/article/india/india-others/govt-admits-hydro-projects-did-affect-uttarakhand-floods/; Bhadra Sinha, 'Uttarakhand Rejects Govt Report on 2013 Floods'. *Hindustan Times*, 17 February 2015. Retrieved from www.hindustantimes.com/india-news/uttarakhand-rejects-govt-report-on-2013-floods/article1-1317550.aspx
8 Indira Jaising (2014). 'Bhopal Gas Leak Tragedy: Disaster in Progress'. *The Indian Express*, 3 December. Retrieved from http://indianexpress.com/article/opinion/columns/disaster-in-progress/
9 Anil Sasi (2014). 'Bhopal Gas Tragedy: 350 Tonnes of Waste and Factory Deaths That No One Even Counts'. *The Indian Express*, 2 December. Retrieved from http://indianexpress.com/article/india/india-others/350-tonnes-of-waste-and-factory-deaths-that-no-one-even-counts/
10 Ministry of Agriculture, Government of India. 'The Report of High Powered Committee on Disaster Management 2001'. Retrieved from http://nidm.gov.in/PDF/pubs/HPC_Report.pdf
11 Verchick Robert (2012). 'Disaster Justice: The Geography of Human Capability'. *Duke Environmental Law & Policy Forum*, vol. 23, p. 51.
12 Verchick, *supra* note 11, p. 38.
13 Cutter Susan and Emrich Christopher (2006). 'Moral Hazard, Social Catastrophe: The Changing Face of Vulnerability along the Hurricane Coasts'. *The Annals of the American Academy of Political and Social Science*. Retrieved from http://webra.cas.sc.edu/hvri/pubs/2006_MoralHazard SocialCatastrophe.pdf, p. 103.
14 The definition of vulnerability and resilience is taken from the Verchick, *supra* note 11, p. 39.
15 Cutter, *supra* note 12, p. 103.
16 Kahn Mathew (2005). 'The Death Toll from Natural Disasters: The Role of Income, Geography, and Institutions'. *The Review of Economics and Statistics*, vol. 87, no. 2, pp. 271–284; Cutter Susan and Emrich Christopher (2006). 'Moral Hazard, Social Catastrophe: The Changing Face of Vulnerability along the Hurricane Coasts'. *The Annals of the American Academy of Political and Social Science*. Retrieved from http://webra.cas.sc.edu/hvri/pubs/2006_MoralHazardSocialCatastrophe.pdf; Enarson Elaine (2000). Gender Issues in Natural Disaster: Talking Point and Research Needs. Retrieved from www.gdnonline.org/resources/ilotalking.doc
17 Verchick, *supra* note 11, p. 39.

18 Ibid., p. 67.
19 For an in-depth comparative analysis of the Indian Constitutionalism and Western Constitutionalism see Bhargava Rajeev (2008. edn.). 'Outline of Political Theory of the Indian Constitution'. In *Politics and Ethics of the Indian Constitution*. New Delhi: Oxford University Press, pp. 1–40.
20 Baxi Upendra (2013). 'Preliminary Notes on Transformative Constitutionalism'. In Baxi Upendra, Viljoen Frans and Vilhena Oscar (eds.), *Transformative Constitutionalism: Comparing the Apex Courts of Brazil, India and South Africa*. Pretoria: Pretoria University Law Press, p. 29.
21 Baxi refers to Article 17 that abolished untouchability and Articles 23 and 24 that invalidated the rural serfdom.
22 Baxi Upendra (2002). 'The (Im)possibility of Constitutional Justice: Seismographic Notes on Indian Constitutionalism'. In Zoya Hasan, E. Sridharan and R. Sudarshan (eds.), *India's Living Constitution: Ideas, Practices and Controversies*. New Delhi: Permanent Black, p. 62.
23 Austin Granville (2002). 'The Expected and the Unintended in Working a Democratic Constitution'. In Zoya Hasan, E. Sridharan and R. Sudarshan (eds.), *India's Living Constitution: Ideas, Practices and Controversies*. New Delhi: Permanent Black, p. 319.
24 Cossman Brenda and Kapur Ratna (1999). 'On Women, Equality and the Constitution: Through the Looking Glass of Feminism'. In Nivedita Menon (ed.), *Gender and Politics in India*. New Delhi: Oxford University Press, pp. 197–261; Galanter Marc (1989). *Law and Society in Modern India*. Delhi: Oxford University Press; Guru Gopal (2008). 'Constitutional Justice: Positional and Cultural'. In Rajeev Bhargava (ed.), (edn.) *Politics and Ethics of the Indian Constitution*. New Delhi: Oxford University Press, pp. 230–246; Jaffrelot Christophe (2008). 'Containing Lower Castes: The Constituent Assembly and the Reservation Policy'. In Rajeev Bhargava (ed.), (edn.) *Politics and Ethics of the Indian Constitution*. New Delhi: Oxford University Press, pp. 249–266.
25 Dr Ambedkar, a chief architect of the Indian Constitution, firmly pleaded for 'social democracy'. He stated, 'We must make our political democracy a social democracy as well. Political democracy cannot last unless there lies at the base of it social democracy. What does social democracy mean? It means a way of life which recognizes liberty, equality and fraternity as the principles of life. These principles of liberty, equality and fraternity are not to be treated as separate items in a trinity. They form a union of trinity in the sense that to divorce one from the other is to defeat the very purpose of democracy. Liberty cannot be divorced from equality, equality cannot be divorced from liberty. Nor can liberty and equality be divorced from fraternity. Without equality, liberty would produce the supremacy of the few over the many. Equality without liberty would kill individual initiative. Without fraternity, liberty and equality could not become a natural course of things'. (Ambedkar B. R. *Constituent Assembly Debates. no. 5*, vol. X–XII. Lok Sabha Secretariat: New Delhi, 2009, 5th Reprint, p. 979).
26 Social vulnerability of these sections has been considerably addressed by Menon Nivedita (1999). 'Rights, Bodies and the Law: Rethinking Feminists Politics of Justice'. In Nivedita Menon (ed.), *Gender and Politics in India*. New Delhi: Oxford University Press, pp. 262–295; Rege Sharmila (2006). *Writing Caste/Writing Gender: Reading Dalit Women's*

Testimonies. New Delhi: Zubaan; Thorat Sukhadeo (February 2002). 'Oppression and Denial Dalit Discrimination in the 1990's'. *Economic and Political Weekly*, pp. 572–578.

27 Farber Daniel (2007). 'Disaster Law and Inequality'. *Journal of Law and Inequality*, vol. 25, p. 298; Verchickt Robert (2012). 'Disaster Justice: The Geography of Human Capability'. *Duke Environmental Law & Policy Forum*, vol. 23, pp. 23–24.

28 Akter Shaheen and Deshingkar Priya (2009). Human Development Research Paper–Migration and Human Development in India. Retrieved from //hdr.undp.org/sites/default/files/hdrp/_2009_12.pdf

29 Naik Asmita, Sigler Elca and Laczko Frank (2007). *Migration, Development and Natural Disasters: Insights from the Indian Ocean Tsunami*. Geneva: International Organization for Migration, p. 38. Retrieved from http://publications.iom.int/bookstore/free/MRS30.pdf

30 E. Hedman (2005). 'The Politics of Tsunami Response'. *Forced Migration Review*, pp. 4–5. Retrieved from //www.fmreview.org/FMRPdfs/Tsunami/full.pdf

31 Nightingale, Katherine (2013). 'Equality in Aid'. *International Dalit Solidarity Network*. Copenhagen: IDSN, p. 4. Retrieved from www.dalits.nl/pdf/EqualityInAid.pdf; Nita Bhalla (2014). 'Lower-Caste People Gets Less Aid When Disaster Strikes–Report'. *Reuters*, 29 January. Retrieved from http://in.reuters.com/article/2014/01/29/ india-low-caste-dalits-idINDEEA0S03M20140129

Part III

International legal framework of disaster management

9 Overcoming the patriarchal insulation of international legal framework

Shiranee Tilakawardane

> We cannot eliminate disasters, but we can mitigate risk. We can reduce damage. We can save more lives.
>
> Ban Ki-Moon, Secretary General, United Nations

Since the dawn of the new millennium, mass disasters have claimed the lives of 1.2 million individuals and affected nearly 3 billion more. The most recent mass disasters that have had a devastating effect on lives and livelihood include the 2004 earthquake and tsunami in the Indian Ocean, the 2010 earthquake in Haiti, the 2011 Tohuku earthquake and tsunami in Japan which caused nuclear accidents that led to further complications and the 2015 Nepal earthquake; the list can be much longer to continue. While it is impossible to eliminate mass disasters or predict their moment of impact, efforts to prepare for such catastrophes can mitigate the damaging effects and reduce devastation, of which gender-sensitive risk assessment and gender-responsive recovery and rehabilitation are integral components, since disasters affect women and men differently as it comes as a double damage upon women as compared to men. They not only lose income with the loss of formal and informal sectors, but they also spend more time and face struggles into unpaid jobs when they look after their children with no schools and support system to take care of them. If they lose their husbands, their single status adds to their vulnerability to the sex markets and trafficking. The tsunami in Sri Lanka demonstrated that a very large majority of those who died were women as many skills such as climbing trees, swimming and understanding or deciphering information was not common with women. Besides social prejudices reduce survivability of women through disasters. In an overall accounting carried out by the World Health Organization more than 75 per cent of displaced persons were women. Post-disaster trauma, psychological sickness and mental problems affect women in a big way.

In case of protecting vulnerable populations such as women, children, the elderly, the sick and the disabled, courts have been playing a proactive role across the world, but this is much less than what is actually needed to awaken laid-back and evasive disaster management institutions particularly in South Asia which has the largest number of poor in the world (551 million) – which is higher than even Africa (436 million and comparable to 15 million in South America and 5.9 million in North America, 0.3 million in Europe) – and has the world's largest population vulnerable to hazards and disasters. In such precarious conditions that millions live, gender-based violence[1] during disasters only erupts to its most uncontrollable and ruthless proportions. This chapter seeks to remind the judiciary about its increased role in preventing these crimes when disaster strikes and also look for more sustainable solutions as cherished by the Hyogo Framework for disaster risk reduction strategies.

Approaching mass disasters

The approach to mass disasters has most recently been typified by the Sendai Framework for Disaster Risk Reduction 2015–2030 (Sendai Framework), adopted at the 2015 Sendai Conference, which outlines the four priorities for action as understanding disaster risk, strengthening disaster risk governance to manage disaster risk, investing in disaster risk reduction for resilience and enhancing disaster preparedness for effective response and to 'build back better' in recovery, rehabilitation and reconstruction. The Sendai Framework is the successor to the Hyogo Framework (2005–2030) adopted at the World Conference on Disaster Reduction in Kobe, Japan, in 2005 and is a culmination of numerous global initiatives since the 1980s. It offers countries with an action plan with which to tackle disasters from assessing risk to effective rehabilitation.

What is predominantly witnessed, particularly with regard to natural disasters that strike developing nations, is the absence of or little preparation for potential catastrophes. This absence of preparation makes the impact on lives and infrastructure greater, slows down the speed of emergency responses that lead to exacerbating the negative impact and makes recovery a difficult prospect. In light of such realities, the priorities outlined by the Sendai Framework provide states and other stakeholders a clear action plan to adopt and implement.

In understanding disaster risk, pre-disaster risk assessments are paramount where hazard characteristics of the immediate environment, vulnerability and the exposure of people must be considered.

In strengthening disaster risk governance to manage disaster risk, the presence of a national disaster risk reduction policy is important, and given the nature of natural disasters in particular, a regional policy or framework could be beneficial in the long terms as well where states can be mobilized effectively, without delay or confusion, in the event of a disaster to minimize loss of life. Investment in resilience measures is also an important aspect of disaster risk reduction, and one of the primary reasons a number of developing countries have poor responses is due to their limited ability to invest in such measures. Viewing such measures as opportunities for innovation and job creation can have the dual effect of strengthening both the economy and disaster management schemes. Such schemes are also important in terms of recovery and reconstruction. Recovery involves an early damage assessment and the reestablishment of infrastructure, while rehabilitation involves post-disaster measures such as socio-economic and environmental impact assessments and prevention and mitigation methods such as hazard prediction and modelling, risk assessment and mapping, and importantly, public awareness and education.

Impact of mass disasters

The Sendai Framework agreed on seven primary global targets which aim at reducing global disaster mortality, the number of people affected by disasters, the direct economic loss suffered as well as damage to infrastructure and services. The targets also include the increasing of countries with national disaster risk reduction strategies and enhancing international co-operation in these areas by 2030.

Unarguably the most topical concern with regard to catastrophes is *impact*, that is, the immediate impact the disaster has on life and infrastructure, and the long-term effects on socio-political and economic concerns such as livelihood. Given these effects, it is often low-income nations and nations with unstable political and economic climate that are most affected because of the limited or lack of disaster management mechanisms and emergency response systems which are further undermined by poor infrastructure facilities. Hazard and vulnerability analyses, which are components of disaster management, shed light on increased devastation being a correlation of human vulnerability to disasters.

Vulnerability analysis not only indicates the high incidence of destruction due to natural calamities in low-income nations but also an increased incidence of devastation felt by the vulnerable and marginalized by society. For instance, it is the poor and the powerless who feel the impact of calamities greatly due to their lack of access to finances that would get them essential healthcare and economic recovery in the long run. Even in the event of influx of foreign financial and medical aid, it is almost always never fully sufficient.

Gender and disasters

Oxfam Report 2005 brought to surface shocking discriminatory dimensions of tsunami disaster. It highlighted that tsunami killed 220,000 people in Asia and displaced 1.6 million according to the IFRC reports. More than 95 per cent of these are found to be women. In Cuddalore in India, almost three times as many women were killed as men, with 391 female deaths, compared with 146 men. In Pachaankuppam village, all deaths were those of women alone. In Sri Lanka too, the findings suggest a similar imbalance between the deaths of men and women.

Therefore, it is required to address the concern that on the peripheries of such human vulnerability lie women. While mass disasters affect the poor the greatest, it is the women who are further marginalised and this claim is backed by the United Nations Development Programme (UNDP) which observes that women, along with children, are 14 times more likely to die during a disaster than men. The reasons for this phenomenon are numerous. From a social rights perspective, certain social prejudices disallow the opportunity for women to develop skills that may assist them during a catastrophe. For instance, Oxfam (2005) noted that the social prejudices and views that existed meant that men and boys were more equipped to survive the tsunami that struck the island in 2004 than women and girls because men are taught to climb trees and are expected to know how to swim. Women are also the subject of victimisation due to a high incidence of domestic and sexual violence following a disaster as a result of social strains and stresses in the nuclear family. For instance, women are exposed to greater risk than men when living in refugee or temporary camps following a disaster, and it is also a likely possibility, as noted by the UNDP, that women avoid such camps for fear of being sexually assaulted. Other inequalities in society, for instance, limited economic power and health concerns such as the nutritional needs of the expectant mother, increase the vulnerability of women in the wake of a natural disaster. Given this impact on women, as well as children, there is an increased need for disaster management initiatives regarding prevention as well as recovery and rehabilitation to be gendered.

Gender-sensitive risk assessment

One of the primary aspects of disaster risk reduction continues to be comprehensive risk assessments. Risk assessment involves the examination of detrimental effects, consequences and magnitude of potential catastrophes and preparing for such an impact comprehensively. In conducting risk assessment, a comprehensive understanding of the existing framework to tackle mass disasters is essential, and risk assessment must be complemented with hazard assessment in order to identify high-risk zones as well as exposure and vulnerability analyses to delineate the population and other assets that are at risk. Such assessments should take into account the community-specific practices and social prejudices, implications of gender roles and gender-specific behaviours and skills, limitations on access to education, inequalities in the dissemination of disaster-specific knowledge such as awareness related to appropriate response to early warnings. Therefore, the need for incorporating a gender perspective to assess impact, both short term and long term, is quite clear and demands attention; it is an important aspect of disaster risk reduction that has received scant attention historically. Attention being paid to identifying and establishing gender-sensitive indicators as a result of vulnerability and risk assessments is still in its early stages and is an area ripe for both research and development. Such indicators can not only assist in the effective reformulation of action plans in preparing for mass disasters, but it will also be of immense assistance in aiding and monitoring the process of recovery of communities in the aftermath of a catastrophe that provides accurate data on progress made. Reducing such inequalities and inaccuracies in information will also assist in tackling recovery processes effectively as vulnerabilities can be identified with greater ease and reduce inappropriate (and ineffective) policy decisions with regard to recovery and rehabilitation.

Gender-responsive recovery and rehabilitation

Gender-responsive recovery and rehabilitation processes are, therefore, a logical extension of gender-sensitive risk assessment. In this context, economic rights and realities are prominent as economic capacity is an essential tool for recovery subsequent to mass disasters. Given socially determined gender roles, limited access to economic structures and markets, limited finances and financial capabilities as well as limited marketable skills due to social prejudices, many women suffer in poverty. This is often compounded by the fact that many women earn income from the informal sector which is often severely affected in the aftermath of a mass disaster. Therefore, the response system subsequent to such an event that aids in the recovery of a district, region or state must have the ability to target such gender-specific concerns in order to ensure that rehabilitation is a holistic exercise.

'In times of upheaval or natural disasters, pregnancy-related deaths and gender-based violence soar,' said Priya Marwah, UNFPA's humanitarian response coordinator in Asia and the Pacific. 'Many women lose access to essential reproductive health services and give birth in appalling conditions without access to safe delivery services and lifesaving care.'[2]

Earthquake in Nepal: April 2015

Given historical earthquake activity in the region, the earthquake that struck the heart of Nepal in April 2015 was not an unforeseen event. Therefore, the importance of gender-sensitive risk assessment and gender-responsive recovery programmes can be seen.

For instance, the United Nations Population Fund noted that over 100,000 pregnant women have been affected by the earthquake. This group is a highly vulnerable group given the medical and healthcare attention they require, their nutritional needs, as well as the risk of potentially life-threatening complications that can arise as a result of the tremendous shock and pressure the calamity produces. Given the physical and social upheaval a mass disaster causes, such an event is fraught with possibilities for human trafficking, women and girls in particular. Given that families are often unaware of the whereabouts of their loved ones after a disaster, it provides traffickers with a window of opportunity.

Source: Compiled from UNFPA-Nepal Reports, http://nepal.unfpa.org/news/life-and-recovery-female-friendly-spaces?page=1%2C3 and http://nepal.unfpa.org/sites/asiapacific/files/pubpdf/UNFPANepalEQ_humanitarianresponsereport27August.pdf

Findings and suggestions

It is ironic that none of the South Asian congregation of judicial officers and judges addresses the issue of gender-based violence during disasters. It is taken for granted that the laws for the normal times would definitely address needs and requirements of women affected by disasters. Judicial attitude has followed the pattern set by the English case of *Rylands v. Fletcher* (1866) which focuses on rising up when there is an injury inflicted upon the public. From this case to the case of Bhopal gas leak in India, the judiciary moved from the rule of 'strict liability' to a doctrine of 'absolute liability'. However, it still failed to broaden it up to take into account the indescribable miseries which women face during disasters.

Despite the statistics revealing a highly disproportionate impact of tsunami on women, the 2012 Round Table of South Asian Judiciaries at Bhurban, Pakistan, again missed taking note of gender concerns in its Bhurban Declaration for a 'Common Vision on Environment of South Asian Judiciaries'. This continued in their subsequent congregations at Thimpu, Bhutan, in 2013 and Sri Lanka in 2014. It is in this direction that this chapter comes up with a demand for judicial attention to gender concerns in a multidimensional manner.

A new legal framework specifically addressing some of the key concerns of gender-based imbalances and violence requires recognition of the facts and to include gender-related information from all directions which they give to governments during disasters such as the one in the *Vasundhara Pathak Masoodi v. Union of India*[3] (2014) after the Kashmir floods in India. A toolkit for gender-sensitive judicial directions to the state would mean the following:

- Supplying health and special needs of women during disasters, that is, toilets, sanitary napkins, analgesics
- Safety of women in crowded camps and settlements especially when they are outnumbered by men
- Giving widows in India access to land once owned by their husbands
- Not forcing younger women to enter into marriages with much older men, as it is happening in some locations now and thus not compromising on their education and reproductive health
- In the fishing communities of South India, to giving rights to surviving women to enjoy under new arrangements and programmes
- Registering newly built houses in their names
- Decreasing women's workloads by asking men to take on domestic work

Conclusion

There is often a misplaced sense of helplessness stemming from the unpredictability of mass disasters and the inability to predict their occurrence, impact and fatalities. I say that this sense is *misplaced* because of the sheer volume of preventive measures that can be taken and the risk management frameworks that can be instituted. While the precise occurrence of a disaster cannot be pinpointed, the response systems of nations can indeed be organised to minimise damage. Such systems have proven to be half-effective as it does not do so from a gender perspective.

Now more than ever a gender perspective must be added to disaster risk management initiatives to effectively tackle related concerns and issues, and female participation in such efforts is vital. It is also a step taken in the direction of accurately identifying vulnerabilities and delineating holistic action plans in the aftermath of mass disasters. Therefore, it is initiatives taken by all to counter the destructive nature of such events that matter. Disaster risk reduction is truly everyone's concern, and a collective effort that pools resources and knowledge will undoubtedly result in the minimisation of devastating consequences; while the frequency of natural disasters may increase, the vulnerability it exposes us to need not.

Notes

1 South Asian findings on gender-based violence are drawn from a recently concluded report: Solotaroff, Jennifer L.; Pande, Rohini Prabha. 2014. Violence against Women and Girls: Lessons from South Asia. World Bank Group, Washington, DC. © World Bank. Retrieved from https://openknowledge.worldbank.org/handle/10986/20153

2 See more on UNFPA website www.unfpa.org/news/tens-thousands-pregnant-women-affected-nepal-dpuf

3 Writ Petition(s)(Civil) No(s). 826/2014, DD NO. 29727 of 2014, See more at www.ifrc.org/en/what-we-do/disaster-law/news/asia-pacific/judicial-action-in-disaster-response

Reference

Oxfam International. (2005). *The Tsunami's Impact on Women*. Briefing Note March 2005. Oxford: Oxfam International.

10 Interrogating the pedagogy of state responsibility and individual rights in disaster law

Stellina Jolly

Learning from the history of disasters

Disasters have always been part of human history and civilization. In the initial phase of human life and settlement, when a man was at the mercy of nature, the disasters were natural and played havoc with the life of people and society. Disasters even paved the way for the extinction of civilization. The biblical account of great flood is believed to have wiped out human life from the planet leaving behind Noah, his family and his selected animals (Pitman, 2000). The most-quoted reasons attributed for the disappearance of Harappan civilization are the floods, earthquakes and climatic variations. With the passage of time, technological developments and industrialization assisted the progress of humanity on earth, and human control on nature got amplified. The industrialization phase also saw the emergence of man-made disasters equalling or even crossing in magnitude and its destructive capacity compared to natural disasters. Bhopal, Chernobyl and Deepwater Horizon are some of the worst man-made disasters in history. The United Nations has estimated the direct economic cost of disasters since 2000 as roughly $1.4 trillion.

Developing norms and principles constitutes one of the prominent mechanics of responsiveness to any situation which requires political, economic or social attention. The significance of putting in place an effective legal norm and principles is not to merely regulate bad and good behaviours. It is also reflective of the values which a society and civilization represent. Domestically, states have addressed the issue of disasters with putting in place an elaborate institutional and legislative mechanism. A peep through international law reveals that there is an almost vacuum of legal mechanism in operation corresponding to natural disasters. Many reasons can be attributed to the lacklustre interest and response of international community to adequately address natural disasters. First, the primary purpose and objective of international law is to regulate the relations between states and to maintain that they function and operate with a sense of responsibility and coexistence. To facilitate peaceful coexistence of states, international law founded some of the fundamental principles. The UN Charter in Article 2 sets forth those principles deemed to be of constitutional importance to the United Nations and its member states: sovereign equality; good faith compliance with agreements to which a state is a party; cooperation in addressing matters of international concern; non-interference in the domestic affairs of states; and peaceful settlement of international disputes. Key to all of these principles is the concept of state sovereignty (Kiss & Shelton, 2007). State sovereignty means that each state has exclusive legislative, judicial and executive jurisdiction over activities on its territory (Kiss & Shelton, 2007). Initially it was perceived that state sovereignty is absolute as propounded under Harmon Doctrine[1] (Kuokkanen, 2002). Although absolute sovereignty on its face seemed a useful tool at least to a party relying on it, in the end it turned out to be a dull sword: an instrument that does more damage than good, and gradually states accepted limitations to their sovereignty (Kuokkanen, 2002). Concept of state sovereignty provided an impetus to the international community to develop a robust and coherent edifice of law to address areas of common concern. Natural disasters were conceived and perceived as ad hoc, spontaneous and short-lived incidents on which states do not have any control, and these incidents were not perceived as a threat to the exercise of sovereignty (Fidler, 2005). The incentive to regulate the activities of states in natural disasters almost never existed. Whereas in the case of industrial disasters it was felt that economic and sovereign interest of nations clashed and the international community came out with an elaborate legal machinery to oversee the preparedness, retentiveness and response mechanism in oil spill, nuclear fallout and so on (Fidler, 2005).

Even though natural disasters cannot be completely avoided, the scientific consensus which later emerged suggests that with an adequate preparation and safeguards, the magnitude and intensity of losses on humanity can be better addressed. The recent cyclone (Cyclone Vardah) which hit the Andhra coast and Tamil Nadu in India in 2016 can be cited as an example of an efficient disaster preparedness as the authorities managed to keep the loss of human lives at a minimum compared to India's previous records in disaster management. In fact, the Uttarakhand landslides in 2013 exposed the fallacies and utter lack of preparedness of India's disaster response system (Bagga, 2013).

Disaster law located within the humanitarian law

Historically, there has been a lack of interest in international law for preventing natural disasters. The disaster was supposed to be responded with relief and not be to prevented and prepared. This also vividly explains the involvement of the philanthropic international community to aid and relief in the aftermath of a natural disaster. The concept of comity[2] dominated the entire relief operations in disaster (Kuokkanen, 2002). The international community equated disasters to a humanitarian crisis and tried to respond to the situation through the legal prism operating in the sphere of humanitarian law (Coppola, 2015). This enabled governmental accountability to take a backseat. The main policies and guidelines to respond to disasters have been developed under the aegis of humanitarian law bodies. In fact, the first coordinated response of international community to disasters came with the establishment of the International Relief Union (IRU) in 1932 (Peaslee, 1977).

The notable feature of IRU mechanism was that the action and aid provided by the IRU was based on the consent of nations and never impinged on the sovereignty of nations (John, 2001). The IRU was expected to play a pivotal role in disaster relief, and it started off with much fancy expectations (Coppola, 2015). The IRU was expected to act as a central agency dealing with disasters and to furnish to the suffering population first aid and to assemble for this purpose funds, resources and assistance of all kinds; given the political scenario and nature of the agency, these expectations were clearly unachievable (Coppola, 2015). However, the IRU could not maintain the momentum and it failed to live up to its expectations mainly because of some fundamental design flaws and could not generate enough financial resources (John, 2001). Further the start of world war untimely snapped the IRU of all its strategies and functions, and ultimately it failed to bring about a positive development of international law (Maraiah, 2014).

The period after the Second World War saw a new phase of development for international law. The world witnessed the formation of a new international organization in the form of United Nations to maintain peaceful coexistence of nations (Gupta, 2009). Unlike the classical approach, the purpose of United Nations was not mere coexistence, but the promotion of cooperation among states was high on its agenda (Brownlie, 1972). In relation to natural disasters the phase was marked by an increasing trend towards the adoption of bilateral treaties (Smith, 1985). The aid and relief was thought of as a mechanism to tackle disaster and was based on the principles of comity, fairness and good neighbourliness rather than on legal obligations and compulsion (Smith, 1985). In fact, it is debatable whether there exists a duty for the states to follow international law (Mccaffrey, 1999). In the voluntary scheme of aid system which operated both assisting and victim states retain virtually unfettered sovereignty (Maraiah, 2014). The absence of a well-planned and mandatory coordinated disaster relief mechanism prompted the International Red Cross and Red Crescent Movement to launch the International Disaster Response Law (IDRL) (Isabelle, 2010). This is also in consonance with the fact that the response to disaster was conceived as a humanitarian law issue. The mandate of IDRL was to evaluate the existing international and national laws in order to determine how law can play a more effective role in helping states and other entities to respond effectively to victims of disasters (Isabelle, 2010). Many focal areas have been identified under the IDRL: the recognition of aid organization and qualification of professionals, the identification of relief supplies, tax relief for relief supplies, and legal liability and accountability (Hoffman, 2000). Based on their work, A Model Act for the Facilitation and Regulation of International Disaster Relief and Initial Recovery Assistance intended to assist states to strengthen their legal preparedness for international disaster cooperation is built upon (International Federation of Red Cross, 2011).

The multitude of disasters forced the United Nations to elevate it as an item of priority. United Nations came out with the declaration of the International Decade (1990–2000) for Natural Disaster Reduction (IDNDR). Various programmes and strategies emanated from the decade-long emphasis. The Yokohama Strategy, 1994, emphasizes that disaster prevention, mitigation and preparedness are better than disaster response in achieving the goals and objectives of vulnerability reduction (Ministry Home Affairs, 2004). In 2005, the Hyogo Framework for Action was adopted to encourage countries to become more resilient in the face of natural disasters (United Nations, 2005) The most striking feature of the decade effort by the international community is the paradigm shift in the concept of disaster management from post-disaster rescue, relief and reconstruction to adopting a pre-disaster proactive approach to include pre-disaster planning, preparedness relief and recovery (Maraiah, 2014). Even after the paradigm shift to a pre-disaster approach it needs no emphasis that the significance of post-disaster relief, recovery and reconstruction cannot be overlooked. Most of the legal mechanisms aimed at disaster relief were soft laws lacking implementation and enforceability. Additionally a well comprehensive and coordinated legal instrument dealing with multiple phases of disaster relief was still a far dream.

Evolution of the 'law to protect'

The international law is based on the fundamental principle of sovereign equality of nations. The sovereign equality is maintained through the principle of prohibition of the use of force and non-intervention. Article 2(7) of the UN Charter of 1945 provides that 'nothing in the present Charter shall authorize the United Nations to intervene in matters which are essentially within the domestic jurisdiction of any state, (United Nations, 1945). Article 2(4) of the UN Charter provides that all members shall refrain in their international relations from the threat or use of force against the territorial integrity or political independence of any state, or in any other manner inconsistent with the purposes of the United Nations (1945). The only exception is envisaged under Chapter VII of the UN Charter which allows for the Security Council to 'determine the existence of any threat to the peace, breach of the peace, or act of aggression' and to take military or non-military action to 'restore international peace and security' (Brownlie, 1972). The existence of the Cold War practically prevented any meaningful intervention even when the situation demanded (Gupta, 2009).

The end of the Cold War brought substantial changes in the normative and procedural framework of international relations (Jolly & Mahajana, 2014). The fall of Soviet Union and the emergence of unipolar world order led to rethinking of many policymakers across the world (Jolly & Mahajana, 2014). The end of Cold War also presented to the world various conflicts, extensive human right violations and devastations to the forefront of humanity. The NATO forces had to militarily intervene, which proved decisive in terminating and finishing the conflict in Serbia (Helal, 2014). NATO justified the military intervention on humanitarian grounds (Helal, 2014). The NATO intervention also brought a substantial discourse on the contours, scope and legalities of international intervention (Helal, 2014). The discourse on the intervention of international communities continued amid the mass killings and human sufferings in Somalia, Rwanda and Sudan and exposed the inadequacy of the international legal order to deal with imminent and then actual, continuing episodes of genocide and ethnic cleansing (Nanda, 2007). But the solutions were not forthcoming as the international community was heavily polarized on the topic of intervention. Many believe that intervention on a just cause and right ground will uphold the dignity of individuals and protect human rights (Lieblich, 2013). They find support to their proposition from the rising importance attached to Individuals as subjects and participants under international law (Lieblich, 2013). But on the other side of the spectrum many expressed the fear that the authority to intervene may be liable to be misused and will be used as an opportunity by the powerful nations to bring new forms of imperialism (Chesterman, 2012).

A concrete step to formulate a principle of the responsibility of international community to protect was taken by the International Commission on Intervention and State Sovereignty (ICISS) which conceived Responsibility to Protect (R2P) as a mechanism of preventing, reacting and rebuilding (Helal, 2014). The ICISS report expounded the threshold wherein the invocation of R2P can be justified.

R2P can be invoked in the following cases:

- Where serious and irreparable harm occurring to human beings
- Right intention to avert more human suffering
- Use of force as part of R2P can be justified only as a last resort
- The scale, duration and intensity of the intervention should be kept to a minimum which is just adequate to secure the human protection
- R2P should have a chance of reasonably halting or averting the suffering
- Authorization from Security Council.

(International Commission on Intervention and State Sovereignty, 2002)

The ICISS report further lists out events where R2P can be applied: genocide, war crimes, ethnic cleansing and crimes against humanity and natural disasters (International Commission on Intervention and State Sovereignty, 2002). The United Nations World Summit in 2005 gave an approval to the doctrine of R2P when it debated and adopted it (United Nations General Assembly, 2005). The international community has a subsidiary obligation to step in when the concerned state fails in its obligation to protect populations from genocide, war crimes, ethnic cleansing and crimes against humanity (Bellamy, 2006). One of the notable differences between ICISS report and the resulting document lies in their differing attitude in relation to disasters. ICISS Report explicitly applies R2P to natural disaster situations, but the outcome document clearly excludes the invocation of R2P in natural disasters (Bellamy, 2006).

The issue of R2P in a natural disaster becomes important in the wake of Cyclone Nargis in Myanmar (Heath, 2011). The disaster brought into focus the inability of international community to organize relief in the face of fierce refusal to aid by Myanmar (Horsey, 2008). It was suggested that a constructive interpretation be given to R2P to extend the applicability to natural disasters (Jarrod, 2009). This approach poses serious challenges to the principles of sovereignty and non-intervention, and has met resistance from governments, scholars and members of the International Law Commission (Jarrod, 2009). ICISS member Ramesh Thakur, in his analysis of the applicability of R2P to Myanmar, concluded that the exclusion of the reference to natural disasters from the Summit Outcome Document clearly suggests that the doctrine was intended to be limited to the affirmative commission of atrocities and armed combat (Jarrod, 2009). The current approach of ILC shows a rejection of the doctrine of R2P in natural disasters. ILC has taken a stand consistent with upholding the concept of state sovereignty. ILC states, 'State affected by a disaster has the freedom to adopt whatever measures it sees fit to ensure the protection of the persons found within its territory. As a consequence no other State may legally intervene in the process of response to a disaster in unilateral manner: third parties must instead seek to cooperate with the affected state in accordance to article 5, as provisionally adopted by the Drafting Committee.' Most of the states still are reluctant to accept the doctrine in case of disasters. Still some are hopeful and argue that the concept of R2P could still be important in developing a legal framework for assessing the appropriate role of the international community in the aftermath of natural disaster (Barber, 2009; Stahn, 2007). The application of R2P becomes complicated if we look at the issue from a state-centric view in which state sovereignty takes the focal point. But this attitude can significantly change if we consider the issue from the perspective of human beings and human security and dignity. In a natural disaster it is the human security which is threatened and violated most. Traditionally the concept of security has, for too long, been interpreted narrowly as a security of territory from external aggression, or as protection of national interests. A state often responds to traditional security threats through amassing more weapons and resorting to a path of conflict. In the human security threats the focus shifts from state-centric approach to individual-centric approach. Moreover the human security issues are not created by another state. This gives an opportunity for the states and international community to co-operate with each other to solve the issues. International community thus owes a solemn responsibility to protect and preserve and rebuild societies struck with disasters. The discourse on human security needs to move from merely confined to the theoretical debates in international relations to be translated into core policy and legal objectives under international law. As of now the international community has not explicitly pronounced in favour of the application of R2P in natural disasters. In the absence of a clear position on the part of international community to invoke R2P in natural disasters, a human right approach emerges as a viable alternative to look for managing disasters. The invocation of human right approach is also pertinent even if the international community develops a framework on R2P applicable to disasters as one of the criticisms advanced against R2P is its inadequate attention to account the human right and specially gender dimension and its failure to acknowledge that women are disproportionately represented among the poor and marginalized in weak unstable states (Sherret, 2005). It is thus imperative that any development of principle of R2P should engage in a deeper understanding of human rights and disaster.

Disasters and human rights

The disasters have always presented to the international community a sight of human sufferings and loss of rights. An intimate relationship exists between disasters and human rights. Disasters often threaten the existence and enjoyment of many human rights like right to life and livelihood directly. At the same time violations of human rights in disasters often result from poor management and poor preparedness to respond to the consequences of the disasters (IASC, 2006). The question is, who is responsible when disasters deny to human beings right to life, liberty and security of person? Who has the primary responsibility to respect, protect and fulfil one's rights, including the right to protection from disaster losses? (Rawinji, 2013).

The human right perspective is operationalized under the disaster management in different ways at domestic and international law. Presently the human right paradigm is used mainly at the domestic level in the context of disaster. The basic human right threatened by a disaster is the right to life which is a wholesome concept. In disaster parlance it can be translated and implemented as the right of a victim to rescue, relief and rehabilitation and a corresponding obligation on the part of state (Alex, 2006). At the domestic context this right can be implemented and justified using the concept of *parens patriae* wherein 'state *as* sovereign is obliged in public interest to protect persons under disability who have no rightful protector' (Alex, 2006). The doctrine can be read as imposing a duty on the state to render adequate relief and rehabilitation to the victims of disaster (Alex, 2006). In the celebrated case of *B.J. Diwan* the Gujarat High Court held that the right to relief and rehabilitation is a guaranteed right under Article 21 of the constitution (*B.J. Diwan v. State of Gujarat*, 2001). Further the principles of non-discrimination with regard to access to basic services including shelter and housing, right to security, health services, clean water, education, compensation are considered as an integral facet of human rights and can easily be claimed in disasters.

The invocation of human rights paradigm to prevention, response and recovery from disasters at the international level has started gaining attention since the last decade. The European Court of Human Rights has ruled that states have obligations to implement preventive measures to protect people from the risks posed by disasters in order to protect the right to life (*Budayeva & Others v. Russia*, 2008). There have also been cases where governments have been held responsible for failing to warn or protect their citizens, most notably by national judicial authorities in the cases of the L'Aquila earthquake in Italy 2009 (Ferris, 2014). The ILC recognized the significance of human right approach in its draft articles on the protection of persons in the event of disasters and affirms that persons affected by disasters are entitled to respect for their human rights (International Law Commission, 2010). The concept of human dignity runs through the breadth and length of ILC draft articles (International Law Commission, 2010). Draft articles lay down duty on the international community to cooperate in disasters and on the affected state to seek assistance and not to arbitrarily withhold its consent for receiving international aid and relief (International Law Commission, 2010). The UN Human Rights Council devoted a special session to human rights issues arising from a natural disaster (Ferris, 2014). In June 2006, the UN Inter-Agency Standing Committee (IASC) adopted Operational Guidelines on Human Rights and Natural Disasters. The guidelines contend that human right protection is not limited to securing the survival and physical security of those affected by natural disasters. Protection encompasses all relevant guarantees – civil and political as well as economic, social and cultural rights – attributed to them by international human rights and, where applicable, international humanitarian law (IASC Operational Guidelines, 2006).

There are ways and mechanisms by which human right paradigm can easily be read into disaster relief strategy in the current legal framework.[3] First, the principle of government accountability can be invoked when it fails to prevent or reduce the risk of disasters. Second, by adopting international law, all states accept the obligation to respect, protect and fulfil human right. A failure by governments and others to take reasonable preventive action to reduce exposure and vulnerability and to enhance resilience, as well as to provide effective mitigation, is therefore a human rights question (United Nations High

Commissioner for Human Rights, 2013). The existing legal documents can be interpreted to augment the human rights paradigm in natural disasters. Prominent among them can be the rules and guidelines on internal displacement. This is pertinent as disasters are known for creating migration at a massive scale and impact many of the human rights (Pratap, 2012). United Nations Framework Convention on Climate Change (UNFCC) Cop in Warsaw in 2013 can be rightfully extended to climate-induced disasters (UNFCC, 2013). Uncoordinated overlap in UN system functions in the humanitarian sector inhibiting the effective delivery of relief in disasters may be remedied by the creation of an intergovernmental body, as found in other economic and social sectors (Isabelle, 2010).

The main objective of human rights is protection of humans. For international law, protection of persons is not a new phenomenon. The classical concept of international law dominated only by state paradigm is on the demise.[4] International human rights law, environmental law, humanitarian law, criminal law are full of developments where individuals are finding a prominent place rapidly. In the context of disasters the ILC draft principles on the protection of individuals gave special emphasis to human rights, including right to protection, safety and security, right to disaster relief and basic needs of economic and social rights (International Law Commission, 2010). With all these advancements of incorporating and elevating the individual concern under international law, the issue of considering disaster relief from a human right perspective suffers from some serious challenges.

First, till date no international human right declaration explicitly recognizes the linkage of human rights and disasters. Further declaration becomes meaningful only when municipal law of a country enacts and adopts it as part of its legal system through treaty application, judicial enforcement and diplomacy. The major problem associated with various human right declaration is the main question of how the individual states will choose to implement it domestically (Kick & Sikkinik, 1999). Further jurisdictional issues also complicate the issue. International courts are open only to nations and not to individuals, and in case of disaster policies having moved into the domain of communities and resilience-building activities, these courts may be more prohibitive than facilitators in addressing serious individual concerns of disasters.

Whatever the way forward, any argument in support of linking human rights and disasters will place considerable reliance on its link with the existing treaty obligations of states in socio-economic rights. Two problems appear prominently in the debate on disasters and human right approach. First, many of the socio-economic human rights are couched in the context of state capability, meaning the enjoyment of these rights is conditional and contingent on the capability of states to provide the same. In terms of disasters, states can always come up with the defense and explanation that they lack the required financial, technical, infrastructural capacities. In fact, many of the human right documents contain the provisions of reservation.[5] Capability argument is a strong point which is indeed difficult to negate. Capability arguments can only be resolved by adopting and promoting a truly international cooperative approach. Second, a real challenge exists in identifying and implementing socio-economic rights relevant in the context of disaster. Irrespective of the difficulties in identifying and enforcing socio-economic rights, the existence of a concrete norm undoubtedly provides a focus for efforts at both the national and international levels to bring pressure to bear on states to fulfil their responsibilities to their citizens. Disaster mitigation and risk reduction is possible only when the institutions managing disasters adopt a rights-based approach and generate vibrant institutions at the grassroots level which resonate with the local issues pertaining to individual perceptions to natural resources use and environmental safety.

Conclusion

This chapter has tried to analyse the international community's response to disaster relief. The disaster relief mechanism had its beginning in the principles of comity and was voluntary. Over the course of time the concept of good neighbourliness and cooperation came to be accepted as the cardinal principles of international law. The international relief in disasters was no more a mere matter of comity but became entrenched under international law. Still the operation of state sovereignty in many cases prevented the effective disbursement of international relief where both the victim and aiding states had to be blamed as evidenced in the refusal of Myanmar for international aid in the wake of Cyclone Nargis in 2009 and the lackluster response of international community in the wake of Pakistan flood in 2010. The international community hotly debated on the possibility of extending the application of the concept of R2P to natural disasters. No consensus could emerge on this contentious issue as the concept of R2P challenges some of the fundamental principles of international law where the legality of interfering in the domestic affairs of a state was prominently questioned. Most of the cited authorities and the work of ILC on the protection of persons in the event of disaster positions against invoking the R2P principle to natural disasters. In a scenario where international community suffers from a lack of clarity to regulate the mode and flow of international relief, the possibility of humanitarian relief during disasters would never be appropriately delivered.

Therefore, human rights approach substantially changes the equation of state sovereignty to establish state responsibility towards its people from which it (in theory) draws its legitimacy (Jolly & Mahajana, 2014). Therefore, the need of the hour is to promote people-oriented, human rights–based disaster relief plans and strategies. Till the time the international community comes up with a clear-cut position on R2P applicable to natural disasters, it should explore the possibility of establishing an international disaster relief fund to which states and transnational corporations can be encouraged to contribute. The trend of establishing financial fund mechanism under the international environmental law could be taken as a guiding point. The loss and damage mechanism envisaged under the United Nations Framework Convention on Climate Change (UNFCC) Cop in Warsaw in 2013 can be rightfully extended to climate-induced disasters (UNFCC, 2013), but the mechanism needs to shed its too much reliance on technicality, and without waiting for the loss and damage mechanism to finalize compensation and relief could be given under several plethora of laws. This argument is embedded in the fact that most of the disaster-prone areas are also the areas of acute poverty and underdevelopment. The disaster is all about human sufferings, and the mandate of international community is to consider the issue from a human right perspective, taking into account the varied social, economic and cultural criteria and promoting cooperation. Cooperation has never been easy for human beings. The mystery is how, despite their history of battling to survive, human beings have learned nonetheless to cooperate with one another (Jolly & Mahajana, 2014). This carries hope for a stronger and clearer disaster law in times to follow the Sendai vision.

Notes

1 Harmon Doctrine: It is named after the American attorney general Judson Harmon. Harmon in the wake of a water dispute between America and Mexico concerning the use of Rio Grande River propounded the doctrine of absolute sovereignty. He stated that a riparian state has complete control over waters lying within its territory and may utilize those waters without regard for the effects of downstream countries. The doctrine is often supported as an example of absolute sovereignty principle.

2 The concept of 'comity' is considered to be one of the bases of international law prompting states to respect each other's laws and actions. Comity is not

a matter of absolute obligation nor a matter of mere courtesy and good will, upon the other. But it is the recognition which one nation allows within its territory to the legislative, executive or judicial acts of another nation.

3 Currently international disaster response law is not a comprehensive or unified framework. It consists of a fragmented and piecemeal collection of various international, regional and bilateral treaties, non-binding resolutions, declarations, codes, guidelines, protocols and procedures.

4 In the beginning sovereign states alone were considered to have international legal personality and subjects under international law. Individuals, international organizations and various non-state actors were not considered to be part of international law. The Second World War and the human right violations, which followed, made the international community deliberate on the efficacy of having only states as a subject of international law. The Nurnberg and Tokyo Tribunals which followed the Second World War ruled that individuals can have legal personality under international law, and this trend was picked up by the later development in international law.

5 Reservation gives a state the option to be a party to the treaty, while leaving aside some specific provision in the treaty to which it has objection. Vienna Convention on law of treaties defines reservation as a unilateral statement, however phrased or named, made by a state, when signing, ratifying, accepting, approving or acceding to a treaty, whereby it purports to exclude or to modify the legal effect of certain provisions of the treaty in their application to that state.

References

Alex, J. P. (2006). *Disaster Management: Towards a Legal Framework*. Retrieved 3 March 2015, from www.iipa.org.in/common/pdf/12.pdf

Bagga, A. B. (2013, June 24). *The Uttarakhand Tragedy Casts Shame on India's Disaster Management: So Why Did the Committee Meant to Plan for Flood Emergencies Fail to Meet for Four Years* Retrieved 13 March 2015, from www.dailymail.co.uk/indiahome/indianews/article-2347624/NDMA-The-Uttarakhand-tragedy-casts-shame-Indias-disaster-management-So-DID-committee-meant-plan-flood-emergencies-fail-meet-FOUR-YEARS.html

Barber, R. (2009). The Responsibility to Protect the Survivors of Natural Disaster: Cyclone Nargis, A Case Study. *Journal of Conflict and Security Law*, *14*, 3–34.

Bellamy, A. (2006). Whither the Responsibility to Protect? Humanitarian Intervention and the 2005 World Summit. *Ethics & Intl Affairs*, *20*, 143–165.

Bellamy, A. (2014). *The Responsibility to Protect: A Defence*. Oxford: Oxford University Press.

B. J. Diwan v. State of Gujarat 2 GLR 1394.

Brownlie, I. (1972). *Principles of Public International Law*. Oxford: Oxford University Press.

Budayeva, & Others v. Russia, App. Nos. 15339/02, 21166/02, 11673/02, 15343/02 (Eur. Ct. H.R. 2008).

Chesterman, S. (2012). *Just War or Just Peace?: Humanitarian Intervention and International Law.* Oxford: Oxford University Press.

Coppola, D. P. (2015). *Introduction to International Disaster Management.* Butterworth-Heinemann.

Ferris, E. (2014, April 10). *How Can International Human Rights Law Protect Us from Disasters?* Retrieved 30 March 2015, from http://reliefweb.int/report/world/how-can-international-human-rights-law-protect-us-disasters.

Fidler, D. P. (2005). *Disaster Relief and Governance after the Indian Ocean Tsunami: What Role for International law.* Retrieved 5 March 2015, from www.repository.law.indiana.edu/facpub/398/

Gupta, S. (2009). *International Law and Human Rights.* Allahabad: Allahabad law Agency.

Heath, J. B. (2011). Disasters Relief and Neglect: The Duty to Accept Humanitarian Assistance and the Work of the International Law Commission. *N.Y.U. Journal of International Law and Politics*, *43*, 419–477.

Helal, M. S. (2014). Justifying War and the Limits of Humanitarianism. *Fordham International Law Journal*, *37*(3), 551–642.

Hoffman, M. (2000). *'Towards an International Disaster Response Law' World Disasters Report.* Geneva: International Federation of Red Cross and Red Crescent Societies.

Horsey, J. B. (2008). *Negotiating Humanitarian Access to Cyclone-Affected Areas of Myanmar: A Review.* Retrieved 30 March 2015, from www.odihpn.org/humanitarian-exchange-magazine/issue-41/negotiating-humanitarian-access-to-cyclone-affected-areas-of-myanmar-a-review

IASC Operational Guidelines. (2006). *Human Rights and Natural Disasters Operational Guidelines and Field Manual on Human Rights Protection in Situations of Natural Disaster. Brookings-Bern Project on Internal Displacement.* Washington DC: The Brookings Institution.

International Commission on Intervention and State Sovereignty. (2002). *The Responsibility to Protect.* Canada: International Development Research Center.

International Federation of Red Cross. (2011). *Model Act on Disaster Relief.* Retrieved 25 February 2015, from www.ifrc.org/en/what-we-do/idrl/model-act-on-idrl/

International Law Commission. (2010). *Draft Articles on the Protection of Persons in the Event of Disasters.* Retrieved 2 March 2015, from http://legal.un.org/ilc/guide/6_3.htm

Isabelle, R. (2010). International Disaster Response Law and the Coordination of International Organisations. *The ANU Undergraduate Research Journal*, *2*, 143–162.

Jarrod, W. (2009). Reconstructing the Responsibility to Protect in the Wake of Cyclones. *Tulane Law Review*, *84*, 219–263.

John, H. (2001). Disasters and the International Order-II: The International Relief Union. *International History Review*, *23*, 253–298.

Jolly, S. & Mahajana, S. (2014). Climate Change and Security: Forging Cooperative Mechanism in South Asia. *International Journal of Public Policy, 10*(6), 315.
Kick, M. E. & Sikkinik, K. (1999). *Transnational Advocacy Networks and the Social Construction of Legal Rules*. Retrieved 12 March 2015, from http://isites.harvard.edu/fs/docs/icb.topic446176.files/Week_7/Keck_and_Sikkink_Transnational_Advocacy.pdf
Kiss, A. & Shelton, D. (2007). *Guide to International Environmental Law*. Leiden: Martinus Nijhoff.
Kuokkanen, T. (2002). *International Law and the Environment: Variations on a Theme*. Biggleswade, UK: Kluwer Law International.
Lieblich, E. (2013). *International Law and Civil Wars: Intervention and Consent*. London: Routledge.
Maraiah, V. (2014). *Disaster Management Law: The Indian experience*. Retrieved 24 March 2015, from http://icehm.org/upload/6782ED0814038.pdf
Mccaffrey, S. C. (1999). Water, Water Everywhere, But Too Few Drops to Drink: The Coming Fresh Water Crisis and International Environmental law. *Denver Journal of International Law and Policy*, *28*(3), 325–337.
Ministry Home Affairs. (2004). *Disaster Management in India*. Delhi: Government of India.
Nanda, V. P. (2007). The Protection of Human Rights under International Law: Will the U.N. Human Rights Council and the Emerging New Norm 'Responsibility to Protect'. *Denver Journal of International Law and Policy*, *35*, 353–365.
Peaslee, A. J. (1977). *International Governmental Organizations: Constitutional Documents*, Part 1, Volume 1. London: Brill.
Pratap, C. (2012, February). *Disaster Management and Law: A Human Rights Perspective*. Retrieved 10 February 2015, from www.lawyersclubindia.com/articles/Disaster-Management-and-Law-A-Human-Rights-Perspective-4497.asp#.VQhd9uEwCUU
Rawinji, F. (2013). *Claiming the Human Right to Protection from Disasters, the Case for Human Rights-Based Disaster Risk Reduction*. Retrieved 30 March 2015, from www.preventionweb.net/files/submissions/31225_righttodisasterprotection.pdf
Ryan, William B. & Pitman, Walter C. (2000). *Noah's Flood: The New Scientific Discoveries about the Event That Changed History*. Simon & Schuster.
Sherret, J. B. (2005). *A Sight for Sore Eyes: Bringing Gender Vision to the Responsibility to Protect Framework, INSTRAW: 22–23*. Retrieved 21 March 2015, from www.un- instraw.org/en/images/stories/SecuritySectorReform/new%20voices%20gender%20r2pdf
Stahn, Carsten (2007). Responsibility to Protect: Political Rhetoric or Emerging Legal Norm? *The American Journal of International Law*, 101(1), 99–120.
UNFCC, U. N. (2013). *Warsaw International Mechanism for Loss and Damage Associated with Climate Change Impacts*. Retrieved 31 March 2015, from

http://unfccc.int/adaptation/workstreams/loss_and_damage/items/8134.php

United Nation Charter. (1945). San Francisco: UNO.

United Nations. (2005). UN World Conference on Disaster Reduction, Building the Resilience of Nations and Communities to Disasters: Hyogo Framework for Action 2005–2015, UN Doc A/CONF.206/L.2/Rev.1.

United Nations High Commissioner for Human Rights. (2013). *Office of the United Nations High Commissioner for Human Rights (OHCHR) 'Organization Profile: Policies and Programmes in DRR'*. Retrieved 30 March 2015, from www.preventionweb.net/english/professional/contacts/profile.php?id=1370

World Summit Outcome United Nations General Assembly. (2005). *World Summit Outcome G.A. Res. 60/1, 1 139, U.N. Doc. AIRES/60/1.*

11 Disaster law, ICT and performance through 'standard-setting' in disaster law

Sanghamitra Nath

Origin of the word 'disaster' may be traced to Latin words *dis* implying bad and *aster* connoting star. The overall meaning conveyed 'a sense of fatalism, which dominated public perception about disasters and even influenced public policies on disaster management, or absence of such policies, in many countries for a long time'.[1] Disaster, therefore, underscores the need for preparedness which finds expression in public policies, plans and laws. Often, response to pending disasters flounders due to procedural confusion, lack of efficacy and poor institutional support.[2]

The Indian subcontinent is vulnerable to disasters both natural and man-made. According to estimates, around 56 million Indians suffer from disasters every year. Though natural hazards are beyond human control, man-made disasters can be mitigated through timely action and preventive measures. At present, emergency governance falls largely on the shoulders of state government. It is responsible for rescue, relief and rehabilitation. However, it is assisted by the central government and the National Disaster Management Authority (NDMA) with resources (physical and financial), guidelines, plans, National Disaster Response Force (NDRF).[3] However, India has a checkered history in disaster management till date. While most of the disasters have reported to be unsatisfactorily managed (e.g. Uttarakhand floods, Pune landslides, Bhuj earthquake), only exceptionally a few have been well-managed (e.g. Odisha Phailin, Andhra Pradesh HudHud).

A well-managed disaster tells of standards of performance, accountability, coordination and dedication at pre-, during, and post-disaster phases. While current disaster laws in India provide a broad overview of duties at central, state and district levels, it does not set standard criteria for assessment of duties. A study of the Uttarakhand disaster in 2013 reveals an immediate requirement of legal parameters in disaster laws as well as in Information and communication technology usage. Construction and legal approval of standards in the Disaster

Management Act, National Disaster Management Plan and State Disaster Management Plans would invigorate disaster legislations and account for governance lapses in meeting predetermined targets.

The conspicuous absence of standard-setting may be attributed to scattered success stories and rampant mismanagement of disasters. This chapter argues that standard-setting is pivotal for implementing and buttressing disaster laws. The chapter is divided into six parts – Standard-setting as a legal parameter of performance, Accountability sans standards of performance, Lessons learnt from Himalayan tsunami in 2013 and CAG Report, Standard-setting: an indispensable tool for implementing disaster law, Findings and recommendations and Conclusion.

Standard-setting as a legal parameter of performance

Any legal action on non-performance or to ensure performance is possible if a standard exists. Standards refer to requirements that state what should and should not be done, how much of the action is desirable and the type of sanctions that 'will apply in the event of non-compliance'.[4] Standards connote a definite rule or principle or measure that is established by authority or enjoys official support. It may be legal or quasi-legal, rigid or flexible. It may not be fair or equitable or scientifically proven, that is, it may be arbitrary and based on insufficient technical data.[5] In addition, there are preferred qualities of standards which emphasize on simple and accurate definition, easy implementation and analysis, possibility of routine checks and reviews, and preclude too much leniency or inflexibility.[6]

A standard becomes the means to achieve predetermined targets. However, '[there is] no point in setting a standard unless we can monitor compliance and assess whether it is achieving its aim'.[7] The Third Report of the Second Administrative Reforms Commission (2006) reiterates making the apparatus of crisis management perform and deliver.[8] It is not enough to proclaim disaster laws or establish legal institutions of disaster management. Consider chapter 10 of Disaster Management Act, 2005, entitled 'Offences and Penalties' which outlines punishments for obstruction of duty, false claim, misappropriation of money or materials, false warning, refusal to comply with directions issued by the government and offences by government departments or private companies. Here, punishment serves dual roles:

1 As punishment follows from dereliction of duties, it indicates monitoring of (non-)compliance by a formal agency that inflicts

the punishment. Hence, punishment serves to attest whether compliance to standard duties gets monitored. Though monitoring compliance may be expensive, this cost is counterbalanced with a certain amount of benefit within the regulatory process.[9]

2 Through punishment of deviance, the Act intends to preserve legally established standardized duties which will presumably facilitate performance and delivery. Thus, punishment serves to ensure that standard duties are fulfilled.

From the preceding list, punishment becomes an instrument to protect standard duties which in themselves need not guarantee realization of predetermined effects. Existence of legal standards of performance can contribute to actual delivery and effectiveness of disaster legislations. It is time to move beyond standard duties to standards of performance. Standards of performance, also referred to as standard-setting, when incorporated into disaster laws, act as necessary criteria of evaluation and accountability.

Accountability sans standards of performance

In the middle of June 2013, the Indian state of Uttarakhand garnered national and global attention. Cloudburst along with landslides, torrential rainfall and massive floods swept away human settlements and livestock; damaged houses, buildings, infrastructures, places of work and worship; and affected tourism, economy and policies. The worse-hit regions of Rudraprayag, Uttarkashi and Chamoli were popular religious sites thronging with pilgrims from India and abroad.[10]

The Uttarakhand tragedy was a combination of natural and man-made disasters. Also called the 'Himalayan tsunami', the consequential devastation was a classic example of emergency un-preparedness. The Comptroller and Auditor General of India (CAG) submitted its report in April 2013 with acerbic remarks on the lack of disaster preparations in the state.

Governance lapses to the makings of the Uttarakhand catastrophe

1 The Uttarakhand Disaster Mitigation and Management Center (DMMC), headed by the chief minister, failed to issue warnings in advance in the state.

2 The report found that the DMMC held no meetings in the past six years.
3 From 2000 onwards, the average tenure of each chief minister had been for two years. This political instability resulted in unplanned development, corruption and disgruntled bureaucracy.
4 The state failed to develop systems of early warning, forecasting and disseminating rainfall- and landslide-related information.
5 The state did not use technology which could predict cloudburst at least three hours in advance. A Doppler radar can discern the intensity of precipitation, direction and speed of wind, and forecast severe storms and heavy rainfall. The information generated by the Doppler radar system facilitates in disseminating weather-related notifications and warnings ahead of disasters. Though funds for the Doppler radar system were sanctioned for Uttarakhand in 2008, it was not purchased due to lack of coordination between the Uttarakhand government, National Disaster Management Authority (NDMA), Indian Meteorological Department (IMD) and Ministry of Earth Sciences.[11]
6 The apex body in disaster management, NDMA, was blamed for non-completion of major disaster preparedness projects on time, selection of projects without proper research work and abandonment of projects midway due to improper planning. The NDMA started an airborne laser terrain mapping and digital camera system, but the CAG report cited inefficiencies in the project implementation. It observed a highly disproportionate technology funding in comparison to the flood-prone areas mapped. The NDMA delayed the installation of the satellite-based communication network for disaster management and Doppler weather radars.[12]
7 The NDMA depends on flood forecasts by the Central Water Commission (CWC). However, the CWC did not have a flood forecasting in Uttarakhand which contributed to lack of information on swelling rivers in the state. The CWC also said that its flood forecasting technology could predict only a few hours in advance.[13]
8 The National Remote Sensing Agency (NRSA) had drawn an action plan for an area of 5 lakh square kilometres in five years. The CAG noticed that survey of the aforementioned area was conducted till August 2010 and data was acquired for only 38,020 square kilometres as against the target of 60,000 square kilometres.

Legal aspects to the makings of the Uttarakhand catastrophe

1 The CAG report indicated neither the state formulated State Disaster Management Plan nor the NDMA outlined National Disaster Management Plan. The latter did not have binding provisions for state governments.[14]
2 The Uttarakhand DMMC lacked resources or infrastructure to carry out disaster management in 2013. Even after seven years of the passage of the Disaster Management Act (2005), the National Disaster Management Plan was absent in 2013.
3 The apex body also suffered from want of strong leadership and coordination in the hierarchy of command.[15] When the Uttarakhand State Disaster Management Plan was eventually formulated, it still lacked in many techno-legal aspects. The plan failed to incorporate guidelines on construction of buildings, mapping of flood-prone regions and safe zones, dissemination of weather warnings in sensitive areas at the earliest to avoid panic and chaos, making people (local and pilgrims) to move towards safe places, protection of telecom lines in disaster-prone places.
4 Finally, reasons for the deadly disaster were also attributed to the extensive proliferation of hydro-power projects and flourishing tourist industry, particularly religious tourism, which brought about unprecedented scale of destruction of forest cover and put immense pressure on land. In short, the disaster was said to be an outcome of unplanned development in the Uttarakhand state.[16]

Hazards may degenerate into disasters due to government negligence, indiscretion and delays. The disastrous tragedy in Uttarakhand seemed to be no less. In the current times, bureaucratic performance remains limited to roles/obligations as given in statutes. Whether these roles/obligations yield desired results is not yet addressed by disaster laws. As disaster laws stop short of standards of performance, it makes accountability nominal. Standard-setting embedded in disaster laws becomes immensely relevant in the light of the aforementioned lapses. Disaster laws must also include provisions for regular review of standards.

Lessons learnt from Himalayan tsunami in 2013 and CAG Report

One of the main reasons for the devastating disaster in Uttarakhand was indifference towards early warning technologies by the state government. For a Herculean task like disaster management, the use of technology contributes to scientific disaster preparedness. Technology must be goal-oriented, and technological performance must be evaluated to ensure that the goal is reached. Disaster laws must incorporate standard-setting in the context of disaster-related technologies too that will help to attain optimal performance in disaster preparedness.

Interrogating Disaster Management Act, 2005

The Disaster Management Act, 2005, is the supreme text on disaster preparedness in the country. An examination of the Act revealed a conspicuous absence of standard-setting in early warning technologies. According to the CAG Report, the NDMA failed to ensure the procurement of equipment in the Uttarakhand state.[17] Particularly, the Doppler radar system could not be procured due to coordination problems between NDMA, the Uttarakhand government, Indian Meteorological Department (IMD) and Ministry of Earth Sciences.[18] Though NDMA's underperformance was an accomplice in the disaster, it also reinforced the need to set standards in the Act for the acquisition of essential technology and routine appraisal of the performance of the available technology.

Interrogating National Disaster Management Policy, 2009

The vision underlined in the National Disaster Management Policy 2009 intends

> to build a safe and disaster resilient India by developing a holistic, proactive, multi-disaster oriented and technology driven strategy through a culture of prevention, mitigation, preparedness and response.[19]

For the realization of the vision, this policy document unequivocally emphasizes the use of a range of technologies. It advocates

1. Risk assessment and vulnerability mapping on the part of all central ministries and departments and national agencies
2. Knowledge-based institutions and disaster management authorities at the state and district levels to demarcate hazardous zones through geographic information system (GIS) in association with National Database for Emergency Management (NDEM) and National Spatial Data Infrastructure (NSDI) and remote sensing data. As the preliminary step, this will facilitate vulnerability analysis within a multi-hazard framework.[20]

3 The establishment, upgradation and modernization of forecasting and early warning technological systems for all kinds of disasters
4 The duty of NDMA entails monitoring and surveillance of specific natural disasters, identifying technological loopholes and formulating projects technological advancement in a timely schedule[21]
5 Collaboration is a permanent feature in disaster preparedness. All the states are bound to set up required infrastructure for upgradation or development of meteorological observation systems for the IMD
6 Collaboration impresses sharing of thematic and spatial data for which the Indian GIS, remote sensing and global positioning systems (GPS) have been connected to a designated electronic clearing house.
7 The centre is encouraged to create partnerships with the World Meteorological Organisation (WMO), Pacific Tsunami Warning System and other regional and global institutions.[22]
8 The NSDI, conceived by the Survey of India, collects, compiles, analyses and prepares value-added maps for multi-organisational usage such as management of natural resources, industrial applications and more. The policy document notes that the NSDI should move towards inter-operability of data and information-sharing protocols to allow valuable policy analysis.
9 The NSDI would be linked with the proposed National Disaster Emergency Communication Network for fast and immediate sharing of spatial and non-spatial databases in a secure environment to overcome information deficiencies in disaster management.[23]
10 The Information and Communications Technology (ICT) must aid decision makers and disaster managers at all levels in emergency governance, disseminate advance warnings and information warnings in real time to the bureaucracy and the threatened community through broadcasting media such as television and radio that have larger geographical reach and audience and ensure reliable connectivity with the site of disaster for rescue and relief operations.[24] The policy document recognizes the utility of state-of-the-art IT infrastructure for successful disaster management.
11 National Disaster Management Policy proposes introduction of emergency operations centres (EOCs) at national, state, metro and district levels equipped with state-of-the-art ICT. It strongly recommends the construction of IT infrastructures inclusive of IT processes, architecture and skills for instant upgradation and updating data sets obtained from several public bodies dedicated to disaster monitoring.

12 National Disaster Management Policy suggests the establishment of a National Emergency Communication Network that combines contemporary space and terrestrial-based technologies 'in a highly synergistic configuration and with considerable redundancy' to circulate real-time warnings and information to the susceptible and affected communities and local authorities.[25]

13 An important dimension in this document is the section on compliance regime. It appreciates the need for a 'sound compliance regime, with binding consequences, to ensure the effectiveness of techno-legal and techno-financial provisions'.[26] The compliance regime should be present at the centre and state levels to inculcate best management practices such as self-certification, social audit, external audit by professional agencies and design of IT-enabled monitoring software to appropriate for disaster management systems in India. It will be the duty of concerned stakeholders to implement the provisions of the compliance regime.[27]

The policy document paints a hopeful picture of emergency governance on the basis of advanced technology as well as myriad collaborations. One only wished that this policy was as true in books as in reality. Like the Disaster Management Act, 2005, this policy too remains silent on the need and procedure for standard-setting to evaluate the effectiveness of all the aforementioned arrangements. Benchmarks help to translate a policy into enforceable actions.

It has a vital role in determining both quality and quantity of technological impact in disaster-prone regions.

Interrogating Uttarakhand's State Disaster Management Plan

Like the National Disaster Management Policy, 2009, the Uttarakhand State Disaster Management Plan calls forth a techno-legal regime. It asserts for appropriate urgent changes to avoid piling on the already-existing vulnerabilities. It necessitates the constitution of a strict compliance mechanism also.[28] In the fifth chapter, 'Early Warning', it specifies the tasks of the State Emergency Operations Centre (SEOC), that is, it must coordinate with IMD, CWC and GSI to obtain the latest information and disseminate warning of any likely emergency. Some of the key responsibilities include:

1 Coordination with local technical agencies which forecast different hazards

2 Establishment of reliable communication system as well as alternative communication systems as back-up in times of collapse of the main system
3 Coordination with media for dissemination of information
4 Creation of awareness among all stakeholders and persuading them to effectively use early warning technologies

The first official oversight that strikes a reader is the absence of the date of publication of the state plan document. One can only assume that this document came after the acerbic CAG report in 2013. The plan document wishes to instill credibility in the system through assured delivery of messages to concerned officials only.[29] Ironically, the state depends on communication equipments only to the neglect of vital early warning technologies such as GIS, GPS, remote sensing, Doppler radar, cloudburst technology and so on.

Standard-setting: an indispensable tool for implementing disaster law

Standards demand compliance to a certain quality of performance. Compliance preserves sanctity of any law. One may deduce that quality of performance imports sanctity to the law. This holds true for disaster laws too. Since standard-setting enhances the value of disaster laws, it becomes an indispensable asset to reckon with. The process of standard-setting is complex. The complexity arises from a host of factors which may be political, financial, cultural, logistical and more. Who decides what kinds of standards should be set, where they should be set and which medium they should be set often trigger rivalry among competing institutions. Questions of cost-benefit ratio in standard-setting prompt economic advisers into heated deliberations, while issues of unintended effects/consequences of standard-setting on subjects ruffle humanist groups. Uncertainties and variations in mathematically testing compliance to standards bring in procedural convolutions.[30] Thus, disaster laws have to meaningfully engage with multiple challenges that come in the wake of construction of standards.

Standards are set on the basis of certain criteria. A criterion suggests a way of trying to make a correct judgement. The nature of criteria depends upon the type of standard needed. Yet, the oft-quoted criteria are attainability and human exposure.[31] There are three approaches which best delineate the standard-criteria typology.[32]

1 Survival approach: Here the main criterion is the survival of the species. The concern is to ensure that pollution or hazardous circumstances remain at a level that avoids chronic irreversible illness and death. This level, generally, alludes to the zone of minimum pollution or hazardous circumstances control where the health zone is either at or just above the level of chronic illness and impaired performance.
2 Cost-benefit analysis approach: Here the prime criterion compares the cost of pollution or hazardous circumstances with the economic loss produced by pollution or hazardous circumstances.
3 Aesthetic approach: Also called the 'luxury strategy', here the essential criterion aims to minimize any effect of pollutants or hazardous circumstances through control measures till health effects or material damage does not manifest. The gap between the cost of control measures and the minimum cost of pollution or hazardous circumstances control measures amounts to 'aesthetic cost'. This cost is uneconomical to be borne by industries and ought to be provided by state sponsorship.

The criteria act as a pointer to public officials regarding levels they should achieve to retain previous quality of environment.[33] Adjudging criteria is difficult for two reasons:[34]

- Technical data on environmental effects may be incomplete or lacking. If data is available, it has limitations and is open to scientific criticism but continues to still be the best available data.
- Consensus on a variety of criteria is ultimately a political decision. Given the broad range of possible figures more or less closely linked to predictable effects, the accepted ones are the outcomes of drawn-out struggles and negotiations among interested parties involved in regulation.

The application of standard-setting helps an environment administrator to judge the extent of achievement of predetermined environmental goals. To an environment administrator, standard-setting acts like an operational information system that assists him or her to determine the extent of progress in the implementation of his or her own managerial goals and policy goals. Further, an impact assessment informs whether the implemented programme improved environmental quality. This knowledge may be fed into the process of standard-setting which could make disaster laws unambiguous, comprehensive and responsive.

How does ICT befit standard-setting?

At present, standard-setting is conspicuously lacking in disaster management law, National Disaster Management Plan and State Disaster Management Plans in India. The need of the hour demands that standard-setting should have legislative support and should be incorporated into technology for the larger cause of optimal disaster preparedness. An example of standard-setting, standard of performance and terminologies would be highly relevant here. Different environment administrators should be on the same page with respect to terminologies. After the fateful Uttarakhand disaster, the NDMA vice chairman blamed IMD: 'Lives could have been saved if the weather office had issued precise forecasts. The IMD followed a standard format of weather forecast and used certain terminologies like rainfall, heavy rainfall, but how are we supposed to translate it into action? They need to pinpoint where and how much it is going to rain.'[35] This urges standardization of terminologies among scientific bodies, weather monitoring agencies and public authorities on disaster management. When same standard terms are interpreted differently by different organizations, it adversely affects performance. If standards were shared among them, the Uttarakhand disaster could have been well managed.

This makes the case for shared methodology in standard-setting in emergency governance. There are five types of approaches in setting quantitative standards:[36]

1 **Safe levels:** This refers to the level where pollutant or human activity will not cause debilitating effect on the subject group or where adverse effects will be exceptional. This approach does not precisely define 'safe', nor does it provide an account of approximate costs. The intention is to derive maximum benefit irrespective of costs.
2 **Prudent reduction:** This refers to reduction in the present level to a practical level. Since a 'safe' level may not be identified due to imperfect scientific understanding or exorbitant costs of achievement, an attempt towards reducing the present levels is a feasible solution.
3 **Precautionary principle:** This is a commonly applied general principle which reiterates the need to follow 'safe' or 'prudent' level. This principle is also linked to the polluter pays principle.
4 **BATNEC:** This refers to the 'Best Available Technology Not Entailing Excessive Cost' approach. This approach acknowledges the high costs involved to achieve a 'safe' level. It, therefore, expresses that the aim is to reduce costs through the use of best available technology. However, it omits any consideration of effects and befits in a formal or explicit manner.

5 **ALARA:** This refers to the 'As low as reasonably achievable' approach. Here, the emphasis is on the use of latest and best technological and other aids and procedures to achieve 'safe' or 'prudential' levels and outcomes that are ALARA.

In the context of India, standards may be set as explained earlier or tailored to suit country-specific features or peculiarities. The development of explicit and comprehensive standards that are legally backed can bring strict commitment and accountability in disaster preparedness among public authorities. These standards relate to plans, procedures, logistics and technological performance, to mention a few. The Third Report of the Second Administrative Reforms Commission (2006) intends to bridge the chasm from despair to hope by suggesting innovative ways that expedite emergency responses of administration and raise effectiveness of the administrative machinery for the purpose of crisis preparedness.[37] There must be adequate investment in technology, early warning systems as well as relief strategies. Nevertheless, it must not be assumed that presence of technology itself is a boon. To what capacity technology is being used will determine its usefulness. This essentially indicates that optimal use of technology is contingent upon standard-setting.

What are best practices in the administration of ICTs for disaster management? On one hand, it was observed that ICTs befit standard-setting through BATNEC and ALARA approaches. On the other hand, effective implementation of ICTs would require pertinent legal and viable parameters whose compliance is regularly checked by a team of experts. Decision makers are dependent on ICTs for cyclone, floods, drought, landslides, earthquake and tsunami warnings. It is not adequate for state-of-the-art early warning systems to be meticulously designed and installed. Whether installed capacities comply with standard operating procedures and standards of performance like data capture, transmission and dissemination should be examined before and after every disaster.[38] Legal parameters of evaluation should focus on improvements that increase precision, prediction, analysis and transmission, as well as rectify areas of coordination problems that yield false or delayed information.

Findings and recommendations

Modern-day disaster management rests on the utilities of sophisticated technology which can forecast and warn in advance. This permits time for preventive and mitigation measures. Developed countries such as the United States, the United Kingdom, Australia and Japan have their respective disaster management legislations and disaster-related technologies. India could do well if it made a comparative study of the laws and technological apparatus used by these countries for prediction, prevention and mitigation of disasters. Human resources should be trained in the scientific application of disaster-related technologies. The training module could include discourse on and best practices from developed countries in disaster management.

An important aspect of developing disaster laws relates to the issue of standard-setting. Standards, incorporated within the legal framework, act as criteria that can pull up performance and facilitate compliance to legal conditions of performance. The compliance factor evinces the element of accountability. In a way, accountability and standards of performance are directly proportional to each other whereby each influences the other similarly. Low accountability will yield low standards of performance and vice versa. In the context of ICTs, standards serve as a two-pronged strategy. First, it insists on maximum output which matches with the desired goals as stated in the policy and plan documents. In doing so, technology is not underused, making the expensive investment worthwhile. Second, it helps to achieve the desired effect on target or vulnerable community.

Conclusion

In this chapter, it was argued that disaster laws require standard-setting to extract optimal performance, plug loopholes and improve accountability in current disaster preparedness. Since standard-setting augments performance of disaster laws, there was a need to legally endorse the same. In the context of ICTs, it intends to respond to failures in achieving optimal emergency governance. Using the case study of the Uttarakhand disaster in 2013, it was highlighted that standard-setting could help to evaluate level of preparedness, attain public goals and measure effectiveness of environmental programmes. Moreover, standard-setting could help to overcome inefficient utilisation of technologies and erroneous or biased measurement of the effectiveness of environmental programmes and facilitate punishment for non-compliance of technical parameters. This chapter aimed to demonstrate that disaster laws could become more forceful with legal parameters that address governance frailties and improve emergency governance.

Notes

1 Chakrabarti (2009, p. 11).
2 Alex (2006, p. 1).
3 Ibid., pp. 1–2.
4 Barnett and O'Hagan (1997, p. 1).

5 Lohani (1984, p. 99); Also refer J. E. McKee and H. W. Wolf (1963). *Water Quality Criteria*, California: California State Water Resources Control Board.
6 Lohani (1984, p. 103).
7 Barnett and O'Hagan (1997, p. 2).
8 Preface, Third Report of the Second Administrative Reforms Commission (2006, September). 'Crisis Management from Despair to Hope'. Second Administrative Reforms Commission, Government of India, New Delhi. Retrieved from http://arc.gov.in/3rdreport.pdf
9 Barnett and O'Hagan (1997, p. 1).
10 Kavita Upadhyay (2013, 22 June). 'Uttarakhand Floods: Disaster Management in Disarray'. Retrieved from www.thehindu.com/news/national/uttarakhand-floods-disaster-management-in-disarray/article4840973.ece (Accessed 20 August 2014).
11 Sreelatha Menon (2013, 20 July). 'Disaster Management Authority a Disaster?' Retrieved from www.business-standard.com/article/economy-policy/disaster-management-authority-a-disaster-113072000633_1.html (Accessed 20 August 2014).
12 Express News Service (2013, 24 April). 'CAG Exposes Underbelly of Disaster Management Authority'. Retrieved from www.newindianexpress.com/nation/CAG-exposes-underbelly-of-Disaster-Management-Authority/2013/04/24/article1558958.ece (Accessed 20 August 2014).
13 Menon, 'Disaster Management Authority a Disaster?'.
14 Krishna Uppuluri (2014, 16 June). 'A Year on after Uttarakhand Disaster, Disaster Management Agencies Yet to Learn'. Retrieved from www.dnaindia.com/india/report-a-year-on-after-uttarakhand-disaster-disaster-management-agencies-yet-to-learn-1995997 (Accessed 20 August 2014).
15 Abhishek Bhalla and Bhuvan Bagga (2013, 24 June). 'The Uttarakhand Tragedy Casts Shame on India's Disaster Management. So Why DID the Committee Meant to Plan for Flood Emergencies Fail to Meet for FOUR YEARS?' Retrieved from www.dailymail.co.uk/indiahome/indianews/article-2347624/NDMA-The-Uttarakhand-tragedy-casts-shame-Indias-disaster-management-So-DID-committee-meant-plan-flood-emergencies-fail-meet-FOUR-YEARS.html (Accessed July 2014).
16 Jyotsna Singh and Soma Basu (2013, 18 June). 'Man-Made Reasons for Uttarakhand Disaster'. Retrieved from www.downtoearth.org.in/content/man-made-reasons-uttarakhand-disaster (Accessed July 2014).
17 Bhalla and Bagga, 'The Uttarakhand Tragedy Casts Shame on India's Disaster Management'.
18 Menon, 'Disaster Management Authority a Disaster?'.
19 National Disaster Management Authority (2009, 22 October). 'National Policy on Disaster Management 2009'. Ministry of Home Affairs, Government of India, p. 7. Retrieved from http://ndma.gov.in/images/guidelines/national-dm-policy2009.pdf
20 Ibid., p. 17.
21 Ibid., p. 19.
22 Ibid.
23 Ibid., p. 17.
24 Ibid., p.19.
25 Ibid.

26 Ibid., p. 24.
27 Ibid.
28 State Disaster Management Authority. 'State Disaster Management Plan'. Government of Uttarakhand, p. 37. Retrieved from http://dmmc.uk.gov.in/files/pdf/sdmp_final.pdf
29 Ibid., p. 42.
30 Ibid., pp. 7, 15.
31 Lohani (1984, p. 99); also refer McKee and Wolf, *Water Quality Criteria*.
32 Lohani (1984, pp. 102–103).
33 Barnett and O'Hagan (1997, pp. 171–172).
34 Ibid., p. 172.
35 Bhalla and Bagga, 'The Uttarakhand Tragedy Casts Shame on India's Disaster Management'.
36 Barnett and O'Hagan (1997, pp. 37–38).
37 Preface, Third Report of the Second Administrative Reforms Commission (2006, September), 'Crisis Management from Despair to Hope'.
38 Ibid., p. 71.

References

Alex, J. P. (2006). *Disaster Management: Towards a Legal Framework*. New Delhi: The Indian Institute of Public Administration. Retrieved from www.iipa.org.in/common/pdf/12.pdf

Barnett, V. & O'Hagan, A. (1997). *Setting Environmental Standards: The Statistical Approach to Handling Uncertainty and Variation*. London: Chapman and Hall.

Bhalla, A. & Bagga, B. (24 June, 2013). The Uttarakhand Tragedy Casts Shame on India's Disaster Management: So Why DID the Committee Meant to Plan for Flood Emergencies Fail to Meet for Four Years? *Daily Mail*. Retrieved from www.dailymail.co.uk/indiahome/indianews/article-2347624/NDMA-The-Uttarakhand-tragedy-casts-shame-Indias-disaster-management-So-DID-committee-meant-plan-flood-emergencies-fail-meet-FOUR-YEARS.html

Chakrabarti, P. G. D. (2009). *Financing Disaster Management In India: A Study for the Thirteenth Finance Commission*. National Institute of Disaster Management. Retrieved from http://fincomindia.nic.in/writereaddata%5Chtml_en_files%5Coldcommission_html/fincom13/discussion/report23.pdf

Express News Service. (24 April, 2013). CAG Exposes Underbelly of Disaster Management Authority. *New Indian Express*. Retrieved from www.newindianexpress.com/nation/CAG-exposes-underbelly-of-Disaster-Management-Authority/2013/04/24/article1558958.ece

Lohani, B. N. (1984) *Environmental Quality Management*. New Delhi: South Asian Publishers.

Menon, S. (July 20, 2013). Disaster Management Authority a Disaster? *Business Standard*. Retrieved from www.business-standard.com/article/economy-policy/disaster-management-authority-a-disaster-113072000633_1.html

National Disaster Management Authority. (22 October, 2009). National Policy on Disaster Management 2009. *Ministry of Home Affairs, Government of India*. Retrieved from http://ndma.gov.in/images/guidelines/national-dm-policy2009.pdf

State Disaster Management Authority. State Disaster Management Plan. *Government of Uttarakhand*. Retrieved from http://dmmc.uk.gov.in/files/pdf/sdmp_final.pdf

Third Report of the Second Administrative Reforms Commission. (September 2006). Crisis Management from Despair to Hope. *Second Administrative Reforms Commission, Government of India, New Delhi*. Retrieved from http://arc.gov.in/3rdreport.pdf

Upadhyay, K. (June 22, 2013). Uttarakhand Floods: Disaster Management in Disarray. *The Hindu*. Retrieved from www.thehindu.com/news/national/uttarakhand-floods-disaster-management-in-disarray/article4840973.ece

Uppuluri, K. (June 16, 2014). A Year on after Uttarakhand Disaster, Disaster Management Agencies Yet to Learn. *DNA India*. Retrieved from www.dnaindia.com/india/report-a-year-on-after-uttarakhand-disaster-disaster-management-agencies-yet-to-learn-1995997

12 Building national resilience through international law

Venkatachalam Anbumozhi

A barrage of shocks – both natural and man-made – has taken its toll on countries and communities in recent years. This raises an urgent question: how communities and governments get better at anticipating, preventing, coping with and recovering from disasters?

For the past 47 years, the Association of Southeast Asian Nations (ASEAN) has been an integral part of Asia's ongoing sociopolitical and economic transformation and remains an example for other regional groups such as the South Asian Association for Regional Cooperation (SARRC) and the Central Asia Regional Economic Cooperation (CAREC) of how carefully crafted cooperation can benefit all members even if these members are extremely diverse in size, geography, culture, income level and resource endowment. Today, the ASEAN needs to consider how to move to new stages of integration, beyond open economic means. It will find merit in forging a longer-term strategy towards the shared prosperity of its members.

Achieving a fully resilient ASEAN by 2030 is an ambitious target. Climate change is becoming one of the greatest economic, social and environmental challenges of our time, the response to which will impact all future generations. To respond to this heightened threat, 168 member states of the United Nations (UN) adopted the Hyogo Framework for Action (HFA) in 2005 as a means of bolstering the resilience of nations and communities against disasters with the objective of reducing disaster risk. Resilience refers to the capacity of Asian member states (AMS) to handle volatility and shocks from within and outside the region, thus reducing the vulnerability of households and economies. The HFA forms part of a growing number of international declarations, frameworks and agreements indicating both recognition of the links between disaster risk reduction (DRR), poverty reduction and climate change and a growing political commitment to address these issues. The global momentum towards greater prioritisation of

DRR has received support from various AMS which now realise that much can be done to minimise the impact of disasters before they occur and that, without action, more extreme weather events in the future are likely to increase the number, scale and impact of disasters. The ASEAN strives to attain its centrality and leadership in these challenges through the ASEAN Agreement on Disaster Management Emergency Response.

In a region already undergoing dangerous climate change and disaster-related ills, there is widespread understanding among policymakers that environmental objectives need a higher profile alongside poverty reduction as all these three are intertwined. The Millennium Development Goals have become a type of global report card for the fight against poverty for the past 15 years. AMS have made substantial progress towards the achievement of the Millennium Development Goals although the progress has been highly variable across AMS. As a successor to the Millennium Development Goals, the world's governments are poised to adopt a set of sustainable development goals (SDGs). The SDGs are an important idea and could help finally move the region into a sustainable trajectory by addressing issues like natural disasters, which are, in part, linked to climate change.

Addressing these three issues simultaneously requires a change from business-as-usual practices to practices that have net positive benefits in terms of disaster risk management (DRM), climate change adaptation (CCA) and sustainable development. ASEAN's economic growth will be rapid and sustainable but can also be made resilient if opportunities for convergence are fully utilised. This chapter reviews regional and global developments on these three frontiers as well as emerging issues post-2015 that will have an impact on the ASEAN cultural community. In that process, it refers to recent ASEAN studies on the regional HFA monitoring of DRR and the ASEAN Agreement on Disaster Management Emergency Response work programmes.

This chapter begins by assessing the similarities and differences among DRM,[1] CCA[2] and SDGs[3] before examining what is at stake if these three agendas do not converge at the regional, national and local levels. It then presents updated evidence where DRM, CCA and SDGs are already converging followed by an analysis of obstacles and opportunities in further convergence. The material presented in this review is drawn from an analysis of the country reports covering progress towards the implementation of the HFA, National Action Plans for Climate Change and National Adaptation Programmes of Action (NAPAs) across ASEAN countries, global literature, consultation with key actors and international organisations, and from the author's own experience of working in this field.

The nexus in disaster risk management-climate change adaptation-sustainable development goals

Over the past 20 years, the ASEAN brought the AMS together in two important global efforts: Agenda 21, which set out a strategy for achieving sustainable development, and the Millennium Development Goals, which were aimed at improving the life of the region's poorest and most vulnerable by 2015. The links between sustainable development, DRM and CCA may be understood with the help of a diagram. Figure 12.1 presents the triangular relationships between DRM, CCA and SDG.

To begin with, a distinction may be made between the two kinds of impact of climate change. One is in terms of a rise in average temperatures and sea levels. This appears to be the focus of discussion and scientific enquiry in much of the climate change literature, at least in the early years when the discipline developed. The other impact takes the form of increased weather variability (e.g. changes in rain patterns and an increase in extreme weather events). It is primarily the latter which has implications for disaster risks facing a community, country or region. In Figure 12.1, these two effects are represented by the arrows cv (denoting rise in average temperatures and sea levels) and cd (denoting increased weather variability).

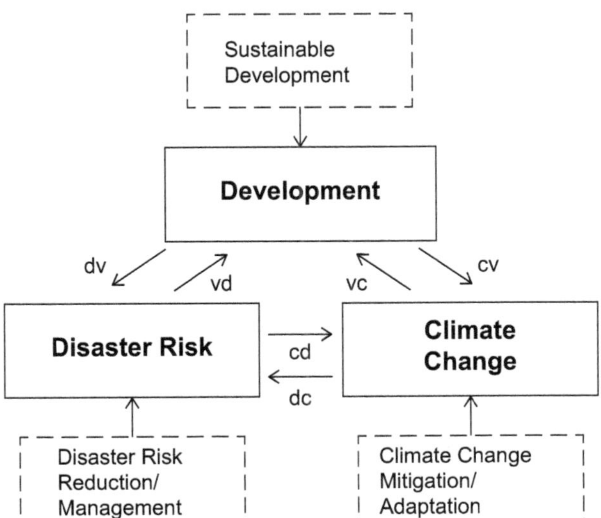

Figure 12.1 Linkage between disaster risk management, climate change adaptation and sustainable development goals

Source: Author.

In the literature, while the first effect is seen as long term, the second is primarily considered as short term. However, this is arguable. The second effect can be long term as well as short term. It may yet to be found that there is insufficient scientific evidence to predict the increased weather variability many decades into the future. Nevertheless, there can be no denial that increased weather variability can happen over the long term as well as the short term. It seems that the second effect is primarily seen as short term because while the predicted long-term changes in temperatures and sea levels will, of course, take time to materialise, the variability effect may already be with us. Additionally, it seems to be because, for various reasons, disasters and our responses to them have historically been treated as a short-term matter. There is, however, no reason why this approach should continue.

Increased weather variability increases disaster risks directly and indirectly. First, increased weather variability can, of course, worsen weather-related hazards. However, coupled with other intervening factors such as environmental degradation and ecosystem destruction exacerbated by particular models of development, it can also change the level of exposure and vulnerability of communities in question to certain hazards, thus raising the combined disaster risks facing a community. In Figure 12.1, such indirect effect would be indicated by the cv arrow to 'development' and then by the vd arrow down to 'disaster risk'.

The impact of a disaster on development has, of course, been well recognised and is indicated in the diagram by the arrow dv. Table 12.1 summarises the lives and property lost in major disasters in Asia from 2004 to 2013.

Table 12.1 Impact of major disasters in Asia 2004–13

Disaster event	*Year*	*Lives lost*	*People affected*	*Economic cost (in US dollars)*
Typhoon Haiyan, Philippines	2013	11,234	350,000 displaced	14 billion
Great East Japan earthquake	2011	19,846	470,000 evacuated	210–375 billion
Thailand floods	2011	813	9.5 million	40–45.7 billion
Cyclone Nargis, Myanmar	2008	138,366	2.4 million	4 million
Wenchuan earthquake, China	2008	87,476	45.6 million	120 million
Indian Ocean tsunami	2004	226,408	1.3 million	2.9 billion

Source: EM-DAT: The OFDA/CRED International Disaster Database.

This direct or indirect impact can be on humans and/or the economy and the livelihoods of people. Even though the impact of a disaster on development is well recognised, it is, in fact, only the direct impact that has been reasonably well recorded and understood thus far. The wider research community and policymakers still have a long way to go to understand the indirect impact of a disaster on development, whether the impact is on a community, a country or economy, and indeed even on other economies and countries through regional and global supply chains and production networks.

Historically, the disaster risk research community has been concerned with studying only this impact. More recently, there has been a growing recognition that there is a reverse impact of development on disaster risks that needs to be considered and understood. How development is managed and achieved can have a profound impact on the disaster risks facing a community, an AMS or the region as a whole. Human-induced climate change is a notable example but only one example. Environmental degradation and ecosystem destruction are other examples. It may even be possible that human actions are exerting an impact on earthquake hazards.

The way development is managed and achieved can impact the disaster risks of a community, nation or region by changing the level and pattern of hazards (e.g. climate change) or by changing the level of exposure and vulnerability to given hazards (e.g. urbanisation and migration to unsafe locations and destruction of local ecosystems). This impact is indicated in the diagram by arrow vd.

Indeed, disaster risks could even have an impact on climate change. A good example of this is the Great East Japan earthquake causing a massive tsunami which, in turn, destroyed the Fukushima Daiichi nuclear plant. This resulted in the cessation of Japan's nuclear power programme and, consequently, increased the use of fossil fuels instead. This cannot be an isolated example. An effect like this is indicated in Figure 12.1 by the arrow dc.

The possible effect of sustainable development – or how it is managed and achieved – on disaster risks has already been noted, and there is, by now, hardly any controversy over the effect of development on climate change as indicated by arrow vc in the diagram. Figure 12.2 illustrates the estimated impact of climate change in five Southeast Asian countries.

At the policy level, the imperatives and objectives of sustainable development must, of course, call for adequate efforts to reduce disaster risks and limit the scale of climate change. However, as long as such risks and change cannot be completely eliminated, appropriate actions to manage the remaining risks as well as to adapt to, and to be prepared for, possible outcomes would be critical.

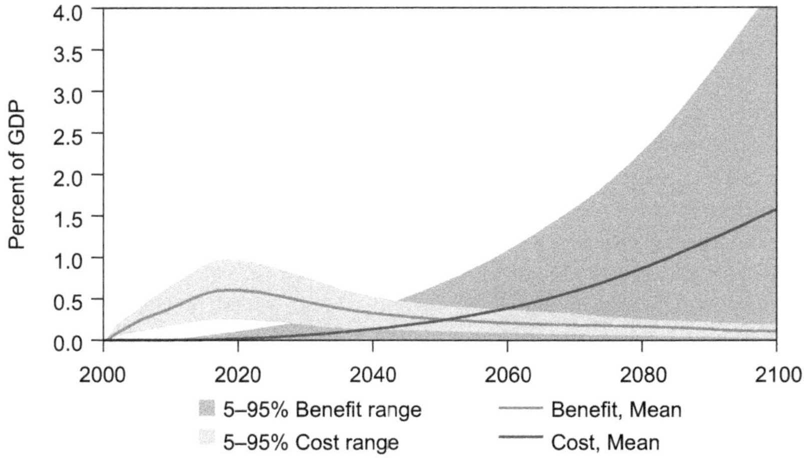

Figure 12.2 Economics of climate change adaptation in five Southeast Asian countries

Source: ADB (2009).

We need to note that the full objectives and imperatives of sustainable development would, in fact, go well beyond a call for necessary actions on the DRM and CCA fronts. Environmental and ecosystem protection and sustainable natural resources management are, for example, some other objectives. However, as indicated previously, these other sustainable development policies can contribute to a strengthened system of CCA and DRM as well.

So while a strong DRM and CCA programme are themselves components of a full and sustainable development agenda for an economy or region, other sustainable development-oriented policies can be instrumental to the achievement of these programmes as well, thus creating new opportunities.

A full agenda for sustainable development must include policies and actions to strengthen DRM and CCA. However, because many of their functions and objectives closely overlap, there is a strong need for these two sub-agendas to integrate. Over the past decade, in parallel with the emergence of 'adaptation' as a critical component of the global response to climate change and the institutionalisation of DRR as signalled by the international agreement on HFA, progressively more attention has indeed been given to converging the DRM and CCA agendas both conceptually and in practice at the international, national and subnational levels. However, despite some considerable work, both academic and policy-focused (e.g. Sperling & Szekely, 2005; the 2006 special edition of Disasters; Few et al., 2006; Yamin et al., 2005), the 2009 United Nations Office for Disaster Risk Reduction's (UNISDR) Global Assessment Report on Disaster Risk Reduction (GAR/DRR) concludes that the majority of national processes for tackling DRR and CCA still exist in parallel and have separate policy and institutional frameworks. For historical reasons, the CCA and DRM agendas have evolved and developed separately in AMS, which is summarised and illustrated in Figure 12.3.

Both DRM and CCA aim to reduce the impacts of shocks by anticipating risks and uncertainties and addressing vulnerabilities. Addressing disaster risk across multiple scales in multiple sectors as well as integrating CCA into planning decisions has now become government policy (Anbumozhi, 2012). Indeed, as noted, a significant portion of climate change impacts will take the form of exacerbating climate variability, and as far as this portion of the impact is concerned, a CCA agenda should be no different from a DRR agenda. Both should have the same functions and objectives. That being so, to avoid duplication, minimise interdepartmental rivalry, exploit potential synergies and increase the effectiveness and efficiency of both programmes, there is an overwhelming case for their close integration.

Disaster risk management in the framework conventions/ conference of the parties' meetings on climate change

There is limited mention of DRM in international frameworks on CCA. The UNFCCC itself mentions the need for special attention for developing countries prone to natural disasters but has no references to the concept of hazard or disaster risk. Climate change, as framed by the UNFCCC, has tended to concentrate on long-term climatic changes rather than extremes and shocks associated with current climate variability. This has made it politically challenging to integrate substantial text tying CCA to DRM in the UNFCCC since DRM is perceived as only being concerned with current climate variability rather than more gradual, long-term changes. In recent years, however, the attention for climate risk management has grown substantially as governments recognise the importance of linking CCA and DRR and as more disasters associated with hydro-meteorological hazards have occurred.

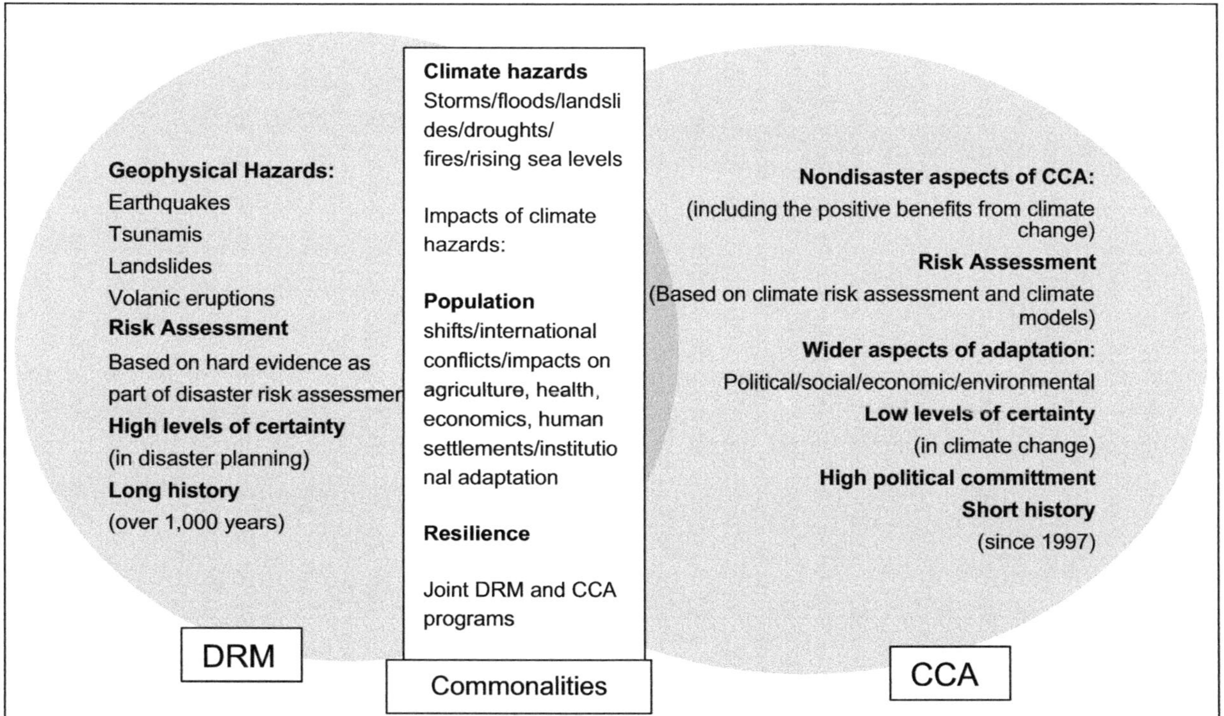

Figure 12.3 Content and commonalities between the disaster risk management and climate change adaptation agendas

Source: Author.

DRM, however, is prominently featured in the 2007 Bali Plan of Action, the 2010 Copenhagen Accord and the 2013 Durban Platform, which highlights DRM as a critical tool for CCA, opening up a range of possibilities for integration of CCA in DRM strategies. The Durban document is a crucial landmark for the 'convergence agenda', recognising the need for enhanced action on adaptation including 'disaster reduction strategies and means to address loss and damage associated with climate change impacts in developing countries that are particularly vulnerable to the adverse effects of climate change' (UNFCCC, 2006). More recently, the Subsidiary Body for Science and Technological Advice of the UNFCCC, in preparation for the 14th COP, produced a series of background papers on issues at the interface of DRR and CCA. These papers informed a session of the UNFCCC Ad Hoc Working Group on Long-term Collaborative Action, the main forum for discussions on the post-2012 agreement. The session on risk management and risk reduction strategies, including risk sharing and transfer mechanisms, focused on the value of DRM and the HFA in supporting CCA in a post-2012 agreement, and parties formally recognised the need for a 'common framework' between DRM and adaptation.

Climate change in the Hyogo Framework for Action

International frameworks on DRM are better at converging DRM with CCA but possess insufficient political clout to alter perceptions on development. The HFA provides an international framework for action on DRR. It is signed by 168 countries, is endorsed by the UN General Assembly and is supported by the UN International Strategy for Disaster Reduction (UNISDR) Secretariat. Unlike the UNFCCC, the HFA does not contain an inherent financial mechanism and is not legally binding. The HFA explicitly integrates the need to anticipate changing risks due to global climate change (even though at the time of the negotiations on the HFA, which took place before the IPCC Fourth Assessment Report came out, certain states objected to using strong language on climate change). The HFA also specifically states that regional and international organisations and other actors commit to promoting 'the integration of risk reduction associated with existing climate variability and future climate change into strategies for DRM and CCA to climate change, which would include the clear identification of climate-related disaster risks' (HFA, 2005). For the past two years, the UNISDR has strongly advocated for the integration of DRM and CCA as a critical component of the HFA's implementation agenda. The UNISDR has published and widely circulated integration approaches and a collection of national-level good practices. It has also become involved in a range of activities designed to enhance convergence, including a mapping of DRR and CCA policies and frameworks at the regional and subregional levels, and has been a key initiator and supporter of the IPCC's special report. However, early indications from the midterm review of the HFA suggest that the UNISDR should be doing more to support convergence. Consequently, the UNISDR launched a series of consultations in 2010 on how CCA can be better integrated into the HFA.

Convergence in financial mechanisms

One of the major issues for DRM that would be addressed through better convergence with CCA is inadequate funding. DRM is funded through humanitarian aid and is ad hoc and insufficient. CCA has sizeable and increasing funding streams due to its political clout and widespread recognition. At the national level, the division of roles between the national and local governments with regard to funding DRM and CCA reduces funding potential. At the international level, funding for CCA and DRM is driven by two actors: international donors and international funds from development banks. Integrating DRM with CCA would give DRM increased access to funding to implement DRM projects that would, with collaboration from CCA, adequately address future disaster risks.

At the national level, DRM and CCA projects are often implemented by the local government while being funded by the national government. Unfortunately, due to DRM's low political presence, it is often not valued by the state as a critical aspect of development. The 2009 Global Assessment Report shows of the 60 reporting countries assessed on their progress towards meeting HFA priorities on a scale of 1 to 5 (with 1 denoting minor progress and 5 for comprehensive achievement); only five countries achieved a level 5 in the indicator measuring plans and policies. Of these five countries, only two managed a 5 in financing disaster risk reduction. Jackson (2011) notes that 'whilst there is evidence of increased international cooperation on DRM, the (relative) scarcity of national resources allocated to DRM remains a common concern in Yokohama (1994), Hyogo (2005), the GAR (2009), and its midterm review (2010)'.

Jackson (2011) also notes that there are three options to fund DRM projects: create a department, enhance the weight given to the function or create a project. One way to finance DRM is to create a department for project financing. Although it would have presentational advantages, its overlapping mandates and unclear lines of command and accountability with existing departments would breed inefficiencies by duplicating activities, which would ultimately result in inefficient resource allocation. The second option would be to increase the resources provided for DRM across departments. Unfortunately, this is dependent on the department's awareness of DRM and can result in the mandate being ignored in favour of other objectives. The third option is to create a project or programme to specifically address DRM. Although projects have administrative simplicity for the government system and can open up possibilities for collaboration with non-government actors, the project can fail to integrate with mainstream activities and become marginalised. These permanent institutions are essential for adequate DRM funding because DRM is often conceptualised as a short-term strategy. DRM activities are often undertaken by local actors with support from national and international humanitarian actors. DRM is thus often funded by humanitarian actors that provide short-term funding for disaster response, and many countries issue permission for aid agencies to work only on short-term basis. Unfortunately, humanitarian actors provide insufficient aid due to their limited budget. Mechler (2013) notes that the brunt of expenses on disasters is dispensed for post-disaster spending. Only $91 billion, or 2 per cent of total official development assistance (ODA) from 1980 to 2009, was allocated to disaster-related activities, of which only 4 per cent was allocated to pre-event risk management (Mechler, 2013).

In contrast, CCA has significant funding even at the national level. As climate change is viewed as an ongoing problem, states that are focused on mainstreaming CCA into development have created funds specifically targeting CCA projects.

How to harness converging opportunities: the Philippine case

The Philippines is one of the most vulnerable states to natural disasters and is thus one of the states focused on mainstreaming both CCA and DRM into its development agenda. Due to its location in the tropics and the Pacific Ring of Fire, the Philippines is exposed to multiple natural hazards such as typhoons, floods, droughts, earthquakes and volcanic eruptions. Unplanned urbanisation, environmental degradation and global climate change have increased the impact of these hazards, with the Philippines suffering over 6,000 casualties, 23 million affected and $1.3 billion in economic damage over the past 10 years (World Bank, 2013). However, the country recently passed legislation focusing on converging CCA and DRM institutions to promote synergy.

The Philippines recognises its high susceptibility to natural hazards. It established the National Disaster Coordinating Council in 1978 which determines priorities in the allocation of funds, services and relief supplies. The National Disaster Coordinating Council is funded through national and local calamity funds, which come from 5 per cent of the annual budget of the national or local governments. These funds are tied to aid, relief, rehabilitation and reconstruction (Lasco & Delfino, 2010). The National Disaster Coordinating Council is a reactive institution, focusing on addressing disaster preparedness rather than the underlying socio-economic factors that might help reduce risk in future disasters. Thus, it can be said that the Philippines has neither converged CCA with DRR within its institutions nor properly integrated CCA with DRR in the past.

The Philippine government's new legislation, the Climate Change Act of 2009, incorporates climate change concepts into policy and development plans. A review of major development plans and policies showed that CCA has not been mainstreamed in the Philippines with the focus being on mitigation where climate change is recognised. However, the 2009 law and the resulting Climate Change Commission have brought attention to the adaptation side of climate change at the local and national levels by promoting climate change risk management initiatives (Lasco & Delfino, 2010). The newly crafted law considers disasters to be of primary relevance to the overall resilience of the country to climate change. In the overall effort to combat the effects of climate change, DRM will be the primary focus and the framework will concentrate on expanding and upgrading the country's capacity to address and anticipate disasters. Although the 2009 act is focused on addressing climate change, the Philippines will address climate change impacts through DRR measures.

Under the new act, a Climate Change Commission headed by the Philippine president will be created as the sole government policymaking body on climate change. Its primary function is to 'ensure the mainstreaming of climate change, in synergy with disaster risk reduction, into national, sectoral, and local development plans and programmes'. The act also gives local governments the primary responsibility for planning and implementing local climate change action plans, which will be consistent with national frameworks. The Climate Change Act of 2009 also resulted in the development of the National Framework Strategy on Climate Change and the National Climate Change Action Plan, both of which serve as the bases for climate change planning, research and development and harmonisation of related policies and institutions. The act explicitly recognises the overlapping objectives between CCA and DRM, declaring that 'further recognising that climate change and disaster risk reduction are closely interrelated and effective disaster risk reduction will enhance climate change adaptive capacity, the State shall integrate disaster risk reduction into climate change programs and initiatives'. However, the act does not provide a fund for DRM initiatives due to the limited appreciation of the linkage between CCA and DRM, both in the Philippines and globally (ADPC, 2013).

The 2010 National Disaster Risk Reduction and Management Law was designed to 'mainstream disaster risk reduction and climate change in development processes'. It emphasises the paradigm shift from reactive to proactive disaster risk reduction, mandating the need to 'develop and strengthen the capacities of vulnerable and marginalised groups to mitigate, prepare for, respond to and recover from the effects of disasters'. It transforms the present National Disaster Coordinating Council into the National Disaster Risk Reduction and Management Council, an inter-ministerial body. The National Disaster Risk Reduction and Management Council is chaired by the secretary of the Department of National Defense with the secretary of the Department of Interior and Local Government as vice chairperson for disaster preparedness. The council's members also include several ministries as well as the executive director of the Climate Change Office of the Climate Change Commission, thereby integrating several ministries to converge with CCA and with DRR. In addition, the law established the Local Disaster Risk Reduction and Management Fund where no less than 5 per cent of estimated revenue from regular sources will be set aside to support DRR activities.

Figure 12.4 shows the convergence between the CCA process and DRM in certain types of sectoral policies in the Philippines, which need to be recognised for scaling up and replication through regional cooperation. Some other sector-specific policy actions in the Philippine framework include:

(i) Land use planning in areas that are sensitive to climate change and disaster risks

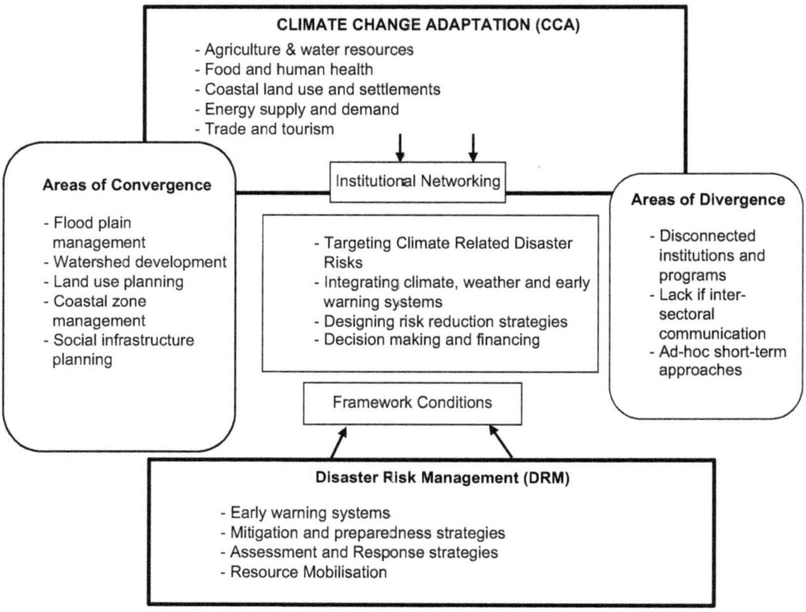

Figure 12.4 Converging and diverging factors of climate change adaptation and disaster risk management in the Philippines

Source: Author.

(ii) River basin floodplain management
(iii) Coastal erosion control and management
(iv) Watershed management programmes
(v) Integrated drought management programmes

The tools and techniques used for DRM such as early warning systems; hazard, risk and vulnerability analysis; risk assessment and monitoring; risk mitigation; and response strategies need to be integrated with critical sectors such as food, water, environmental security, agriculture and tourism. There are success stories and good practices demonstrating such integration, which should be replicated and further scaled up.

On the other hand, there are also many forces that create divergence between CCA and DRM. The institutional arrangements that exist are such that DRM and CCA experts and functionaries are usually different, respond to different needs and to different constituencies and do not have the authority to implement policy decisions in the areas other than their specific responsibilities. Such structural barriers also exist at the regional and international levels. Furthermore, DRM and CCA policies, planning and programmes often take place or exist in isolation without sharing their respective goals, methodologies and objectives. CCA information is inherently complex. For most DRM projects, risks to investments are not considered for the full lifetime of the project, thus ignoring climate change risks, impacts and adaptation factors.

Although the Philippines still faces challenges in integrating CCA with DRR, it has successfully established an inter-ministerial body and fund to promote their convergence. Philippine laws on CCA and DRR have been lauded as the 'best in the world', by the United Nations special DRR representative Margareta Wahlstrom (Ubac, 2012). There are enabling mechanisms for converging DRM and CCA through the integration of appropriate technologies such as information and communications technology (ICT), automatic weather stations, weather radars and so on. Similarly, the networking of DRM and CCA institutions at the national, ASEAN and international levels coupled with multi-stakeholder communication and dialogues as well as exchange of information and expertise may catalyse such integration.

What is at stake if disaster risk management and climate change adaptation agendas do not fully converge in ASEAN member states?

Although CCA and DRM have distinct core differences and convergences, their shared objectives include protecting development gains; maintaining effective resilience planning and programming; and managing risks and uncertainties for all kinds of shocks. On the other hand, as experiences in the ASEAN and elsewhere are showing, neither government-led DRM nor CCA will happen automatically. There is often little political will or financial incentive to invest human and financial resources in government-led DRM or CCA, compared to investing in visible and popular infrastructure or social programmes. Whatever incentives are given is even more skewed given the fact that external donors and the international community provide generous humanitarian assistance after disasters such as tsunamis and floods but largely fail to provide similar support for reducing the risk in the first place. Attention to incentives, institutions and instruments to promote good, risk-aware development is urgently needed. Both the

DRM and CCA agendas have suffered from lack of political influence and human capacity to raise the profile of risk management and mainstream development planning and practice. Nevertheless, the higher international political profile of CCA and the conduct of the Sendai summit meeting may generate additional momentum for innovations and institutional structure, which may potentially bring DRM and CCA closer together.

The overall goal to mitigate disaster risk is the same, providing collaborative perspectives on addressing future risk. By virtue of it being studied for a much longer period of time than CCA and the availability of past cases for analysis, DRM has developed sufficient tools and strategies to adapt to future disaster risks, assuming that the variability of those extreme events remains the same. Unfortunately, climate change is altering that variability, increasing the magnitude and severity of future disasters analysed under CCA. The lack of coordination between CCA and DRM can increase administrative burdens; prevent the efficient use of financial, human and natural resources; and decrease the overall effectiveness of efforts to reduce risk. DRM and CCA need greater integration institutionally and through funding to benefit from their synergy.

It has been observed that one of the major reasons for the lack of coordination between DRR and CCA is the lack of clarity in how integration is to be achieved. Although experts have recognised the synergies between CCA and DRR, it is unclear when, at what level and to what extent coordination is required. CCA and DRR are institutionally segregated, resulting in parallel efforts in developing new tools to address future risk. Institutional integration would require greater coordination, possibly an inter-ministerial body at the national level and more treaties recognising the integration between CCA and DRR at the international level.

In most countries, CCA and DRM typically have separate institutional 'homes', often the Ministry of Environment for CCA and the Ministry of Interior or similar agencies for DRM (Table 12.2).

These sectoral institutions, CCA and DRM, often possess their own administrative (i.e. technical and financial) groups, have their own channels of funding and have separate entry points in different international agreements (UNFCCC and HFA, respectively). While sharing similar objectives and similar challenges in raising the profile of their agendas, they typically fail to coordinate for better delivery. Such duplication of efforts and even competition among various groups not only hamper DRM and CCA objectives but compromises the overall effective use of resources. Hence, opportunities for joint work towards

Table 12.2 National platform for disaster risk management and climate change in the ASEAN

Country	*DRM platform*	*CCA platform*	*Related act*
Brunei Darussalam	National Disaster Management Centre, Ministry of Home Affairs	Department of Environment, Parks and Recreation, Ministry of Development	–
Cambodia	National Committee for Disaster Management – General Secretariat	Climate Change, Department of the Ministry of Environment	Subdecree No.35 ANK
Indonesia	National Agency for Disaster Management (BNBP)		Presidential regulation
Lao PDR	Ministry of Labour and Social Welfare	Ministry of Natural Resources and Environment	–
Malaysia	National Security Division, Prime Minister's Office (PMO)	Ministry of Natural Resources and Environment	National Security Council Directive
Myanmar	Ministry of Social Welfare	Ministry of Natural Resources and Environment	Rehabilitation Board Act
The Philippines	Department of National Defence	Climate Change Commission, Office of the President	Disaster Risk Reduction, Management, and Recovery Act
Singapore	Ministry of Home Affairs	Ministry of Natural Resources and Environment	Civil Defence Act
Thailand	Ministry of Interior	Ministry of Natural Resources and Environment	Disaster Prevention and Mitigation Act
Viet Nam	Ministry of Agriculture and Rural Development	Ministry of Natural Resources and Environment, Climate Change	Decree No. 168

Source: Compiled by the author.

the common objective of reducing the risk to development must be seized wherever feasible.

One case of institutional segregation despite significant progress towards DRM and CCA is Bangladesh. Bangladesh is one of the most disaster-prone countries in the world due to its geophysical location, land characteristics, multiplicity of rivers and monsoon climate variability. In response, Bangladesh has made significant progress in both DRR and CCA to manage these disaster risks. In 2010, the Government of Bangladesh developed the National Plan for Disaster Management which articulates specific DRM responsibilities and roles for all relevant stakeholders at different levels of government with punitive measures for non-compliance (Shamsuddoha et al., 2013).

At a more technical level, the rapid expansion of climate change–related efforts may waste time and risk reinventing older approaches if they neglect learning from the experiences, methods and tools already developed for DRM. On the other hand, efforts related to addressing the frequency and magnitude of hazards, exposure and vulnerability may not only fail to achieve their objectives but even increase vulnerability. For instance, flood defences may give a false sense of security but actually fail to provide lasting protection against rising flood risks.

Hence, each country should create a platform to coordinate various organisations at different levels. They are needed to properly design and implement DRM, CCA and SDG strategies. UNISDR defines 'national platform' as a nationally led forum or committee of multi-stakeholders. A national platform needs some critical elements such as (1) political, (2) technical, (3) participatory and (4) resource mobilisation components.

How can AMS governments and agencies at the national and regional levels coordinate?

A wide range of stakeholders must be coordinated because resilience is everybody's business. DRM, CCA and SD require a multi-sectoral approach, which covers agriculture, water, urban development, infrastructure, education, health and many other sectors. Single-sector development planning cannot address the complexity of challenges and opportunities available, nor can such plans build resilient societies. For example, DRM plans and CCA agendas should be linked to urban planning and to the teaching of urban and development planning in school. The idea that DRM and CCA are effective measures to increase resilience and reduce casualties should be promoted. Since no single organisation can have the ultimate responsibility for managing risks, various stakeholders and sectors should share the risks.

A thematic vision of a resilient future viewed through a sector lens is illustrated in Figure 12.5.

Sectoral ministries should strengthen the linkages with local governments to guide and support the latter in the promotion of DRM, CCA and SDGs in an integrated way by creating appropriate coordination mechanisms.

There are seven ways by which coordination could be achieved. Based on the regional analysis, these efforts are identified and briefly explained.

1 National platform – This is the highest decision-making body, usually chaired by the head of the state which gives it a high-profile leadership. This will decide specific policies, draft policies and formulate long-term plans and medium-term actions (e.g. the Philippines).
2 Subcommittees – They play important roles in coordinating specific issues. These technical committees consist of offices of government organisations, the academe, the private sector and international organisations (e.g. Japan).

Supportive thematic/sectoral vision

Resilience is integrated into thematic and sectoral strategies; policies; plans; legal, regulatory, and institutional arrangements; projects; budgets; and monitoring and evaluation frameworks

Livelihood	Land use	Transport	Education	Housing
- Routine risk assessment informing livelihood policies, plans, programs, and individual interventions - Strengthened resilience of assets - Access to microcredit and microinsurance - Diversification of livelihood opportunities	- Risk-sensitive land-use planning, policies, laws, and regulations - Coherent supporting institutional arrangements - Strong capacity and public-private incentives for compliance	- Risk-sensitive transport policy, investment decisions - Strict construction and maintenance of quality control - Adequate capacity and funding for routine maintenance - Post-disaster institutional arrangements	- Risk-sensitive school site planning and construction - Strict control with compliance to building codes - Retrofitting of existing schools - University catastrophe insurance pool - Adequate capacity and funding for safe school construction and routine maintenance	- Strong public, private, and community risk assessment - Training of local builders and crafts people trained in safe building techniques - Incentives for the construction of safe new homes and retrofitting old ones - Regularised tenure for illegal and informal settlements

Figure 12.5 Integrated policies for improving the disaster resilience

Source: Author.

3 Political commitment – This facilitates the reporting of the resilience situation to the head of the state or parliament through the publication of white papers. It covers the status and issues of DRM, CCA and SDGs and specifies budgetary allocations (e.g. Indonesia).
4 Budget allocation – Agencies coordinate and lead integrated policies through budget allocation to line ministries. This is separate from the emergency budget allocated for post-disaster rehabilitation activities (e.g. Bangladesh).
5 Drills and training – A wide range of organisations such as defence, civil society organisations (e.g. Japan), public work organisations and education ministries conduct training and drills to strengthen communication and networks with other organisations.
6 Local office – They send staff to and receive staff from line ministries and local governments or recruit staff from other ministries or from the private sector (e.g. Japan).
7 Decentralisation – It devolves powers and budgets for CCA, DRM and SDGs from national governments to local governments while considering the limited capacity of local governments (e.g. India).

Barriers to mainstreaming disaster risk management and climate change adaptation in developmental planning

DRM and CCA international frameworks, political processes, funding mechanisms, information exchange fora and practitioner communities developed independently and generally continue to be separate (Thomalla et al., 2006). While the trajectory towards convergence has been reasonably rapid and evidence of integration is growing, a number of significant barriers to full convergence remain.

Barriers at the international level

Despite the relevance and importance of DRM to CCA agreements, strategies and approaches, the incorporation of DRM into UNFCCC decision texts on adaptation has been, on the whole, ad hoc and piecemeal. There are a number of reasons for this. Key donor governments and institutions are still struggling to ensure good communication and collaboration between their own disaster management and climate change departments and units, affecting their ability to influence UNFCCC processes.

DRM proponents use the HFA as the international justification and architecture for scaling up DRM efforts in the UNFCCC. However, the HFA is not legally binding and has little recognition outside the DRR community. Efforts to have more explicit linkages to the HFA in the UNFCCC may help engage the DRR community in the adaptation arena and would possibly ensure greater attention for DRM in climate change debates. Adopting a negotiating/advocacy position solely based on the strength of the HFA is unlikely to be successful. Instead, the case for DRR in the context of the UNFCCC should be made in terms that will engage the real stakeholders that need to come on board to implement adaptation in developing countries: sectoral stakeholders and the ministries of finance and planning.

Furthermore, anecdotal evidence suggests that key donor governments (and the major polluters) are opposed to further integrating DRM and humanitarian assistance language into UNFCCC text because the UNFCCC only talks about human-induced climate change while the IPCC also includes climate variability. In the view of some of the major polluters, commitments to link CCA with DRR and humanitarian assistance more closely under the UNFCCC would create complex and potentially expensive overlaps associated with commitments to finance disaster relief. This leaves the unhelpful spectre of working out what proportion of disasters can be attributed to anthropogenic climate change and how much to existing climatic variability.

Barriers in multilateral and bilateral institutions

Within major bilateral and multilateral institutions, CCA and DRM commonly reside in different parts of the organisation and may even be managed in different geographic locations although steps are being taken to address this. For instance, UNDP's Bureau for Crisis Prevention and Recovery is based in Geneva (closer to many humanitarian agencies), while the adaptation-oriented UNDP/GEF is administrated from the Bureau for Development Policy headquartered in New York. However, UNDP has expressed a clear intention to more closely align and even integrate its support on DRR and CCA with developing countries and is also taking concrete steps to ensure closer collaboration between BCPR and BDP at the headquarters as well as in the field. In the World Bank, the Climate Change team, the Hazard Management unit and the GFDRR team are now located under the office of the vice president for sustainable development. These three teams were previously separated. However, there is limited day-to-day interaction, joint development of tools or analyses or joint programming on climate risk management. This is also similar to the Asian Development Bank (ADB) where climate change and DRM units are under the Regional and Sustainable Development Department. A number of the author's consultations with policymakers pointed to the fact that the convergence of CCA and DRM should start with reorganisation within organisations.

Many felt that bringing DRM and CCA into the same organisational home would send a clear message to other multilateral, bilateral and civil society organisations to do the same. Some expressed concern that the persistence of the close relationship between humanitarian assistance (mainly disaster response) and DRR in terms of organisational structures is damaging the profile of DRR as a development issue and is inhibiting the ability of DRM people to communicate effectively with their key counterparts in development and climate change. Seeing DRM primarily as a humanitarian concern was described as 'an anachronism that must be countered'.

Barriers in financing mechanisms

Multilateral adaptation financing mechanisms are closely tied to the UNFCCC which, in the past, has not paid much attention to extremes, partly due to the lack of scientific clarity on the attribution of changes in extremes to anthropogenic climate change. This has changed in recent years, and many requests for funding from the GEF-managed adaptation funds include attention to the management of extremes.

Nevertheless, a remaining barrier preventing DRM-oriented actors to start using the adaptation funding is the need to demonstrate 'additionality'. This means that the project, or at least the portion of it for which financing is sought, needs to address the changes in climate rather than just variability and extremes in the current climate. In practice, the GEF has demonstrated substantial flexibility in its treatment of this requirement, but some rationale must be included. This is often a challenge for DRR-oriented programmes. DRR actors perceive these requirements as ineffective, forcing attention on climate change rather than the most urgent disaster risk.

Another challenge for integrating DRM in adaptation financing mechanisms is the strong role of the national climate change and GEF focal points, which have to approve the applications for funding from the adaptation funds. They are usually based in environment ministries and often prefer projects with a strong role for their own ministry. They also prefer that coordination be done through the climate change mechanisms in the country rather than leave the initiative to the DRM actors and/or their intersectoral coordination mechanisms.

The World Bank–managed Pilot Program for Climate Resilience, part of the Climate Investment Funds, is less constrained by UNFCCC guidance and more closely aimed at integrating into development and establishing useful examples of how integrated climate risk management can be mainstreamed into development, particularly through budgetary support modalities. Within DRR funding mechanisms, especially the GFDRR, the integration faces less formal obstacles although the GFDRR guidelines, for instance, emphasise the need for coordination through the national platforms for DRR rather than allowing more flexibility regarding the use of other coordination mechanisms (as long as these achieve integration of risk reduction into development). Within regular development financing, especially within budget support and policy dialogues, both CCA and DRR face the same obstacles: they lack strong demand from recipient countries and are often perceived as donor interests. Both need to make a stronger case for the economic and planning dimensions of integrated risk management in order to focus policy attention at that level. This has worked, for instance, in the Pacific Islands region.

Barriers at the national level

In practice, the implementation modality for the GFDRR and much of the HFA are the so-called national platforms for disaster risk reduction promoted by the International Strategy for Disaster Reduction. The UNFCCC, on the other hand, has focal points in ministries of environment or sometimes the meteorological office. The preparation of national reports for the UNFCCC (e.g. National Communications and NAPAs) does require some form of inter-ministerial coordination process, but the UNFCCC focal point has typically assumed the lead. In most countries, these coordination mechanisms exist largely in isolation from each other. Both coordination mechanisms struggle to influence planning and budgeting in major sectors. Climate change is very explicitly integrated in guidance for the GFDRR. However, there is no explicit role for climate change focal points or coordination mechanisms.

As a contribution to the interagency Vulnerability and Adaptation Resource Group, the European Community funded a research project to look at links between climate change and DRR in Viet Nam, the report for which was published in 2006 (Few et al., 2006). It found no concrete evidence of the systematic integration of DRM and CCA in terms of project activities, coordination and fundraising. At the project's wrap-up workshop, participants stressed the need for national DRM and CCA budgets to enable joint programming. However, in order for this to be achieved, a clear cost-benefit, cost-effectiveness case needs to be made to convince finance ministries that public spending is justified. In stimulating better risk management, there is no one-size-fits-all solution such as the integration of the DRR agenda into climate change coordination structures or vice versa. Instead, donors should build on existing capacities. This may mean working with well-functioning DRR mechanisms where they exist, particularly when they are well integrated in sectoral planning. A review of the 2009 national HFA reports reveals that even countries with strong DRR mechanisms and political commitment towards integrated efforts are lacking financial support, appropriate processes, frameworks and programme guidelines for the integration of DRR in CCA at the policy level.

This can be seen in the segregated ministries of Bangladesh. Despite the significant awareness of both DRM and CCA, there is relatively minimal collaboration between the two ministries at present. Due to the more developed and robust DRR plans and institutions of Bangladesh, the country's Ministry of Disaster Management and Relief is focusing on managing and coordinating pre-disaster preparedness and post-disaster response measures. Rather than focus on planning and implementing CCA activities, the entities working on CCA are focused on mainstreaming policy and coordinating finance from various national and international sources.

This is accentuated by a lack of capacity to understand and implement climate risk management approaches. In other cases where DRR infrastructure is still weak, it may be better to focus on the institutions coordinating new adaptation funding, using them as entry points for better DRR through existing climate change coordination mechanisms.

Where political will for the joint agenda is strong, another solution may be the top-down integration of both agendas, for example, under the leadership of the prime minister or head of state.

Barriers in sharing knowledge and experiences

Historically, there are separate communities of policymakers, practitioners and researchers working on DRM and CCA with limited overlap in networks, meetings, methods or tools. Some DRR specialists are sceptical of the sudden popular interest in adaptation and the adaptation community's perceived focus on a long-term agenda that only encompasses part of the entire array of hazards (excluding earthquakes, for instance). Some DRR experts feel that the adaptation community often focuses too much on climate as the main driver and fails to acknowledge the social factors behind vulnerability. Adaptation experts have tended to focus on longer-term issues, particularly on changing averages (which are easier to get from the use of a General Circulation Model) and feel that the DRR community fails to address these. An additional complication is that the two communities often use different words for similar issues.

The lack of coordination between the ministries has resulted in several lost opportunities in Bangladesh. Since CCA is focused on mainstreaming policy and coordinating finances, the DRR framework of the Government of Bangladesh does not adequately account for how climate change processes will induce loss and damage and affect risks and vulnerability to extreme events. Although both DRR and CCA acknowledge the importance of mainstreaming both DRR and CCA into national planning efforts, their disparate bureaucratic bases make it difficult to coordinate on issues where mandates and interests overlap. This lack of coordination is a result of bureaucratic 'turf wars' between ministries who are unwilling to cede control to others (Shamsuddoha et al., 2013). One example of the negative effect of these turf wars is the Ministry of Environment and Forests' inhibiting the ability of the Ministry of Disaster Management and Relief to learn from an important network of researchers and practitioners on new tools to adapt to future risk. The Ministry of Environment and Forests serves as the focal point for all UNFCCC engagements.

It is clear that the driver for closer integration is the growing demand from the applications side where projects or plans want to address the full spectrum of risk at once (but currently fail to find proper guidance or documented experience). In recent years, there has indeed been an increase in mutual interest and a growing number of joint sessions at major events, knowledge portals and guidance documents, but there is still some way to go. Bilateral and multilateral donors can support the emerging initiatives for integrated knowledge, experience and guidance, particularly by focusing on applications rather than theoretical explorations.

How to remove the barriers in DRM and CCA

Role of knowledge institutes

The knowledge community in AMS is primarily focusing efforts on DRM and CCA forecasting at the national level. Quantitative modelling is an essential tool to assess impacts, estimate systems sensitivity in response to climate change extremes and reduce uncertainties concerning forecasts and the costs and benefits of integrating CCA and

DRM measures (OECD, 2009). AMS with limited scientific capacity are frequently compelled to apply generic and global methods that do not necessarily fulfil their needs (Box 12.1).

Box 12.1. An Assessment of the Current Status of Scientific Capacity for Climate Change Adaptation

The following have been reported as constraints to undertaking effective research on climate change adaptation in the ASEAN:

- Lack of programming skills: Most research and educational activities undertaken are on a short-term basis. There is very little long-term planning to continue the development of solutions.
- Inadequate monitoring and evaluation: Keen on activities but unenthusiastic in monitoring the impact of research and education.
- Inadequate communication skills: For example, downscaling the climate forecast at the subregional level and communicating with decision makers.
- Lack of effective networking, experience sharing and dissemination skills.
- Inadequate leadership, governance and management capacities: Undefined roles of team members and lack of accountability.
- Inadequate capacity to raise adequate international resources, mobilise local resources, manage finances and report effectively.

Therefore, global models need to be downscaled, taking into consideration regional data, the increasing participation of local research centres and scientists and local community knowledge of local DRM (current and historical perspective). Inventory activities and field campaigns must be sponsored to fill knowledge gaps in observing networks and data collection methodologies. Although significant attempts have been made to develop methodologies and models to focus on ASEAN sociocultural and ecosystems, this field is still under investigation. To this end, multidisciplinary subregional knowledge platforms or networks must be formed. Scientists who measure physical impacts of climate change and DRM strategies should work with economists and social scientists, filling the need to include economic impacts and the perspectives of local communities. However, the lack of programming skills and the insufficient expertise in predicting events (due to the short-term basis of activities) result in unreliable surveys that do not support the decisions of policymakers.

There are also regional research networks such as the SysTem for Analysis Research and Training, the Asia-Pacific Network for Global Change Research and the Economy and Environment Program for Southeast Asia as well as institutes like the Atmospheric Data Receiving & Processing Centre, the Economic Research Institute for ASEAN and East Asia (ERIA) and the Asian Development Bank Institute (ADBI) that support regional research. Organisations such as these will be among the most important in implementing any research and educational programme. Building the capacity of knowledge institutions will be particularly important for those that are concerned with the current policy environment and for producing the 'graduates' who will ultimately populate government, national sector or policy organisations and private business entities. Such organisations train future generations of sector-specific and integrated DRM and CCA planning and economic development experts (i.e. the individuals who will ultimately actualise systems). An indicative system of such capacity building programmes is shown in Table 12.3.

Due to the wide array of issues involved and the actors that need to be influenced, partnerships that involve diverse combinations of academic, government and private sector actors are likely to be particularly

Table 12.3 Capacity building and training indicators towards disaster risk management and climate change adaptation

Indicators	*International partnership*	*New knowledge*	*Integration*	*Stakeholders*	*Dissemination*
Workshops and seminars	o	o	o	o	o
Books and websites	o	o	o	o	o
Decision support systems	o			o	
Joint cross-sector actions			o	o	o
Guidelines and handbooks		o	o	o	o
Joint studies	o	o	o	o	o
Graduate courses		o		o	o

important in supporting national adaptation. Where such networks (as illustrated in Figure 12.3) do not currently exist, encouraging their formation will have greater impact than attempting to work on a one-on-one basis with individual organisations, however strong they may be.

Conclusion and the way forward

Substantial economic opportunities exist by integrating the concepts and shared goals of DRM, CCA and SD. In the past, the ASEAN has seen some progress in the convergence of these three areas of practice, at least in terms of intentions and policy statements as well as in some on-the-ground activities. However, significant barriers to convergence in critical institutions remain and the risks of duplication of efforts and competing institutional structures are still significant. Nevertheless, the growing attention and funding for both areas and the clear local interest in a coordinated approach offer ample opportunities for the continued integration of DRM, CCA and SDG agendas and shared learning.

Broader gap also exists between the theoretical understanding of disaster risk management and formulation of officials policies and laws that are actually taken in the course of routine exercise. The critical transitional functions where most vulnerable communities are exposed to disaster and climate risks are easily assumed in the advocacy, but they are much more difficult to realise in national and international laws. Today, in many developing countries there is awareness of the need for better disaster risk policies. But, of course, this often means investment, and there is strong competition for the use of public resources. National resilience will not be accomplished unless until sufficient incentives can be provided through credible institutional, governance and financial systems embedded. Risk management has to be led by the top political level. It should also involve other key stakeholders such as business. Many infrastructure projects, for example, are carried out between the government and the private sector, which include large insurance companies and global businesses.

To achieve a broad vision of a resilient, inclusive and competitive *region*, a wide range of steps should be taken at the regional, national and local levels. There are five critical steps that can accelerate the community process of overcoming a number of barriers or gaps in convergence:

- Strengthened legal frameworks for improved coordination and to lead concerned subcommittees of line ministries. Devolution of power and finance to local governments is also needed to effectively respond to the needs of the people. Capacity of local government could further be improved by the legal framework, putting in place seconded-staff programmes across the social development, environment and economic ministries.

- Integrated risk assessment through the DRM and CCA lens for all new investments, whether financed by the government, by the private sector or by the international community, in order to protect communities against hazards and economic risks.
- Formulating a detailed framework to monitor and evaluate the progress of integrated resilience capacity, potentially covering a wide array of legislative, regulatory, policy planning, institutional, financial and capacity-building instruments and mechanisms regularly.
- Regional institutions like ASEAN, SAARC, CAREC working with other bilateral and multilateral facilities such as the World Bank and Asian Development Bank as well as the United Nations to establish public programmes of financial support for improving the resilience of communities in leveraging private financing.
- Countries and communities should also work with regional and local institutes to establish a knowledge hub for facilitating, developing, exchanging and disseminating DRM data, best practices and climate modelling tools.

Notes

1 Disaster risk management: The broad development and application of policies, strategies and practices to minimise vulnerabilities and disaster risks throughout society through prevention, mitigation and preparedness.

2 Climate change adaptation: An adjustment in natural or human systems in response to actual or expected climate stimuli or their effects, which moderates harm or exploits benefit opportunities.

3 Sustainable development goals: One of the main outcomes of the Rio+20 Conference, which will build upon the Millennium Development Goals and converge with the post-2015 development agenda.

References

ADPC Annual Report '(2013), *'Asian Disaster Preparedness Report'*, Bangkok: Asian Disaster Preparedness Centre, available at www.adpn.net.

Ahmed, A. K. (2010). *Mapping of Climate Change Adaptation and Disaster Risk Management-Related Governance in Three South East Asian Countries: Cambodia, Indonesia and the Philippines*. Brighton, UK: Institute of Development Studies.

Anbumozhi, V. (2012). *Enhancing Adaptive Capacity in Asia and the Pacific Region: Opportunities for Innovation and Experimentation*. New Delhi: Sage.

Asian Development Bank. (2009). *Economics of Climate Change in South East Asia: A Regional Review*. Manila: Asian Development Bank.

Few, H., Anderson, J., Balzer, N., Hastrup Clemmensen, A., Hess, U. & Rispoli, F. (2006). *Potential for Scale and Sustainability in Weather Index*. Rome: International Fund for Agricultural Development.

Organisation for Economic Co-Operation and Development. (2009). *Integrating Climate Change Adaptation into Development Co-Operation: Policy Guidance*. Paris: OECD Publishing.

Shamsuddoha, M., Roberts, E., Hasemann, A. & Roddick, S. (2013). *Establishing Links between Disaster Risk Reduction and Climate Change Adaptation in the Context of Loss and Damage: Policies and Approaches in Bangladesh*. Dhaka: Center for Participatory Research & Development (CPRD).

Sperling, F. & Szekely, F. (2005). *Disaster Risk Management in a Changing Climate*, Discussion Paper Prepared for the World Conference on Disaster Reduction in Kobe, Japan, on behalf of the Vulnerability and Adaptation Resource Group (VARG). Reprint with Addendum on Conference Outcomes, Washington, DC.

Thomalla, F., Downing, T., Spanger-Siegfried, E., Han, G. & Rockström, J. (2006). Reducing Hazard Vulnerability: Towards a Common Approach between Disaster Risk Reduction and Climate Adaptation. *Disasters*, *30*(1), 39–48.

World Bank. (2013). *Philippines*. Washington, DC: World Bank. Retrieved from www.worldbank.org/en/country/philippines

Part IV

The wide-eyed slippages of disaster law

13 Corruption in humanitarian assistance

Challenges and opportunities

Sumaiya Khair

Corruption in humanitarian operations has featured on the agenda of international aid agencies given the almost routine dilemma aid practitioners face in reconciling the need to quickly reach the needy with aid in an environment of competing management priorities and capacity stretched beyond limits with integrity challenges at various levels; however, the seriousness of the matter reached a new height when the tsunami-hit countries around the Indian Ocean in December 2004 and aid agencies were confronted with corruption in their operations in a much larger and more public way than ever before.[1] While aid agencies have over time developed mechanisms and adopted measures to minimise corruption risks in their operations by strengthening procurement, logistics and financial systems, they are believed to have had little impact on the ground given the diversity of contexts, urgency to deliver aid, size of the affected population and so on. The most palpable impact of corruption in humanitarian action is that it prevents assistance from reaching the people who most need it and instead facilitates collusive forces to capitalise on human plight.

In an attempt to bridge the gap in knowledge about the extent and consequences of corruption in humanitarian assistance, the present chapter draws on experiences from Bangladesh and elsewhere to underscore *inter alia* perceptions and practices of corruption in humanitarian assistance, the conditions which make humanitarian action vulnerable to corruption, the significance of incorporating integrity standards and benchmarks in humanitarian work and the role of the regulatory framework. The chapter also provides directions for the future.

Why set good governance standards in humanitarian action?

Humanitarian interventions traditionally respond to humanitarian crises/emergencies; however, what constitutes a humanitarian crisis or emergency is largely determined by the normative fabric of political life and standards of acceptable behaviour in the world.[2] Notwithstanding, expectations of how a state or aid agency ought to manage a crisis are often at odds with the established normative framework in the face of the severity, frequency and scale of a crisis, all of which play a key role in setting standards of acceptable forms of humanitarian response. The basic principles of humanitarian action are premised on humanity (saving lives and alleviating suffering), impartiality (implementation of actions solely on the basis of need), neutrality (assistance without fear or favour) and independence (autonomy of humanitarian objectives from the political, economic, military or other considerations of any actor in the area where humanitarian action is being implemented).[3] These various principles are played out by a wide range of actors comprising donor organisations, bilateral and multilateral agencies, NGOs, Red Cross/Crescent societies, private contractors and military forces, each operating under set norms and guidelines but with diverse approaches.[4] It is believed that the diversity of actors and implementation modalities creates scope for corruption which may vary in terms of typology and nature.

While the need to address human rights abuses during emergencies, particularly in conflict situations, has customarily featured prominently in humanitarian interventions, good governance is increasingly being recognised as an essential criterion for guiding international aid work. This is premised on the understanding that corruption in humanitarian aid undermines the fundamental purpose of humanitarian action by way of, for example, diversion of relief supplies away from affected communities, inequitable distribution of aid and sub-standard or inappropriately located infrastructure.[5] These various actions essentially exacerbate the deprivation experienced by victims of humanitarian emergencies and enhance their vulnerabilities in different ways.

Humanitarian action has been criticised for a wide array of shortcomings ranging from undermining the accountability of governments to their people, destroying markets, creating dependency, failing to reach the neediest and being inequitable to providing poor-quality and insufficient assistance to people in desperate need.[6] Taken together these deficiencies seemingly make emergency aid 'one of the largest unregulated industries in the world'.[7] It is in this context that humanitarian reformers believe that by making aid more accountable, aid actors (international and local) will no longer be able to abuse their power and exploit the people they are there to help, and aid work will be more effective, context-specific, responsive, empowering, needs-driven, rights-enforcing, high-quality and dynamic, as well as timely, efficient and equitable.[8] In this regard, transparency and accountability in terms of fund flow, information dissemination, decision making, disbursement planning, stakeholder (aid recipient) identification/

selection and aid utilisation/distribution are some of the critical elements for ensuring good governance in humanitarian interventions. While every situation is different, in all cases humanitarian aid actors need to strike a balance between their commitment to humanitarian principles and the need to control corruption in order to be truly accountable to their beneficiaries and donors – in so doing they need to be transparent with stakeholders about corruption challenges and how they may affect their work.[9]

Recent years have witnessed a proliferation of codes of conduct in the humanitarian sector which essentially demonstrates the degree of concern among humanitarian actors to improve quality and performance by applying basic principles and 'standards of behaviour' in humanitarian action. Some examples in this context include but are not limited to the 2010 HAP Standard in Accountability and Quality Management, the Code of Conduct for the International Red Cross and Red Crescent Movement and NGOs in Disaster Relief, the Sphere Handbook Core Standards and the Humanitarian Charter and the Organisation for Economic Co-operation and Development's (OECD) Development Assistance Committee (DAC) Criteria for Evaluating Development and Humanitarian Assistance. These and other initiatives focus on different aspects of emergency action and provide guidelines to strengthen the elements that are intrinsic to humanitarian assistance. For instance, while some of these initiatives are guided by core humanitarian principles, others promote evaluation and learning, set standards and norms and aim at improving management and accountability.[10] The *Core Humanitarian Standard on Quality and Accountability (CHS)* is yet another initiative that has evolved in sync with these various standards and on the basis of a global consultation. It outlines nine fundamental principles that actors involved in humanitarian response can use to improve the quality and effectiveness of their aid work.[11] Notwithstanding these developments, there is still quite a lot to be done in terms of facilitating greater accountability to all stakeholders generally and affected communities in particular. Being accountable to crisis-affected people helps aid agencies develop quality programmes that respond to their needs and at the same time reduces the possibility of mistakes, abuse and corruption.[12]

Scope and understanding of corruption in humanitarian emergencies

Humanitarian emergencies that demand international aid and assistance typically occur in vulnerable contexts characterised by poverty, deprivation, inadequate coping mechanisms and, more often than not, poor governance. When crisis hits a given country or region, it is common for governments, NGOs and international humanitarian agencies to react swiftly and come to the aid of affected populations. Indeed, developing economies tend to rely considerably on international aid agencies which often dole out substantial amounts of resources to mitigate the impact of the crisis. It has been argued, however, that the influx of humanitarian assistance is at risk of both being diverted by corrupt means and exacerbating existing corruption.[13] The situation gets more complicated if the particular aid agency has little or no idea of the local landscape in terms of social, political and economic exigencies and priorities. In other words, rapid and uninformed entry of large amounts of supplies, whether in cash or kind, into a resource-deficient environment is believed to be counter-productive. Aid agencies, however, would argue that their course of action in emergencies is determined by the scale, seriousness and urgency of the crisis; therefore, in the final assessment the risk of loss of human lives clearly outweighs corruption risks.[14]

Indeed, differences in opinion regarding corruption risks among aid workers and aid recipients shape the discourse on corruption in humanitarian aid. Findings of a perception study commissioned by Transparency International (TI) in 2007–2008 and undertaken by a team from TI, Feinstein International Centre and the Humanitarian Policy Group of the Overseas Development Institute (ODI)[15] in seven countries – three in Africa, three in Asia and one in the Middle East – reveal that the aid agencies are reluctant to actively engage on the subject of corruption primarily because they feel it might potentially undermine aid operations and erode public trust – factors that cannot be ruled out entirely. One of the interesting findings from this study was that the majority of the aid staff interviewed across most of the participating agencies did not consider corruption prevention as being particularly important; rather, corruption was generally perceived as an unavoidable aspect of emergency situations and, as such, was just another part of routine business. This attitude essentially demonstrates the lack of incentives within existing systems of humanitarian aid for reporting corruption and demanding accountability. Aid practitioners argue that humanitarian agencies appear to be in state of denial about the scale of the problem, largely because they fear that public acknowledgement of the existence of financial mismanagement would lead to a loss of confidence among donors, tax-payers and politicians in the aid system, and eventually threaten their income.[16] Also, corruption scandals are believed to pose potential reputational risks for aid workers and adversely impact their activities in the field.[17] This notion contributes to the promotion of systemic under-investment in corruption control measures which in turn produces a systematic under-reporting of fraud and corruption; unless therefore the scale of corruption is measured and acknowledged, control of financial malfeasance by humanitarian agencies will be untenable.[18]

The TI-led study also found that corruption perceptions of employees of aid agencies differed considerably from that of aid recipients. For example, while aid agency staff tended to view corruption primarily in terms of financial irregularities (rather than abuse of power), aid recipients were found to relate corruption to lack of transparency and nepotism in aid distribution, theft or sale of aid goods, wastage by aid agencies through renting expensive houses or using expensive vehicles and so on. The understanding of corruption among aid recipients in the study is found to mirror the spirit of TI's definition of corruption: 'the abuse of entrusted power for private gain'. This definition essentially transcends the stereotypical view that corruption only involves fraud, embezzlement and other illegal financial transactions. Recognising that there is no one definition of corruption for societies and cultures across the world, TI adopts an inclusive approach in defining corruption by adding non-financial forms of corruption to the more widely acknowledged forms of financial corruption. In the context of humanitarian emergencies these would mean, for example, the manipulation or diversion of humanitarian assistance to benefit non-target groups; the allocation of relief resources in exchange for sexual favours; preferential treatment in assistance or hiring processes for family members or friends (nepotism and cronyism); and the coercion and intimidation of staff or beneficiaries to turn a blind eye to or participate in corruption.[19] In contrast to the concept of public good, 'private' refers not just to individuals but to families and communities; ethnic, regional or religious groups; political parties and organisations; corporate bodies; professional or social associations; and warlords and militias. Similarly, 'gain' is not always financial but can very well centre on the abuse of power for the enhancement of personal or organisational reputation or for social and political purposes.[20]

Factors contributing to corruption in humanitarian assistance

There are various factors – institutional, systemic and contextual – that directly or indirectly contribute to corruption in different phases of humanitarian assistance. The need for urgency perceivably overrides the need for accountability as manifest from aid managers' aversion to acknowledging cases of corruption, absence of due diligence in staff recruitment for field operations, anomalies in procurement and lack of compliance with basic standards of due process by law enforcement agencies and judicial systems in addressing corruption.[21]

Based on experiences of national chapters of corruption risks in humanitarian emergencies during the tsunami in the Indian Ocean in 2004 and the severe earthquake in Pakistan in 2005, TI identified some of the key reasons why corruption occurs or is likely to occur in aid work: conditions inherent in humanitarian emergencies; characteristics of the humanitarian aid system; and levels of transparency and accountability in recipient countries.[22] The conditions in which humanitarian agencies work are characterised by damaged or destroyed infrastructure, disrupted community services, mass population movements, outbreaks of disease and actual or anticipated conflicts. These elements erode local governance structures, rule of law and integrity systems which in turn lead to the growth of parallel and often illegal outfits, for example, black markets that operate in the political and economic vacuum created by an emergency. The need to reach affected populations quickly results in inaccurate disbursement of relief goods in terms of quantity, location and beneficiary. In such circumstances, aid flows tend to be manipulated and misused.

Led by diverse actors including international donors, international aid implementing agencies (e.g. UN bodies, the ICRC and international NGOs), national and local NGOs and governments of affected countries, the international humanitarian aid framework often contributes to integrity lapses in humanitarian assistance. The normative practice of resource-rich countries channelling aid to resource-poor countries creates a power imbalance which divests aid recipients of powers to hold aid providers accountable for failure to detect all types of corruption on the ground and take measures accordingly. Indeed, the engagement of multiple actors in humanitarian work (donors and implementing agencies) and consequently the demand for multiple reporting requirements increase administrative burden, particularly for the smaller, newly set up agencies; lacking in robust governance structures and internal/external controls, these agencies become vulnerable to malpractice and corruption.

Humanitarian aid is particularly susceptible to corruption in countries with low levels of transparency and accountability. This coincides with the fact that humanitarian aid is often provided in environments with weak governance structures. This poses heightened challenges for humanitarian aid agencies in their attempts to ensure that reasonably robust control mechanisms are in place. Unfamiliarity with local contexts and practices makes it difficult for aid actors to manage corruption, particularly the subtler forms.

Although the risks of corruption have been rarely explicitly analysed, monitored or evaluated in the public domain,[23] empirical evidence supports the notion that the preceding conditions create entry points for corruption and governance deficits in aid work. TI's multi-country study in 2007–2008[24] discovered corruption and irregularities in administrative, financial and operational aspects of humanitarian assistance. To cite a few examples, food aid operations were found to be particularly vulnerable to corruption and diversion to unintended destinations due to involvement of multiple and divergent actors in the supply chain; mismanagement of food aid also occurred due to inadequate staff strength in food disbursement processes; similarly, post-emergency homes were constructed with substandard building material and the process was led by inexpert contractors and workers; irregularities and corruption were evident in beneficiary assessment and relief distribution, finance and procurement, transportation, port clearance and forwarding and so on.[25] Findings of the TI study were reinforced when Médecins du Monde (MDM) led a study in 2008 in which 17 of the largest French NGOs were interviewed regarding their perceptions of corruption, procedures to identify corruption risks and approaches to risk management and prevention. Among the NGOs that participated in the study, most conceded that corruption indeed posed a significant challenge to humanitarian operations, particularly in respect of procurement, transport and distribution of medicines, food, building materials and other consumables, particularly in large, rapid-onset emergencies.[26] While joint work by external donors and local organisations (like civil society organizations and community-based organizations) is believed to strengthen service delivery mechanisms in emergency situations, many perceived that 'the trade-off between too much trust and too much oversight is often a tricky balance for external agencies to manage' and that 'partnerships are a way of outsourcing corruption risk by external agencies'.[27] On the whole, humanitarian crises occur in intensely complex environments where rapidly changing resource levels, survival instincts and fear factors merge to create scenarios that are susceptible to corruption.[28]

Corruption risks in emergency response: lessons from Transparency International Bangladesh

Bangladesh is a disaster-prone country that experiences some form of natural calamity annually in the form of floods, torrential rains, erosion or cyclones. Disaster management has received considerable attention of policymakers in Bangladeshi view of recurring natural disasters in the country. Accordingly, the capacity to manage disasters has improved within concerned agencies of the government manifest, for example, from the significant reduction in cyclone deaths in the past few decades due to enhanced disaster risk reduction (DRR) efforts undertaken by the government, primarily by constructing multi-purpose cyclone shelters and introducing improved early warning systems.[29] The practice of collaboration with non-governmental organisations and other stakeholders in disaster management in terms of relief operations, rehabilitation, social reintegration and so on, has also risen. While these developments respond to fundamental aspects of humanitarian action, they do not address the more covert aspects of malgovernance that can potentially and adversely affect the humanitarian assistance process. This omission might well stem from the notion that altruism naturally takes precedence over malpractice and corruption in conditions of human misery. Unfortunately, experiences on the ground appear to negate this perception.

In 2006 TI conducted a study in 10 countries, including Bangladesh, for mapping corruption in humanitarian action. The survey for Bangladesh was conducted by Transparency International Bangladesh (TIB), accredited chapter of TI. The survey results revealed a wide range of irregularities that are usually committed during disaster management processes. In response to the question whether they had any knowledge of abuse of relief assistance, people came up with a number of disquieting examples which are summed up here:

- Selection of agencies based on individual and personal relationship, misstatements of achievements and biased beneficiary evaluation resulting in diversion of assistance for personal gain or creation of fields of influence to mislead donors, employers and intended beneficiaries.
- Involvement of local government structures in corrupt practices in beneficiary selection and distribution of relief goods. Relief goods were distributed less than what recipients were entitled to.
- Misappropriation of relief goods by local government functionaries, who, instead of distributing them in affected communities, diverted them to areas which housed their supporters or vote bank.
- Creation of fake names and addresses of relief recipients by government officials. No objection was raised as government officials at all levels were involved in siphoning off relief allocations.

- Political influence on government officials to distribute relief goods to party members. On refusal to comply, suspension of relief distribution was ordered by Member of Parliament.
- Supporters of the ruling political party were given priority in accessing shelters.
- Collusion of local government officials, Members of Parliament and ministers in malpractice in relief operations.
- Credit claims by NGOs against farmers' own investments in post-disaster recovery.
- Bribery of government officials by NGOs for getting selected as partner NGOs and receiving funds from government programmes.
- Distribution of relief goods by selected NGOs to unaffected people.[30]

Following the survey in 2006, Bangladesh witnessed recurring natural disasters in 2007. The country was ravaged by two rounds of floods between July and September 2007, affecting 46 districts, with a death toll rising to over 1,000 people, affecting about 10 million people and damaging crops worth $86 million.[31] Before the country could recover from the effects of the floods, Cyclone Sidr hit the southwest coast of Bangladesh on 15 November 2007, with winds up to 240 kilometres per hour. This was accompanied by tidal waves up to five meters high and surges up to six meters in some areas, breaching coastal and river embankments, flooding low-lying areas and causing extensive physical destruction. This onslaught essentially set the stage for TIB to conduct an independent research to examine the integrity challenges in post-disaster humanitarian assistance.

Loss and damage caused by Cyclone Sidr

The loss and damages caused by Cyclone Sidr were immense. It destroyed crops, property, essential services. Lives were lost, diseases spread and people were robbed of livelihoods and subjected to psycho-social trauma. In addition to harming the environment generally, Cyclone Sidr caused extensive damage to housing, communication, transport, power and other infrastructure. It also wreaked havoc in the productive sector (crops, livestock, fisheries, commerce, industry, tourism) and the social sector (health, nutrition, education).

While a total of 30 districts took the brunt of the cyclone, 12 districts hosting an estimated population of 18.7 million were more severely affected. In the wake of the cyclone, the Government of Bangladesh, together with the international donors, undertook a comprehensive assessment to gauge the extent of damage and loss and to develop a feasible recovery plan. According to the Joint Damage, Loss, and Needs Assessment (JDNLA), the total damage and losses caused by the cyclone was an estimated BDT 115.6 billion (US$1.7 billion).[32] It claimed 3,406 lives, 1,001 people went missing, and more than 55,000 were injured.[33] Damage, which is an expression of the destruction of physical assets, was estimated at BDT 79.9 billion (69 per cent of total effects), while losses, depicting the flows of the economy that arise from the temporary absence of the damaged assets, were estimated at BDT 35.7 billion (31 per cent of the total effects).[34] The most affected individual sectors, in the order of decreasing magnitude of total effects, were housing (BDT 57.9 billion), agriculture (BDT 30.2 billion), transport (BDT 9.7 billion), water resource management and control (BDT 4.9 billion) and education (BDT 4.7 billion). When only losses are considered, the most affected were agriculture (BDT 28.7 billion), industry (BDT 2 billion), transport (BDT 1.7 billion) and commerce (BDT 1.3 billion).[35]

Actors and initiatives in post-Sidr humanitarian assistance

The enormity of the Cyclone Sidr galvanised collective humanitarian action as international and national actors came together to address the loss and damage caused by the disaster. The JDNLA, undertaken by the Government of Bangladesh with assistance from international development partners, captures the wide range of actors that have contributed to post-Sidr humanitarian aid.[36] The Government of Bangladesh, in collaboration with the United Nations, the National Red Crescent Society and the International Red Cross and Red Crescent Societies, undertook several humanitarian assessment missions and started aid operations primarily focusing on food, nutrition, water and sanitation, shelter and disease. The government allocated BDT 450 million (US$6.7 million) for relief and housing construction, distributed relief items and dispatched medical teams to affected areas.[37] According to a compilation by Office for the Coordination of Humanitarian Affairs on the basis of information provided by donors and appealing organisations, total funding received as humanitarian assistance for Cyclone Sidr as of 16 March 2015 amounted to US$215,214,297 and outstanding pledges accounted for US$22,528,778.[38]

The JDNLA reveals that a total of 49 countries, including Australia, Canada, China, India, Italy, Japan, Kuwait, the Netherlands, Norway, the Kingdom of Saudi Arabia, Sweden, UK, USA and the European Union, provided emergency assistance for the victims, while the US

Marine Forces took part in rescue and relief operations. These actions were reinforced by international donors, such as United Nations Development Programme, United Nations Children's Fund, OXFAM, Save the Children Fund Alliance, World Vision, Care Bangladesh, Islamic Relief, Caritas, Christian Aid, Concern Worldwide and ActionAid Bangladesh. National NGOs contributed in different ways. Some like BRAC and Adventist Development and Relief Agency International (ADRA) provided affected families with edible and non-edible items, while others, for example, Grameen Bank, BRAC and ASA waived loan payments for members who were affected by the cyclone. The entire process was coordinated by the Bangladesh government's Disaster and Emergency Response (DER) subgroup of the Local Consultative Group (LCG). The Ministry of Foreign Affairs and the Economic Relations Division (ERD) organised meetings for development partner countries and organizations in order to brief them about the impact of Cyclone Sidr.[39]

Integrity challenges in post-Sidr emergency work

Drawing upon experiences from the TI-supported survey in 2006, TIB sent six teams of researchers to Sidr-affected areas of Barisal, Jhalakathi, Pirojpur, Bagerhat, Madaripur and Chandpur during ongoing relief operations with the aim of documenting the governance challenges in post-Sidr humanitarian action. The research team found that many of the governance deficits inherent in post-Sidr humanitarian assistance were similar to the ones uncovered by the TI-led survey in 2006. It may be noted that TIB's research was premised on field observations, key-informant interviews and secondary reports and, as such, did not provide any specific measure of corruption. An attempt is made here to summarise the key findings:[40]

- i The assessment of local conditions was flawed and, in some instances, inappropriate. This, compounded by incorrect or lack of requisite information, impeded the process of setting strategic priorities for humanitarian aid and assistance. There was evidence that in some cases relief was distributed on the basis of exaggerated or unsubstantiated information.
- ii The process of selecting beneficiaries of relief was beleaguered by irregularities. The selection criteria were guided by vested interests, political patronage and connections with influential quarters within or outside the government. This resulted in the distribution of relief material among families that did not qualify to receive

assistance whereas those who genuinely needed it were deprived. While some affected families were saturated with relief goods, others, particularly in remote and inaccessible areas, received none. Middle-class families too were left out of the relief net as they were unable to reconcile with the social embarrassment of reaching out for aid.

iii There was evidence of lack of coordination and corruption among relief workers. Allegations were levelled at them *inter alia* for inequitable distribution of relief goods, misappropriation by fake relief outfits and pilferage of relief goods and sale in the black market. Medicines meant for affected populations were sold in local drug stores. Brisk business was also carried out with expired relief goods. Relief work was manipulated by local government representatives to benefit their respective constituencies unduly. Local body members allegedly embezzled relief goods.

iv The procurement of relief goods and other logistical support suffered from lack of transparency and failure to comply with conflict of interest principles. Concerned actors were reluctant to divulge information. Internal control and proper monitoring of relief distribution were largely absent.

v Irregularities were also committed by NGOs that were disbursing aid. Preferential treatment by NGOs was evident from the fact that relief operations were confined to members within their own constituencies or coverage areas. NGOs were found to give out loans in the name of relief, subsequently exerting pressure for loan repayment. Pursuant to government request, some NGOs stopped collecting installments on micro-credit but also stopped issuing new loans to those who genuinely needed for resuming economic activities. This created scope for traditional moneylenders to charge a much higher interest.

TIB maintains that the preceding scenario was influenced by three fundamental elements: *first*, lack of capacity to absorb large amounts of resources pumped into aid operations within a short span of time; *second*, disregard for conventional tools of accountability given the urgency of the situation; and *third*, asymmetric power relations at all levels between relief providers and intended recipients.[41] In addition to creating scope of corruption, these factors are believed to impede choice and decision making by aid recipients and free flow of information, potentially leading to loss or reduction of funding flows which, in turn, results in loss in opportunities and income.[42]

Benchmarks of integrity standards: TIB's recommendations

Based on the findings of its independent research and secondary literature, TIB came up with a set of benchmarks of integrity standards[43] perceived as critical for preventing corruption in humanitarian interventions:

i *Transparency and Access to Information*: In many disaster contexts, few people know what they are entitled to receive, or how to complain if they cannot access it, and are unable actively and meaningfully to participate in the planning and delivery of assistance.[44] The process and mechanism of needs assessment and relief distribution must be transparent and made public locally and nationally in a simple language and through a harmonised and comprehensible system. The intended beneficiaries must be able to access need-based information on *inter alia* what they are entitled to in terms of aid and compensation, who to ask for help and guidance, where to lodge complaints in case of deviation and so on. Citizens' groups are particularly useful to help local communities demand transparency and accountability in relief operations. Actions in this regard would include proactive and/or on request disclosure of the whole range of issues connected to emergency assistance starting from *inter alia* the criteria of beneficiary selection, the means of conducting the selection, names of donors and the amount of funds committed and received from each, reporting guidelines, costs of carriage, storage and disbursement of relief goods to monitoring and grievance redress mechanisms.

ii *Tracking of Relief Distribution Process*: Relief goods may be stolen, diverted or simply siphoned off during repackaging for distribution.[45] In order for efficient and effective disbursement of relief goods, it is imperative to establish a transparent and accountable system for tracking the disbursement process with active collaboration of all stakeholders. This would help them follow the relief trail, recognise the bottlenecks, identify the gaps in coordination and monitoring and ultimately see if relief goods were reaching the intended beneficiaries. Ownership of the tracking process by all stakeholders and dissemination of the results is essential for the effectiveness, credibility and acceptance of the system.

iii *Proficient Monitoring and Evaluation*: It is crucial for concerned institutions to develop internal control systems to facilitate monitoring and evaluation, both internal and external, of the various assistance programmes, initiatives and resource flows. In this context it is important that all stakeholders involved in relief disbursement meticulously maintain their books of account and other information and ensure people's access to them. Social audits with participation of the intended beneficiaries are another means of assessing impact and effectiveness of humanitarian assistance. However, the capacity with respect to M&E, internal control and audit, financial management, oversight and accountability is often lacking in key institutions engaged in delivering relief goods. Adequate investments must therefore be made to strengthen the internal capacity of these institutions through training, orientation, digitisation of systems and so on.

iv *Complaint Mechanisms*: The humanitarian assistance landscape is largely devoid of effective complaint mechanisms, and even where such mechanisms exist, they are found to be inadequate or inappropriate. Beneficiaries often find it difficult to complain or communicate concerns to relevant agencies and/or are simply reluctant to do so for fears that this will negatively impact on assistance or just will not be acted upon.[46] As such, in the absence of an enabling environment they are put off from lodging complaints and seeking redress for irregularities and inequities in relief operations. Options and opportunities should be provided to affected communities/individuals for reporting irregularities, filing complaints and seeking redress through a user friendly and independent grievance-handling apparatus which they can access and use without fear or favour. Protective measures must be available against potential retribution and for whistle-blowers.

v *Participation of Affected Populations*: It is common for humanitarian assistance programmes to be externally driven offering little or no scope for participation of affected communities in the planning, design and implementation of aid projects. Knowledgeable about local contexts and power dynamics, affected populations are in a better position to distinguish and guard against potential corruption risks than external aid agencies. Strengthening community involvement in the planning, implementation and evaluation of humanitarian programmes essentially promotes transparent and accountable local governance, which reduces corruption opportunities on the one hand and develops ownership over aid efforts on the other. Involving beneficiaries meaningfully in project planning, implementation, evaluation and reporting can contribute to minimising corruption by increasing both beneficiaries' awareness of their entitlements and their stake in the success of aid programmes.[47]

vi *Code of Conduct*: Corruption is one factor that can potentially induce actors in decision making, resource allocation and control to put personal gain before their official duties.[48] Efforts must be made to strengthen the integrity of public officials who are in charge of and/or at the frontline of relief operations by institutionalising anti-corruption codes and practices in public service. In order for the code of conduct to be effective, it must have inbuilt negative and positive incentives to provide a fine balance of reward and punishment for officials on the basis of their performance. Needless to say, codes of conduct are not adequate in themselves unless supported by a strong oversight mechanism and decent compensation package for officials.

vii *Ethics and Integrity*: Given the diversity of humanitarian actors (government, NGOs, donors, private sector, civil society), mechanisms must be developed to guide and coordinate their efforts, ensure due diligence and internal oversight and foster mutual trust among stakeholders for maximum impact and for ensuring integrity, transparency and accountability in humanitarian assistance. Pursuant to this, a code of ethics with customised principles and tools promoting zero tolerance against corruption should be developed in a participatory process and made strictly applicable to all concerned stakeholders involved in humanitarian assistance. The commitment not to engage in corruption and to resist it in all its forms can also manifest in public pledges of integrity.

Needless to say, the preceding points do not necessarily provide a magic formula or a definitive prescription for preventing and eliminating corruption in humanitarian work. For all of them to work it is imperative that relationships are forged among all stakeholders and ownership developed to make room for integrity practices in humanitarian assistance. The utility and benefits will be realised only when emergencies occur next. Standards and protocols are developed on the basis of current knowledge – this knowledge will change – accordingly, standards and benchmarks must also evolve with the passage of time and in response to particular operational realities.

Integrity standards in the disaster management regulatory framework in Bangladesh

Successive governments in Bangladesh have undertaken various policy initiatives to strengthen the resilience of the country against disasters. Some of the key developments in the area include the issuing of Standing

Orders on Disaster (SOD) in 1997 and revised in 2010, the drafting of the National Disaster Management Policy 2008, the adoption of the National Disaster Management Plan (2010–2015), the development of Guidelines for Humanitarian Assistance Programme Implementation 2012–2013 and, finally, the enactment of the Disaster Management Act in 2012.

While the regulatory framework broadly provides legislative, policy and best practice directions that are critical for the implementation of disaster risk reduction and emergency response activities, the policies have no specific reference to integrity practices during humanitarian crises. This essentially demonstrates a general lack of recognition of corruption risks in disaster management and humanitarian assistance despite that among the many challenges besetting the disaster management system in Bangladesh, the absence of good governance at all levels of disaster management and risk reduction is regarded by experts as being the principal challenge.[49]

More recently, a shift in the law and policy environment guiding disaster management is discernible. For example, the Guidelines for Humanitarian Assistance Programme Implementation 2012–2013 provide that any person aggrieved by beneficiary list or assistance rendered may lodge a grievance with the concerned authority, to be disposed of within 15 days of the complaint. This initiative has more or less set the ground for actively recognising that disaster management systems and processes are not completely free from risks of mismanagement and governance lapses. This policy possibly provided a watershed for the adoption of a law that more distinctly focused on essential elements of good governance during disaster management.

The Disaster Management Act 2012 provides certain elements that seek to prevent mismanagement and corruption in humanitarian assistance. This law enables any individual, family or group to lodge a complaint with the committee set up for the purpose at the national or local level if any irregularities, negligence or mismanagement in disaster management is observed (Section 29). The committee must dispose of the complaint within 30 days from the date of its receipt, through a proper investigation where necessary. If the complainant is aggrieved by the committee's decision, he or she may appeal to the government in case of a decision at the national level and to divisional commissioner or district administrator as applicable in respect of decisions at the local level. Decisions of the appellant authorities shall be regarded as final. The act prescribes penal sanctions of rigorous imprisonment for up to one year or fine of up to BDT 100,000 or both for individuals or organisations making false or baseless claims in an attempt to secure assistance or benefits within the disaster management framework (Section 38). Penal sanctions are also applicable to designated managers of disaster resources if they misuse or use them for personal interest or incite others to do the same (Section 39) and to any individual who inflates the price of basic commodities or creates conditions for such inflation in disaster-hit areas for illegal profit (Section 40).

While these initiatives are indeed a step in the right direction, they can at best be regarded as elementary and somewhat tentative evident from the somewhat broad brush approach at addressing only some selected forms of corruption during emergencies without considering the non-monetary forms (e.g. violence and gender-based persecution) and the more intangible forms of corruption (e.g. nepotism, misuse of power, use of political influence and indifference or failure of public officials to discharge their duties) that are commonly associated with humanitarian assistance. The Disaster Management Act 2012 refers to 'irregularities' 'mismanagement', 'negligence' without providing any working definition for the same or any guidelines indicating what would constitute the said offences in the context of disaster management. It does not indicate how provisions of this law would be aligned with those in existing administrative, penal and anti-corruption laws. It speaks of a committee for handling complaints but does not specify its membership and constitution. However, it is expected that these gaps will be mitigated once rules have been framed and capacities of relevant stakeholders have been developed for practical implementation of the law.

Conclusion

Clearly corruption is a serious and often unavoidable aspect of humanitarian assistance processes and practices although until fairly recently humanitarian assistance has not been considered an important arena for anti-corruption discourse. Corruption is considered a threat to humanitarian action because it can prevent assistance from getting to the needy, and because it can potentially undermine governance structures dedicated to such assistance. While it may be difficult to completely eliminate the risks given the constraints and demands associated with humanitarian emergencies generally, the recognition that corruption risks do exist and preparedness to deal with them are essential first steps to addressing the problem. Strong and capable management, with the necessary systems and procedures, is as important for mitigating corruption risks in humanitarian assistance as are greater levels of transparency and accountability to affected communities. In order for these steps to translate into action, it is necessary to have integrity standards and benchmarks in place to address corruption or chances of corruption at different levels and phases of humanitarian assistance. Civil society activism through joint and coordinated advocacy is also crucial for ensuring that government and humanitarian agencies do their job and for educating affected populations about their rights and entitlements so that that they can seek relevant information, participate in the planning and implementation of relief operations and complain when they come across corruption and irregularities. Above all, the issue of corruption in humanitarian work needs to be openly discussed by and among all stakeholders, particularly at the policy level. There is a tendency to shy away from the topic lest it erodes public trust in aid operations and impedes the work of humanitarian agencies on the ground, but conversations in this context are critical for learning about good practices and the development of anti-corruption measures for reducing the risks inherent in the systems.

Notes

1 Maxwell et al. (2008, p. 4).
2 Finnemore, 14 April 2000 (revised September 2000).
3 Ewins et al. (2006, pp. 10–11).
4 Ibid., p. 11.
5 Transparency International (2006, p. 1).
6 Davis (February 2009, p. 1).
7 Buchanan-Smith, December, 2002.
8 Davis (2009, p. 1).
9 Larché (1999).
10 Davis (2009, p. 8).
11 See *Core Humanitarian Standard on Quality and Accountability* (2014), published by Groupe URD, HAP International, People in Aid and the Sphere Project.
12 The 2010 HAP Standard in Accountability and Quality Management, Switzerland, p. 1.
13 Maxwell Walker, Maxwell, CMI (2009). U4 Anti-Corruption Resource Centre. Retrieved from www.u4.no/themes/ces
14 Ibid.
15 For details see Maxwell et al. (2008).
16 Nicholas Stockton (2005). 'Preventing Corruption in Humanitarian Relief Operations', Issue Paper Presented at the 5th Regional Anti-Corruption Conference, 28–30 September 2005, Beijing, ADB/OECD Anti-Corruption Initiative for Asia and the Pacific, p. 1.
17 Calossi et al. (2012, p. 664).
18 Stockton (2005, p. 10).
19 Transparency International (2014, p. 11).

20 Ibid.
21 Stockton (2005, pp. 2–3).
22 Transparency International (2014, pp. 1–3).
23 Harvey et al. (2010, p. 43).
24 Maxwell et al. (2008).
25 CMI, U4 Brief (2009).
26 Larché (1999).
27 Walker and Maxwell (2009).
28 Maxwell et al. (2008, p. 9).
29 Shamsuddoha et al. (2013, p. 7).
30 Ewins et al. (2006, p. 7).
31 *The Daily Star*, Dhaka, 13 December, 2007.
32 Government of Bangladesh. 'Cyclone Sidr in Bangladesh. Damage, Loss and Needs Assessment for Disaster Recovery and Reconstruction', a report prepared by GoB, assisted by the International Development Community with financial support from European Commission, Dhaka, April 2008, p. xvii.
33 Ibid., p. 4.
34 Ibid., p. 14.
35 Ibid., p. 15.
36 Ibid., p. i.
37 Ibid.
38 Financial Tracking Service. Tracking Global Humanitarian Aid Flows, 'Bangladesh – Cyclone Sidr – November 2007'. Retrieved from http://fts.unocha.org/reports/daily/ocha_R10_E15382_asof___1503250301.pdf
39 See Government of Bangladesh (2008, p. i).
40 Drawn from Mahmud, Akram and Iftekharuzzaman, 'Integrity in Humanitarian Assistance: Issues and Benchmarks', paper presented at a seminar organised by Transparency International Bangladesh (TIB) in Dhaka, 18 December 2007, pp. 9–10.
41 Ibid., p. 7.
42 Ibid.
43 Ibid., pp. 11–12.
44 Harvey et al. (2010, p. 39).
45 *Preventing Corruption in Humanitarian Operations*. Pocket Book of Good Practices, p. 36. Retrieved from www.rodekors.no/Global/HK%20-%20Hovedkontoret/Organinsasjon/Dokumenter/Pocket%20Guide_corruption.pdf
46 Harvey et al. (2010, p. 40).
47 Transparency International (2006, p. 6).
48 Calossi et al. (2012, p. 663).
49 Rahman et al. (2013, p. 41).

References

Akram, S. M., Mahmud, T. & Iftekharuzzaman. (2007). *Integrity in Humanitarian Assistance: Issues and Benchmarks*, Paper Presented at a Seminar Organised by Transparency International Bangladesh (TIB), Dhaka, 18 December.

Buchanan-Smith, M. (2002). Interrelationships between Humanitarian Organizations. *FORUM: War and Accountability*, ICRC, 31 December.

Retrieved from www.icrc.org/eng/assets/files/other/icrc_002_808_forum_war_and_accountability.pdf

Calossi, Enrico, Sberna, Salvatore & Vannucci, Alberto. (2012). 'Disasters and Corruption, Corruption as Disaster' in A. de Guttry, et al. (eds.) *International Disaster Response Law*. The Hague, Netherland: Springer.

Davis, A. (February 2009). *Concerning Accountability of Humanitarian Action*, HPN Network Paper, No. 58, London, UK: ODI.

Ewins, P., Harvey, P., Savage, K. & Jacobs, A. (2006). *Mapping the Risks of Corruption in Humanitarian Action*, Report for Transparency International and the U4 Anti-Corruption Resource Centre UK: Overseas Development Institute and Management Accounting for NGOs (MANGO). Retrieved fromwww.odi.org/sites/odi.org.uk/files/odi-assets/publications-opinion-files/874.pdf

Government of Bangladesh. (2008). *Cyclone Sidr in Bangladesh: Damage, Loss and Needs Assessment for Disaster Recovery and Reconstruction*, Report prepared by GoB. Dhaka: The International Development Community & The European Commission, Dhaka, April.

Harvey, P., Stoddard, A., Harmer, A., Taylor, G., Domenico, V. D. & Brander, L. (2010). *The State of the Humanitarian System: Assessing Performance and Progress: A Pilot Study*. London: Overseas Development Institute.

Larché, J. (1999). *Corruption in the NGO World: What It Is and How to Tackle It*. Retrieved from www.odihpn.org/humanitarian-exchange-magazine/issue-52/corruption-in-the-ngo-world-what-it-is-and-how-to-tackle-it

Maxwell, D., Walker, P., Church, C., Harvey, P., Savage, K., Bailey, S., Hees, R. & Ahlendorf, M.-L. (2008). *Preventing Corruption in Humanitarian Assistance*. Final Research Report. Berlin: Transparency International.

Rahman, M., Chakraborty, B. & Chakraborty, T. C. (2013). *An Overview on Gaps and Opportunities of Disaster Management in Bangladesh Managing Climate Induced Disasters*. Dhaka: Network on Climate Change, Bangladesh (NCC,B).

Shamsuddoha, M., Islam, M., Haque, M. A., Rahman, M. F., Roberts, E., Hasemann, A. & Roddick, S. (2013). *Local Perspective on Loss and Damage in the Context of Extreme Events: Insights from Cyclone-Affected Communities in Coastal Bangladesh*. Dhaka: Center for Participatory Research and Development (CRPD).

Stockton, N. (2005). *Preventing Corruption in Humanitarian Relief Operations*, Issue Paper Presented at the 5th Regional Anti-Corruption Conference, 28–30 September 2005, Beijing, ADB/OECD Anti-Corruption Initiative for Asia and the Pacific. Retrieved from www.oecd.org/site/adboecdanticorruptioninitiative/regionalseminars/35592702.pdf

The Sphere Project. (2014). *Core Humanitarian Standard on Quality and Accountability*. London, UK: The Sphere Project.

Transparency International. (2006). *Corruption in Humanitarian Aid*, Working Paper No.03, p. 1. Retrieved from www.transparency.ca/9-Files/Older/Reports-Older/Readings/SR-P-working_paper_humanitarian_aid.pdf

Transparency International. (2014). *Preventing Corruption in Humanitarian Operations*. London: Handbook of Good Practices.

Walker, P. & Maxwell, D. (2009). *Confronting Corruption in Humanitarian Aid: Perspective and Options*. Bergen: Chr. Michelsen Institute (U4 Brief 2009:3) U4 Brief No. 3, March 2009, U4 Anti-Corruption Resource Centre. Retrieved from www.u4.no/themes/ces

14 A legal framework to prevent trafficking of women and young girls during disasters in India

Manjula Batra

> In this crucial year for global development, as Member States work to craft a post-2015 agenda and a new set of sustainable development goals, let us do our utmost to eradicate all forms of human exploitation. Let us strive to build a world of social justice where all people can live and work in freedom, dignity and equality.
>
> UN Secretary-General Ban Ki-Moon[1]

Globally, natural disasters are the result of ecological imbalance and climate change, and it has also been observed that the number of hydro-meteorological disasters has increased considerably (Henry, 2012; Shaw & Krishnamurthy, 2009). Further, the Sendai discussions reveal that more than 700,000 people have lost their lives across the world, over 1.4 million have been injured and approximately 23 million have been made homeless as a result of disasters across the world.[2]

In India more than 1.5 billion people have been affected by disasters in different ways, and that women, children and people in vulnerable situations have been affected the most.[3] Disasters affect men and women in different ways, which reflects the existing gender discrimination between the two sexes (Oxfam International, 2005). In times of a disaster, the fact of biological and physiological differences between men and women coupled with the variations in their socio-economic status poses a big challenge that has to be dealt with by the affected state and its people (Neumayer & Plumper, 2007). It is also true that devastations caused by a disaster lead to a depletion of resources and a temporary breakdown of social order, and create adverse conditions of competition within the community (WHO, 2002). Moreover, it aggravates the existing gender inequality among the affected population that further increases the vulnerability of women and young girls (Enarson, 2007). Unfortunately, devastation caused by a disaster is also considered as the most advantageous period for the stakeholders of the trafficking industry as they can exploit women and young girls for commercial reasons.

The present chapter attempts to establish the cause and relation between the occurrence of the disaster and human trafficking. It also lays down the modalities and recommends steps necessary for addressing the occurrence of disasters and for combating human trafficking in India.

Relationship between disaster and human trafficking

Disasters impede progress towards sustainable development (Shaw & Krishnamurthy, 2009). They often pull families apart make the lives of women, young girls and children more vulnerable; and cause the death of loved ones, or make them arrive at unusual and hostile surroundings (Todres, 2011).

A disaster has a direct impact on human trafficking. The conditions created by a disaster enable the stakeholders of the trafficking industry to thrive and trade in women and girls across countries. At least 225,000 women and children are trafficked from the Southeast Asian countries every year, thereby accounting for approximately one-third of the global human flesh trade (Perry & McEwing, 2013). India has often been a destination and transit point for trafficking victims from Bangladesh, Nepal and Bhutan (UNODC, 2009). The challenge of human trafficking during disasters is a threat to the security of the inhabitants of the destination region, besides impacting the moral system of the destination country (Enarson & Dhar, 2009). However, human trafficking is an organized crime round the globe and can be best described as 'modern-day slavery' (Nair, 2009). An amalgamation of disaster and human trafficking results in the infringement of human rights of the poor, the marginalized and the vulnerable population (Zommers & Singh, 2014). It often leads to a violation of the socio-economic, cultural and other rights of the people affected by the disaster.

The modus operandi of traffickers engaged in human trafficking has become very advanced over the years which makes the fight for combating the evil of human trafficking more difficult (Bhat, 2009). It has been observed that the trauma related to the post-disaster period affects the vulnerable group, especially their health, livelihood and psychological state of mind (Oxfam International, 2005). The recent earthquake that hit Nepal led to an exodus of thousands of young girls who were either lured or smuggled to be sent into brothels across South Asia through human traffickers (*The Guardian*, 2015).[4] While death may harm women and young girls during a disaster, it has been seen that the mortality figures in the post-disaster period significantly increase due to violence against women and neglect of issues of women's health (Hobson et al., 2014).

During the post-disaster period sexual violence against women can be seen in various forms. In the aftermath of the Indian Ocean tsunami, women who were pulled out of water were 'raped' as payment for being saved (Thomas et al., 2013). Further, displaced women who are kept in 'rescue camps/shelters' are also and sexually assaulted (Nasreen, 2008). Women who are kept in refugee camps without men are more vulnerable to being sexually exploited (Dasgupta et al., 2010). Also, as a consequence of disasters striking in Indonesia, it has been seen that displaced women are sexually harassed, as well as forced or rushed into marriage with much older men (Bacalla, 2010). Moreover, female children both in refugee and outside camps and especially those who have lost one or both parents in the disaster are forced into child marriage for economic and cultural reasons (Norlha, 2015). All these factors, including others, may lead to an increase in the trafficking of women and children in disaster-hit regions. Both the World Bank and UN divisions for the advancement of women have issued warnings on increasing trafficking due to displacement of women and girls (Dasgupta et al., 2010).

Modalities for disaster risk reduction

The hon'ble prime minister of India Narendra Modi in his address at the United Nations Summit in September 2015, for the adoption of Post-2015 Development Agenda, highlighted the importance of collective action at the international level to resolve issues relating to development or combating climate change or protecting the poor from the repercussions of natural disasters. He emphatically stated that 'we all believe that international partnership must be at the centre of our efforts, whether it is development or combating climate change. And, the principle of common but differentiated responsibilities is the bedrock of our collective enterprise . . . resolve to secure the future of the poor from the perils of natural disasters'.[5] The words to secure the perils of natural disasters clearly include the peril of human trafficking that woman and young girls are subjected to at the time of natural disasters.

For ages, India has been always known for its diversity both in terms of culture and in terms of its geological vicinity. Starting from Kashmir to Kanyakumari, India has a land border of 15,106.7 kilometres and a coastline of 7,516 kilometres, including island territories.[6] Given its geographical conditions, India is vulnerable to natural disasters.

India follows a 'zero-tolerance' approach towards the loss caused to human development at the outset of major storms (UNISDR Annual Report, 2014).[7] India follows the United Nations (United Nations Office for Disaster Risk Reduction) concept of 'disaster risk reduction',[8] as a practice of reducing disaster risks through systematic efforts to analyse and reduce the causal factors of disasters. In the journey from Hyogo Framework for Action[9] to the Sendai Framework for Disaster Risk Reduction,[10] it has been observed that it is very necessary to foresee, plan and lessen the disaster risk for promotion and protection of human rights of persons globally. The collective approach of stakeholders for 'disaster risk reduction' would indirectly help to restrain the mass outflow of affected citizens into the gallows of human trafficking through the launch of sensitization and awareness programmes regarding the modus operandi of the traffickers in the trafficking industry (Price, 2015).

It is evident that many countries have failed to formulate gender mainstreaming policies and strategies to deal with the aftereffects of disasters (True, 2012). In fact, it is surprising that the United Nations Framework Convention on Climate Change has not even included bodies of most countries' perspectives on gender mainstreaming (Basic Facts-UN, 2011). It is also surprising to note that the legislatures in most countries are lagging behind in framing women-centric plans and policies that should be considered as an integral part of any disaster management plans (Green, 2012). Therefore, it becomes imperative that the global leaders are urged to make gender-responsive legislations pertaining to climate change and disaster risk reduction (Manila Declaration, 2008).[11]

In India, the Ministry of Home Affairs through its 2010–2011 annual report has endorsed a comprehensive scheme called 'Strengthening Law Enforcement Response in India against Trafficking in Persons' which focuses on training and capacity building. Currently under this scheme different states and union territories have established anti-human trafficking units throughout the country.[12] Likewise, the Ministry of Women and Child Development (MWCD) is the nodal ministry responsible for the holistic development of women and children. MWCD promotes advancement, development and betterment of women through its different schemes such as the National Policy for the Empowerment of Women 2001, the National Mission for Empowerment of Women and *Ujjawalla* (towards light).[13]

Further, the Ministry of Home Affairs is actively participating in meetings of International Strategy for Disaster Reduction – Asia Partnership (IAP) to discuss the disaster risk reduction. The upcoming IAP meeting will also provide an opportunity to discuss substantive issues related to the implementation of the Sendai framework at the regional, national and local levels. These discourses will be considered as an important platform to discuss the inclusion of gender issues in disaster risk reduction.[14]

Combating human trafficking: international dimensions

Human trafficking for commercial sexual exploitation is the worst form of violence against women as it violates the most basic human rights to sexual autonomy and integrity.[15] Today commercial sexual exploitation may not be the only reason for human trafficking. Some of the other identified reasons for trafficking include (1) child labour, (2) bonded labour, (3) domestic helps and maids, (4) forced marriages, (5) kidnapping by de-notified tribes engaged traditionally in sex trade, (6) adoption and running of orphanages, (7) begging and (8) organ transplant (NCW, 2012). Undoubtedly, when the sexual and reproductive rights of women or girls are exploited as a commodity, it not only amounts to infringement of her socio-economic and cultural rights, but it also amounts to an infringement of her moral as well as basic human rights.[16]

The United Nations Declaration of Human Rights, 1948;[17] the Vienna Declaration, 1993;[18] and the Convention on the Elimination of All Forms of Discrimination against Women (CEDAW)[19] ensure human dignity and protection from violence caused due to the act of trafficking, *in toto*. Besides the different United Nations Organizations like the United Nations Office of Drugs and Crimes (UNODC) and the United Nations Global Initiative to Fight Human Trafficking (UN GIFT), and the World Bank, the International Organization on Migration (IOM), the Asian Health Agency (TAHA) and the Asian Development Bank (ADB) have consistently been sponsoring various programmes for the rehabilitation and reintegration of the trafficked victims in the country (UNODC, 2008).

Recently, India ratified the United Nations Convention against Transnational Organized Crime (UNTOC) and its three protocols.[20] The implementation of the said Convention along with municipal laws[21] can help the prevention of cross-border human trafficking and resilience of its victims. The victims of human trafficking in India consequent to disasters must be repatriated to their native place as India has ratified the South Asian Association for Regional Cooperation (SAARC) Convention on Preventing and Combating Trafficking in Women and Children for Prostitution, 2002,[22] and the SAARC Convention on the Regional Arrangements for the Promotion of Child Welfare, 2002, in South Asia that advocates to opt a victim-centric approach irrespective of the fact that they have been nabbed by the concerned authorities on the pre-text of human trafficking.

Strong constitution and weak enforcement in combating human trafficking in India

The Indian Constitution guarantees the right to life and personal liberty of every citizen of the country under Article 21, but the thriving flesh trade and human trafficking belies all the promises made to the vulnerable sections trapped in disasters.

It is a well-known fact that in India the victims of human trafficking[23] are forced to enter into sex slavery, forced marriage, bonded labour (for brick kiln and begging), prostitution and domestic slavery. Moreover, the fact that prostitution (a clandestine affair) is not legalized in India[24] further aggravates the condition of the displaced victims. Furthermore, it is a gigantic and impractical task to rescue victims from the red-light areas of GB Road in Delhi, Kamatipura and Bhivandi in Mumbai, Sona Gachi in Kolkata and other southern regions where commercialized prostitution is prevalent (Nair, 2009). In the wake of vulnerability, it has been observed through last decade, nearly 250,000 Nepalese women and girls have been found in Indian brothels (Wadhwa, 1998).[25] The local NGOs in Nepal estimate that every year between 5,000 and 7,000 Nepalese girls are trafficked into the red-light districts of Indian cities and are compelled to work in horrendous circumstances. Many of these girls are between nine and ten years of age.[26]

The Supreme Court of India through its various landmark judgements has indirectly read the sexual exploitation of women and girls as violation of their right to life and personal liberty and to live with dignity under Article 21 of the Indian Constitution. In the case of *Chandrima Das v. Railway Board*, the apex court observed that sexual exploitation of women violates the right to life and liberty of women under Article 21 and was applicable as much to foreigners as to Indian citizens. In this case a Bangladeshi woman was gang-raped in *Yatri Niwas* (motel) at the railway station in Kolkata, which was considered violation of her right to life. The apex court directed the state to give the victim of rape compensation for the wrong committed against her.

Likewise, to protect the rights of vulnerable women languished in the web of sexual exploitation, the Supreme Court in *State of Maharashtra v. Madhukar Narain Mardikar*[27] has held that even a prostitute has a right to privacy, which is an integral part of the right to life under Article 21 of the constitution of India and no one could be allowed to invade this right. In *Vishal Jeet v. Union of India,*[28] the apex court issued directions to the state governments and union territories for eradicating the evil of child prostitution and for evolving programmes for the care, protection, treatment, development and rehabilitation of the young fallen victims. Even in *Gaurav Jain v. Union of India,*[29] the Supreme Court held that the problem of prostitution had become a serious one and required considerable and effective attention. The court issued directions to the concerned authorities to constitute a committee to examine the problem of prostitution and to segregate the children of prostitutes from their mothers living in the prostitute homes so that they could mingle with others and become part of the society.

It is important to note that the Supreme Court has considerably widened the scope of Article 21 of the constitution of India to include within its ambit all the rights as mentioned earlier. By giving such a wide interpretation to Article 21, the Supreme Court has cast a non-delegable duty upon the central and state governments to prepare effective disaster management policies and programmes so that the problem of human trafficking of women and girls could be curtailed during disasters. Besides Article 21, there are other provisions in the Indian Constitution which directly or indirectly enjoin a duty upon the government to combat human trafficking in the country. Article 23 of the constitution of India explicitly prohibits 'trafficking in human beings and *beggar* and other similar forms of forced labour'. Article 24 of the constitution specifically prohibits the employment of children below 24 years of age in factories, mines and other hazardous employment. Further, Article 14 assures each and every citizen of the country equality before law and equal protection of laws, while Article 15 (1) prohibits discrimination on grounds of religion, race, caste, sex and place of birth. In fact, Article 15 (3) of the constitution of India makes it obligatory for the government to make laws and policies for the welfare of women and children.

Further, the Directive Principles of State Policy embodied in the constitution of India enjoin a duty on the Government of India to lay down socio-economic policies that could secure social justice to all and prevent all forms of exploitation of the people of country. Article 39 of the constitution of India categorically states that 'men, women and children should not be forced by economic necessity to enter unsuitable avocations and that child and youth should be protected against exploitation'. Article 39A of Indian Constitution directs that the legal system should ensure that opportunities for securing justice are not denied to any citizen because of economic or other disabilities. Besides this, Article 51 (A) (e), which is one of the fundamental duties embodied in Part IV-A of constitution of India, imposes a duty on all citizens of the country to renounce practices that are derogatory to the dignity of women.

Unfortunately, despite having one of the world's most unambiguous set of constitutional provisions that accord protection to women and young girls against human trafficking, the problem still remains unresolved and there is no evidence of reduction in their being trafficked. Considering that the forms of human trafficking have changed over the years, the prevalent measures seem inadequate to deal with the issue of human trafficking. For example, the Immoral Traffic (Prevention) Act, 1956, is the only available law which only recognizes the trafficking of commercial sexual exploitation. Also, there is a dearth of proper implementation of the act, and quality of services rendered is poor. Many districts don't have shelter homes for trafficked survivors, and the government-run shelter homes are inadequate and insufficient (NCW, 2012). In fact, the Government of India has been expressing its concern over the increasing and persistent changes in the trends of human trafficking in India especially in the disaster-hit regions.

The DMA 2005: needs to resonate with women and girls

Until recently, there was no legislation in India which dealt specifically with disaster management. It was only in December 2005 that the Indian legislature enacted the DMA which especially deals with matters related to disaster. The objective of the Act is to provide for the effective management of disasters, including disaster risk reduction and for matters therewith and incidental thereto. The enactment of the DMA 2005 was followed by the adoption of the National Disaster Management Policy in the year 2009. Both these instruments have helped in adopting a proactive prevention-driven approach towards disaster management and relief-centric approach following a disaster which means that the centre and states are obliged to directly and indirectly address the issue of combating human trafficking of women and children in disaster-hit regions. Section 2(d) of the DMA defines disaster:

> as a catastrophe, mishap, calamity or grave occurrence in any area, arising from natural and man-made causes, or by accident or negligence which results in substantial loss of life or human suf-

fering or damage, or degradation of environment, and is of such a nature or magnitude as to be beyond the coping capacity of the affected area.

Section 2(e) of the said Act defines disaster management as a continuous integrated process of planning, organizing, co-ordination and implementing measures which are necessary or expedient for

- i prevention of danger or threat of any disaster;
- ii mitigation or reduction of risk of any disaster or its severity or consequences;
- iii capacity building;
- iv preparedness to deal with any disaster;
- v assessing the severity or magnitude of any disaster;
- vi evacuation, rescue and relief; and
- vii rehabilitation and reconstruction.

Even if trafficking is not clearly mentioned in the Act, the subclauses (v) and (vi) of Section 2(e) read with Section 2(d) impose a duty on the authorities established under the Act to plan, organize, coordinate and implement measures which are necessary or expedient for the evacuation, rescue and rehabilitation of the victims of the disaster-hit regions. This duty indirectly extends to undertaking measures for preventing and combating human trafficking of women and young girls. Considering the inadequacy of existing laws to curtail the issue of sexual exploitation of women and young girls in the context of natural disasters, the proper implementation of the Act can to a large extent reduce and prevent human trafficking during and in the aftermath of disasters.

The DMA provides a legal and institutional framework for disaster management in India at the national, state and district levels. However, as India is quasi-federal in nature,[30] the primary responsibility for disaster management rests with the state government though the Act makes it obligatory for the state to implement the policies and guidelines as laid down by the central government. It is in fact the district administration that carries out most of the operations related to disaster management in consonance with the central and state-level authorities.

The DMA has created several new authorities at the national, state, district and local levels to manage disaster and deal with the adverse situations arising due to the disaster. A brief discussion on these authorities along with their powers and functions is given here:

- i The National Disaster Management Authority (NDMA) which has been established under the chairmanship of the prime minister is the apex body responsible for laying down policies, plans and guidelines for disaster management and for coordination and implementation of the same throughout the country. The State Disaster Management Authority is responsible for ensuring the taking of integration measures for disaster management at the state level, while at the district level it is the District Disaster Management Authority. The guidelines for the prevention, mitigation, preparedness and response measures laid down by the NDMA and SDMA are followed by all the departments of the state, district and local levels.

ii The National Executive Committee (NEC) which is another important body constituted under the DMA is mandated to assist the NDMA in the discharge of its functions and ensure compliance of the directions issued by the central government. The NEC comprises the Union Home Secretary as the chairperson, and the secretaries to the Government of India in the Ministries/Departments of Agriculture, Atomic Energy, Defense, Drinking Water Supply, Environment and Forest, Finance (Expenditure), Health, Power, Rural Development, Science and Technology, Space, Telecommunications, Urban Development and the Chief of the Integrated Defense Staff of the Chiefs of Staff Committee as members, secretaries in the Ministry of External Affairs, Human Resource Development, Mines, Shipping, Road Transport and Highways and secretary of NDMA are special invitees in the meetings of the NEC. It is responsible to prepare the national plan, coordinate and monitor the implementation of the national policy and the guidelines issued by the NDMA. The Ministry of Home Affairs in the central government has the overall responsibility for disaster management in India.[31]

iii The National Institute of Disaster Management (NIDM) established under the DMA has the mandate for human resource development such as training needs, educational and research material for capacity building for disaster management within the broad policies and guidelines laid down by the NDMA.

iv The National Disaster Response Force (NDRF) established under the DMA is the specialized force for disaster response that works under the overall supervision and control of the NDMA. The specialized force can be utilized in rescuing and rehabilitating women and children who become victims of human trafficking.

According to the scheme of the Act, if measures to control and prevent human trafficking are included in the plans and policies evolved by the NDMA, the state, district and the local authorities would be bound to implement them. Moreover under Section 12 of the Act, the NDMA is obliged to recommend guidelines for the minimum standards of relief to be provided to persons affected by disaster and also make special provisions for widows and orphans. It is also important to mention here that while giving compensation and other forms of relief to the victims of disaster, the authorities established under the Act cannot discriminate anybody on grounds of sex, caste, community, dissent and religion as embodied in Section 61 of the Act.

In the light of the aforementioned provisions, it is explicit that the DMA imposes immense responsibility on both the local authorities *viz.* the rural local self-governing institutions (Panchayati Raj Institutions) and urban local bodies (municipalities, cantonment, boards and towns planning authorities) to ensure capacity building of their officers and employees for managing disasters, carry out relief, rehabilitation and reconstruction, rehabilitation in the affected areas and will prepare disaster management plans in consonance with guidelines of the National, State and District Disaster Management Authorities.

A careful analysis of the DMA is that it enjoins a duty upon the aforementioned authorities established under it to carry out the relief, rehabilitation and reconstruction activities in the disaster-affected areas in accordance with the guidelines of the NDMA operations which also extends to the victims of disasters including women and children in the affected regions. Therefore, it is the duty of the chief secretary, SDMA secretaries and the rural and urban local self-government to play a pro-active role in preventing and curbing human trafficking of women and children. It is also their duty to evacuate and rescue women and children from the clutches of the traffickers. These local self-governments must disseminate information about the modus operandi of the traffickers and maintain a special register for the women and children of the affected area so that their whereabouts can be established. This is a task which should be completed during pre-disaster time as part of preparedness. The registers should be saved at the NIC servers at the centre.

However, for specific types of disasters the concerned ministries have the nodal responsibilities to manage the disasters and NDMA should appropriately stay connected with them. For example, for drought – Ministry of Agriculture; for epidemics and biological disasters – Ministry of Health and Family Welfare; for chemical disaster – Ministry of Environment and Forests; nuclear disasters – Ministry of Atomic Energy; for air accidents – Ministry of Civil Aviation; and for railway accidents – Ministry of Railways.

A way forward towards combating human trafficking in women and young girls in the context of disaster

Human trafficking during and after disasters can be prevented by a collaboration of the community-based system with the effective working of the administration. Timely availability of resources and the rehabilitation processes taken by the concerned authorities could be an important measure in saving the marginalized and vulnerable population from being trafficked. There is a need to draw special attention towards the disaster management programmes with the active participation of the affected communities. Many vulnerable communities revert to coping with risk, often in the same or worse conditions even before a disaster actually strikes. There is a wide gap between what the affected community needs and what the authorities provide (Pant, 2012).

Both at the international and national levels, policies and plans, which are gender specific, need to be formulated on a priority basis if the havoc of human trafficking during and after disasters is to be overcome. Keeping this view in mind, the disaster management plans to combat human trafficking must be made in a manner that can deal with the problem in three stages: namely, at the pre-disaster stage, the disaster stage and the post-disaster stage. To achieve this, a multidisciplinary institutional association between all stakeholders is necessary. In this regard, the NDMA set up under the DMA can take help from civil society organizations, recognized international and national NGOs, the meteorological departments and the administration for the purpose of making gender-responsive management strategies for specific disaster-prone areas as well as for unprecedented disasters.

Preparedness against trafficking

The time before a disaster strikes in an area is crucial to deciding the preparedness[32] of the administration of India. At this stage, the disaster management plans mainly include the preparedness, prevention, mitigation and other pre-disaster planning strategies. The following are some strategies that can be undertaken by the authorities to reduce the incidences of human trafficking of women and young girls when a disaster strikes:

- Engendering pre-disaster strategies such as training, strategies, sensitization programmes, environmental laws and standard operating procedures (SOPs) on the subject of human trafficking due to disasters should be devised and developed through training, seminars and mock drills as described under the National Disaster Management Policy. Under the capacity-building[33] clause, a list of young girls, children and women residing in the disaster-prone area should be developed for ready reference for the use of the administration before any disaster strikes the area. NDMA should add 'Gender Sensitization and Vulnerabilities of Women in Disasters' as a special module in their training of trainers programme for disaster management.

- Seminars and trainings on the issue of human trafficking should be organized, at all educational institutions, offices (government and non-government both) in collaboration with civil society organizations and other stakeholders.
- Methods to engender 'information and communication technology' used in disaster management at various levels should be made mandatory. Information about impending disaster should be aired on television and radio and help may be sought from volunteers to communicate to the people living in the region where disaster is about to strike. Satellite phone and battery-operated walkie-talkie should be arranged in advance for the use of officers of administration.

Taking lessons from vulnerabilities encountered during disasters

The real test of preparedness of any community and administration appears during or immediately after disaster strikes an area. One of the best practices which evolved during the gigantic and devastating Hanshin Awaji earthquake of 1995 (SEEDS, 2009) could indicate that there are more such practices one could search for. Fortunately, community participation during a disaster ensures local ownership, ponders over the regional needs and promotes volunteerism and mutual help to prevent and minimize the damage caused due to disaster. It calls for a prompt response to any threatening disaster situation or disaster[34] through the community and local authorities.[35] For the purpose of preventing human trafficking at this stage local authorities and volunteers must consider many concerns indigenous to women per se such as camp location, sanitary and medical needs, health workers primarily women, cultural connections in approaching women in distress, sensitization of the police and local home guards on how to deal with a list of young children, girls and women which has been provided to them and how to find their lost families. Only government-recognized medical staff and nurses should be allowed to visit the camps where the displaced and young population is taking shelter. They should not be handed over in distress to lessen administrative work to unidentified people till women and girls have overcome trauma, temporary mental disability or physical lack of capacity.

Post-disaster stage

The community-based system and local authorities play a significant role in the post-disaster stage. Collectively, they can precisely comprehend the damage caused to the person and property. This stage calls for a rigorous concentration on community health (assessing the severity or magnitude of effects of any disaster,[36] evacuation, rescue and relief[37] and rehabilitation and reconstruction).[38] For the purpose of dealing with the trafficked women and young girls, the District Disaster Management Authority in collaboration with the local authorities, community people and the recognized NGOs should be sensitive to the needs of such population and proceed on a future course of action collectively so that the socio-economic and cultural rights of the affected population are protected. This stage calls for the dedicated services from psychologists/volunteers for psycho-social support, and counselling of the victims of disaster should be arranged. Passionate teachers should be identified to set up temporary schools for the victims in the disaster-affected areas to help victims overcome the trauma of the disaster. Local administration should look for, restore and create livelihood of the victims of the disaster. An orphaned child who is below 18 years of age should be registered with the Central Adoption Resource Agency and Local Child Welfare Committee. Orphaned young girls above 18 years of age should be sent to Nari-niketans or similar agencies. Strict vigil should be maintained at transit stations like railway stations or bus stops, checkposts in cross-border areas and special women officers should be deployed at checkposts. Investigation of suspected migrants (especially females) of cross-border area as per the rules of SAARC Convention that requires a victim-centric approach to deal with suspects of human trafficking should be carried out.

From the discussion and suggestions made thereon it is explicit that the present approach of Government of India is towards undertaking relief operations only when disaster strikes. While the DMA in its present form can be made effective in preventing sexual exploitation of vulnerable women and young girls in disaster-affected areas, it is suggested that a specific provision which deals with the issue of human trafficking be incorporated in the Disaster Management Act. Undoubtedly, if this approach is put into action with sufficient community involvement, the vulnerable groups, such as, women and young girls, could be protected against different forms of exploitation.

Notes

1 The United Nations marks 20 February each year as the 'World Day of Social Justice'. The theme for the year 2015 was to end human trafficking and forced labour.
2 UNGA – A/RES/69/283, The Sendai Framework for Disaster Risk Reduction 2015–2030.
3 National Disaster Management Authority, Ministry of Home Affairs, Government of India, Retrieved from http://ndma.gov.in/en/disaster-data-statistics.html (Accessed 30 July 2015).
4 *The Guardian*, 2015, 'Nepal Quake Survivors Face Threat from Human Traffickers Supplying Sex Trade', Retrieved from www.theguardian.com/world/2015/may/05/nepal-quake-survivors-face-threat-from-human-traffickers-supplying-sex-trade (Accessed 3 July 2015).
5 Retrieved from www.narendramodi.in/text-of-pm-s-statement-at-the-united-nations-summit-for-the-adoption-of-post-2015-development-agenda-332923 (Accessed 1 October 2015).
6 Ministry of Home Affairs, Department of Border Management, Ministry of Home Affairs, India. Information can be retrieved at: www.mha.nic.in/sites/upload_files/mha/files/BMIntro-1011.pdf. India shares its land border with the neighbouring countries like Bangladesh (4,096.7 kms), the People's Republic of China (3,488 kms), Pakistan (3,323 kms), Nepal (1,751 kms), Myanmar (1,643 kms), Bhutan (699 kms) and Afghanistan (106 kms in Pak-Occupied Kashmir). Its coastline runs through the states of Gujarat, Maharashtra, Goa, Karnataka, Kerala, Tamil Nadu, Andhra Pradesh, Orissa and West Bengal and the union territories of Daman & Diu, Lakshadweep, Puducherry and Andaman & Nicobar Islands.
7 United Nations, Retrieved from www.unisdr.org/files/42667_unisdrannualreport2014.pdf (Accessed 20 September 2015).
8 This mechanism helps to reduce exposure to hazards, lessening vulnerability of people and property, wise management of land and the environment and improving preparedness and early warning for adverse events, which are all examples of disaster risk reduction, Retrieved from www.unisdr.org/who-we-are/what-is-drr
9 A/CONF.206/6. Hyogo Framework for Action 2005–2015: Building the Resilience of Nations and Communities to Disasters.
10 Supra Note ii.
11 Manila Declaration for Global Action on Gender in Climate Change, Retrieved from www.unisdr.org/files/8731_maniladeclarationforglobalactionongenderinclimatechangeanddisasterriskreduction1.pdf
12 Ministry of Home Affairs, Government of India website, Retrieved from http://mha.nic.in/sites/upload_files/mha/files/MOM-HumanTrafficking-230813.pdf (Accessed 20 September 2015).

13 This scheme prevents trafficking and concentrates on rescuing, rehabilitating and re-integrating the victims along with providing them the basic amenities at the community level.
14 Business Standard e-paper, Retrieved from www.business-standard.com/article/government-press-release/india-to-host-asia-partnership-meeting-on-disaster-risk-reduction-next-115101601236_1.html (Accessed 17 October 2015).
15 General Assembly of the United Nations in resolution *317 (IV)2* of 2 December 1949. 1949, 'The Convention for the Suppression of the Traffic in Persons and the Exploitation of the Prostitution of Others' declares prostitution and the accompanying evil of trafficking for prostitution to be incompatible with the dignity and worth of every human being.
16 Finnish Report on Trafficking in Human Beings: Report to the Informal Group on Gender Equality and Anti-Trafficking, PC.DEL/654/02.
17 Article 1 declares that 'all human beings are born free and equal in dignity and human rights'; Article 5 prohibits 'cruel, inhuman or degrading treatment or punishment'.
18 Article 1 of Vienna Declaration, 1993, defines as violence against women 'any act of gender-based violence that results in, or is likely to result in, physical, sexual or psychological harm or suffering to women, including threats of such acts, coercion or arbitrary deprivation of liberty, whether occurring in public or in private life'.
19 Article 6 states that 'state parties shall take all appropriate measures including legislation, to suppress all forms of traffic in women and exploitation of prostitution of women'.
20 India is among five countries (Afghanistan, Pakistan, Sri Lanka and Nepal) of South Asia that ratifies the UNTOC that came into force in year 2003, a first comprehensive and global legally binding instrument to fight transnational organized crime. The following protocols supplement the UNTOC to combat specific forms of organized crime:

    a The Protocol to Prevent, Suppress and Punish Trafficking in Persons, Especially Women and Children,
    b The Protocol against the Smuggling of Migrants by Land, Sea and Air,
    c The Protocol against the Illicit Manufacturing of and Trafficking in Firearms, Their Parts and Components and Ammunition.

21 The Immoral Traffic (Prevention) Act, 1956, the Indian Penal Code, 1860, the Criminal (Amendment) Act, 2013 and so on.
22 The scope of the SAARC Convention focuses on trafficking in women and children for commercial sexual exploitation along with other organized crime organ trade, servitude or forced labour.
23 Sections 370 and 370 A of the Criminal Law (Amendment) Act, 2013, define the act of human trafficking and punishment for the exploitation of its victims. They are as follows.

    'Sec 370 (1) Whoever, for the purpose of exploitation, (a) recruits, (b) transports, (c) harbours, (d) transfers, or (e) receives, a person or persons, by –

        First. – using threats, or
        Secondly. – using force, or any other form of coercion, or

Thirdly. – by abduction, or
Fourthly. – by practicing fraud, or deception, or
Fifthly. – by abuse of power, or
Sixthly. – by inducement, including the giving or receiving of payments or benefits, in order to achieve the consent of any person having control over the person recruited, transported, harboured, transferred or received,

commits the offence of trafficking.

Explanation 1. – The expression "exploitation" shall include any act of physical exploitation or any form of sexual exploitation, slavery or practices similar to slavery, servitude, or the forced removal of organs.
Explanation 2. – The consent of the victim is immaterial in determination of the offence of trafficking.

(2) Whoever commits the offence of trafficking shall be punished with rigorous imprisonment for a term which shall not be less than seven years, but which may extend to ten years, and shall also be liable to fine.
(3) Where the offence involves the trafficking of more than one person, it shall be punishable with rigorous imprisonment for a term which shall not be less than ten years but which may extend to imprisonment for life, and shall also be liable to fine.
(4) Where the offence involves the trafficking of a minor, it shall be punishable with rigorous imprisonment for a term which shall not be less than ten years but which may extend to imprisonment for life, and shall also be liable to fine.
(5) Where the offence involves the trafficking of more than one minor, it shall be punishable with rigorous imprisonment for a term which shall not be less than fourteen years but which may extend to imprisonment for life, and shall also be liable to fine.
(6) If a person is convicted of the offence of trafficking of minor on more than one occasion, then such person shall be punished with imprisonment for life, which shall mean imprisonment for the remainder of that person's natural life, and shall also be liable to fine.
(7) When a public servant or a police officer is involved in the trafficking of any person then, such public servant or police officer shall be punished with imprisonment for life, which shall mean imprisonment for the remainder of that person's natural life, and shall also be liable to fine.'

'Section 370 A – (1) Whoever, knowingly or having reason to believe that a minor has been trafficked, engages such minor for sexual exploitation in any manner, shall be punished with rigorous imprisonment for a term which shall not be less than five years but which may extend to seven years, and shall also be liable to fine.

(2) Whoever, knowingly by or having reason to believe that a person has been trafficked, engages such person for sexual exploitation in any manner, shall be punished with rigorous imprisonment for a term which shall not be less than three years but which may extend to five years, and shall also be liable to fine.'

24 64th Law Commission of India Report.
25 S. Wadhwa (1998). For Sale: Childhood. Retrieved from www.outlookindia.com/article/for-sale-childhood/205123 (Accessed 4 July 2015).
26 Retrieved from www.outlookindia.com/article/for-sale-childhood/205123 (Accessed 4 July 2015).
27 AIR (1991) SC 207.
28 AIR (1990) SC 1412.
29 AIR (1990) SC 292.
30 Kuldeep Nayyar v. Union of India, AIR (2006) SC 3127.
31 Supra Note vii.
32 Section 2(m) of the Disaster Management Act, 2005, defines preparedness as the state of readiness to deal with a threatening disaster situation or disaster and the effects thereof.
33 Section 2(b) of Disaster Management Act, 2005, 'capacity-building' includes –

   i) identification of existing resources and resources to be acquired or created;
   ii) acquiring or creating resources identified under sub-clause(i);
   iii) organization and training of personnel and coordination of such training for effective management of disasters.

34 Section 2(e)(v) of Disaster Management Act, 2005.
35 Section 2(h) of Disaster Management Act, 2005, defines local authorities which includes Panchayati Raj Institutions, municipalities, a district board, cantonment board, town planning, authority or Zila Parishad or any other body or authority, by whatever name called, for the time being invested by law, for rendering essential services or, with the control and management of civic services, within a specified local area.
36 Section 2(e)(vi) of Disaster Management Act, 2005.
37 Section 2(e)(vii) of Disaster Management Act, 2005.
38 Section 2(e)(viii) of Disaster Management Act 2005.

References

Bacalla, T. (2010). *[Indonesia] Women Tough It Out in Post-Disaster Situation*. Bangkok: Southeast Asian Press Alliance. Retrieved 25 September 2015 from www.seapa.org/?p=3216

Bhat, P. I. (2009). *Law and Social Transformation in India*. New Delhi: Eastern Book Company.

Dasgupta, S., Siriner, I. & Sarathi De, P. (eds.) (2010). *Women's Encounter with Disasters*. Kolkata: Frontpage Publications Limited.

Enarson, E. (2007). Toward a Feminist Perspective on Women and Disaster. *Women's Rights Law Reporter*, *28*(1), 1–11.

Enarson, E., & Chakrabarti, P.G. Dhar (2009). *Women, Gender and Disaster: Global Issues and Initiatives*. London: Sage Publications.

Green, D. (2012). *From Poverty to Power: How Active Citizens and Effective States Can Change the World*. Rugby, UK: Practical Action Publishing and Oxford: Oxfam International, 2nd ed.

Henry, S. (2012). *Impasses of the Post-Global: Theory in the Era of Climate Change*. London: Open Humanities Press.

Hobson, C., Bacon, P. & Cameron, R. (eds.) (2014). *Human Security and Natural Disasters*. London: Earthscan from Routledge.
Nair, P. M. (2009). *Human Trafficking: Dimensions, Challenges & Responses*. New Delhi: Konark Publications.
Nasreen, M. (2008). *Violence against Women during Flood and Post-Flood Situations in Bangladesh*. Dhaka: ActionAid Bangladesh.
National Commission for Women. (2012). Standard Operating Procedures – Part-I (Human Trafficking). New Delhi: National Human Rights Commission.
Neumayer, E. & Plumper, T. (2007). The Gendered Nature of Natural Disasters: The Impact of Catastrophic Events on the Gender Gap in Life Expectancy, 1981–2002. *Annals of the Association of American Geographers*, *97*(3) (Sep.), 551–566. Retrieved from www.jstor.org/stable/4620289
Norlha. (2015). *Impact of Natural Disasters on Girls and Women*. Retrieved 15 October 2015, from http://norlha.org/wpcontent/uploads/2015/04/Impact_of_natural_disaster_on_girls_and_women_Norlha_June_2015.pdf
Oxfam International. (2005). The Tsunami's Impact on Women. *Oxfam Briefing Note*, 7. Retrieved 15 August 2015, from www.oxfam.org.uk/what_we_do/issues/conflict_disasters/downloads/bn_tsunami_women.pdf
Pant, V. (2012). *Community Based Disaster Management Planning (CBDMP) in Uttarakhand*. Uttarakhand, India: Department of Geology, Kumaon University.
Perry, K. & McEwing, L. (2013). How Do Social Determinants Affect Human Trafficking in Southeast Asia, and What Can We Do about It? *Health and Human Rights*, *15*(2), 138–156.
Price, S. (ed.) (2015). *Global Implications of Development, Disasters and Climate Change: Responses to Displacement from Asia-Pacific*. London: Routledge.
Sachs, J. (2015). *The Age of Sustainable Development*. New York: Columbia University Press.
SEEDS. (2009). *Community as First Responder: Building CBDM at District Level*. Retrieved 15 September 2015 from www.seedsindia.org/pdf/cbdm%20manual%20low.pdf
Shaw, R. & Krishnamurthy, R. R. (2009). *Disaster Management: Global Challenges and Local Solutions*. New Delhi: CRC Press.
Thomas, D., Phillips, B., Lovecamp, W. & Fothergill, A. (eds.) (2013). *Social Vulnerability to Disasters Second Edition*. New Delhi: CRC Press.
Todres, J. (2011). Mainstreaming Children's Rights in Post-Disaster Settings. *Emory International Law Review*, *25*, 1233–1261
True, J. (2012). *The Political Economy of Violence against Women*. Oxford: Oxford University Press.
UNISDR (United Nations Inter-Agency Secretariat of the International Strategy for Disaster Reduction). (2004). *First Announcement, World Conference on Disaster Reduction, 18–22 January 2005, Kobe, Hyogo, Japan*. Retrieved 6 August 2015 from www.unisdr.org/wcdr/preparatory-process/Ist-announce/First-Announcement-WCDR-eng.pdf

United Nations. (2011). *Basic Facts about the United Nations*. New York: United Nations.

UNODC. (2008). *Compendium of Best Practices on Anti Human Trafficking by Non Governmental Organizations: Government of India*. Retrieved 2 October 2015 from www.unodc.org/documents/human-trafficking/India_Training_material/Compendium_of_Best_Practices_by_NGOs.pdf

UNODC. (2009). *Prevention of Human Trafficking*. Retrieved 10 August 2015 from www.unodc.org/southasia/en/topics/frontpage/2009/preventin-of-human-trafficking.html

Wadhwa, S. (1998). For Sale: Childhood. *Outlook India Magazine*, Delhi. Retrieved from www.outlookindia.com/article/for-sale-childhood/205123 (Accessed 4 July 2015).

Wisner, Ben., Adams, John., (eds.) (2002). Environmental Health in Emergencies and Disasters: A Practical Guide, New York, London: Springer.

Zommers, Z. & Singh, A. (eds.) (2014). *Reducing Disaster: Early Warning Systems for Climate Change*. New York, London: Springer.

15 Disability, disaster and the law

Developing a mandate for disability inclusive law making process for disaster risk reduction

Deepa Sonpal

Disaster laws ignore 'disability'

Is there a legal right for a person with disability to be protected against disasters? Is there a state liability in failing to ensure this right? Adrien A. Weibgen (2015) analyses the legal responsibilities of state agencies and departments towards marginalized communities in times of crisis and argues that people with disabilities (PWDs) have a 'right to be rescued', 'a legal right to have their unique needs accounted for and addressed in emergency planning' (p. 2202). He has argued that 'such planning is not merely morally correct; it is legally required, and it is critical that local governments get their plans in order before the next storms, and lawsuits, come' (p. 2202).

During post-tsunami, the news crew for Japan Broadcasting Corporation's Fukushi (Welfare) Network program disclosed the much-anguished data that 'the mortality rate due to the Great East Japan Earthquake for persons with disabilities (2.06%) was twice that for the general population (1.03%). In addition, at facilities with many bedridden elderly residents, more than half of the residents perished. A survey of Hyogo prefecture clearly reveals that for the Great Hanshin-Awaji Earthquake, half of the fatalities were 65 or older, and according to the National Police Agency, at least 65% of victims in the Great East Japan Earthquake were 60 or older' (Nogiwa, 2013). Inclusive disaster policies and a disability-sensitive disaster law and management are a serious concern involving more and more researchers now from those who work on children, on the elderly, on various categories of disabilities. Disability is a much-debated concept globally as well as in the Indian context. There is no acceptable definition of disability that is followed, and hence there are variations in the enumeration and the prevalence rate. The World Health Organisation (WHO-ICF, 2001; WHO-WB, 2011) has evolved an International Classification of Functioning, Disability and Health or ICF which emphasises that environmental factors lead to disability – socio-cultural, economic, political and physical barriers in the environment – causing activity limitation and restricting participation in many aspects of life. The United Nations Convention on the Rights of Persons with Disabilities (UNCRPD) recognises that 'disability is an evolving concept and that disability results from the interaction between persons with impairments and attitudinal and environmental barriers that hinders their full and effective participation in society on an equal basis with others'.

The World Report on Disability (2011) claims that 15 per cent of the global population comprises of persons with disabilities. In India the Census 2001 and 2011 claims it to be a little above 2 per cent. Other informal sources have estimated around 5 to 6 per cent (WB, 2007). Disability is a phenomenon that may occur to any one at any point of time in their life cycle. Hence, the actual extent remains to be computed to be able to derive effective strategies of redressal, provisioning for budgeting and formulating any programme of action and for advocacy.

In recent times, the understanding of disasters has expanded due to issues faced in the context of global warming. Disasters are both natural and man-made which affect different sections of the populations differently depending on their coping mechanism and the context in which they are situated. Among the vulnerable/marginalised groups that are excluded from development processes, persons with disabilities remain the most alienated, specifically in disaster situations. Persons with disabilities are disproportionately affected by disasters, and disasters, in turn, can result in an increase in the number of persons with disabilities, from both direct and indirect actions (HI, 2005; CBM, 2013). For both these groups, the process of overcoming the short-term and long-term consequences of disaster is rather cumbersome due to their already-vulnerable states – the socio-economic status, lack of voice and the inaccessible evacuation, response and recovery efforts in most disaster situations. There is a greater likelihood of persons with disabilities being abandoned due to lack of planning, inaccessible transport, facilities (camps/shelters) and services (HI, 2005; CBM, 2013). Disaster situations create new impairments and disabilities. While persons impaired during a disaster may be visible, those that are more likely to be neglected are persons with disabilities existing prior to the disaster.

Persons with disabilities face stigma, abandonment, neglect and invisibility (Dalal, 2000), and this is enhanced during emergency and disaster situations where survival of the fittest prevails. Persons with disabilities are poorest of the poor and are entrapped in a vicious cycle of poverty and disability that gets aggravated in disaster situations (DFID, 2000; Elwan, 1999; Yeo, 2005). All vulnerable populations have specific needs. As persons with disabilities are not a homogenous segment, they are always confronted by intersectionality of class, caste, religious ethnicity, gender, type of disability and environmental context. Each person has specific needs depending on the type and extent of disability, socio-economic background, skills and orientation per se of the sensory, cognitive, psychological and mobility-related disability. (UNNATI, 2006; HI, 2009; CBM, 2013). This chapter explores the specific international legal frameworks that aim to protect the rights of persons with disabilities, and at the same time emphasises the need for mainstreaming, integrating and including the rights of persons with disabilities within the global and national frameworks, policies and laws. It is absolutely essential to include the voices of persons with disabilities in the process of law making so that their needs, potentials and aspirations are considered to enable them to lead a dignified life on an equal basis with others (IFRC, 2010, 2013; UNDP, 2014).

International frameworks protecting the rights of persons with disabilities

The UNCRPD marks a paradigm shift in uplifting disability from a medico-charity approach/model to a social and rights-based model/approach rendering full and equal participation to persons with disabilities on an equal basis with others. Article 11 of the UNCRPD focuses on the situation of risk and humanitarian emergencies and proposes all state parties to introduce a mandate in international humanitarian and human rights laws to include all measures to enhance the participation of persons with disabilities in situations of risk, including situations of armed conflict, humanitarian emergencies and the natural disasters.

United Nations Economic and Social Commission for Asia and the Pacific (UNESCAP), while launching the third Asia Pacific Decade of Persons with Disabilities (2013–2023), signed a treaty, the Incheon Strategy, to 'Make the Right Real' for the 650 million persons with disabilities in Asia and the Pacific (UNESCAP, 2012). Goal 7 of the Strategy ensures disability-inclusive disaster risk reduction and management. While clearly setting out the goal and targets to be achieved, specific indicators have been set for tracking progress that includes disaster risk reduction plans, training for service providers, provisioning for accessible goods and services in all the phases of disaster risk reduction – relief, shelters, assistive devices and technologies and ensuring the participation of persons with disabilities in preparation of community-based disaster management plans.

The Sphere Standards (2011) launched by a group of international NGOs for humanitarian aid has developed several tools to improve the quality of assistance to people affected by disasters and accountability of states including that of humanitarian aid to beneficiaries and donors. The Sphere Standards have included persons with disabilities including disability linked to age, gender and HIV/AIDS. The specific standards relate to participation and representation of all groups in assessment, response, targeting, monitoring and evaluation of programmes. The standards also refer to aid workers' competencies and responsibilities, management and support of staff.

The Asia-Pacific region is most adversely affected by disasters, including those caused by climate change. Persons with disabilities and other vulnerable groups are at higher risk of death, injury and additional impairments, as a result of exclusion from disaster risk reduction policies, plans and programmes. Public service announcements are often issued in formats and language that are not accessible by persons with disabilities. In addition, emergency exits, shelters and facilities tend not to be barrier-free (UNNATI, 2006; CBM, 2013). Regular participation of persons with disabilities in emergency preparedness drills and other disaster risk reduction measures at the local and district levels could prevent or minimize risk and damage when disasters occur (HI, 2005). Physical and information infrastructure that incorporates universal design principles would improve the chances of safety and survival.

Disability is not as yet a part of the agenda of most development organisations, even though the social model (Albert, 2004) has led the focus away from the person-centred, health and welfare approach followed until very recently. Most examples of mainstreaming disability during disasters are reactive and not proactive wherein persons with disabilities need to be included before, during and after the disaster. Even the Hyogo Framework for Action (2005–2015) adopted by the World Conference on Disaster Reduction to make the world safer from natural hazards is not inclusive of disability. The Guidelines for the Domestic Facilitation and Regulation of International Disaster Relief and Initial Recovery Assistance – International Disaster Response Laws, Rules and Principles (also known as the IDRL Guidelines) – have mentioned disability as a sign of vulnerability (IFRC, 2011). Every framework needs to acknowledge the specific needs of persons with disabilities from a rights-based perspective on an equal basis with others basing the UNCRPD as the guiding and overarching framework. The Sendai Framework for Disaster Risk Reduction 2015–2030 – adopted on 18 March 2015 at the Third World Conference on Disaster Risk Reduction, held from 14 to 18 March 2015 in Sendai organised by United Nations Office for Disaster Risk Reduction (UNISDR) – is a step in this direction.

Developing national frameworks for disaster risk reduction from a disability lens

Articles 11 and 32 of the UN Convention on the Rights of Persons with Disabilities (CRPD) require that persons with disabilities benefit from and participate in disaster relief, emergency response and disaster risk reduction strategies. Article 11 states that 'States Parties shall take in accordance with their obligations under international law . . . all necessary measures to ensure the protection and safety of persons with disabilities in situations of risk, including situations of armed conflict, humanitarian emergencies and the occurrence of natural disasters'. Further, Article 32 of the Convention ensures that any initiative on international cooperation should be inclusive of and accessible to persons with disabilities.

Disasters are affecting about 40 per cent of the global population residing in South Asia largely due to the inability or lack of adequate mechanisms to cope with them (IFRC, 2010). Persons with disabilities experience profound exclusion during disaster situations. Experience suggests that robust and stringent laws play a vital role in putting in place coping mechanisms demonstrating the power to equip vulnerable communities build better resilience (IFRC, 2010). Over-regulation leads to unnecessary bottlenecks, and under-regulation leads to uncoordinated efforts. Disruption of services post-disaster affects all and particularly persons with disabilities, as they are excluded from the mainstream services as well as processes of relief and rehabilitation. Moreover, the needs of persons with disabilities are likely to be ignored, more because other survival needs assume higher priority both among people and relief organisations (Unnati, 2006; HI, 2005; CBM 20113). Also when resources are scarce, there is a possibility that persons with disabilities face neglect and discrimination. The kind and degree of follow-up and referrals that are required for physical and psycho-social rehabilitation are difficult as people relocate, and tracking processes are not so organised. Re-integration into normal activities of the community life like attending formal/informal education centres or earning livelihood, accessing services of health and education is much slower due to the impairments and issues of accessibility.

Efforts for community-based disaster risk reduction and disaster preparedness are recent, and the role of vulnerable groups in disaster management processes, including that of persons with disabilities, remains unexplored. The needs of persons with disabilities continue to be excluded over the more long-term recovery and reconstruction efforts; thereby the opportunity to ensure that towns/cities are accessible and inclusively resilient to future disasters is often missed.

Even in normal situations, there is a dearth of trained rehabilitation experts, more so in rural areas. Mustering adequate human resources in disaster situations is even more difficult, especially on a sustained basis. Community-based skills in these areas are not honed to be able to fill in the gap. Girls and women with disabilities and persons with mental illness and multiple disabilities are the most vulnerable in disaster situations: disabilities that are not so obvious tend to be completely ignored.

In India there are no anti-discrimination laws to protect the rights of persons with disabilities. Currently, there are four laws related to disability – Persons with D (Equal opportunities, Protection of Rights and Full Participation) Act 1995, the National Trust for Persons with Autism, Cerebral Palsy and Multiple Disabilities Act 1999, the Mental Health Act 1999 and the Rehabilitation Council of India Act 1992. All these acts emanate from a medico-welfaristic perspective, offering rehabilitation support to persons with disabilities. As a signatory to the UNCRPD all laws of the country need to be harmonised with the spirit enshrined in this. Far from doing so, none of the laws related to disability even speak about the plight of persons with disabilities during and after disasters. Even the Nation Disaster Management Act, 2005, fails to acknowledge the rights of persons with disabilities and fleetingly mentions them as one of vulnerable. The Draft on Rights of Persons with Disabilities, 2014, too does not legally bind the state to take necessary steps for persons with disabilities during disasters. State is not bound by any responsibility towards the disabled during disasters. Whereas specific laws, policies, protocols need to be developed from a disability lens, it is also crucial to disaster management policies that there exist documented evidences for non-compliance along with penalties for non-implementation of disability law. The following suggestions may be incorporated at each of the phases – relief, rehabilitation and reconstruction and disaster preparedness outlining the specific steps/protocols in consultation with persons with disabilities and their representation organisations. These need to be incorporated within the disability-specific and disaster management, laws, policies, rules and regulations and protocols, circulars and government orders issued at the national as well as the specific state-level policies. All programmes and schemes related to disability need to be revised and developed from a right-based perspective that aims to empower and enhance the dignity of persons with disabilities in consultation with persons with disabilities and their representative organisations.

Administrative accountability and public liability during the 'relief – rehabilitation-reconstruction phase'

It is the responsibility of local administration to identify persons who have been injured at all rehabilitation centres and camps before developing an area-specific database. After surviving the disaster the harsh life of an evacuee does not end. They struggle desperately with toilets and other basic facilities inaccessible to them in temporary shelters; many of them who are provided wheelchairs as philanthropic measures of state activity get their wheel chairs stuck at fatal points, and some who survive the disaster die of this trauma and accident. While the visually challenged have no access to fliers posted as instructions, the hearing impaired are considered as silent and quiet people who are left behind to die unnoticed.

While it is the joint responsibility of the Ministries of Labour Welfare, Social Justice, and Health to come together under the umbrella of State Disaster Management Authority (SDMA), it is equally a mandatory task for SDMAs to design a structure where they could all plan a concerted action.

The SDMA should be collaborating with local hospitals and district administration for providing trauma care, curative, therapeutic and other supportive services like physiotherapy, occupational therapy, corrective surgery to persons with injuries to minimise the possibilities of these resulting into a disability; assistive and mobility devices, support services such as caretakers, sign language interpretation, adapted/accessible transportation services and information in accessible formats like Braille, large print, audio and visual announcements including early warning systems that can be understood by different persons with disabilities.

The same exercise is equally relevant for identifying the specific health care needs of persons with existing disabilities and providing them services at accessible centres or through community-based mechanisms and information in accessible formats. Developing a community-based mechanism for identification and rendering support to persons with disabilities works best by encouraging their participation. SDMAs and DDMAs (District Disaster Management Authority) should plan for developing a protocol for issuing/retrieving disability certificates for obtaining benefits of government schemes related to disability. Mapping of community-level resources and assets and strengthening the resources for sustained support to persons with disabilities for their basic health care and rehabilitation need to be added to the efforts on strengthening the implementation of social safety net programmes for most vulnerable groups. Enhancing and investing in recovery schemes especially psycho-social care and training, ensuring that the built environment is made barrier-free based on the principles of universal design for all in the reconstruction process and involving persons with disabilities and other vulnerable groups in the development, implementation and monitoring of the programmes improve efficiency and sustainable development, but the Disaster Management Act, 2005, fails to incorporate even the most basic needs of disability management. Much of this management requirement could be supported simply through a mandatory requirement from SDMAs and DDMAs for maintaining a gender and disability disaggregate date and facilitating proactive disclosure of the same at all service provider levels. This could go a long way towards vulnerability and capacity assessments, contingency planning, constituting task force and disaster risk reduction committees by investing in capacity building such as developing places for rescue shelters within 2–3 kilometres vicinity that are accessible and this could even be the local school to help the evacuation process.

Laws have failed to create an enabling environment for mainstreaming disability through inclusive policies, bye-laws, information systems, infrastructure, attitudes of society on an ongoing basis. Therefore laws have drastically failed to curb violence and sexual harassment against children, senior citizens and women with disabilities. Administration follows no code of conduct in the absence of supervision, performance assessment and penalties for inflicting any form of ill treatment/violence/neglect/discrimination of persons with disabilities and specifically girls and women with disabilities.

Scientific tools have been missing for measuring progress by effectively designing indicators for monitoring the Hyogo Framework for Action, Sustainable Development Goals, Incheon Strategy, the Sphere Standards, national and regional disaster management plans and disability action plans developed by inter-agency groups. The disaster management curriculum in colleges and universities, school safety plans as well as in the training of first-responders, such as fire-fighters, ambulance and police personnel throughout the state, has yet to draw focus of the mainstream disaster laws.

In conclusion one could reiterate the words of Weibgen (2015, 2676) that 'the task of listening to marginalized people is not that of city agencies or federal judges alone – court orders cannot take the place of our own consciences. We must all continue to combat prejudice against people with disabilities outside of the courtroom, taking responsibility for meeting everyone's needs in times of disaster and in those of lesser crisis. While the law may serve to concretize and remind us of our obligations to each other, in the end, it is up to us to ensure that no one is left behind when the next storms come'.

References

Albert, B. (2004). Briefing Note: The Social Model of Disability, Human Rights and Development. *Enabling Disabled People to Reduce Poverty*, Disability KaR Research Project. Retrieved 24 January 2016 from www.enil.eu/wp-content/uploads/2012/07/The-social-model-of-disability-human-rights-development_2004.pdf

Christoffel Blindenmission (CBM). (2013). *Disability Inclusive Disaster Risk Management: Voices from the Field and Good Practices*. Retrieved 1 January 2016 from www.asksource.info/resources/disability-inclusive-disaster-risk-management-voices-field-and-good-practices

Dalal, A. K. (2000). Social Attitudes and Rehabilitation of People with Disabilities: The Indian Experience. *Journal of Rehabilitation*, 5, 15–21.

Department for International Development (DfID). (2000). *Disability, Poverty and Development*, Issues Paper. London: Overseas Development Group.

Elwan, A. (1999). *Poverty and Disability: A Survey of the Literature*. Washington, DC: The World Bank.

Handicap International and European Commission Humanitarian Aid and Civil Protection DG. (2009). *Mainstreaming Disability into Disaster Risk Reduction: A Training Manual*. Nepal: Prevention Web. Retrieved from www.un.org/disabilities/default.asp?id=1546

HI, Handicap International. (2005). *How to Include Disability Issues in Disaster Management, European Commission: Handicap International*. Retrieved from www.globalprotectioncluster.org/_assets/files/tools_and_guidance/age_gender_diversity/HandicapInt_Including_Disability_Disaster_Management_EN.pdf

IFRC. (2010). *Disasters in Asia: A Case for Legal Preparedness*. Geneva: International Federation of Red Cross and Red Crescent Societies.

IFRC. (2011). *Introduction to the Guidelines for the Domestic Facilitation and Regulation of International Disaster Relief and Initial Recovery Assistance*. Geneva: International Federation of Red Cross and Red Crescent Societies.

IFRC Annual Report (2010) Saving Lives, Changing Minds, Geneva: International Federation of Red Cross and red Crescent Societies.

IFRC. (2013). *Better Laws, Safer Communities? Emerging Themes on How Legislation Can Support Disaster Risk Reduction*. Geneva: International Federation of Red Cross and Red Crescent Societies.

Nogiwa, S. (2013). 'Issues and Lessons Learned from the Relief Activities for Persons with Disabilities Affected by the Great East Japan Earthquake' Tohoku Office: Association for Aid and Relief, Japan (AAR Japan), September. Retrieved 1 July 2016 from http://donate-japan.com/articles/view/458.html

UNESCAP. (2012). *The Incheon Strategy to 'Make the Right Real' for Persons with Disabilities in Asia and Pacific 2013–2022*. New York: United Nations.

UNNATI. (2006). *Mainstreaming Disability Issues*. Ahmedabad: UNNATI.

UNNATI – Organisation for Development Education. (2004). *Understanding Disability – Attitude and Behaviour Change for Social Inclusion*. Ahmedabad: UNNATI.

Weibgen, A. A. (2015). The Right to Be Rescued: Disability Justice in an Age of Disaster. *Yale Law Journal*, *124*(7), 2202–2679. Retrieved 1 July 2016 from www.yalelawjournal.org/note/the-right-to-be-rescued

World Bank. (2007). *People with Disabilities in India: From Commitments to Outcomes*. Washington, DC: World Bank.

World Health Organization. (2001). *The International Classification of Functioning, Disability and Health (ICF)*. Geneva: WHO. http://www.who.int/classifications/icf/en/.

Yeo, R. (2005). Disability, Poverty and the New Development Agenda. *Disability Knowledge and Research*, 1–33.

16 Anthropogenic disaster economics and the non-human species

Subhalakshmi Sircar

Overwhelming disasters and unprotected weaker species

India is one of the most disaster-prone countries in the world because of its geo-climatic conditions and its socio-economic vulnerability. The approach to disaster management in India has evolved over the years from one of relief-based operations to a multi-dimensional proactive response of mitigation, relief, rescue and rehabilitation. Disaster Management Act of 2005 defines 'disaster' as

> a catastrophe, mishap, calamity or grave occurrence in any area, arising from natural or manmade causes, or by accident or negligence which results in substantial loss of life or human suffering or damage to, and destruction of, property, or damage to, or degradation of, environment, and is of such a nature or magnitude as to be beyond the coping capacity of the community of the affected area.[1]

Natural disasters include floods, drought, earthquakes, cyclones and landslides. In India, about 60 per cent of landmass is susceptible to earthquakes of various intensities, over 40 million hectares is prone to floods, about 8 per cent of the areas are prone to cyclones and 68 per cent of the total area is prone to droughts. This causes huge loss of the lives of humans and other non-human species and extensive damage to private, community and public assets. Non-human species include cattle stocks, stray animals, wildlife and flora and fauna of different kinds in the natural environment. Therefore, disasters not only cause extensive economic loss but also impede the process of sustainable development. One study by the World Bank puts the cost of disasters, adding up to 2 per cent of GDP of the country.[2] According to the Annual Report of Ministry of Home Affairs, during 2014–2015, 21 states had seen damages due to various natural calamities. As a result, 1,674 human lives were lost, 92,180 cattle perished, 725,390 houses were damaged and 26.72 lakh hectares of cropped area was affected. The Al Jazeera report gives a rough estimate of the loss of about 7,000 cattle heads and 7 lakh poultry during Kashmir floods in 2015.

In view of the colossal damage and loss of lives, the United Nations General Assembly declared the decade of 1990–2000 as the International Decade for Natural Disaster Reduction with the objective to minimize the loss of lives and property through concerted efforts particularly in the developing countries. The Government of India initiated efforts in the early 1990s to develop a comprehensive disaster management framework which includes preparedness, rescue, relief, rehabilitation and mitigation as key components.

In India, the approach to disaster management is based on the understanding that mitigation of disaster is more cost-effective than rescue and rehabilitation. This was adopted only after the Hyogo Framework for Action of 2010–2015. Hence the policy of disaster management should be guided by the idea of sustainable development and should be multi-disciplinary in nature spanning across all sectors of development. This was echoed in the Tenth Five-Year Plan Document (2002–2007), which has a separate chapter on disaster management – 'Disaster management – the Development Perspective'.

The idea of sustainable development needs to be understood in terms of the symbiotic and interdependent relationship between humans and all other species which form the ecosystem. Therefore, human development can be sustainable only if it recognizes development in harmony with nature and is built around the idea of conserving all the constituents of natural habitat.

For disaster management in any country to be successful, it requires

a An effective legal and institutional framework
b Reliable database for different kinds of disasters happening in the country and their impact on the economy and environments
c Sufficient resources to build capacities for preparedness, response and mitigation at all levels

The impact of disasters is higher on economically weaker sections of the population. In India, almost 50 per cent of the population depends on agriculture directly or indirectly for livelihood and sustenance. Most of them are small and marginal farmers or landless labourers. Animals, being a source of livelihood, nutrition and sustenance, form an integral part of their lives and economic well-being. There are reports that after Koshi floods in Bihar, villagers refused to leave their homes without their cattle.

The chapter seeks to explore how disaster management policy and disaster risk reduction plans in India address the issues of rescue, relief, rehabilitation and preparedness for all animals during and the aftermath of disasters. The focus would be on pets, strays, livestock and poultry. Here we try to address two questions: (1) whether the approach to disaster management in India is broad enough to incorporate all types of animals and (2) whether public investments made for disaster management and mitigation have any component which are specifically meant for animals.

The chapter purports to do this by looking at the disaster management in India at three levels. First, we look at the institutional framework provided by the Disaster Management Act of 2005 and the National Plan of 2009 to understand how policies related to disaster management deal with animals in developing capacities for preparedness, prevention, mitigation and response. Second we examine the database on damages caused during disasters in India which is very critical to developing a holistic approach to disaster management. The third is to track the public investments made for disaster management by the central government and devolution of resources to states for undertaking rescue and relief operations.

Institutional Framework lacks Coordination: The disaster management in India has evolved over the years from activity-based relief work to proactive response of prevention, mitigation, preparedness and reconstruction. The Disaster Management Act of 2005 has created an institutional-based framework to address disaster management in India. This act provides for the setting up of National Disaster Management Authority (NDMA) under the chairmanship of the prime minister and State Disaster Management Authority (SDMA) under the chairmanship of chief ministers as well as constituting District Disaster Management Authorities (DDMAs) at district levels. The NDMA is responsible for laying down policies for disaster management, approval of the National Plan and issuing guidelines for the effective response and mitigation of disasters which would be followed by various ministries, departments of the Government of India and state governments. In addition, the Act of 2005 led to constituting the Disaster Response Force at the central and the state level for effective response mechanism.

NDMA as the apex body

The Disaster Management Act of 2005 adopts a multi-pronged approach to disaster management which includes prevention of any danger of disaster, mitigation of risk, capacity building, preparedness and response to deal with calamities, evacuation, rescue and relief, rehabilitation and reconstruction.

However, the Disaster Management Act is conspicuously silent on the issue of non-human species in its definition of disaster management or in the provisions of the National Plan drafted by the NDMA. The definition fleetingly mentions the destruction or degradation of the environment which can be left to interpretations in various ways. The overwhelming focus on human life and properties which are of economic value to the people and society at large makes it highly skewed. Although the basis of this approach to disaster management is based on the understanding that any policy of disaster management should be integrated into the process of development, the formulation lacks any broader interpretations of development which includes the close relationship of humans to the other inhabitants of the ecosystem including animals.

Even the relief and rehabilitation measures focus on food, drinking water, shelter and medical facilities only for affected people. There is a provision for compensating for the loss of life, damage to property or loss of economic livelihood. Therefore, any such compensation can be provided for the loss of other non-human lives to the extent that it directly affects the economic livelihood of the people. There is no such explicitly mentioned provision for rescue, relief and rehabilitation of other species, namely strays, pets or other animals, in disaster-affected areas. People living in rural areas and also tribal population share a close relationship with their natural surroundings which include both domesticated and free animals.

Any institutional framework which underscores the need to build a systemic and strategic framework to reducing vulnerabilities and risks to disasters should develop a meaningful method of coordination between various agencies which are entrusted with carrying out the policies for disaster response and mitigation. The NDMA as the apex body should build a meaningful coordination between various ministries under the Government of India such as Ministry of Agriculture, Ministry of Rural Development, Ministry of Panchayati Raj and the Animal Welfare Board of India. The various ministries in the structure of the Government of India are responsible for formulating and implementing policies for disaster mitigation and risk reduction. Department of animal husbandry, dairying and fisheries under the Ministry of Agriculture and the Ministry of Environment, Forest and Climate Change are responsible for formulating and implementing policies related to cattle, poultry, fish and wildlife and stray animals which are worse affected during disasters. Here it is important to mention the Animal Welfare Board of India, which is the statutory advisory body entrusted with formulating laws of animal welfare and protection. The NDMA should assign a greater role to the AWBI for formulating policies related to animal rescue and rehabilitation during and in the aftermath of disasters across the country.

Database on disasters

There is a lack of centralized statistical database on the past disasters and their impact on the economy in terms of the loss of lives and property. Developing a centralized system of various kinds of disasters and their impact on the economy is critical to objective risk assessment. The national plan does not talk about creating any statistical database on the damage caused to various forms of life other than humans. Until such information is available, the system of disaster management in India cannot address the true extent of damage which hampers economic growth and the overall development of the nation.

Table 16.1 gives the year-wise data on damages caused due to disasters in India from 2001–2002 to 2010–2011. The second column pertains to the loss of cattle because they are the source of economic livelihood to people mainly in rural areas. There is no reference to the destruction or loss of any other forms of life which are more vulnerable than humans in most cases and many of such species may even become extinct as a result of natural calamities.

Table 16.1 Year-wise damage caused due to disaster

Year	*Lives lost (human)*	*Cattle lost*	*House damaged*	*Cropped areas affected*
	In nos	*In nos*	*In nos*	*In lakh hectares*
2001–2002	834	21,269	346,878	18.72
2002–2003	898	3,729	462,700	21.00
2003–2004	1,992	25,393	682,209	31.98
2004–2005	1,995	12,389	1,603,300	32.53
2005–2006	2,698	110,997	2,120,012	35.52
2006–2007	2,402	455,619	1,934,680	70.87
2007–2008	3,764	119,218	3,527,041	85.13
2008–2009	3,405	53,833	1,646,905	35.56
2009–2010	1,677	128,452	1,359,726	47.13
2010–2011	2,310	48,778	1,338,619	46.25

Source: Ministry of Home Affairs.

Any accounting system which tries to estimate the losses incurred due to any disaster, solely on the basis of economic criterion, is lopsided just like the established methods of estimation of gross domestic product (GDP) of any country. GDP measure in terms of per capita GDP is considered to be a measure of economic well-being of the residents of a country. As GDP rises, it is assumed that people are better off. However, this does not include the value of leisure. For example, if the GDP of a country falls, it may be due to the fact that residents of that country prefer to work less and enjoy more leisure time. This is not necessarily a sign that they are worse off. In 2009, the French Statistics Agency decided to incorporate new indicators like high-quality health service, long holidays and sense of happiness. This was in response to a report commissioned by the then French president Nicholas Sarkozy. The commission, headed by the Noble Prize winner economist Joseph Stiglitz, suggested a number of measures to improve the widely used GDP accounting method. It suggested accounting for people's well-being and the sustainability of the economy of a country and its natural resources. Many economists and analysts even prefer Human Development Index (HDI) over per capita GDP to look into the overall well-being of a country. Similarly, any accounting system for measuring loss in disaster-related situations should go beyond the mere use of economic loss and attempt to measure intangible losses associated with disasters. It should be based on the very notion of conserving the ecosystem. It is imperative to acknowledge and design a framework for disaster response and mitigation which treats non-human species as essential part of the ecosystem.

Anthropogenity in funding for disaster management in India

The main responsibility of funding the post-disaster-related work lies with state governments. The central government provides a supportive role in terms of financial, technical and material assistance whenever necessary. The entire funding to the states is made by annual allocations for five-year fiscal cycle based on the recommendations of the finance commissions.

The allocation of resources from the central government to various state governments is done through the Union Budget. These resources include sharing of taxes between the central government and states and also the grants-in-aid from the Consolidated Fund of India. The principles that govern the sharing of taxes and the devolution of grants-in-aid are decided by finance commissions every five-year period. Every finance commission constituted so far has awarded a specified amount to the states for disaster management. In addition, there are various schemes under ministries/departments of the Government of India which have allocations earmarked for disaster management. These schemes can be grouped into two categories – one is 'dedicated' schemes under which the 100 per cent allocations are meant for disaster response and relief. The other is 'embedded' schemes which have components that can help to promote risk reduction.[3] The expenditures of various ministries and departments for the fiscal year are listed under Plan and Non-Plan heads of the Union Budget.

Our focus would be limited to devolutions of resources from the central government to the states to analyse the trends in public investments in India which are primarily used for disaster response, relief and mitigation. We would look at the awards of finance commissions and various budget documents to ascertain how far public investments in India have dealt with the issues of disaster management specific to non-human species. First we will look at the sources of funding for relief-and-rescue operations which are given to the states. Then we will track the allocations under various schemes of different departments and ministries of the Government of India which are used for disaster management and disaster risk reduction plans.

The second finance commission created a separate fund of 'margin money' to finance the relief operations of natural calamities. This was continued by the next six finance commissions with certain modifications. Under the Ninth Commission, the scheme of margin money was replaced with the 'Calamity Relief Fund' (CRF) to which the contributions made by the central government and the state government would be 75:25. The CRF was meant for the sole purpose of on-disaster response, relief and rehabilitation. The National Calamity Contingency Fund (NCCF) was created on the recommendation of the Tenth Finance Commission with an initial corpus of Rs 500 crores to be funded by the central government. The Thirteenth Finance Commission (2010–2015) made the recommendation of merging the NCCF with the National Disaster Response Fund (NDRF) and the CRF with the State Disaster Response Fund (SDRF), with effect from 1 April 2010.

The Disaster Management Act calls for the setting up of two types of funds: one for disaster response and relief and the other for disaster mitigation. The National Disaster Response Fund (NDRF) and the State Disaster Response Fund (SDRF) are created for disaster response and relief. The National Disaster Mitigation Fund (NDMF), the State Disaster Mitigation Fund (SDMF) and the District Disaster Mitigation Fund (DDMF) at all district levels are created for the purpose of disaster mitigation. So far, only the NDRF has been created at the national level. All states have constituted SDRFs, but only very few SDMFs have been created. The NDRF and SDRF constitute the bulk of funding for disaster response and relief. The NDRF and SDRF fall under the dedicated schemes.

Currently the NDRF is financed by levying a National Calamity Contingency Duty (NCCD); a levy of cess on selected items and any additional budgetary support is provided as and when necessary.

Table 16.2 shows that during the period of 2002–2003 and 2011–2012 there has been an additional release of Rs 2,051.03 crores through budgetary provisions.

The SDRF is the primary source of funding available to states for undertaking relief operations in the affected areas. Whereas the Disaster management Act provides for two sources of funding for NDRF, the funding of SDRF at the state level is made on the basis of grant-in-aid recommended by finance commissions under the Article 275(1) of the constitution. The states have shared their concerns regarding the increase in the frequency and intensity of disasters in the recent past and escalation of costs for post-disaster rescue and rehabilitation work due to rising inflation. Taking into view of the concerns of different states as well as the observations made by the Ministry of Home Affairs, the Fourteenth Finance Commission has

Table 16.2 Collection of NCCD and release from NCCF/NDRF

Year	*(Rupees crores)*	
	NCCD collected	*Release from NCCF/NDRF*
2002–2003	1,648.45	1,600
2003–2004	1,740.13	1,587.42
2004–2005	1,484.44	2,583.12
2005–2006	1,274.67	3,061.44
2006–2007	1,727.88	1,962.05
2007–2008	2,268.36	373.38
2008–2009	2,319.73	2,279.92
2009–2010	2,619.56	3,261.52
2010–2011	2,966.51	4,179.25
2011–2012	3,246.16	2,458.12
Total	**21,295.89**	**23,346.92**

Source: Ministry of Finance.

recommended for an aggregate corpus of all SDRFs to the amount of Rs 61,219 crores for the award period. The commission (Figure 16.1) has further reduced the share of contributions made by states to the SDRF to 10 per cent and the rest 90 per cent has to be financed by the central government.

The commission has made a recommendation of increasing the disaster relief grants to the states (Table 16.3) under the grants-in-aid from Rs 5,791 crores in 2014–2015 to Rs 12,120 crores in 2019–2020, an increase of 109 per cent in nominal terms.

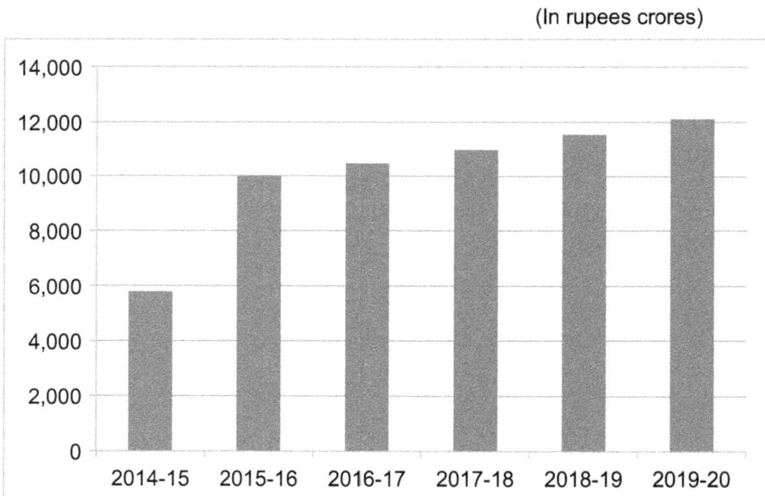

Figure 16.1 Disaster relief grants to state governments awarded by the Fourteenth Finance Commission, 2013

Source: Ministry of Finance.

Table 16.3 Disaster relief grants to states (as percentage of GDP)

Disaster relief grants to states	*2014–2015*	*2014–2015*	*2015–2016*	*2016–2017*	*2017–2008*	*2018–2019*	*2019–2020*
	(BE)	(reassessed)					
	0.04	0.04	0.07	0.06	0.06	0.05	0.05

Source: Ministry of Finance.

However, as a per cent of GDP it is only 0.04 per cent in 2014–2015, and it is further reduced to 0.05 per cent in 2019–2020 from 0.07 per cent in 2015–2016.

It is also important to study the different schemes of the Government of India available for disaster-related issues and analyse the trends in expenditures made under such schemes. It is difficult to track investments under embedded schemes because they are spread over numerous departments and ministries of the Union Government.

There are two nodal agencies in the structure of Union Government which are entrusted with formulating and overseeing the implementation of policies related to animals and forests. One is Department of Animal Husbandry, Dairying and Fisheries, Ministry of Agriculture, and the other is the Ministry of Environment, Forest and Climate Change.

The key focus of the Department of Animal Husbandry, Dairying and Fisheries is production, preservation and protection of livestock through medical facilities and development of dairies and fisheries.

Among the broad objectives of the Ministry of Environment, Forest and Climate Change are conserving flora, fauna and wildlife and ensuring the welfare of animals. Disasters cause extensive damage to the environment by the destruction of flora, fauna and animals including wildlife. Protection and rescue and rehabilitation of animals should be an integral part of any holistic approach to disaster management. There should be separate provisions of funding for such operations within the budgetary allocations of the central and state governments.

The various schemes under the Department of Animal Husbandry, Dairying and Fisheries can be put under the category of 'embedded' schemes which can be used for disaster risk reduction. There is no specific scheme which deals directly with disaster response and relief.

The Ministry of Environment, Forest and Climate Change has one scheme for 'relief to animals during natural calamities and unforeseen circumstances'. The allocation for this scheme is Rs 10 lakhs in 2013–2014, and this has been raised to Rs 30 lakhs for the year 2015–2016. The allocation under this scheme has been increased from 0.43 per cent to 0.97 per cent of the total allocations for various schemes related to stray animals and wildlife protection.[4]

If we look at the items of permissible expenditure under NDRF/SDRF, we find that any disaster response-and-relief operations pertaining to animals entail the disposal of carcasses, care of cattle/poultry against epidemics and assistance to animal husbandry sector.

Table 16.4 shows that the allocations made to these nodal agencies which are responsible for any schemes meant for either disaster response or mitigation for non-human species have come down in 2015–2016 (BE) compared to the year 2013–2014 (actual).

The Twelfth Plan outlay (2012–2017) for forest and wildlife is Rs 4,818.80 crores, and for animal welfare the amount is Rs 200.20 crores (Table 16.5). There is a marginal increase to Rs 623.37 crores for 2014–2015 compared to the outlay of Rs 606.09 crores for 2012–2013 for wildlife and forest. For animal welfare, the budgetary allocation is reduced to only Rs 17 crores for 2014–2015 from an allocation of Rs 25.20 crores in 2012–2013.

Table 16.4 Central plan outlay by ministries/departments

Central plan outlay	*(Rupees crores)*		
	2013–2014 Actual	*2014–2015 RE**	*2015–2016 BE***
Department of Animal Husbandry, Dairying and Fisheries	1,748.67	908.91	1,133.14
Ministry of Environment, Forest and Climate Change	1,808.55	828.98	995.05

* RE is the revised estimate.

** BE is the budget estimate.

Source: Union Budget 2015–2016.

Table 16.5 Twelfth Plan outlay (in rupees crores)

	Forest and wildlife	*Animal welfare*
XII Plan approved outlay	4,818.80	200.20
2012–2013		
Outlay (BE*)	606.09	25.20
Actual expenditure	577.81	25.09
2013–2014		
Outlay (BE*)	719.14	25.20
Outlay (RE**)	580.31	7.40
2014–2015		
Outlay (BE*)	713.11	23.2
Revised estimates	623.37	17.0

Source: Annual Plan (2014–2015), Ministry of Environment, Forest and Climate Change.

The allocations under various schemes of the central government meant for either disaster management or disaster risk reduction for animals show an overall declining trend in recent years.

Conclusion

There has been a paradigm shift in the approach to disaster management from one of rescue and relief to developing an institutionalized system of proactive response which includes preparedness, rescue, relief, reconstruction and mitigation. This approach is built on the premise of sustainable development to reduce vulnerabilities across all sectors of the economy. However, this approach is overwhelmingly human centric, often ignoring the fact that development cannot be sustainable without developing the environment and acknowledging the relationship of humans with other non-human species. This is more so in rural areas where people depend on animals, particularly livestock and poultry, because they are a source of livelihood, nutrition and sustenance.

The Disaster Management Act of 2005 and the National Plan of Disaster Management of 2009 fail to develop a development strategy which recognizes the relationship of human beings to all species irrespective of their economic usefulness. There are two aspects to any strategy to handle disasters either natural or human-made. One is the immediate response after disasters in terms of rescue, relief and rehabilitation. The other and more important is the focus on disaster mitigation or risk reduction. There have been concerted efforts to address such issues through the Disaster Management Act of 2005 and setting up of National Disaster Management Authority at the national level and Disaster Management Authorities at the state level and also at district levels. Even there has been substantial increase in the devolution of resources from the Union Government to states and union territories to deal with challenging situations faced in the wake of disasters and carry out rescue-and-relief operations. However, the rescue, relief and rehabilitation of animals are left mostly to NGOs which are equipped to deal with animals in distress. There is a lack of database on the impact of different disasters on all types of animals. The definition of disaster needs to be broadened to include loss or damage to various other forms of life. The concept of sustainable development should recognize the fact that people in India share a special affinity with nature and its inhabitants. When disasters strike, their losses go beyond what can be measured by only economic criterion. Disaster risk reduction measures and policies should focus on preparedness and developing capacities for addressing issues related to animals including wildlife.

There has been some progress on the part of the nodal agency like the NDMA to incorporate animal protection into disaster planning. The NDMA is in the process of setting up Veterinary Emergency Response Unit (VERU) in association with World Society for the Protection of Animals (WSPA) to rescue animals during disasters. Now there is a growing acceptance of the fact that people in rural India depend on livestock for their livelihood. Therefore, protection of animals during disasters should be made an integral part of rescue and rehabilitation plans. More needs to be done in terms of allocating funds and preparing national disaster response force to evacuate and rehabilitate animals during disasters. We must start to acknowledge that all non-humans are the responsibility of the state.

The key components of any disaster response plans for animals should focus on these key areas:

a Arranging for the rescue of stranded animals in non-accessible areas and providing for food and fodder
b Arranging for temporary shelters for homeless animals
c Treatment of sick animals
d Mass vaccinations to prevent outbreaks of disease
e Compensating the owners for the losses of their animals

There needs to be enhanced focus on developing the existing disaster management policies and risk reduction plans which would deal with animal welfare and protection during and in the aftermath of disasters. This can be done by reframing the National Plan on Disaster Management and increasing the funds under various schemes of departments and ministries for building an adequate infrastructure for effective rescue, relief and rehabilitation of animals.

Notes

1 This definition is provided in Disaster Management Act, 2005.
2 This is an estimated economic loss in India due to various disasters as observed by the World Bank study.
3 Dhar Chakrabarty (2012) has given a detailed account of various sources of funding at the national and state levels.
4 Annual Report (2014), Ministry of Environment, Forest and Climate change.

References

Dhar Chakrabarty, P. G. (2009). *Financing Disaster Management in India, a Study for the Thirteenth Finance Commission, New Delhi: National Institute of Disaster Management.*

Dhar Chakrabarty, P. G. (2012). Understanding Existing Methodologies for Allocating and Tracking DRR Resources in India. Available from http://www.unisdr.org/files/32376_32376indiadraftdrrinvestmenttrackin.pdf.

The Disaster Management Act. (2005). *National Institute of Disaster Management.* Delhi: Government of India.

Fourteenth Finance Commission Report. (2013), Ministry of Finance. Delhi: Government of India.

Government of India, Annual Report of the Ministry of Environment, Forests and Climate Change (2014), New Delhi: Government of India Publications.

Government of India, Ministry of Home Affairs, Annual Report (2014–15). New Delhi: Government of India Publications.

Government of India, Union Budgets. (2014–15 and 2015–16) New Delhi: Government of India Publications.

17 Gender and trafficking

Mondira Dutta and Manika Kamthan[1]

Human trafficking has been an issue of concern whenever disaster strikes. Disasters never restrict to administrative boundaries and does not recognize international borders. These areas, therefore, become the most vulnerable from that point of view. During a disaster, women move across the countries in search of livelihood options and, therefore, become even more vulnerable to trafficking for sexual exploitation. There is minimal compliance to law at borders since most of them are difficult to implement across the countries and international borders, thus being unable to protect the cross-border victims. Field visits have shown that most of the victims of human trafficking are often lured or abducted from one country or from their homes and subsequently forced into prostitution, bonded labour in agricultural and manufacturing settings, domestic services, organ trade and other transnational crimes and servitude in another country or a place where the victims are a complete alien. Human trafficking has been prevalent in areas which reel under abject poverty, food insecurity, insensitive social and cultural milieu and displacements due to natural and human-made disasters. Disaster only doubles the hardships faced in such areas. Although human trafficking can take different forms in different regions and countries around the world, most human trafficking cases follow a similar pattern; that is traffickers use acquaintances or false advertisements to recruit men, women and children in or near their homes and then transfer them to and exploit them in another city, region or country.[2]

South Asian region, in particular, has witnessed the exploitation of women and children under the garb of fraudulent marriages, false job promises, culture and religious beliefs and deceit. They become even more vulnerable in a situation as a result of a disaster which takes away their land, house and the few livelihood options that were prevalent in their places of residence.

The present chapter attempts to identify the vulnerability to trafficking among women and girls in India for sexual exploitation, especially during a natural calamity that hits the region. The study is based mainly on secondary sources of information with selected indicators of vulnerability. The study also relies upon field visits undertaken in some of the sample districts for the authentication of the secondary sources of information vis-à-vis the micro-level data.

Although there are sufficient studies to establish that women are more vulnerable to disasters, there is not sufficient research to establish that it is during disasters that the risk of human trafficking reaches its peak. When disaster renders people shelterless, the women, in particular, become vulnerable to all kinds of exploitation including trafficking which becomes a business for people who are involved in this illegal trade.

Significance of disaster law in combating trafficking

Many of such studies remain unattended in the absence of a law, which is the first and foremost factor in providing a preventive measure in risk reduction process towards the disaster-related victims who have been forced to leave their hearth and home in search of livelihood options. The purpose of any law is manifold. It establishes and maintains the order, resolves disputes if there are any and finally protects the rights and liberties of people. The disaster law, or more appropriately called as 'disaster response law', also aims for serving these purposes. It aims for the mitigation of disasters, protection and rescue of victims and rehabilitation of the victims. A disaster response law framework consists of international treaties, municipal laws of countries which provide guidelines for mitigation, protection, rescue and rehabilitation work.

> International disaster response law is found in treaties, municipal law and regulations. Its development is facilitated through resolutions adopted by the International Conference of the Red Cross and Red Crescent, the UN, other intergovernmental organisations, and learned societies, and through public and private codes and standards adopted to guide humanitarian action. (IDRL, 2003)

In India, we have 'Disaster Management Act' which forms the bulwark of the disaster response law. However, in this chapter we are looking into the problem of trafficking of women, which is accelerated during disasters. Thus, the anti-trafficking laws will also be included in the disaster response laws. Thus, the scope of disaster response laws is much wider than merely those laws which directly relate to disasters. They contain various other laws which become useful in different circumstances created by the occurrence of natural disasters.

In countries where gender discrimination is tolerated, women and girls are particularly vulnerable to natural hazards. Not only are the percentage of women and girls who die higher in these countries, but the incidence of gender-based violence – including rape, human trafficking and domestic abuse – is also known to increase exponentially during and after disasters.[3] Their extreme vulnerability can be made from the fact that during tsunami in the Karakai region of Puducherry, adult female fatalities outnumbered adult male fatalities nearly 2:1.[4]

It is often suggested that women and girls post disaster will be forced into sex work. However, sufficient (reliable and robust) studies do not exist to support the extent of this outcome. Haider (2013) suggests that the post-earthquake period in Haiti was linked with a rise in the number of women and girls engaging in sex work. In May 2011 UNHCR conducted several focus groups with women and adolescent girls in a selection of IDP camps. Based on the testimonies of participants, the study found that the practice of women and adolescent girls engaging in 'transactional sex' in Port-au-Prince was 'widespread' (UNHCR, 2011). The 2012 World Disasters Report (IFRC, 2012a) provides several other examples of 'transactional' or 'survival' sex following disasters and conflict where women and girls are coerced into providing sex in exchange for food and other relief items or 'protection'. However, it is not clear the extent to which levels of such sexual exchanges increase post event, or if the nature of these exchanges changes in terms of with whom women engage in sex or which women engage in such transactions.[5]

A pioneering report developed by the Lawyers Collective[6] supported by UNIFEM examines the role and function of law enforcement and the adjudication machinery in dealing with the problem of trafficking for CSE, the lacunae specific to each component, namely the police, the prosecution, the judiciary and the correctional institutions, those that are responsible for the ineffective functioning of the criminal justice system (CJS) and suggest that changes can be made to improve the functioning of various components of the CJS in dealing with the issue. The report presents vast data from two metropolitan cities of India, namely Mumbai and Delhi, which host a significant proportion of the victims for sexual exploitation. The respondents include police, advocates and officials of the state homes, and the report analyses of reported cases under ITP Act in Kamla Nagar Police Station, New Delhi, and Nagpada

Police Station Mumbai. The report presents the profile of law enforcement machinery in the two cities for CSE cases registered under the ITP Act. It analyses the procedures for reporting CSE cases and sections of ITP act used for booking the cases and highlights excessive use of sections 8 and 20 of ITP Act which criminalizes the victims. The report suggests reasons for acquittals of criminals like unworthy witnesses, lack of collaboration, discrepancy in witnesses, procedural problems and absence of women officers. It also highlights the demographic, social, economic and spatial characteristics of victims staying in government shelter homes and the innumerable problems faced by the victims in these homes including poor living conditions and other associated survival coping mechanisms. The research report suggested invaluable recommendations for improving the law enforcement machinery especially the effective training for police and prosecution.

Factoring in gender perspective into Hyogo Framework for action

Gender is a cross-cutting principle of the Hyogo Framework for Action 2000–2015: on Building Resilience of Nations and Communities to Disaster, which states that 'a gender perspective should be integrated into all disaster risk management policies, plans and decision-making processes, including those related to risk assessment, early warning, information management and education and training'. In addition, the Beijing Agenda for Global Action on Gender-Sensitive Disaster Risk Reduction (2009), adopted following the 23rd special session of the General Assembly, entitled 'Women 2000: Gender Equality, Development and Peace for the Twenty-First Century', calls for gender-sensitive approaches to disaster prevention, mitigation and recovery strategies and natural disaster assistance.

Gender priorities were integrated into the report of the World Conference on Disaster Reduction, January 2005, in Kobe, Japan, and the Framework for Action 2005–2015: Building the Resilience of Nations and Communities to Disasters: now abbreviated to HFA (Hyogo Framework for Action). In the opening section, the HFA states that a gender perspective should be 'integrated into all disaster risk management policies, plans and decision-making processes, including those related to risk assessment, early warning, information management, and education and training' (HFA, 2005, 4). However, while it has been suggested that this provides the 'most explicit reference to gender than any other international policy frameworks for DRR' (UNISDR, 2009, 10), it is not without limitations. Most importantly its call to integrate gender into all areas of DRR did not result in gender being integrated even into the HFA itself, and in the remainder of the document 'gender'/'women' is mentioned only twice: once when discussing early warning systems and once when discussing the need to ensure equal access to appropriate training and educational opportunities. This suggests a lack of real commitment to adopting a gender perspective that has not changed much in the intervening years.

The third edition of the United Nations Global Assessment Report on Disaster Risk Reduction: From Shared Risk to Shared Value: The Business Case for Disaster Risk Reduction makes scant mention of gender matters; in fact, the word 'gender' is not mentioned at all; neither is 'girl'; and 'women' is mentioned three times in 288 pages. The three occurrences of 'women' are all in the same place: they concern the after-effects of the Great East Japan Earthquake of 2011 in which employment for women recovered more slowly than for men, due to the slow recovery of the female-dominated food-processing sector, while the many new employment opportunities in the construction sector were mainly for men. This is disappointing considering that the 2011 Global Assessment Report had previously noted that gender was still not being adequately addressed in disaster risk reduction.

However, we are unable to trace any imprints of these guidelines when it comes to law making. The disaster management laws have turned a blind eye to the specific needs of women and especially women in agriculture. In India, the Disaster Management Act 2005 does not even mention the word 'women' or 'gender'. There are no gender-specific post-disaster studies, and the special needs of women are not highlighted. While gender mainstreaming has entered the disaster rhetoric, gender is far from mainstreamed in policies and gender is still not part of mainstream disaster risk reduction and response practice (Bradshaw & Fordham, 2013, 30).

Human trafficking is usually exacerbated by the lack of legal assistance services available to victims and by the lack of awareness concerning the existing legal protection available to victims of trafficking. Victims and witnesses of human trafficking are often not aware of the mechanisms available to obtain justice and redress. On the other hand, law enforcement officials and judicial organs may not have adequate resources and training to ensure full victim protection. The issue of trafficking and displacements caused by disasters is closely related. It is the displacement caused by natural disasters which result in massive trafficking. It has been estimated by WHO that women and children are particularly affected by disasters, accounting for more than 75 per cent of displaced persons.

A composite disaster response law is still trying to be developed which addresses the problem of trafficking during disasters. The Disaster Management Act 2005 in India neither mentions anything about special needs of women nor addresses the problem of trafficking during disasters. A well-meaning disaster law shall address the problem of trafficking and shall also aim for its control. The basis for such a law lies in the positive rights of citizens. There are two kinds of rights: positive rights and negative rights. A positive right bestows a positive duty upon the state to do something, whereas a negative right bestows a negative duty upon the state to not to do something. For example, the right to education bestows the duty upon the state to provide compulsory primary education to every child of India. The right to religion, on the other hand, bestows the duty upon the state not to interfere with the religion of the citizens of India. In case of disasters it is the positive duty of the state to protect its citizens from the disasters and also during and post disasters. Thus there exists a right against disasters in the citizens. Since we are focusing on the problem of trafficking, we shall widen the scope of the disaster response law to include the anti-trafficking laws and the guidelines for the displaced persons for the purpose of providing an unbreakable shield against the traffickers.

Factors of post-disaster vulnerability

Disasters do not occur in vacuum. Disasters affect everyone differently depending upon the different vulnerabilities. The different vulnerabilities are shaped by existing discriminatory socio-economic conditions. Disasters result from the combined factors of natural hazards and people's vulnerabilities. These vulnerabilities take the form of physical exposure, socio-economic vulnerability and limited capacity to reduce vulnerability and disaster risk. Capacities to reduce vulnerabilities and risks arise out of a complex mix of factors, which include poverty, social class, age group, ethnicity and gender relations. Women are made more vulnerable to disasters through their socially constructed roles. As Elaine Enarson states, 'Gender shapes the social worlds within which natural events occur'.[7] Women are tied down by the gender roles ascribed to them by the society. They are responsible for the children and elderly people at home and are doubly burdened. Women, themselves being vulnerable, are left destitute in the case of destruction of their homes and become far more vulnerable to hazards. Many families are forced to relocate to shelters. Inadequate facilities for simple daily tasks such as cooking means that women's domestic burden increases at the same time as her economic burden, leaving her less freedom and mobility to look for alternative sources of income. They are less informed and do not possess skills (including literacy) which act as life-saving mechanisms in times of disasters.

Designation of '25 November' in 1999 as UN International Day for the Elimination of Violence against Women was of major significance. The UN adopted in the 23rd Special Session of General Assembly a document entitled 'Women 2000: Gender Quality, Development and Peace for the Twenty-First Century'.[8] It clearly spelt out the action needed to address the problem of violence against women, especially human trafficking of women and children. The United Nations Convention against Transnational Organized Crime (UNCTOC) was adopted in November 2000, along with two optional protocols by which countries would undertake in-depth measures to combat smuggling of migrants and the trafficking of women and children. The protocol to Prevent, Suppress and Punish Trafficking of Persons, especially women and children, is the first attempt to address trafficking of persons in a comprehensive manner based on the expanded understanding of the term 'trafficking' and its multiple dimensions. The protocol applies to the prevention and combating of trafficking as well as to the protection of and assistance for victims and cooperation among state parties.[9]

The passing of the 'Victims of Trafficking and Violence Protection Act of 2000' by the US Senate was another important development in the global process designed to address human trafficking. The act provided a good assessment framework for multiple agencies to review progress on anti-trafficking initiatives. The Trafficking in Persons (TIP) report, brought out by the Government of United States every year, is based on the assessment of government and civil society action in each country to combat trafficking. It places different countries in different tiers depending on the action their governments have taken to combat the problem of human trafficking.

> UN Millennium Declaration in 2000, resolving to combat all forms of violence against women and the subsequent 2005 World Summit Outcome; the first-ever 2004 Security Council Open Debate devoted to sexual and gender-based violence in conflict and post-conflict situations (in follow up to Resolution 1325), and the momentous Security Council Resolution 1820 adopted in June 2008, establishing sexual violence as a priority global security concern have provided significant inputs for UNIFEM's role towards developing appropriate strategies for reducing human trafficking especially for women and children.[10]

Trafficking is the process of recruiting, contracting, procuring or hiring a person for CSE. Therefore, trafficking is a process and CSE is the result. The 'demand' in CSE generates, promotes and perpetuates trafficking which is a vicious circle. The victims of trafficking during disasters are not pushed into CSE as soon as they are trafficked. Thus, as a matter of fact, the ITPA proves to be quite ineffective for curbing trafficking during disasters. The ITPA envisages only trafficking for CSE. Commercial activity need not be in a brothel but could also occur in places including a residential dwelling and a vehicle. Therefore, a police officer who is acting under the ITPA has powers to take steps in all such situations where trafficking leads to or is likely to lead to CSE in any form, including those under the facade of massage parlours, bar tending, 'tourist circuit', 'escort services' and 'friendship clubs' (Nair, 2007).

The ITPA needs to be amended for making the act of trafficking per se punishable. The pushing of victims into trafficking should not be a prerequisite for applying for the prevention of trafficking. Moreover, the ITPA should be made a self-sufficient law and made in link with the Disaster Management Act 2005 (DMA). A separate chapter on 'Trafficking during Disasters' can be added in the ITPA and can establish a machinery of its own which is independent of the local police of the area where the disaster occurs; for example, it can link itself with the National Disaster Relief Force (NDRF) under the DMA. The victims of trafficking during disasters should not be prosecuted under the ITPA which is what the ITPA actually do. The role of the NDRF should be extended to preventing trafficking during disasters, and the wrongdoers should be harshly punished.

It is interesting to study three major factors of vulnerability that affect women and girls most as a result of disaster. Each one of these has been discussed here.

Cultural component

It need not be mentioned that when a disaster hits it is the women who are the worst sufferers and take upon themselves the responsibility to carry forward the society, family and children in the name of legacy of protecting their culture and tradition on behalf of the whole community. So at such times the cultural factor becomes even more influential in taking the women victims towards being sexually exploited in order to make a living. It is for the first time that the Census of India has documented a few of these communities and their distribution pattern in space. Field visits further unravelled a plethora of such communities that exist today. The Rajnats, Bedia, Dommara, Lambada, Joigini, Satnami, Kanjar, Sansui, and the list goes on. Culture and tradition thus at times plays a dominant role in the lives of the women in the disaster-hit areas.

The cultural factor perhaps is the one which has been ignored and goes unnoticed from the perspectives of vulnerability to trafficking of women and children. With sanction from the society this system has become accepted by the community as part of the cultural norm. The traditional cultural practice of dedication of girls to gods and goddesses in temples has been in existence for ages. As these norms gained social sanction, prostitution as a system became institutionalized. After an initial persuasion into the profession, girls either become the property of wealthy men or a wage earner for their family.[11] Though many states have banned this practice, various reports indicate that this dedication still continues in the form of *Jogini, Devadasi* and *Basavi* in Orissa, Andhra Pradesh, Maharashtra and Karnataka. In some other communities the practice of prostitution has been accepted as traditional and given the name of *Parivarik Dhandha* (traditional family occupation) like that practised by some of the communities such as the *Bedia, Rajnats, Kolta, Banchra, Mahar, Matang* and *Sansi*. These are socially sanctioned and accepted.

The *Bedia* boys marry in *Kanjar* or *Sansi* communities. They protect their daughters-in-law keeping them indoors under *pardah*. They believe that their *Bahus* are the pride of their families. However, the same attitude and sentiments are not extended to their daughters.[12] They are pushed into the flesh trade immediately after puberty. This practice is socially sanctioned. Rituals symbolizing womanhood are performed. Nearly 95 per cent of these communities belong to the scheduled castes and the scheduled tribes. 'India is so far the only land where women/girls are worshipped as well as marketed by their own parents and brothers as a commodity in the name of caste and suffer inequalities and shame for no fault on their part.'[13] A disaster-hit region promotes such a culture even more as there are no livelihood options left for the women. The society and family justify such occupations in the name of culture and traditions.

Age-specific sex ratio (10–24 years)

A situation where disaster hits a place having a strong cultural factor especially for the age group of 10–24 is a deadly combination. This fact can be found from the secondary sources of information. The Census of India 2001 provides the data on sex ratio under various age groups. The map shows that the districts where the age group 10 to

24 years are conspicuous by their absence. Girls and women who have gone missing belong to the age group 10 to 24. Several studies show the importance of such an indicator for asserting the age group that is the most vulnerable.

This fact was authenticated during the field visit. Some the women interviewed at the brothels of Sonagachi in Kolkata belonged to Murshidabad in North Bengal. They stated that floods were a regular feature in their region every year, forcing them to move out. Women and girls thus end up in the brothels. The women who arrive make sure to bring with them another one in the subsequent years. Similarly other districts from Bihar and Uttar Pradesh also displayed a similar picture. Data from the Census of India clearly display these phenomena.

Hazard-prone vulnerable districts

Disaster proneness is characterized by vulnerability to drought, flood or any type of natural calamity, which has a direct impact on production and productivity of crops, livestock or human life or any kind of tangible loss that might affect the economy of the region, resulting in a mass exodus of population. Disasters lead to a breakdown of social institutions, making food securing and humanitarian supplies 'difficult'. This leaves women and children 'vulnerable to kidnapping, sexual exploitation and trafficking'. The 2008 devastating floods in Bihar had left children vulnerable to trafficking, and many girls ended up being 'sold as brides'.[14] Natural hazards like floods, droughts, earthquakes and typhoons enhance displacements and forced migration. The hazard-prone areas create conducive conditions for such large-scale displacements year after year. The Kosi belt of Bihar and Brahmaputra and Ganga flood plain areas in Assam, Meghalaya and West Bengal are inundated year after year due to floods, displacing a large number of people. Similarly drought situations in central parts of India, Rajasthan and Gujarat also force people to look for outside support. The coastal belts are also prone to inundation of saline water due to cleaving.

Such an indicator includes all the hazard (natural)-prone areas of the country which have been hit by natural calamity such as drought, floods and earthquake. Owing to natural disasters such as droughts, floods and hailstorms, there is a loss of crop, cattle and property, leading to the decrease in family income and forcing the population to migrate. The present study has utilized the data created on the map prepared by the National Atlas Thematic Mapping Organization (NATMO). There have been two distinctions made between those that are hit by a disaster and those that are not. The type of hazard that had been considered for the study was only natural hazards and does not consider the conflict-ridden zones and riot-hit regions. This indicated a positive relation showing that the higher the value the higher is the vulnerability. Areas include most of the coastal plains, Andhra Pradesh, Kerala, Odisha, Assam, Bihar, Chattisgarh and parts of Gujarat and Himachal Pradesh.

Recommendations

- Dissemination of reports with concerned ministries such as the Ministry of Women and Child Development, Ministry of Social Welfare and Empowerment, Ministry of Home Affairs and several others, so that preventive measures are imbibed into their ongoing schemes and inter-ministerial policies are made to tackle the problem in the right perspective.
- There is a need for greater convergence of the ongoing schemes in the various ministries of the vulnerable districts. It is important that the capacity build of governance institutions be initiated in order to bring together all existing programmes for achieving a greater impact on people's lives. It is recommended that courses be introduced in training institutions such as the 'Lal Bahadur Shastri National Academy of Administration' (LBSNAA), Mussoorie, and the 'National Institute of Rural Development' (NIRD).
- Initiatives must be developed to build capacity and support grassroots level NGOs for linking government initiatives on poverty alleviation programmes like MGNREGA, Swadhar and Ujjawala for addressing the needs of women under difficult circumstances and in providing alternative sustainable livelihood opportunities during a disaster.
- Local village-level committees must be constituted for regular interaction with young girls and other women as a preparation to cope up with any calamity.
- Women NGOs must conduct constant training for women for awareness and self-rescue preparedness.
- A strong infrastructure needs to be set up in the most vulnerable districts for disaster preparedness. The Ministry of Women and Child Development in collaboration with the Ministry of Home Affairs should establish community referral mechanisms such as short-stay home facilities, along with counselling to the trafficked victims by trained practitioners. Such initiatives will go a long way in the smooth reintegration of the survivor victims during a post-disaster scenario.

Conclusion

Among the major reasons that contribute towards creating conducive conditions for vulnerability to human trafficking are abject poverty, landlessness, lack of income opportunities, economic exploitation of labour, food insecurity, insensitive social and cultural milieu and, most importantly, mass-scale displacements due to natural and human-made disasters. Disasters leading to mass displacement of vulnerable population year after year pose as the greatest challenge with hundreds of missing people, particularly women and children, in the flood-hit areas. This is extremely challenging not only for the state government but also for the non-governmental organizations involved in the relief and rehabilitation.

Preventive measure is the key to overcome the widespread net of human trafficking. A continuous ongoing effort is necessary to strengthen and create awareness at the grassroots level. A close coordination between societies, parents' organization, women's group, local self-government machinery, police, mass media, civil society and non-governmental organization is warranted to keep traffickers at bay. Such coordination has worked wonders in several regions of Nepal-India and Bangladesh-India borders. The need of the hour is to strengthen such co-ordination mechanisms at the identified vulnerable areas to create awareness related to safe migration procedure requirements (like seeking identity proofs of persons offering jobs, job offer letters and finding out the whereabouts of prospective grooms). This method has been found to be extremely useful in creating the right kind of awareness in comparison to other methods as traffickers try to avoid luring an awakened community. Involvement of adolescent boys and girls in creating awareness on safe migration has been effective to identify fraudulent marriages as vulnerable groups usually share their anxiety with their peer groups in villages. Several instances show where girls reported to their teachers in schools about scrupulous marriages of their friends that were being formalized. Teachers in turn convince the parents to seek proper identification and whereabouts of the prospective groom before marriage can be solemnized. Such actions have saved several cases of human trafficking.

These collaborations can be forged ahead with other stakeholders, and building of capacities for effective awareness on safe migration with NGO partners in the local areas, local self-governments (PRI), community/religious leaders and women's groups create the necessary environment for safe migration. This necessitates the development of tool kits, action guides and publicity material on safe migration procedures and consequences of human trafficking to create appropriate awareness and knowledge-sharing mechanisms. Facilitating networking among NGOs for learning and sharing information and developing mechanisms for joint collaborative monitoring in the border areas, vulnerable districts and states would go a long way to generate knowledge against human trafficking.

Enforcing and strengthening of community initiatives like maintaining of social registers for all marriages (with unknown partners and community members) will create the necessary security environment against scrupulous and fraudulent marriages.

Initiatives of building capacities support grassroots-level NGOs to enable them to link government initiatives on poverty alleviation programmes like MGNREGA, Swadhar and Ujjawala, to help providing sustainable livelihood opportunities and access the due entitlements from the government programme.

These government schemes are an innovative approach in order to address the requirements of women under difficult circumstances. The National Commission for Women should support in establishing the community referral mechanisms such as providing short-stay home facilities along with counselling by trained practitioners to the trafficked victims. Regular imparting of basic knowledge skills on possible methods being adopted by traffickers, legal entitlements and so on will ensure that the anti-trafficking squad remains not only informed but vigilant as well. Such initiatives will contribute in the smooth reintegration of the survivor victims into the society.

Notes

1 With acknowledgement to UN Office on Drugs and Crime and UN Women (2011).
2 The UN Convention on Trafficking (Palermo Convention, 2000).
3 UNDP (2010) Gender & Disasters.
4 Tsunami Analysis (2004). A Comprehensive Analysis. Retrieved from http://apps.searo.who.int/PDS_DOCS/B4998.pdf?ua=1
5 Bradshaw and Fordham (2013).
6 Lawyers' Collective (2003).
7 Pan American Health Organization (1997).
8 United Nations (2008).
9 The UN Convention on Trafficking (Palermo Convention, 2000) defines 'trafficking in persons' as the recruitment, transportation, transfer, harbouring or receipt of persons, by means of the threat or use of force or other forms of coercion, of abduction, of fraud, of deception, of the abuse of power or of a position of vulnerability or of the giving or receiving of payments or benefits to achieve the consent of a person having control over another person, for the purpose of exploitation. Exploitation

includes, at a minimum, the exploitation or the prostitution of others or other forms of sexual exploitation, forced labour or services, slavery or practices similar to slavery, servitude or the removal of organs.

10 United Nations (2008).

11 Mondira Dutta (2001).

12 Pandey (2004).

13 Saanlap (2008).

14 Indo-Asian News Service (IANS): 19 August 2009.

References

Bradshaw, S. & Fordham, M. (2013). *Women, Girls & Disasters – A Review for DFID*. London: Gender and Disaster Network.

Dutta, M. (2001). *Evaluation Study on 'Devadasis – Mainstreaming & Empowerment' a Project Implemented by MYRADA*. Bangalore, Karnataka: NOVIB.

Haider, H. (2013). *International Legal Frameworks for Humanitarian Action*. UK: GSDRC, University of Birmingham.

Hyogo Framework for Action (HFA). (2005–2015). *Building the Resilience of Nations and Communities to Disasters*. Kobe: UNISDR.

Indo-Asian News Service (IANS) (19 August 2009).

International Disaster Response Law, Project Report. (2003). *International Fedof Red Cross and Red Crescent Societies (International Federation)*. Geneva: International Committee of the Red Cross.

Lawyers' Collective Womens' Rights Initiative. (2003). *Trafficking in Persons for Commercial Sexual Exploitation: Legislation, Role and Effectiveness of the Law Enforcement and Law Adjudication Machinery*. New Delhi: UNIFEM.

Pandey, S. P. (2004). *A Study of Children Dependent on Prostitutes in Selected Areas of Uttar Pradesh, Pandit Govind Ballabh Pant Institute of Studies in Rural Development*. Lucknow: Department of Women and Child Development, Government of India.

Saanlap. (2008). *Withering Flowers – A Criminal Tradition in India: A Study on Caste Based Prostitution among Bedia and Banchhara Community in Madhya Pradesh*. Kolkata: Sanlaap.

Tsunami Analysis. (2004). *A Comprehensive Analysis*. Retrieved from http://apps.searo.who.int/PDS_DOCS/B4998.pdf?ua=1

UNDP. (2010). *'Gender & Disasters', Bureau for Crisis Prevention & Recovery*. New York: UNDP.

UNHCR Global Report. (2011). Available at http://www.unhcr.org/gr11/index.xml

UNISDR. (2009). *Making Disaster Risk Reduction Gender-Sensitive: Policy and Practical Guidelines*. Geneva: UNISDR; IUCN; UNDP.

United Nations. (2003). *United Nations Convention against Transnational Organized Crime, General Assembly Resolution 55/25 of 15 November (Palermo Convention, 2000)*. New York: United Nations.

United Nations. (2008). *Women, Peace and Security, Security Council Resolution 1820*. S/RES/1820. New York: United Nations.

United Nations Population Fund. (2006). *State of World Population, a Passage to Hope, Women and International Migration*. New York: UNFPA.

UNO. (2008). *Women, Peace and Security: United Nations: Security Council Resolution 1820*. S/RES/1820. New York: United Nations.

World Disasters Report. (2012). *Focus on Forced Migration and Displacement*. Geneva: International Federation of Red Cross.

18 Techno-legal regime for safety against natural hazards

Ved Mittal

Introduction

The human settlements in the recent past are effectuated by the natural disasters, be it devastating floods in Australia where the land area of settlements exceeds the area of France or Germany or floods with mud slide in Brazil or high-intensity earthquake in Indonesia triggering tsunami with devastating effect far away in the coastal belt of India. Most recent is the devastating earthquake, tsunami and nuclear disaster in Japan. Therefore, preparedness and mitigation measures are necessary for a safer world.

Indian case

India is a vast country with a geographical area of about 3.2 million sq. km and having 29 states and 7 union territories (UTs) for administration. The total population is 1,210 million (2011). There are 7,935 towns and cities and about 638,590 villages. The degree of urbanization was at 27.8 per cent in 2001, and it is anticipated that 50 per cent of the population would reside in urban areas by 2021 (Mittal, 2009). According to the Ministry of Housing and Urban Poverty Alleviation, Government of India, the total housing shortage in India (till 2007, beginning of 11th Five-Year Plan) was about 24.71 million dwelling units (DUs).

The development and construction of high-rise buildings and other structures in various sizes of settlements is continuing at a rapid pace, which are vulnerable to various forms of hazards. Recent past earthquakes in India (Uttarkashi, 1991, Latur, 1993 and Bhuj 2001) have exposed the vulnerability of building stocks, causing widespread damage resulting in the loss of lives and property. This is mainly due to faulty construction practices which do not follow earthquake-resistant features complying with structural design codes.

Vulnerability Atlas of India – 2005

Vulnerability Atlas of India was brought out in 1997 by BMTPC (Building Materials and Technology Promotion Council, Ministry of Housing and Urban Poverty Alleviation, Government of India) and has since been revised in 2005. This atlas has served as a useful tool for policy planning on natural disaster prevention and preparedness especially for housing and related infrastructure.

According to the Vulnerability Atlas, Indian subcontinent is among the world's most disaster-prone areas. The Vulnerability Atlas of the region against three major disasters and subsequent damages is as follows:

a. Land

- 59 per cent of land vulnerable to earthquakes
- 8.5 per cent of land vulnerable to cyclones
- 5 per cent of land vulnerable to floods

One million houses damaged annually + human, social and other losses

b. Earthquakes

- 10.9 per cent land is liable to severe earthquakes (intensity MSK IX or more)
- 17.3 per cent land is liable to MSK VIII (similar to Latur/Uttarkashi)
- 30.4 per cent land is liable to MSK VII (similar to Jabalpur quake)

Biggest quakes occur in Andamans, Kuchchh, Himachal, Kashmir, North Bihar and the North-East

c. Wind and cyclones

- 1877–2005: 283 cyclones (106 severe) in a 50-km wide strip on the east coast
- Less severe cyclonic activity on the west coast (35 cyclones in the same period)
- In 19 severe cyclonic storms, death toll was more than 10,000 lives

In 21 cyclones in Bay of Bengal (India + Bangladesh) 1.25 million lives have been lost.

d. Floods

- Floods in the Indo-Gangetic-Brahmaputra plains are an annual feature; on an average, a few hundred lives are lost.
- Millions are rendered homeless.
- Lakhs of hectares of crops are damaged every year.

Role of the town-planning process

A town-planning process is the basic framework of urban locales of disaster law which fixes roles, responsibilities and accountability of concerned offices and departments. The prime objective of any town planning and urban development activity is to achieve a planned development of an urban area that assures comfort, convenience and safety to the inhabitants. This is achieved by regulating and directing the physical development in relation to the social, economic and environmental goals of the community; therefore, the development plans are formulated under the provisions of town-planning legislations.

To direct and regulate development at the layout and building levels within the framework of development policies and land use control contained in the development plan, a set of development control regulations or development code or development promotion regulations are prescribed in the development plan, according to which development is carried out by the public and private agencies.

The development control regulations, including the land use control, sub-division control, height, plot coverage, FAR, density and parking provisions, exist practically in every state, but certain additional provisions in DCR and land use zoning for safety in natural hazard-prone areas and additional provisions for structural safety in building bye-laws are essential.

Classification of urban land uses is based upon the requirements of the various plans. For example, a perspective plan, which is a policy document, need not show many details of a specific land use and may show only the main use which could be, say, residential or commercial. In the case of a development plan, which is a comprehensive plan indicating the use of each parcel of land, there is a need to show more details of a specific land use. It has to indicate for the land designated as, say, commercial the further details as to which land is for retail commercial or for wholesale trade or for godowns. In the case of layouts of projects of a shopping centre, further details shall be necessary, indicating which block of retail commercial is for, say, cloth or electronics or vegetables. There could be three levels in land use classification:

Level I For Perspective Plans/Regional Plans
Level II For Development Plans
Level III For Layouts of Projects/Schemes

Land use zoning

The next step to urban land use planning is land use zoning which clarifies the legal arena in disaster management. The main purpose of the land use zoning is to provide regulations for the development of a particular area to serve the desired purpose efficiently and to preserve its character. It also provides for the kind of buildings to be constructed. Zoning regulations are legal tools for guiding the use of land and protection of public health, welfare and safety. Such regulations also include provisions for the use of premises/property and limitations upon the shape, size and type of buildings that are constructed or occupy the land. Further, these provide both horizontal and vertical use of the land. These regulations also improve the quality of life in urban centres by preventing flooding during monsoons and heavy rains and helping water harvesting in urban habitats. For instance, in flood zones, the land may be used for parks, playgrounds and gardens while restricting any building activity in such vulnerable areas which contain drainage and water channels. Imaginative administrators and decision makers who have a prospective disaster perspective would prefer to emphasize green belts along the natural drainage channels which may facilitate improvements of these drains as well as the urban groundwater levels. Zoning also identifies lifeline structures which should also be protected while either proposing land uses or otherwise.

City and 'use zones'

In order to promote a healthy and balanced development, it is necessary to apply reasonable limitations on the use of lands and buildings. For desirable development, the city is divided into a number of 'use zones' such as residential, commercial, industrial and recreational. For each zone, specific regulations are provided. A single set of regulations cannot be applied for the whole city. It is here that the law is expected to absorb human requirements into development processes in a city.

Objectives of land use zoning

The objective of land use zoning is to regulate land use in hazard-prone areas to minimize the damage caused to the habitat, as a result of natural hazards, namely earthquakes, cyclonic storms and floods, which recur from time to time. Land use zoning, therefore, also aims at determining the locations and the extent of areas likely to be adversely affected by the hazards of different intensities and frequencies and to develop such areas in a manner that the loss to the development is reduced to the minimum.

Land use zoning envisages certain restrictions on the indiscriminate development of the 'unprotected' hazard-prone areas and specifies conditions for safer development by protecting the area from severe losses. In the former case, boundaries of different zones are to be established to prevent unrestricted growth there. Another objective of land use zoning in the hill areas will be to ensure the forest cover and to preserve the green areas for environment protection. In coastal areas the role of 'costal regulation zone' prohibits construction and other developmental activities as much as it does in the riverbed areas; besides it also facilitates prevention of erosion, protection of mangroves, fish catch, livelihoods and multifarious other activities which feed into sustainable progress of a society. Another objective of the land use zoning in the coastal areas is to protect inland stretches that are influenced by tidal action, tsunami and other disasters at sea.

Applicability of zoning

Areas are planned under State Perspective Plan/Regional Plan/Master Plan/Development Plan as part of 'Master Plan or Zonal Development Plan'. While formulating Perspective Plan/Regional Plan/Development Plan (Master Plan/Zonal Development Plan) for any notified area, the proposals should indicate the natural hazard-prone areas with the type and extent of likely hazards. In such areas where there are no Master Plans or Development Plans, general guidelines and recommendations on natural disaster mitigation should be issued to the various local bodies, municipalities and town area committees and panchayats to enable them to take these into consideration while sitting various projects and deciding on construction of buildings and so on. Technical help may be required by some of the local bodies in implementing plans. Many model guidelines were recommended by expert committees[1] for the Town and Country Planning Organization (TCPO) along with the formulation of Model Town and Country Planning Act in the year 1960. Thereafter, it was revised in 1985 as a Model Regional and Town Planning and Development Law, which has largely been the basis for the enactment of comprehensive urban and regional planning legislation in the states and UTs.

Based on the previously referred model development law, the revised model guidelines on Urban Development Plan Formulation and Implementation (UDPFI) have been formulated to include the provisions of 73rd and 74th constitutional amendments. These guidelines with suggested changes pertaining to safety in natural hazard zone should be the basis for amendment in all the existing TCP Acts and the enactment of new TCP Act in the states.

How to identify natural hazard-prone areas as a precursor to regulations

Identifying earthquake-prone areas

Intensities of VII or more on Modified Mercalli or MSK intensity scale are considered moderate to high. Areas under seismic zones III, IV and V, as specified in IS 1893,[2] will be considered prone to earthquake hazards. In these zones the areas which have soil conditions and the level of water table favourable for liquefaction or settlements under earthquake vibrations will have a greater risk to buildings and structures which will be of special consideration under land use zoning. Under these zones, those hilly areas which are identified to have poor slope stability conditions, where landslides could be triggered by earthquake, where, due to prior saturated conditions, mud flow could be initiated by earthquakes and where avalanches could be triggered by earthquake will be specially risk prone.

The earthquake hazard-prone areas as defined earlier are identified on the map given in IS 1893 on a small scale and more easily identified on a larger scale by state-wise maps given in the Vulnerability Atlas of India. The special risky areas as defined earlier have to be determined specifically for the planning area under consideration through special studies to be carried out by geologists and geo-technical engineers. If an active fault trace is identified by GSI (Geological Survey of India), a structure for human occupancy should not be placed over the fault trace and must be set back by a minimum of 15 m on either side of fault trace.

Identifying cyclone-prone areas

Areas prone to cyclonic storms are along the sea coast of India where the cyclonic wind velocities of 39 meter per second or more are specified in the wind velocity map given in IS 875 (part 3) on a small scale and easily identified in the Vulnerability Atlas of India where the maps are drawn state-wise on a larger scale. In these cyclone-prone areas, those areas which are likely to be subjected to heavy rain–induced floods or to flooding by seawater under the conditions of storm surge are especially risky due to damage by flood flow and inundation under water. Whereas areas under cyclone threat are easily identified, those with special risk have to be identified by special contour survey of the planning area under consideration and the study of the past flooding and storm surge history of the area. These studies may have to be carried out through the Survey of India or locally appointed survey teams, and by reference to the Central Water Commission, Government of India, and the departments of the state or UT dealing with the floods.

Identifying flood-prone areas

a The flood-prone areas in river plains (unprotected and protected by bunds) are indicated in the Flood Atlas of India prepared by the Central Water Commission and reproduced on a larger scale in the state-wise maps in the Vulnerability Atlas of India.
b Besides the previous flood-prone areas, other areas can be flooded under the conditions of heavy-intensity rains, inundation in depressions, backflow in drains, inadequate drainage, failure of protection works and so on.

Whereas the flood-prone areas under 'a' are identified on the available maps as indicated, the areas under 'b' have to be identified through local contour survey and study of the flood history of the planning area. Such studies may be carried out through Survey of India or local survey teams and by reference to the Central Water Commission and the departments of the state or UT dealing with the floods.

Identifying landslide–prone areas

While it is known that most hilly areas are prone to landslides and landslips, the susceptibility of the various areas to landslide varies from very low to very high. Landslide zoning naturally requires mapping on a large scale. Normally medium scale of 1:25,000 is at least chosen. In preparation of the landslide zone map, two types of factors are considered important as listed here:

1 Geological/ topographic factors/parameters
2 Triggering factors

Approach for land use zoning

Having identified the hazard-prone areas, the following alternatives can be adopted for dealing with the disaster risk problems.

a *Leaving the area unprotected.* In this case it will be necessary to specify land use zoning for various development purposes as recommended under herein
b Using protection methods for the areas as a whole or in the construction of buildings, structures and infrastructure facilities to cater for the hazard intensities likely in the planning area
c To prioritize buildings, structures and infrastructures in terms of their importance from the point of view of impact of damage on the socio-economic structure of the society as recommended under Regulation no. 6[3]

How to prioritize

In regard to land use zoning, different types of buildings and utility services are grouped under three priorities as indicated here:

Priority 1 Defence installation, industries, public utilities, lifeline structures like hospitals, electricity installations, water supply, telephone exchange, aerodromes and railway stations, commercial centres, libraries, other buildings or installations with contents of high economic value.
Priority 2 Public and semi-public institutions, government offices and residential areas.
Priority 3 Parks, playgrounds, woodlands, gardens, green belts and recreational areas.

As far as the Land Use Zoning for Flood Safety is concerned the following recommendations of the Expert Committee become important (2007).

Preparation of flood contour maps

The following actions should be taken to prepare the flood contour maps by taking up special studies/surveys as found necessary in the development area:

i Prepare detailed contour plan of the area liable to flood on a scale of 1:15,000 or a larger scale showing contours at an interval of 0.3 to 0.5 m.

ii Fix reference river gauges or maximum flood levels due to heavy rains with respect to which areas are likely to be inundated.
iii Demarcate areas liable to flooding by *floods in rivers* of return periods of 5, 25, 50 and 100 years or by *excessive rainfall* of return periods of 5, 10, 25 and 50 years.
iv Mark on the maps the submersion contours for these flood stages.

Regulation for land use zoning

i Installations and buildings of priority 1 should be located in such a fashion that the area is above the levels corresponding to a 100-year flood or the maximum observed flood levels, whichever higher. Similarly they should also be above the levels corresponding to a 50-year rainfall flooding and the likely submersion due to drainage congestion.
ii Buildings of priority 2 should be located outside the 25-year flood or a 10-year rainfall contour, provided that the buildings if constructed between the 10- and 25-year contours should have either high plinth level above 25-year flood mark or been constructed on columns or stilts, with ground area left for the unimportant uses.
iii Activities of priority 3, namely play grounds, gardens and parks, can be located in areas vulnerable to frequent floods.

Note: In natural hazard-prone areas identified under the land use zoning regulations, structures, buildings and installations which cannot be avoided, protective measures for such construction/development should be properly safeguarded.

Planning in hill areas

In order to ensure environmentally sound development of hill towns, the following restrictions and conditions may be proposed for future activities. An integrated development plan may be prepared taking into consideration environmental and other relevant factors including ecologically sensitive areas, hazard-prone areas, drainage channels, steep slopes and fertile land. Water bodies including underground water bodies in water-scarce areas should be protected. Where cutting of hill slope in an area causes ecological damage and slope instability in adjacent areas, such cuttings shall not be undertaken unless appropriate measures are taken to avoid or prevent such damages. No construction should be ordinarily undertaken in areas having slope above 30°, areas which fall in landslide hazard zones or areas falling on the spring lines and first-order streams identified by the state government on the basis of available scientific evidence. Construction may be permitted in areas with slope between 10° and 30° or spring recharge areas or old landslide zones with such restrictions as the competent authority may decide.

Conclusion

The amendments in Town Planning Legislations of all the states and UTs and framing of land use zoning regulations, in development control regulations and structural safety measures and provisions to follow BIS codes for structural safety against earthquakes, cyclone/wind protection and landslide protection in building bye-laws, will go a long way to ensure safety in the development and construction for safer settlements in India. Provisions are required in legislation for compliance, enforcement, accountability and liability. A weak enforcement throws a city into irretrievable vulnerability to varying disasters.

Notes

1 Expert[0] Committee (2004). Constituted by Ministry of Home Affairs, Govt. of India. Proposed Amendment in Town & Country Planning Legislation, Regulations for Land Use Zoning, Additional Provisions in Development Control Regulations for Safety & Additional Provisions in Building Regulations/Byelaws for Structural Safety – in Natural Hazard Zones of India – Volume 1.
2 IS 1893–1 (2002): Criteria for Earthquake Resistant Design of Structures, Part 1: General Provisions and Buildings (CED 39: Earthquake Engineering).
3 Generally, the structural design of foundations, elements of masonry, timber, plain concrete, reinforced concrete, prestressed concrete and structural steel shall conform to the provisions of part VI Structural Design Section – 1 Loads, Section – 2 Foundation, Section – 3 Wood, Section – 4 Masonry, Section – 5 Concrete and Section – 6 Steel of National Building Code of India (NBC), taking into consideration the Indian Standards (National Disaster Management Division, 2007).

Reference

Mittal, V. (2009). Intelligent Cities: Planning for Urban Future, Proceedings of the World Habitat Day, 5 October 2009, pp. 20–23.

National Disaster Management Division, MHA, Government of India. (2007). Model Town and Country Planning Legislation Zoning Regulations Development Control Building Regulation Bye-laws for Natural Hazard Zones of India – Volume 1, July 2007 updated 2008, p. 15.

19 Post-disaster medical services

Can law ensure services?

Sunita Reddy and Shishir Kumar Yadav

Understanding disasters and its relationship to law

Disasters have been defined and redefined, yet there is no consensus on what is the right definition for disasters (Quarantelli, 2005). Historically there have been changes in the ideas about disasters, seen as events, which are 'supernatural' or 'acts of God' or 'acts of man'. Now there are ongoing debates on development and disasters. Definitions for disasters are either too broad or too narrow. Cutter (2005) says that instead of spending too much time and intellectual capital in defining disasters, it is important to do research on more fundamental concerns. Instead of trying to know 'what is disaster?' it is better to ask 'what is our vulnerability', resilience to environmental threats and extreme events. A book by Quarantelli (2005) named *Disaster* tries to define 'what is disaster'. Thirty different academic disciplines look at disasters and understand differently. For lay perception, everything and anything under the sun is called disaster. However, in academic discourse, naturalness of 'natural' disasters is also questioned, due to the anthropogenic development models, which trigger 'natural' disasters. Categories of disasters as 'slow' or 'sudden', 'natural' or 'man-made' are all questioned much more critically; however, as social scientists, we understand disasters as social phenomenon. Therefore, the relationship to law becomes more intricate to the lives of those encountering disasters.

While disasters kill people, those who survive need emergency medical care. While a lot depends on the pre-existing medical care system in the location of disasters, emergency medicine and its preparedness is an important aspect for mitigating and managing disasters. Disasters not just affect all the public health services, but there are serious public health consequences post disasters.

Gunn (1990) and Lechat (1984) cited in Noji (1997) emphasize the definition of a 'disaster' from the standpoint of healthcare providers. They define 'disasters' as:

> A disaster is the result of a vast ecological breakdown in the relation between humans and their environment, a serious and sudden event (or slow, as in a drought) on such a scale that the stricken community needs extraordinary efforts to cope with it, often with outside help or international aid.

Disasters have different stages, and it has a different impact on the affected population. Noji (1997) had marked out different stages in disaster cycle and formulated five such cycles: the non-disaster or inter-disaster phase, pre-disaster or warning phase, The impact phase, the emergency phase (also called the relief or isolation phase) and, last, reconstruction or rehabilitation phase.

It has been observed from the past experiences that the medical services themselves gets incapacitated at the time of large-scale disasters. Tsunami 2004 was a breakthrough in the Indian history to come up with the Disaster Management (DM) Act 2005. With the formation of a National Disaster Management Authority (NDMA) at national level, State Disaster Management Authority (SDMA) at the state level and District Disaster Management Authority (DDMA) at the district level. The district level officers have been given powers to exercise in case of emergencies, subject to ex-post facto ratification of the district authority.

Given the large population of India with high vulnerabilities for disasters in different districts and poor health care services, it is important to take stalk of the existing laws, policy guidelines on one hand and the practical challenges on the ground situation which fails all the policies, unless there is a proactive effort to put systems in place. In such a situation what would be the role and responsibility of law? Who should be held accountable? What could be the penalties for non-performance? How could human and non-human bodies be evaluated, and who should pay the cost of their losses, maiming and death?

This chapter explores the existing emergency medical preparedness in India and suggests legal framework and laws to strengthen medical emergency response. In the whole cyclic approach to disasters, from preparedness – event, rescue, relief-rehabilitation, mitigation – interface with medical system is an important spoke in the wheel. This chapter limits itself to looking at only the medical emergency aspects. Taking examples from the previous disasters in India, like the Bhopal gas disaster, the chapter will see the need for emergency medical preparedness, especially when the deaths were more due to not handling the medical emergencies well than the deaths due to the disaster itself. The chapter tries to analyse the lacuna in the existing frameworks and makes suggestions to fulfil the gap in the same.

Unlearnt lessons from Bhopal gas disaster

Bhopal gas disaster[1] can be seen as a watershed disaster that raised issues of management of emergencies and availability of public health facilities. In a way it has posed a challenge for disaster preparedness, and lacunae in the planning and handling medical emergencies. It is very important then to critically examine the existing laws and medical emergency plans related to disasters. Three decades have passed; the living memory of the Bhopal gas disaster[2] is fresh in minds, and the community is still fighting for justice. Government records to 2,500 deaths, whereas activists and other groups estimate to 25,000 deaths. More than the leak of the poisonous gas, itself, many died due to lack of emergency medical response. In the case of Bhopal gas leak, the medical staffs were unprepared for the thousands of casualties. Doctors and hospitals were not informed of proper treatment methods for methyl isocyanate (MIC) gas inhalation. They were told to simply give cough medicine and eye drops to their patients. 'Operation Faith': on 16 December, the tanks 611 and 619 were emptied of the remaining MIC. This led to a second mass evacuation from Bhopal. Complaints of a lack of information or misinformation were widespread. The Bhopal plant medical doctor did not have proper information about the properties of the gases.

A movie on Bhopal gas disaster, released in 2014, *A Prayer for Rain*, raises the issue of medical emergencies and ends with a pertinent question

> What was the truth behind Bhopal tragedy? That the case between our government and Carbide went for four years or our government did not file a criminal case against them and they were acquitted. Or maybe, people died due to not getting timely treatment and not only because of Carbide.

This incident reflects the classic case of the existing lack of preparedness in emergency medical services in India. Not just post disasters, lack of medical care in normal situations is also a major concern and reason for higher morbidities and mortalities in India. In this case of

Bhopal gas disaster, people died not only because of the disaster but because of the lack of emergency medical facilities.

It is pertinent to take stock of the risk and vulnerability because of hazardous chemical units in India. There are 1,861 Major Accident Hazard (MAH) Units in 301 districts across the country. There are thousands of hazardous material factories in unorganized sector, with serious and complex disaster risks. Though there are various acts, which can be related to hazardous chemical units and its regulation, they are not comprehensive and not enacted in true spirit.

The laws have existed much before Bhopal Gas Accident: Explosive Act 1884, Petroleum Act 1934 and Insecticides Act 1968. Post Bhopal, Environmental Protection Act 1986; Motor Vehicles Act 1988; the Manufacture, Storage and Import of Hazardous Chemical Rules 1989; Public Liability Insurance Act 1991, which provides damage to victims of an accident, handling any hazardous substance,[3] were enacted. The recent Disaster Management Act 2005 envisages a holistic and integrated approach to disaster management. Instead of only relief-centric response, it looks forward for proactive role in prevention, mitigation and preparedness-driven approach for conserving developmental gains and to minimize loss of life, livelihood and property.[4] Though on ground most often we end up with firefighting and respond only after disaster has occurred.

Government of India reinforced the legal framework of chemical safety and management of chemical accidents, by enacting new rules such as MSIHC Rules, EPPR Rules, SMPV Rules, CMV Rules, Gas Cylinder Rules and Hazard Waste Rules. The National Disaster Management Authority (NDMA) of India has come up with Chemical Disaster Management.[5] Though we have various acts, there is a lack of comprehensive act as present in the United States to check any disasters. In the last decade itself, 130 significant chemical accidents were reported in India, which resulted in reported cases of 259 deaths and around 563 major injuries.[6]

Emergency preparedness in other countries

In the late 1960s, after the increase in the number of road accident causalities, the federal government in the US decided to bring a law that would standardize the emergency medical services in the country. A major NAS (National Academy of Sciences) report, published in 1966, urged that a national program to improve emergency care be launched. Emergency Medical Services Systems Act (EMSSA) was passed in 1973 with the agenda to develop systems that would encompass all phases of patient care. The new law, however, faced several challenges at the implementation stage where disaster concerns especially were raised. Disaster is given less attention in the law. It views the requirements of a disaster situation as only quantitatively different from normal EMS operations – that is, as similar to daily emergency treatment, only larger in magnitude. The law also fails to clear the ambiguity regarding the roles assigned to various groups and organizations during a disaster, which can cause confusion (Tierney, 1985).

The US Congress, Environmental Protection Agency (EPA) and the chemical industry came forward with a law The Comprehensive Environmental Response, Compensation and Liability Act (CERCLA) of 1980, commonly known as Superfund, enacted on 11 December 1980. This law created a tax on the chemical and petroleum industries and provided broad federal authority to respond directly to releases or threatened releases of hazardous substances that may endanger public health or the environment.[7] Several reasonable provisions are given for assuring an adequate emergency response to a major chemical spill. These include developing comprehensive emergency and evacuation plans by the manufacturer with the involvement of state and local officials. These measures should necessarily include a detailed description of the health effects of any hazardous substance, the specific measures to be taken to mitigate and minimize risks to human health and the environment, specification of an emergency notification plan for hospitals and the public, an evaluation of available medical, police and, firefighting resources and, if appropriate, recommendations for additional resources. It also calls for the formation of 'Emergency Response Districts' and 'Emergency Response Committees' to be designated by the governor of each state for the purpose of developing a comprehensive emergency response plan for the designated districts (Editorial, 1986). Therefore, it establishes that the immediate crucial response in the case of a chemical disaster comes from the manufacturing plant. Moreover, the Chemical Manufacturers Association has established the Chemical Response and Information Centre to organize information, train non-industry local personnel on the local level and coordinate industry responses (ibid.).

In Japan, emergency medical services are provided by the fire defence headquarters of the local government. It has one-tiered emergency medical service system. The ambulances are kept ready with three crew members, who are trained in rescue, stabilization, transportation and advanced care of traumatic and medical emergencies. There are three levels of care services provided by ambulance personnel, which are the basic-level ambulance crew (First Aid Class 1), a second level (Standard First Aid Class) and the highest level (Emergency Life Saving Technicians). Further, the medical emergency facilities are classified into three levels on the basis of the resources, administration, staff and so on Primary emergency facilities provide care for walk-in patients, secondary emergency facilities provide in-hospital care for acute illnesses and trauma and tertiary emergency facilities, called 'Life-Saving Emergency Centers', provide total care for critically ill and severely traumatized patients. An Emergency Medical Information Service is also available at all centres useful for the proper management of the system. Appropriate training is provided to the citizens for ensuring their participation in the emergency health medical service system (Tanigawa & Tanaka, 2006).

Emergency preparedness in India

Post the formation of NDMA, it came up with 18 guidelines on the management of various disasters. There are also guidelines on 'Medical Preparedness and Mass Casualty Management' and also 'The Guidelines on Incident Response System' to handle any medical emergencies in disaster scenario. The National Policy on Disaster Management 2009 approved by the Union Cabinet on 22 October 2009 stated:

> Medical preparedness is a crucial component of any DM Plan. The NDMA, in close coordination with the Ministry of Health and Family Welfare, States and premier medical research institutes plans to formulate policy guidelines to enhance capacity in emergency medical response and mass casualty management. Which include developing and training of medical teams and paramedics, capacity building, trauma and psychosocial care, mass casualty management and triage. The surge and casualty handling capacity of all hospitals at the time of disasters will be worked out and recorded through a consultative process, by all the States/UTs in the pre-disaster phase. The State and District authorities will be encouraged to formulate appropriate procedures for treatment of casualties by private hospitals during disasters. These plans will also address post-disaster disease surveillance systems, networking with hospitals, referral institutions and accessing services and facilities such as availability of ambulances and blood banks.[8]

The guideline further adds that the

> Medical response has to be quick and effective. The execution of medical response plans and deployment of medical resources warrant special attention at the State and District level in most

> of the situations. The voluntary deployment of the nearest medical resources to the disaster site, irrespective of the administrative boundaries, will be emphasized. Mobile medical hospitals and other resources available with the center will also be provided to the States/UTs in a proactive manner. Post-disaster management of health, sanitation and hygiene services is crucial to prevent an outbreak of epidemics. Therefore, constant monitoring of any such possibility will be necessary.[9]

Very clearly the National Disaster Management Guidelines on 'Incident Response System' gives a well-planned duties and responsibilities. At the lowest level a 'Medical Unit Leader' is also envisaged under Service Branch Director (SBD); (i) that have to prepare the Medical Plan and procurement of required resources as per Incident Action Plan, (ii) provide medical aid and ambulance for transportation of victims and maintain the records of the same, obtain a road map of the area from the PS for the ambulance services, transportation of medical personnel and victims; (iii) Respond to requests of the OS for medical aid, transportation and medical supplies etc. under intimation to the SBD and Logistic Section Chief (LSC); (iv) maintain the list of medical personnel who could be mobilized in times of need; (v) requisition more human resources as and when required to meet the incident objectives; (vi) prepare and circulate list of referral service centres to the entire medical team leaders; (vii) maintain record of various activities and send to SBD; and (viii) perform any other duties assigned by the SBD and LSC.[10]

However, the challenge is to put this plan into action, given the three-tier system of primary, secondary and tertiary sector with improper referral services and especially when the health service systems have been weakened. There are no standards maintained and are very heterogeneous in nature, with wide disparities across geographical locations. Most places they are inaccessible, unaffordable and unavailable.

The private health sector too is very heterogeneous; from a single doctor unit to multi and super specialty hospitals in most of the metropolitan cities. Though, the capacities to meet the medical emergencies in these multi and super-specialty hospitals is adequate, however, the response at the time of disasters, is yet to be seen, without the profit motive.

Though the 'Incident Response System' is well planned and with clear guidelines at the national level, it is important for the states to adopt these guidelines and put in place the system to respond, given any emergencies. However, one can see that every time we fail, given any disaster, the most recent being the Chennai floods, where the tertiary care hospital itself could not save its own in-patients.

There is no uniform ambulance service. In Delhi, the Centralized Accident and Trauma Service (CATS) provides the ambulance services via two numbers (102 and 1099), and in Andhra Pradesh, the ambulance system is run by the Emergency Management and Research Institute (EMRI), through 108 service. Apart from these two, most of the ambulances are not fully equipped; they are just little more than transport service.[11]

Apart from the lack of preparedness at the Health Service System levels, in the Indian context, all the Hazardous units should have on-site and off-site preparatory and disaster mitigation plans. Though these plans are present on paper, however, drills are not practiced with required seriousness. Many of the managers from the Hazardous units reported[12] that they are keen to share the hazards of the chemicals in their factories to the local communities who reside in the nearby areas, but fear that they will demand closure of these units. Thus, in most places, the local population is unaware of the hazardous material in their vicinity; leave alone the health institutions being aware of the antidote and emergency medicine, in case of any impending disasters. This shows that despite three decades of Bhopal disasters, we have not learned the lessons.

In 2008, UNDP and Government of India brought a report with series of guidelines for hospital emergency preparedness planning in India.[13] The guidelines ensure a central role for the hospital to deliver to medical services at the ground level. It suggests training for staff and personnel in the hospital for dealing with mass casualty situations according to the triage method of classification, which is widely accepted in the world. It also proposes the communication and networking between the nodal officers and other institutions such as blood banks, private hospitals, railway hospitals, media and radio stations etc. However, despite the good intentions, these guidelines have failed to translate into reality because it is not practiced at the normal times or there are hardly any mock drills done to know the division of the roles and responsibilities of specific authorities which leads to ambiguity, chaos and lack of coordination at the time of disaster.

Emergency phase

'The Emergency Phase' (also called the relief or isolation phase) is the most important phase because it starts immediately after impact of disaster and is the time for providing relief and assistance to the victim.

This phase requires actions that are necessary to save lives, search and rescue operation, evacuation of the vulnerable population from the hazards situation and places, emergency medical services, restoration of communication and transportation network and public health surveillance (Burkle et al., 1984 cited in Noji, 1997).

The emergency medical services are very crucial in a post-disaster situation. While a well-attended post-disaster situation can reduce the risk of epidemics and reoccurrence of a disaster, a failure in providing adequate medical services at the end of a disaster can simply worsen the situation and survival for the 'sufferers'[14] of a disaster. A post-disaster site is a serious breeding ground for diseases and epidemics. There are several diseases that can emerge immediately after a disaster such as diarrhoea, cholera and other water-borne diseases in case of disasters like floods and tsunamis. Rise in malaria cases were reported in Andaman and Nicobar Islands post-tsunami (Reddy, 2013). Some diseases emerge over a period of time after the disaster, such as genetic diseases that occurred after the Hiroshima and Nagasaki disaster. Massive accidents are common in a post-disaster situation. Emergency medical services are important because of providing immediate relief and assistance after a disaster. However, in some disasters like floods, earthquakes, tsunamis, the health services themselves can be crippled, and there are losses of lives of the medical and paramedical professionals. The most recent example is of the Chennai floods, where the breakdown of ICU and emergency services in MIOT hospital led to the death of 18 critically ill patients.[15] In such scenario, even the emergency medical services are helpless, given the nature of disasters, like floods, where all the lifelines based on communications, electricity become dysfunctional, raising the challenge to provide emergency services.

Medical emergency planning in India

In Indian context, when the primary and secondary public health services are already precarious in normal times, standing up at the time of emergencies is even more challenging. Presence of large private sector across rural and urban can be more resourceful, provided they come forward in emergency situation without the ulterior motive of profit making. This chapter argues that there has to be a law to monitor and regulate both public and private health care institutions to rise to the occasion in emergency situation, as disasters are going to be everyday experiences. Thus, there is an emergency to build institutional mechanisms in the form of Law and organizations to attend to the medical emergencies with utmost attention.

In the wake of a disaster, the interaction between vulnerabilities and disaster hazards may result in significant injuries and the loss of human lives. Since a large number of casualties can easily overwhelm the existing but partly destroyed medical facilities, establishing an emergency health services is critical. The type of health services provided depends on whether the emergency situation is post-natural disaster, a complex emergency or protracted refugee health; but it must guarantee basic physical and mental care as well as prevention. In all emergency situations, the prioritization of health services must focus on meeting both the short-term and long-term health needs of the survivors (The Johns Hopkins and Red Cross Red Crescent, 2008).

The legal framework of medical services

According to Seventh Schedule of Indian Constitution, the issue of health comes under the state and concurrent lists. Public Health, hospitals, sanitation, and so on fall in the state list and the items having wider ramifications at the national level like population control and family welfare, medical education, prevention of food adulteration, quality control in manufacture of drugs etc. have been included in the Concurrent list. The Ministry of Health & Family Welfare is instrumental and responsible for the implementation of various programmes on a national scale in the areas of Health & Family Welfare, prevention and control of major communicable diseases and promotion of traditional and indigenous systems of medicines. Apart from these, the Health Ministry assists states in preventing and controlling the spread of seasonal disease outbreaks and epidemics through technical assistance as health is a State subject. The ministry is also responsible to bring out laws and enactments for grappling with medical emergencies during disaster (NIDM, 2012).

Indian health care services are run through programmes based on diseases or services. Most of these programmes are carried out in normal situation: preventive, promotive, rehabilitative and curative services. Some of the programmes listed are *Pradhan Mantri Swasthya Suraksha Yojana* (PMSSY), Reproductive & Child Health, National Rural Health Mission (NRHM), *Janani Suraksha Yojana, Naav Jat Shishu Suraksha Karyakarm* (NSSK), Integrated Management of Neonatal & Childhood Illness (IMNCI), School Health Programme, National Cancer Control Programme, National Tobacco Control Programme, National AIDS Control Programme, National Sexually Transmitted Disease (STD) Control Programme, National Mental Health

Programme, National Programme for Prevention and Control of Diabetes, Cardiovascular Disease & Stroke 2008, National Programme for Health for the Elderly, National Disease Control Programme, National Vector Borne Disease Control Programme (NVBDCP). Various Projects like Integrated Disease Surveillance Project, Emergency Medical Relief (EMR), Health Education, Training & Capacity Building, AYUSH too are running. Most of these health programmes in India talk about the disaster at large.

The National Mental Health Policy 1982 & National Mental Health Act 1987 has some preparatory part for the disaster emergencies. There are also several Acts passed in the parliament that set the standard for maintaining the quality of human health. Some of these Acts are Food Safety & Standard Act 2006, National Alcohol Policy and Drug-de-Addiction Programme.

After reviewing each of these programmes, we find that in NRHM, the disaster management is given some attention on preparatory part at different levels. National Urban Health Mission (NUHM) also focuses on community level monitoring of resources while promoting public health measurements. The National Policy on HIV/AIDS & the World of Work (2009) Report brought out by Ministry of Labour and Employment, however, only mentions skill development/livelihood and other social security schemes in disaster situation.[16]

National Council for Human Resources in Health in 2009[17] is an overarching regulatory body to achieve the objective of enhancing the supply of skilled personnel in the health sector. However, surprisingly in spite of being the latest and extremely crucial document for the future of human resource creation and planning in health, it does not mention any thing about the planning of 'emergency medicine' or 'disaster medicine' education or capacity building of existing health professionals for effective management of post-disaster mortality and morbidity. Food Safety and Standard Act 2006, does mention about food safety and nutrition during disaster or emergency situations. Other programmes also have some sections and guidelines on preventive measurements about disaster management but they do not have any institutional mechanism to ensure the disaster's medical emergencies (NIDM, 2012).

After reviewing the basic frameworks of all programmes, we learn that all programmes have not been given enough attention to draw any specific guideline for medical emergencies. Medical emergency is merged under the larger ambit of the public health service systems with no specific focus on emergencies like large scale disasters.

A medical disaster response: triage and golden hour

In emergency medical care, response time is critical. Several studies have shown that in the case of disasters, among the dead, the potentially savable people were those who died slowly over several hours from otherwise treatable conditions. By the time, outside medical assistance arrives it is already too late for lack of medical emergency facility. The conventional medical health care system relies on hospitals and the primary health care centres, in the event of disasters. It has been observed that in earthquakes and other major disasters, there is an incapacitation of hospitals and their staff and thus cannot be relied upon. An alternative model in the form of the National Medical Disaster Response Force (NMDRF), like the NDRF (National Disaster Response Force) can also be formed, however, to reach this NMDRF would take time and the golden hour is lost.

The NMDRF model can be designed in such a way that they be trained for 'Triage'[18] and then treating the survivors according to the need. An operations plan needs to be designed, which directs the initial management of personnel and casualties, and a training course to educate health care providers about the unique medical problems of different disasters and their particular effects. Ex. earthquake survivors have more orthopaedic problem, compared to fire/chemical/radiological/nuclear disaster survivors. The medical teams have to have prior knowledge of medical/clinical protocols to treat the patients. In the Delhi Mayapuri Scrap Market case of radiological exposure, doctors took some time to diagnose the cause and decipher the treatment, in the process one patient died.[19]

Schultz (1996) gives the Operations plan, which is divided into three phases according to the time elapsed since the initial disaster and the location of treatment: hour 0 to 1 (Golden hour) -solo-treatment areas; hours 1 to 12 – disaster-medical-aid centres; and hours 12 to 72, casualty-collection points. In the first phase, solo treatment locations would be established where physicians will stabilize the patients with the available medical resources in their backpacks and the patients will be immediately sent to centres depending on their conditions. In the second phase, patients will be provided with the triage depending on their requirements (Schultz et al., 1996).

However, the triage should be done right at the spot of disaster, before taking them to the medical facility.[20] The disaster-medical-aid centres would be the principal sites for the delivery of medical care after any disaster. An initial triage area would be established immediately outside the centre. In accordance with the Simple Triage and Rapid Treatment system, the 'walking wounded'[21] would be identified first. The remaining patients would then be divided into three categories with colour coding: those requiring immediate care (coded in red), those for whom care might be delayed (yellow), and the dead (black) respectively. From here, they would be sent to their respective places, medical aid centres, casualty collection centres and to morgue respectively. In the third phase, the casualty collection point performs two functions. First, it serves as a staging area for the arrival of medical supplies and personnel and the evacuation of patients. Second, it contains a medical area for triage and treatment. Under the second part or the training phase, the subjects that are covered would be mass-casualty triage, airway management, use of intravenous fluids, anaesthesia and analgesia in the field, crush-injury treatment, and command and control. This way, the disaster medical emergency response is helpful in reducing the mortality after any disaster (Schultz et al., 1996).

India is still struggling to put the model in function in case of major disasters, where golden hour is lost, resulting in huge causality. The long-term medical care too is not so effective and planned in disaster scenario, due to lack of resources and manpower. Psychosocial care is another major and important area to be addressed in the post-disaster situation, under the rehabilitation stage.

Existing Indian laws and medical emergency

Disaster Management (DM) Act 2005, though talks of paradigm shift from response centric to a holistic cyclic approach of preparedness, relief, rehabilitation and mitigation, is still not prepared to absorb medical emergencies as mentioned earlier. Due to the limited resources and lack of adequate health services in the normal times, there is no expectation for any medical emergencies response in disaster scenario or to have disaster medicine. However, given the increase in frequencies of disasters, it is pertinent to prepare for disaster at all levels with well-equipped medical emergencies plans, which will go long way in improving the medical emergency services in normal times.

National Disaster Management Authority (NDMA) came with a laundry list of Laws, called 'Compendium of Laws on Disaster Management' 2015 in their website. The Compendium has four parts and 22 chapters. It has covered different legislations which have been enacted at the State and Central levels to deal with different types of disasters. This compendium has a range of general Acts, but not specifying either the health or medical emergency. Within the compendium the list goes on about ill-connected set of laws, that is, The

Indian Penal Code 1860, The Indian Evidence Act 1872, The Civil Defense Act 1968, The Wild Life (Protection) Act 1972, The Code Of Criminal Procedure 1973, The Water (Prevention And Control Of Pollution) Act 1974, The Water (Prevention And Control Of Pollution) Rules 1975, Forest (Conservation) Act 1980, The Air (Prevention And Control Of Pollution) Act, 1981 and so on, which comprise of better human health through laws, but they do not have any specific laws for a medical emergency situation.

Dispersed laws brought in to address a specific need situation

There is a need for a comprehensive law in disasters, which can cover insurance, remuneration plan, accidental relief fund, regular inspection, welfare commission and communication responsibility as major plans to manage peoples' health under these laws. These laws are silent on the emergency situation including a medical emergency. They do not consider medical emergency situation in the first place because of which there is no clause on it. The Mines Rescue Rules, 1985 is the first law, which has separate section on emergency. Under this Law, there is some communication and instruction on emergency and later look for the medical assistance. However, whether they have any tie-up with medical institutions for their medical emergency or not, is not reflected from the law. The Oil Mines Regulations 2011 is another law, which specifies the emergency plan, in case of any emergency. They focus on alarm and communication system, system of notifying the authorities, duties and responsibilities of each key personnel and how the action shall be carried out.

Remote laws to account for personnel and staff management: The Atomic Energy Act 1962 and Atomic Energy (Working of the mines, minerals and handling of prescribed substances) Rules, 1984 focus on ensuring the availability of adequate staff at all time in order to ensure safety of normal operations, for dose evaluation, for management of accidents, if any, and for medical care and attention of the employees and ensure that adequate protection is provided at all times to safeguard the health and safety of the employees. It also arranges pre-employment and post-termination/retirement medical examination of all employees. It also maintains complete and update records of personal, medical and occupational histories of radiation workers and workers in mines, in such form, as may be prescribed by the Competent Authority. Radiological Safety Officer chalks out an emergency plan, which will lay down instructions for the guidance of the employees in the event of emergency and/or accident conditions and shall get the plan approved by the Competent Authority.

Complex jungle of laws, weak accountability

There are number of rules to follow under the numerous laws mentioned in the compendium, such as Hazardous Wastes (Management and Handling) Rules 1989, The Gas Cylinder Rules 2004, Hazardous Wastes (Management, Handling And Trans-boundary Movement) Rules 2008, Atomic Energy (Safe Disposal Of Radioactive Wastes) Rules 1987, Bio-Medical Waste (Management And Handling) Rules 1998, rules for 'The Manufacture, Use, Import, Export And Storage Of Hazardous Micro Organisms' Genetically Engineered Organisms Or Cells (1989). The Insecticides Rules 1971, Epidemic Diseases Act 1987, Management of Chemical (Terrorism) Disasters guideline, also have some sections on emergency planning. However, for the execution of all these laws there is a need for a comprehensive legal framework which makes it mandatory to carry on the Incident Response System in mitigating disaster. However, equally important is the legal frameworks for medical preparedness for ensuing disasters.

Most of the Acts and rules mentioned in the website are there for emergency planning along with a well plan IRS. However, detailed rules on these Acts, have to be chartered and executed, like What is the role and responsibility of different health care institutions; public, private and corporate at all levels – primary, secondary, tertiary level health care during a disaster? There is no mention about this in any Act or rule. What is the guarantee that the private sector will not exploit the situation of disaster and over charge the disaster survivors, in case the public health facilities fail or get destroyed. There are instances where the prices shoot up and the cost of the essential items like food and water itself is overcharged, seeing the desperation and shortage of it. There are food riots in the post-disaster scenario.

Though on paper, there is Incident Response Systems to carry on with the medical emergencies, however, there are no efforts on preparation before the disasters. It should be made mandatory by law to carry out mock drills in all the vulnerable districts for medical emergency response. Increase in the resources to fill the gaps in health care services in normal times to mitigate better at disaster times. It is important to document the lessons learnt from the past experiences. Under the comprehensive law, it is pertinent to spell out the strategies for mitigating disasters effectively in disaster situations. The role of private sector to treat the disaster survivor under the Corporate Social

Responsibility (CSR) and design under the public–private partnership (PPP) model, a well thought of disaster medicine. The PPP is very much prescribed in the US to involve private sector, as disaster cause huge losses to private resources too, thereby, their involvement in disaster mitigation and Disaster risk reduction, as complied in the book 'Seeds of disaster, roots of response' (Auerswald et al., 2011).

The emergency medicine or disaster medicine foundation lies in the basic health care infrastructure and resources. It is high time to put in adequate resources in health care. All the medical institutions should be empanelled and be equipped for any emergency. Modalities should be chalked out on the mode of the remuneration (monetary or by other means) to the medical service provider, small or big, a one-doctor clinic to a corporate-tertiary care, super specialty hospital. Strong Laws to pin down liability if there is any delay in the treatment. Though there are many laws on Health per se, can we now also have one on medical emergencies in disaster in particular? There is an urgency to draft one.

Notes

1 I have used 'disaster' for Bhopal event, purposively due to the scale of devastation. However, it is seen as tragedy, or as an accident in most literature, it was not as trivial as an accident, nor a tragedy, as inevitable but host of factors led to 'Bhopal Gas Disaster'; one among them is the lack of preparedness in medical emergency which this chapter focuses.

2 During the night of 2–3 December 1984, large amounts of water entered tank 610, containing 42 tons of methyl isocyanate. The resulting exothermic reaction increased the temperature inside the tank to over 200 °C (392 °F), raising the pressure to a level the tank was not designed to withstand. This forced the emergency venting of pressure from the MIC holding tank, releasing a large volume of toxic gases into the atmosphere. The gases flooded the city of Bhopal, causing great panic as people woke up with a burning sensation in their lungs. Thousands died immediately from the effects of the gas, and many were trampled in the panic.

3 Ministry of Environment, Forest and Climate Change (2015). Retrieved from http://envfor.nic.in/rules-regulations/public-liability-insurance (Accessed 19 December 2015). Government of India.

4 National Disaster Management Authority (2015). Ministry of Home Affairs, Government of India. Retrieved from www.ndma.gov.in/images/ndma-pdf/DM_act2005.pdf (Accessed 19 December 2015).

5 National Disaster Management Authority (2015). Ministry of Home Affairs, Government of India. Retrieved from http://ndma.gov.in/en/learn-about-disasters/man-made-disaster/chemical-disaster.html (Accessed 29 August 2015).

6 United States Environment Protection Agency (2015). Retrieved from www.epa.gov/superfund/policy/cercla.htm (Accessed 29 August 2015). Washington DC

7 United States Environment Protection Agency (2015). Retrieved from www.epa.gov/superfund/policy/cercla.htm (Accessed 29 August 2015). Washington DC
8 National Disaster Management Authority (2015). Ministry of Home Affairs, Government of India. Retrieved from www.ndma.gov.in/images/guidelines/national-dm-policy2009.pdf, p. 20 (Accessed 20 December 2015).
9 National Disaster Management Authority (2015). Ministry of Home Affairs, Government of India. Retrieved from www.ndma.gov.in/images/guidelines/national-dm-policy2009.pdf, p. 26 (Accessed 20 December 2015).
10 National Disaster Management Authority (2015). Ministry of Home Affairs, Government of India. Retrieved from http://ndma.gov.in/images/guidelines/incidentresponsesystemjuly.pdf, p. 80 (Accessed 20 December 2015).
11 A. K. Das, S. B. Gupta, S. R. Joshi, S. Galwankar, B. Arquilla and R. Mittal (2008). White Paper on Academic Emergency Medicine in India: INDO-US Joint Working Group (JWG) Vol. 56, October, JAPI., p. 789. Available at www.indusem.org/wp-content/uploads/2015/01/pdf/u_789_new.pdf
12 During various FICCI conferences in collaboration with NDMA, where the first author spoke on community preparedness in Chemical disasters, the managers shared their concern.
13 GOI-UNDP DRM Programme (2008). 'Guidelines for Hospital Emergencies Preparedness Planning', New Delhi: Government of India.
14 The term 'sufferer' is more appropriate than the term 'victim' which is often used. As victim suggests lack of any agency by the people, those who survived disasters are called as 'sufferer'.
15 Aljazeera (2015). 'India: Heavy Floods Kill Chennai Hospital Patients' 5 December. Retrieved from www.aljazeera.com/news/2015/12/india-heavy-floods-kill-chennai-hospital-patients-151204163134270.html (Accessed 19 December 2015).
16 Ministry of Labour and Employment (2009). 'National Policy on HIV/AIDS and the World of Work'. New Delhi. Retrieved from www.ilo.org/wcmsp5/groups/ . . . **aids**/ . . . /wcms_117318.pdf
17 www.prsindia.org/uploads/media/Draft_Bill_The_National_Council_for_Human_Resources_for_Health_Bill,_2009.pdf (Accessed 20 August 2015).
18 Triage is the process of determining the priority of patients' treatments based on the severity of their condition. This rations patient treatment efficiently when resources are insufficient for all to be treated immediately.
19 National Center for Biotechnology Information, U.S. National Library of Medicine (2015). US National Library of Medicine National Institutes of Health Rockville Pike, Bethesda MD, available at www.ncbi.nlm.nih.gov/pubmed/22914329 (Accessed 29 August 2015).
20 First author was an observer for the mock drill at Bangalore, where the private hospital 'Ramaiah Medical College' participated along with the DDMA and SDMA organized in collaboration with NDMA.
21 Walking Wounded refers to those people who will need medical attention later after some critical injuries have been treated.

References

Andrulis, D. P. et al. (2007). Preparing Racially and Ethnically Diverse Communities for Public Health Emergencies. *Health Aff*, *26*, 1269.

Auerswald, H., Konrad, K. A. & Thum, M. P. (2011). Adaptation, Mitigation and Risk-Taking in Climate Policy. SSRN, e-Library.

Burkle, F. M., Jr., Sanner, P. H. & Wolcott, B. W. (1984). *Disaster Medicine: Application for the Immediate Management and Triage of Civilian and Military Disaster Victims*. New Hyde Park, NY: Medical Examination Publishing Co.

Cutter, S. L. (2005). 'Pragmatism and Relevance: A Response to Wolf R. Dombrowsky' in W. R. Perry & E. L. Quarantelli (eds.) *What Is a Disaster? New Answers to Old Questions*. USA: International Research Committee on Disasters, pp. 39–48.

Editorial. (1986). Preparing for Disaster. *American Journal of Public Health*, *76*(3), 233–235.

Gunn, S. W. A. (1990). *Multilingual Dictionary of Disaster Medicine and International Relief*. Dordrecht, the Netherlands: Kluwer Academic Publishing.

The Johns Hopkins and Red Cross Red Crescent. (2008). *Public Health Guide in Emergencies*. Switzerland: International Federation of Red Cross and Red Crescent Societies.

Lechat, M. P. (1984). 'Disasters: A Public Health Problem', Workshop on Health Aspects of Disaster Preparedness' 15–20 October, Trieste Brussels Centre for Research on the Epidemiology of Disasters.

NIDM. (2012). *Mainstreaming Disaster Risk Reduction into Health: Strategies, Methodologies & Tools*. New Delhi: National Institute of Disaster Management.

Noji, E. K. (1997). 'The Nature of Disaster: General Characteristic and Public Health Effect' in K. Noji Eric (ed.) *The Public Health Consequences of Disasters*. New York: Oxford University Press, pp. 3–20.

Quarantelli, E. L. (2005). 'A Social Science Research Agenda for the Disasters of the 21st Century: Theoretical, Methodological and Empirical Issues and Their Professional Implementation' in W. R. Perry & E. L. Quarantelli (eds.) (2005) *What Is a Disaster? New Answers to Old Questions*. New York: International Research Committee on Disasters, pp. 325–396.

Reddy, S. (2013). *Clash of Waves: Post Tsunami Rehabilitation in Andaman and Nicobar Islands*. New Delhi: Indos. ISBN-978-81-908972-2.

Schultz, C. H., Kristi, M. D., Koenig, L. & Noji, Eric K. (1996). A Medical Disaster Response to Reduce Immediate Mortality after an Earthquake. New England Journal of Medicine. Feb 15; 334(7): 438–44.

Tanigawa, K. & Tanaka, K. (2006). Emergency Medical Service Systems in Japan: Past, Present, and Future. *International Ems Systems*, *69*, 365–370.

Tierney, K. J. (1985). Emergency Medical Preparedness and Response in Disasters: The Need for Inter Organizational Coordination. *Public Administration Review*, *45*, Special Issue, 77–84.

Part V

Case-specific studies

20 Interrogating right to compensation in disaster laws

A case study of Jammu and Kashmir floods

Himanshu Shekhar Mishra

India is one of the most disaster-prone countries in the world. According to the National Policy on Disaster Management,

> 58.6% of the landmass is prone to earthquakes of moderate to very high intensity; over 40 million hectares (12% of land) is prone to floods and river erosion; of the 7,516 km long coastline, close to 5,700 km is prone to cyclones and tsunamis; 68% of the cultivable area is vulnerable to drought and hilly areas are at risk from landslides and avalanches.[1]

What is more alarming is the fact that India is part of the most disaster-prone region of the world. As the International Federation of Red Cross and Red Crescent Societies (2010) has argued,

> Disasters are a part of everyday life and they are increasing. Nowhere are they increasing faster and with greater ferocity than in Asia Pacific, the world's most disaster-prone region where, on average, 40 per cent of the globe's 'natural' catastrophe occurs.[2]

In fact, India has faced the wrath of nature and paid a heavy price in terms of the loss of human life and property in the last three decades. According to a Report of the Ministry of Home Affairs (2011),

> India due to its geo-climatic and socio-economic condition is prone to various disasters. During the last thirty years' time span the country has been hit by 431 major disasters resulting into enormous loss to life and property. According to the Prevention Web statistics, 1,43,039 people were killed and about 150 crores were affected by various disasters in the country during these three decades.[3]

A World Bank study has argued that India lost about 2 per cent of its GDP between 1991 and 2005 due to disasters.[4] It is ironic that despite a high degree of vulnerability to disasters, for almost six decades after independence, India's disaster response strategy was 'reactive' and 'relief-centric' approach. The enactment of the Disaster Management (DM) Act in 2005 was the first serious effort to restructure India's disaster response strategy from a 'relief-centric' approach to a more proactive 'prevention, mitigation and preparedness-driven' approach.

The DM Act brought upon a paradigm shift in India's approach to disaster management by laying down a legal framework to set up new disaster risk reduction structures, at both the central and the state level, and put in place an institutional response mechanism to deal with disasters. It has been almost 10 years since the DM Act was enacted. But serious questions have arisen in recent times about the effective implementation of this legislation, especially in the wake of the devastating floods in Jammu and Kashmir in September 2014.

Worst floods since 1902

In terms of the scale of devastation, the floods in Jammu and Kashmir are considered the worst to hit the state in more than a hundred years. The Parliamentary Standing Committee on Home Affairs in its report tabled in parliament in December 2014 argued that such a flood situation in Jammu and Kashmir, particularly in Srinagar, had not been witnessed since 1902. The scale of devastation was so huge that large parts of Srinagar city remained submerged in flood waters for more than three weeks. It followed above normal rainfall in 10 out of 22 districts of Jammu and Kashmir. A Home Ministry note reveals that the volume of rainfall was recorded highest in Shopian district which received an unprecedented 2,953 per cent above normal rainfall while Srinagar district received 1,410 per cent above normal rainfall.[5]

The crisis was exacerbated by the absence of any actionable warning from the Met Department. Security officials involved in relief-and-rescue operations were caught off-guard in the absence of any specific early flood warning alert from Met Department.[6]

The huge devastation caused by floods was visible everywhere in and around Srinagar: all major hospitals in the capital city were submerged deep in water and had become dysfunctional. As health care infrastructure collapsed, the fear of an epidemic loomed large in many places, with dead bodies of animals floating in stagnant flood waters. I saw many dead bodies of animals floating in the canal adjoining the Jawahar Nagar locality a week after the flood waters had entered this part of the Srinagar city. The state government did not seem to have the wherewithal to deal with the serious threat it posed to the hundreds of families living in open make-shift tents along this canal. In fact, mobile towers to power and gas supply stations: most of the critical infrastructure laid submerged in flood waters for many days making it difficult for state agencies to provide basic civic amenities to the flood victims.

Costliest natural disaster in 2014

The scale of devastation unleashed by these floods was unprecedented in the history of Srinagar. It turned out to be the worst natural disaster in the world in terms of the quantum of economic loss it caused. The Annual Disaster Statistical Review 2014 conducted by the Centre for Research on the Epidemiology of Disasters (CRED), Institute of Health and Society (IRSS) and the Université catholique de Louvain in Brussels argued after assessing the economic damage caused by disasters in different parts of the world: 'The costliest natural disaster in 2014 was the flood in the Jammu and Kashmir region, in India, which cost US$ 16 billion.'[7]

Significantly, these floods severely disrupted the income generation in the state. The Jammu and Kashmir finance minister Haseeb Drabu said in his budget speech in the state assembly on 22 March 2015:

> The total income of the state has declined by 1.5 per cent in 2014–2015 to a little less than 88,000 crore. With this the average per capita of a common man in J&K has declined from 59,279 to 58,888. These are advanced estimates. The actual figures which will come out next year will be much worse.[8]

Haseeb Drabu went on to add:

> As a result of the decline in SDP, the tax and the non-tax collection, the revenue collection of the state too has plummeted. With incomes of people and businesses taking such a massive hit, it is but natural that revenues of the state government would also have suffered. The total receipts of the state decreased by 4,100 crore.

The economic loss was so huge that the state government could not release two instalments of dearness allowance (DA) due from January 2014 to the State Government Employees and Pensioners till March 2015.

Fault lines in disaster management strategy

In many ways, the unprecedented floods in Jammu and Kashmir showed that nine years since the DM Act was enacted by parliament, the mandatory legal provisions enshrined in this law had not been effectively implemented in this strategically important border state.

The DM Act clearly specifies the role of states in putting in place a disaster response mechanism. Section 23(4) of the DM Act clearly specifies[9]:

> The State Plan shall include,-
>
> a the vulnerability of different parts of the State to different forms of disasters;
> b the measures to be adopted for prevention and mitigation of disasters;
> c the manner in which the mitigation measures shall be integrated with the development plans and projects;
> d the capacity-building and preparedness measures to be taken.

Section 24 of the DM Act is more specific. It categorically states:

> For the purpose of, assisting and protecting the community affected by disaster or providing relief to such community . . . the State Executive Committee may
>
> a control and restrict, vehicular traffic to, from or within, the vulnerable or affected area;
> b control and restrict the entry of any person into, his movement within and departure from, a vulnerable or affected area;
> c remove debris, conduct search and carry out rescue operations;
> d provide shelter, food, drinking water, essential provisions, healthcare and services in accordance with the standards laid down by the National Authority and State Authority;
> e take such measure or steps for rescue, evacuation or providing immediate relief saving lives or property, as may be necessary in its opinion;
> f establish emergency communication systems in the affected area.

The DM Act assigns this specific responsibility to the District Disaster Management Authority (Section 34). As I travelled from one flood-affected area of Srinagar to another, I saw that there was no mechanism to regulate the movement of traffic or public in Bemina and in Jawahar Nagar localities, two of the worst-affected areas of Srinagar. A large number of flood victims had no access to shelter, clean drinking water and other basic civic amenities like health care in many flood-affected areas.

I saw thousands of people forced to live out on the roadside in open makeshift tents in Bemina. No viable epidemic prevention strategy seemed to be in place. The flood victims had no option but to line up for aid at makeshift medical camps. The collapse of telecom towers had led to a virtual collapse of the communication network in most of the flood-affected areas, making it difficult for flood victims to reach out to relief agencies.

The state government had made no concerted effort to initiate disaster mitigation measures in disaster-prone areas. In fact, it had blatantly ignored a specific warning from the National Institute of Disaster Management (NIDM), India's premier research institution dealing with disaster management. In a report released in 2012, the NIDM had specifically warned:

> The state is a multi hazard prone region with natural disasters like earthquakes, floods, landslides, avalanches, high velocity winds, snow storms . . . the unauthorized and unplanned construction on the river banks has disturbed the river ecosystem. Sand and gravel dredging or top soil denudation for brick industry to support growing real estate industry have significantly enhanced the human induced disaster risk in the eco-sensitive zones of the State.[10]

The abysmal failure of the state government in launching an effective relief-and-rescue mission led to violent protests especially in areas where people had been stranded for days without any help and support from the relief agencies. At some places irate mob of flood victims pelted stones and attacked security personnel involved in relief work. More than 40 boats of National Disaster Relief Force (NDRF) were destroyed as anger rose over late arrival of relief and rescue effort in many flood-hit areas.

Some air force choppers involved in relief-and-rescue operation were even pelted with stones. The New Delhi Television (NDTV) crew filmed one such attack when they were flying in an air force chopper involved in relief-and-rescue effort. The video footage shot by the NDTV cameraperson showed a small group of youth attacking an air force chopper with stones from the ground. These attacks raised concerns about the safety of security forces and media personnel working in a disaster zone.[11]

Intervention by Supreme Court

As the flood crisis unfolded in Jammu and Kashmir, the plight of thousands of flood victims soon caught the attention of the judiciary. In an order issued on 12 September 2014 during a hearing on petitions filed by Prof. Bhim Singh, Colin Gonsalves and Dinesh Kumar Garg, respectively, demanding immediate rescue, relief and rehabilitation of the flood-affected persons in Jammu and Kashmir, the Supreme Court said:

> The petitioners do not dispute the commendable work being done by the Armed Forces in rescue operations but they submit that the current rescue operations are too inadequate for such huge disaster. It needs no emphasis from us that a calamity and disaster as huge as this deserves national response so that immediate relief is made available to the victims of floods.[12]

The Supreme Court went on to order the central government to urgently set up a national agency to coordinate relief operations. The Court observed:

> The Government of India may also consider forming a Unified Agency for proper co-ordination of rescue, relief and rehabilitation operations. It goes without saying that supply of food, drinking water, medicines, fuel and other essential supplies deserve top-most priority and so also the restoration of communication and provision for health-care facilities. After all, lives of people who are affected by such disaster have to be saved.[13]

The apex court went ahead and constituted a special five-member committee to assess the damage caused by the floods. The committee was asked to visit all the flood-affected areas and submit its report in two weeks.[14] Significantly, the SC-appointed committee after an independent evaluation of the flood-affected zones in Kulgam, Pulwama, Anantnag, Jammu, Udhampur, Rajouri and Poonch districts, claimed in its report dated 9 October 2014,

> no effective steps were taken to warn people residing in vulnerable areas of Srinagar city of the fast-approaching deluge of flood and

> to evacuate them . . . people remained stranded for days together without food and drinking water, waiting for rescue, which was being elusive.[15]

No consensus on reconstruction package

Even a year after the worst flood tragedy in the state in more than a century, no political consensus exists on the quantum of the reconstruction and rehabilitation package required to reconstruct the economy, infrastructure and the lives of tens of thousands of flood-affected families. The previous Omar Abdullah Government initially made an official demand to centre for approximately Rs 44,000 crore rehabilitation and reconstruction package last year. But the new government which subsequently took over in March 2015 in the state termed this figure as 'incomprehensive'.

Jammu and Kashmir finance minister Haseeb Drabu categorically told the state assembly in March this year that he disagreed with the methodology of quantifying the total economic loss caused by the floods and the quantum of funds required to restore normalcy in the State. Haseeb Drabu told the state assembly:

> The biggest issue facing us today is the rehabilitation of the flood victims. The previous Government had submitted a Memorandum to the Central Government seeking financial assistance of 43,960 crore over and above the SDRF-NDRF framework. In the interest of speedy disbursement, we have no choice but to endorse it. But the fact is that it I am neither convinced by the method in which it has been estimated nor the manner in which it has been designed. It is far too adhoc and arbitrary for comfort.[16]

The absence of political consensus on the quantum of economic loss caused by the floods means that no acceptable figure exists with regard to the quantum of compensation package required to reconstruct lives of disaster victims as well.

No time frame for compensation

There is no provision in the Disaster Management Act 2005 for initiating any 'short-term' or 'long-term' reconstruction and rehabilitation measures to rebuild lives and infrastructure in disaster-affected areas and provide compensation to victims within a specified time frame. This perhaps explains why more than nine months since the floods destroyed critical infrastructure and made millions homeless in Jammu and Kashmir, the Home Ministry was still in the process of releasing funds for what it called 'a short term relief/reconstruction'. An official release issued by Home Ministry on 16 June 2015 said,

> A total of Rs. 5039 crore has been provided for short term relief/ reconstruction measures for the flood affected State of J&K.[17]

Importantly, a Finance Ministry release issued on the same day said,

> The Government of India is sympathetically considering the request of the State Government for undertaking long term measures to improve the infrastructure in the State. . . . A team of Central Government officers led by CEO, NITI Aayog and Secretary (Expenditure), Ministry of Finance, Government of India will visit the State in the next week (that is, the fourth week of June) to explore the possibilities in taking into account the requirements of the State.[18]

Considering the huge scale of devastation caused by floods and the financial losses incurred by the Jammu and Kashmir state, a decision to send a central team to assess the quantum of post-disaster reconstruction package required to rebuild the critical infrastructure should have been taken much earlier.

More than 14 months after the flood tragedy, Prime Minister Narendra Modi announced an 80,063 crore developmental package for Jammu and Kashmir on 7 November 2015, with a specific allocation of Rs 7,854 crore towards the 'flood relief, reconstruction and flood management' in the state.[19] It is aimed at reconstructing damaged houses and infrastructure and restore the livelihood of traders and small businessmen. But the delay in allocation of funds has led to a considerable delay in initiating the requisite measures to rebuild lives. The local industrialists and traders have termed this package as inadequate. The Kashmir Chamber of Commerce and Industry (KCCI) has termed this package as too little too late. As the president of the KCCI Mushtaq Ahmad Wani said in a statement on 9 November 2015,

> Hon'ble Prime Minister in his inordinately belated announcement has come out with a baffling allocation of funds in the name of package. The Chamber has noted with concern that the amount of money earmarked for flood relief and reconstruction including flood management is mere Rs. 7854 crores as against the

requirement of Rs. 37000 crores demanded by the State Government exclusively for losses suffered while the flood management is estimated to involve a separate huge expense of over Rs. 30,000 crores.[20]

Struggle for relief and compensation

It is the poor who suffer the most during a natural disaster. When the flood waters entered Srinagar and nearby areas, the weak and fragile homes of poor migrant labourers were one of the first structures to get washed away. Thousands of migrant labourers, especially from Uttar Pradesh and Bihar, lost their homes and their source of livelihood. They could be seen desperately seeking aid from the state agencies in different parts of the Srinagar city. To make matters worse, many of them lost their identification documents which made it difficult for them to stake the claim for any form of compensation from the official relief agencies.

With the highways blocked because of landslides at several places, they were at the mercy of air force to airlift them out of the disaster zone. At the Srinagar air force base, thousands of such poor migrant labourers and their families had to wait for many days in the open to fly to safer zones while the more affluent citizens had the easy option of flying out in commercial flights. Already fragile and financially insecure, floods had further aggravated their problem. Many of them could be seen pleading with relief agencies and government officials for urgent aid.

The struggle of the poor and the underprivileged migrants in Jammu and Kashmir to seek urgent compensation to survive the aftermath of floods leads us to an important question: should the existing official norms to grant relief and rehabilitation to disaster victims need to be urgently amended to ensure prompt award of compensation?

The existing law empowers the National Disaster Management Authority (NDMA) and State Disaster Management Authority (SDMA), the primary nodal agencies to deal with disasters, to just formulate and 'recommend' guidelines for grant of relief to the disaster victims.

According to section 12 of the Disaster Management (DM) Act 2005[21]:

> The National Authority (NDMA) shall recommend guidelines for the minimum standards of relief to be provided to persons affected by disaster, which shall include,-

(i) the minimum requirements to be provided in the relief camps in relation to shelter, food, drinking water, medical cover and sanitation;
(ii) the special provisions to be made for widows and orphans;
(iii) Ex-gratia assistance on account of loss of life as also assistance on account of damage to houses and for restoration of means of livelihood;
(iv) Such other relief as may be necessary.

Similarly, section 19 of the DM Act clearly specifies the role of SDMA in the grant of relief:

> The State Authority (SDMA) shall lay down detailed guidelines for providing standards of relief to persons affected by disaster in the State:
>
> Provided that such standards shall in no case be less than the minimum standards in the guidelines laid down by the National Authority (NDMA) in this regard.

The aforementioned provisions in the DM Act clearly indicate that nodal disaster management agencies at both central and state levels can only 'recommend' guidelines for finalizing minimum standards of relief for disaster victims. Also, the process of granting relief and compensation is cumbersome and time-consuming as it has to be routed through a complex web of official procedures.

A right to compensation to disaster victims

The struggle of the flood-affected people in Jammu and Kashmir to seek urgent relief and rehabilitation leads us to two important questions: (a) Should the existing Disaster Management Act be amended to incorporate a legal right to relief and compensation to disaster victims? (b) Should there be a fixed timeline in the DM Act for fixing the quantum of compensation to the worst-affected disaster victims?

Some countries have sought to codify the rights of disaster victims to seek compensation by incorporating specific provisions in their Disaster Laws. In the United States, for instance, the 'Robert T. Stafford Disaster Relief and Emergency Assistance Act' (broadly referred to as 'The Stafford Act') clearly outlines the broad responsibilities of the state in providing compulsory relief and compensation to disaster victims. The Section 410 of 'the Stafford Act' has a provision for grant of an 'Unemployment Assistance' to disaster victims who have lost their source of livelihood. The act says,

> The President is authorized to provide to any individual unemployed as a result of a major disaster such benefit assistance as he deems appropriate while such individual is unemployed for the weeks of such unemployment with respect to which the individual is not entitled to any other unemployment compensation (as that term is defined in section 85(b) of title 26) or a waiting period credit. Such assistance as the President shall provide shall be available to an individual as long as the individual's unemployment caused by the major disaster continues or until the individual is reemployed in a suitable position, but no longer than 26 weeks after the major disaster is declared.[22]
>
> (pp. 44–45)

'The Stafford Act' also provides for 'Reemployment Assistance' by states. According to section 410 of this act,

> 1) State Assistance – A State shall provide, without reimbursement from any funds provided under this Act, reemployment assistance services under any other law administered by the State to individuals receiving benefits under this section.[23]

In fact, 'the Stafford Act' also incorporates a detailed provision for 'Emergency Grants to Assist Low-Income Migrant and Seasonal Farmworkers (42 U.S.C. 5177a)'. The act says,

> The Secretary of Agriculture may make grants to public agencies or private organizations with tax exempt status under section 501(c)(3) of title 26, that have experience in providing emergency services to low-income migrant and seasonal farmworkers where the Secretary determines that a local, State or national emergency or disaster has caused low-income migrant or seasonal farmworkers to lose income, to be unable to work, or to stay home or return home in anticipation of work shortages. Emergency services to be provided with assistance received under this section may include such types of assistance as the Secretary of Agriculture determines to be necessary and appropriate.[24]

Tardy pace of post-disaster reconstruction

The absence of such specific provisions in the DM Act has complicated the process of granting relief and compensation to disaster victims in India in an effective manner. In recent months, serious questions have been raised with regard to the failure of state agencies to effectively address the needs and concerns of flood victims in Jammu and Kashmir. Significantly, no official assessment has been made public as to how far the reconstruction and rehabilitation work has moved forward in the entire state.

The Home Ministry had informed the parliament in December 2014 that 2.54 lakh houses had been partially or fully damaged in these floods. But, as of date, no data have been made public as to how many of these houses have been reconstructed by the central or the state agencies in Jammu and Kashmir. The information that exists in public domain is limited to the data of beneficiaries made public separately by district administrations on an individual basis. The data made available by the Srinagar district administration, for instance, show that up to 22 August 2015, 5,730 pucca and kutcha houses had been identified as fully damaged while the total number of houses identified as partially damaged was 24,521.[25] As per the information made public by the Srinagar district administration, only 9,872 households had been paid compensation till 22 June 2015, that is, 32.63 per cent of the total affected households. This means that of the total 30,251 affected households, 67.37 per cent households had not been paid any compensation till 22 June 2015.

Serious questions have also been raised about the quantum of compensation and the methodology employed to calculate the loss suffered by flood victims. In Saroora village in Jammu, the agriculture department issued cheques worth Rs 47 to Rs 400 as relief to the flood-affected villagers for their crop and poultry losses nine months after the floods destroyed their livelihood.[26] Poultry farmer Darshan Lal told NDTV that he had birds worth Rs 4 lakh when flood waters hit this village but he has been given a paltry compensation of Rs 400.

In the wake of these structural weaknesses in the existing mechanism to dole out compensation to the disaster victims, it has become imperative to reform the existing system of granting relief by devising a new rights-based paradigm to award compensation. This would require a national debate on the broad definition of compensation per se and delineation of an acceptable legal framework for the identification of beneficiaries.

Such a rights-based paradigm should include a right to every disaster-affected person to reconstruct their dwelling and recreation of livelihood opportunities especially for the underprivileged and poor among the disaster-affected populace. A legal mechanism to scientifically assess the quantum of loss suffered by flood victims must also be incorporated in the DM Act. It would also be necessary to incorporate a fixed time frame for grant of compensation to every disaster victim. The broad focus should be on constructing a legislative framework which respects the right of every citizen to seek relief and compensation.

Such a legalized institutional mechanism to grant compensation to disaster victims would be especially important for the underprivileged and poor citizens who live in high disaster-prone zones. In such regions, millions of such people have to face the wrath of nature almost every year which often wipe off their meagre assets. As a Home Ministry Report argued in 2011,

> Poverty and risk to disasters are inextricably linked and mutually reinforcing. The poor section of the society is worst affected in case of disaster. . . . Poverty also compels the poor to migrate and live at physically more vulnerable locations, often on unsafe land and in unsafe shelters. These inhabitations of the poor at such locations are either due to the fact that there is no other land available at reasonable cost or it is close to the employment opportunities. The inhabitations of the poor people on marginal land are prone to all types of disasters. The type of construction of these houses further deteriorates the condition. These dwellings made up of low cost material without giving much consideration to technical aspect are easy targets of various hazards.[27]

Notes

1 National Policy on Disaster Management (22 October 2009). Retrieved from http://ndmindia.nic.in/NPDM-101209.pdf. p. 1.
2 International Federation of Red Cross and Red Crescent Societies (2010). *Disasters in Asia: The Case for Legal Preparedness*. Geneva.
3 Ministry of Home Affairs (2 August 2011). *Disaster Management in India*, p. 8. New Delhi. Retrieved from http://ndmindia.nic.in/UNDP-020811.pdf
4 Ibid., p. 13.
5 Parliamentary Standing Committee on Home Affairs, 182nd Report (22 December 2014). 'Rescue, Rehabilitation and Reconstruction in the Aftermath of the Floods and Landslides in Jammu & Kashmir'.
6 Ministry of Home Affairs (2014). Southwest Monsoon-2014: Daily Flood Situation Report. Report No.32–20/2014-NDM-I.

7 Global Humanitarian Overview (2015) Prepared by Appeals Coordination and Analysis(ACA), Programme Support Branch(PSB), Office for the Coordination of Humanitarian Affairs (OCHA). Retrieved from http://reliefweb.int/sites/reliefweb.int/files/resources/ADSR_2014.pdf, p. 2. (Accessed September 2015).
8 Retrieved from http://jakfinance.nic.in/Budget15/speechEng.pdf (22 March 2015).
9 Retrieved from www.ndma.gov.in/images/ndma-pdf/DM_act2005.pdf (23 December 2005).
10 National Institute of Disaster Management (2012). Jammu and Kashmir. Retrieved from http://nidm.gov.in/PDF/DP/JAMMU.PDF
11 NDTV News Report (14 September 2014). Retrieved from www.ndtv.com/cheat-sheet/stone-pelting-stalls-food-drops-in-parts-of-srinagar-10-latest-developments-666418
12 Supreme Court of India. Record of Proceedings (12 September 2014). Retrieved from www.sci.nic.in/outtoday/wc82614p-2014_09_12.pdf
13 Supreme Court of India. Record of Proceedings (12 September 2014). Writ Petition(s) (Civil) No(s). 826/2014. Retrieved from http://supremecourtofindia.nic.in/outtoday/wc82614p-2014_09_12.pdf
14 India Abroad News Service (24 September 2014). Supreme Court Forms Panel to Assess Jammu and Kashmir Flood Damage. Retrieved from www.thehindu.com/news/national/other-states/supreme-court-forms-panel-to-asses-jammu-and-kashmir-flood-damage/article6441747.ece
15 Krishnadas Rajagopal (12 October 2014). As Floods Struck, J&K Government Went Missing. Retrieved from www.thehindu.com/news/national/as-floods-struck-jk-govt-went-missing-sc-panel/article6492694.ece
16 Government of Jammu and Kashmir, Civil Secretariat (2015). Retrieved from http://jakfinance.nic.in/Budget15/speechEng.pdf (March 22)
17 Ministry of Home Affairs (16 June 2015). Release ID: 122551. Retrieved from http://pib.nic.in/newsite/erelease.aspx?relid=0
18 Ministry of Finance (16 June 2015). Retrieved from http://pib.nic.in/newsite/PrintRelease.aspx
19 Prime Minister's Office (7 November 2015). Retrieved from http://pib.nic.in/newsite/erelease.aspx?relid=0
20 Kashmir Chamber of Commerce and Industry (9 November 2015). Retrieved from http://thekcci.com/thekcci/newsitem.aspx?id=76
21 Retrieved from www.ndma.gov.in/images/ndma-pdf/DM_act2005.pdf (23 December 2005).
22 Retrieved from www.fema.gov/media-library-data/1383153669955-21f970b19e8eaa67087b7da9f4af706e/stafford_act_booklet_042213_508e.pdf
23 Ibid.
24 Ibid.
25 Government of Jammu and Kashmir, Civil Secretariat (2015). Retrieved from http://srinagar.nic.in/ (August 22).
26 NDTV news Report (4 June 2015). Retrieved from: www.ndtv.com/india-news/9-months-after-floods-jammu-and-kashmir-farmers-get-compensation-amount-rs-47–768484. NDTV news Report.
27 Ministry of Home Affairs (2 August 2011). Disaster Management in India. p. 14. New Delhi. Retrieved from: http://ndmindia.nic.in/UNDP-020811.pdf

References

Amin, S. & Goldstein, M. (2008). *Data against Natural Disasters, Establishing Effective Systems for Relief, Recovery and Reconstruction*. Washington, DC: The World Bank.

Clements, B. W. (2009). *Disasters and Public Health, Planning and Response*. Cambridge, MA: Butterworth-Heinemann.

Gaur, V. K. (2000). 'Disaster Mitigation' in P. S. Roy, C. J. Van Westen, V. K. Jha, R. C. Lakhera & P. K. Champati Ray (eds.) *Natural Disasters and their Mitigation, A Remote Sensing and GIS Perspective*. Dehradun: Indian Institute of Remote Sensing, p. 195.

Gopalakrishnan, C. & Okada, N. (2007). *Water and Disasters*. London and New York: Routledge.

Jain, N. K. (2000). 'Floods in a South Asian Context, Critical Reflections on the International Decade and Local Community Participation in Flood Disaster Reduction' in D. J. Parker (ed.) *Floods*, Volume 2. London: Routledge, pp. 255–259.

Karan, P. P. & Subbiah, S. P. (2012). *The Indian Ocean Tsunami, the Global Response to a Natural Disaster*. New Delhi: Cambridge University Press India Pvt. Ltd.

Merriman, P. A. & Browitt, C. W. A. (1993). *Natural Disasters: Protecting Vulnerable Communities*. London: Thomas Telford Services Ltd.

Zweynert, A. (2013). *The Key Role of Mainstream Media in Disaster Management*. London: Thomas Reuters Foundation.

21 Unanswered questions in disaster preparedness and the Right to Information

Abha Yadav

The Right to Information (RTI) has often been seen as a link between disaster preparedness and post-disaster rehabilitation. It acts as the repository of information which can be used to prevent the colossal losses that disasters often are associated with and also to build back the lives of the sufferers of these losses post disaster.

The theme of the book is 'Law builds community resilience', and this chapter attempts to draw attention to the importance of the RTI in resilience building to counter the effects of any disaster, both pre and post disasters.

Some examples of neglect towards disaster prevention plans revealed through RTIs

Srinagar

Roger G. Bilham (www.scidev.net/global/earth-science/news/kashmir), the US-based seismologist, warned on 21 December 2011 that Kashmir is likely to be hit by a mega quake while quoting from his GPS-based study about gradual movement of rocks in Zanskar Mountains north of the valley. He, however, didn't specify any time frame. Since then there have been many RTI applications filed by concerned citizens to know about the state of J&K's disaster preparedness. However, various functionaries of the public authorities where these RTIs have been filed did not answer the queries.

RTI applications filed by advocate Mir Imaad Rafi have shown that there is a violation of policy by non-implementation of National Building Code or any other code laid by the Bureau of Indian Standards by relevant departments in existing building bye-laws. The RTI application reveals that in Shopian district alone, the government has failed to establish an 'emergency operating centre' which is mandatory for post-disaster response under the Disaster Management Act. Withholding of such information from the public is unconstitutional and undemocratic (GK News Network, Srinagar, 27 December 2015).

Uttarakhand

The RTI application filed post the Uttarakhand disaster has revealed how bureaucrats have misused the state government relief funds frivolously over personal expenses. RTI filed by activist Bhupendra Kumar on 30 May 2015 (www.dailymail.co.uk/indiahome/indianews/article-3103978/Kedarnath-flood-RTI) has revealed that Rs 25.19 lakhs was spent for the food and accommodation of bureaucrats by the Rudraprayag district administration. The Uttarakhand chief minister has ordered an inquiry into the matter.

Post disaster, many missing people have been tracked using the RTI act. Names of people missing and lost in the Uttaranchal floods have been recovered through the RTI Act. Public information officer of Zonal Police Headquarters, Jammu (ZPHQ-J), has apprised the information seeker that three persons namely Sham Lal Gupta S/o Hakumat Rai (62), Neelam Gupta w/o Sham Lal Gupta (60), both residents of Sarwal Colony, Jammu, and Ramesh Gupta (62) S/o Des Raj who is resident of Kashmiri Mohalla Akhnoor, Jammu, are still missing at Uttarakhand. It is easier for the families to track their relatives from the information received through the RTI Act. The reply also mentions the name of Late Bhim Singh S/o Late Padhu Singh of Hiranagar in Kathua, an inspector in ITBP who sacrificed his life during the rescue operations on 25 June 2013. It also states that except Jammu and Kathua districts, no person from other district of the state is missing or died there in Uttarakhand.

Chennai

The tsunami that occurred in 2004 led to major displacements across many states in India. For the 628 families in Nochinagar, Chennai, near Marina Beach, life post tsunami in 2004 was full of despair, and they have almost lost hope until through the RTI they were able to retrieve crucial information regarding the rehabilitation promised by the government. The families were relying on the large compensation promised by the state government, but none seemed to be in sight. Rehabilitation which was the need of the hour was getting delayed because of which basic facilities were not being delivered to the disaster-affected population.

Through the RTI, information on the Tamil Nadu Slum Clearance Board's housing project for the coastal communities was accessed, and it was found out how the government had planned to deprive the poor coastal dwellers of their traditional land.

Sundari, who belongs to the non-fishing Dalit community, says

> We got to know that the TNSCB planned to relocate the non-fishing community to Thoraipakkam and Semmenchery, areas far away from the coast. Their plan was to provide housing near the coast only to the fishing community. Our predominant livelihood activities are related to fishing and we need to stay close to the coast. Why should we be discriminated against?

As other Dalit women came to know of this, more than 500 of them came together to complain. Then their protests grew louder with other Dalit community leaders joining hands, which led to the formation of the Chennai Dalit People's Federation (CDPF). Sundari, who was elected president of the Chennai Coastal Dalit Women's Federation, led the campaign to expose the bid to divide the fishing and non-fishing communities. Through these massive efforts aided largely by the RTI, the government was forced to provide concrete shelters to the disaster-affected people (14 November 2014, www.thebetterindia.com).

Thiruvavanthapuram

Through the Right to Information Act, it has been found that three years after tsunami hit Indian shores on 26 December 2004, the Kerala government has found that Rs 17.16 crores of the relief money spent for rehabilitation programmes is unaccounted for. Though a commission formed by the LDF government to probe allegations of irregularities in tsunami fund allocation submitted its report, prepared by former chief secretary M. Vijayan Unni, in January, it was not made public till advocate D. B. Binu resorted to the RTI Act.

The commission also blamed the previous Congress-led government for diverting Rs 8.3 crores for priorities other than tsunami relief and rehabilitation. The government spent Rs 2.41 crores in Idukki, Rs 2.94 crores in Wayanad and Rs 1.13 crores in Pathanamthitta districts, which do not have an inch of coastline. Former chief minister Oommen Chandy's home district Kottayam got Rs 2.75 crores.

Even in the tsunami-affected coastal districts, the expenditure was flawed. Thiruvananthapuram district got Rs 5.33 crores, while Kollam, Alappuzha and Ernakulam got Rs 3.36 crores, Rs 5.57 crores and Rs 1.94 crores, respectively. Chandy had earlier said Rs 36.25 crores of the Rs 40.2 crores received in the relief fund was spent. The state had also spent Rs 88 crores received as central relief fund (2 November 2007, www.dnaindia.com).

Gurgaon (Haryana)

In an RTI filed by RTI activist Aseem Takyar, the application filed in the district commissioner's office seeking copy of the District Disaster Management Plan (DDMP) received a response that the document is extremely secretive and cannot be provided. Such attitudes need to be condemned (7 June 2015 http://timesofindia.indiatimes.com).

The work of the land mafia in an attempt to destroy the Mangar Bani forests is exposed through the RTI Act. Hundreds of trees have reportedly fallen in Mangar, a part of the Aravalis off the Gurgaon-Faridabad highway. Though some trees are cut for fuelwood every winter, there has been large-scale fall even in the dense parts of the forest. In a complaint to the Haryana Forest Department, activists have alleged that logs are being transported out for commercial purposes and property owners are helping in clearing the trees.

The complaint has been made by RTI activist Sarvadaman Oberoi which mentions GPS readings of areas where trees have fallen and photographs documenting the gradual clearing of forest patches taken by a few villagers and activists. Other environment activists like Chetan Agarwal say the Haryana government's apathy towards protecting Mangar is obvious. An RTI inquiry had revealed that Haryana had tried to remove the 0.5 per cent restriction on construction in the natural conservation zones, which include Mangar from the Regional Plan 2021 that is being amended. 'Instead of identifying deemed forests and protecting the tree cover in the Aravalis as directed by SC and reiterated by MoEF, the government is trying to divide the Mangar hills into zones for commercial, residential, and tourism uses,' said Agarwal (25 December 2013, www.rtiindia.org).

RTI and disaster preparedness of PWD

The results of the first-ever UN global survey 2013 of persons living with disabilities on how they cope with disasters reveal a disproportionate number suffer and die in disasters because their needs are ignored and neglected. They are often left totally reliant on the kindness of family, friends and neighbours for their survival and safety. Just 17 per cent of respondents were aware of a disaster management plan in their city/town/community, and just 14 per cent said they had been consulted on it. At the same time, 50 per cent of respondents expressed a wish to participate in community disaster management. The RTI filed by Abha Khetrapal (17 September 2014, www.indiaamericatoday.com) highlighted the unpreparedness of National Institute of Disaster Management (NIDM). In continuation of this Dr Satendra Singh, a medical doctor with Guru Teg Bahadur Hospital in Delhi, asked NIDM through an RTI the action taken on the previous TOI story. NIDM's response was that 'they are not yet directly involved except preparing TOT module for disabled person'. Sai Padma, founder of Global AID and a wheelchair user, was stuck in her house for 20 days as a tree fell at their entrance in the recent Hud Hud Cyclone at Vizag (http://theenablist.blogspot.in).

Disaster preparedness results in building resilience against disasters. Resilience is the ability of a community to look after itself post disaster. There is an accepted link between the development of a country and disasters. Each step forward towards development engages a lot of resources, and the trade-off between disaster spending and development spending has often been discussed and debated. Anderson (1990), in her working paper submitted to the World Bank in 1990, argues that the neglect shown towards disaster planning and prevention while allocating funds for development planning is a retrograde step. She clarifies that disaster planning and development planning are not trade-offs but both sides of the same coin. Both the aspects help in building resilience in a community.

In development planning it is very important to note that poverty and disasters are usually mutually reinforcing (Anderson, 1990). For any country whether developed or developing, it is very important to avoid the cyclical trap that disasters and poverty reinforce. Huge amounts of resources are invested in the building of a nation. Allocation of these resources is to be done in the most judicious manner. It is seen in most cases that money allocated towards building infrastructure to support freedom of information is seen as wasteful expenditure by most policy makers. However, development investment needs to include measures that reduce disasters and build governance resilience to counter disasters. Anderson (1990) has stated that preventive methods that are adopted for disaster management are vital and imperative for sustainable long-term development. This chapter attempts to develop the argument that resilience towards disasters can be built through the freedom of information in a democratic set-up.

To be able to analyse this argument at a deeper level, it is important to also take note of development vis-à-vis disasters. 'Development' has been defined as the process by which a nation's capacities are increased and its vulnerabilities are reduced (Anderson & Woodrow, 1989). The interlink between development and disasters is clear from this definition.

Governance plays a big role in development and disaster prevention. It is pertinent to mention here that most of the literature available on the subject and the practical experiences has shown that there has to be consultative process between various groups to arrive at preventive measures to be taken for disaster preparedness. It has to be a joint exercise between policy-makers such as legislators, bureaucrats, academicians, nongovernmental organizations and other stakeholders to arrive at governance techniques that mitigate disasters. Fothergill has stated that 'working in separate cultures does not mean that there cannot be communication and respect' (2000, 97). The joint effort has been a success in many countries such as New Zealand. The collaborative exercise in New Zealand's emergency management legislation fine-tuned and refined the duties and responsibilities of officials and citizens which led to the portraying of gaps within the existing system (Neil, 2005).

David Alexander (2005) has highlighted the failure of academicians to reach out to the general public in a simple language and only being able to communicate to their kind. He further states that disaster studies are unique in the sense that they are an amalgamation of experiences of theorists and practitioners. He confesses how difficult it is to get the two groups to communicate although he focuses on the importance of the exercise.

The role of the RTI Act can only be highlighted through academicians and bureaucrats who have to come forward to take charge of the debate and offer solutions, one of which could be in the form of freedom of information laws. It is pertinent to mention here that till now the role of the practical implementers of the disaster policies has not been heard, but now it is important to take their viewpoint into consideration. A case in point here could be of Anthony Oliver-Smith and Hoffman (2002), who while encouraging his fellow anthropologists to become engaged, stated that 'in grappling with the problematic of disasters, anthropologists . . . can clarify the important distinction between symptoms, the disaster events and the processes themselves, and their underlying and largely systemic cause' (2002, 46). The same can be applied to bureaucrats and other policy-makers who can be encouraged to be a part of the change that disaster management policy requires. This shall boost the implementation of legislations such as the RTI Act in matters of disaster and their management. As Quarentelli (1993, 37) reminds us, we can all learn from one another if we but listen.

Suppressing the quantum of devastation during disasters

There has been an attempt at all levels to reduce the number and devastating effects of disasters. Some disasters are unavoidable, however, in a lot of spaces; there is a possibility of mitigating or lessening the impact of disasters. Of late, there has been a trend to identify such areas where losses can be reduced. The reason to ask this question can be supported by the arguments of Susan L. Cutter who advances another strategy. She simply redefines the question: The question is not what is a disaster, but what is our vulnerability (and resiliency) to environmental threats and extreme events? Susan L. Cutter has turned this question in to another innocent question: what is a car? She replies by saying that the question is not what is a car, but what is your danger of an accident and of the vehicles pollution potential and extreme speed? She takes inspiration perhaps from science; it is important to avoid answering questions by deflecting them and redirect attention to the original question, Dombrowsky (2005).

Redefined that way, Cutter becomes systematic: what makes human and environmental systems vulnerable and more or less resilient to threats and extreme events? In elaborating conceptual frameworks, she posits that vulnerability and resiliency imply an examination of human systems, natural (or environmental) and technological systems, and the interconnectedness between them . . . it is, in fact, the linkages and interdependencies between these three systems and the built environment that amplify or attenuate vulnerability. The challenge is to balance prevention and resilience to organize for the unknown. This article argues that this is possible through the RTI Act which results in transparency and accountability in all spheres including pre and post disaster losses and collection of data.

Conservative estimates show that on an average about 220 natural catastrophes, 70 technological disasters and 3 new armed conflicts occur every year (Alexander, 2005). All of these can be termed as 'disasters' where steps need to be taken for restoration of conditions back to their previous stage by the concerned authorities.

For the purpose of this chapter, it is most important to define disaster and resilience. Most scholars have found it an uphill task to define disaster in the real sense of the word. There is no escaping the subjectivity involved while giving definition to the word disaster. Also, in the course of lengthy discussion, it is clear by now that a 'legalistic' or objective definition will no longer suffice (cf. Kroll-Smith et al., 1998).

It is needless to add that upon the occurrence of a disaster there is a subjective feeling of loss which cannot be quantified through a legal definition with objective indicators because the subjective feeling of loss rarely correlates consistently across time and space (Barton, 1969; Ellemers, 2001).

All authors in the Quarantelli (1998b) volume agree that disasters must be defined in terms of social disruption, whether as cause, characteristic or consequence. This approach provides for the inclusion of both objective and subjective parameters.

Boin (2005) has tried to explain the trajectory from crisis to disaster and has emphasized that it negates what actually happens in practice. The situation pre and post disaster is very fluid, and Boin has concluded by saying that a useful definition of crisis takes into account the changing nature of the crisis. The 9/11 terrorist attacks in New York and Washington have been a watershed moment in the study of disaster and crisis. He places a lot of importance on institutional crisis management capacity. It is this capacity enhancement of public institution that this article seeks to elaborate upon.

David Alexander has identified six distinct schools of thought and expertise on disasters (Alexander, 1993, 13–14). The broad classifications that can be made are geography, anthropology, sociology, development studies, health sciences and the geophysical sciences with engineering. Possibly social psychology can be added as a seventh. Individually, disaster brings people back to the basics of survival, deprivation, injury or bereavement (Erickson, 1994)

According to David Alexander (2005), resilience to disasters has increased very slowly because it does not have a strong democratic base. This article focuses on building the resilience against disasters through the RTI Act.

Good governance which includes transparency and accountability are important in post-disaster remedial measures. The so-called high reliability theorists present us with an optimistic vision (Rochlin, 1996). This group of researchers maintains that smartly designed and well-maintained organizations are capable of absorbing human errors and external pressures while preventing common organizational pathologies. Through a mixture of strategies, organizational leaders can turn their high-risk systems into high-reliability organizations. This line of research finds support in the literature on institutions, which strongly suggests that the right kind of administrative architecture will lead to effective organizations (Selznick, 1957). The debate between optimists and pessimists continues to generate powerful insights.

It is in this space that the role of right to information has to be seen. Disasters leave devastating aftermaths that need to be addressed in a proper and timely manner. Broken infrastructure needs to be rebuilt, hospitals have to be equipped to deal with enormous numbers of wounded and grievously injured electricity, water and other essential supplies need to be restored and the dead need to be buried. It is in this sphere that administration and bureaucracy plays a major role.

Most of the information in terms of literature that is available has focussed attention on the environmental disasters and their impact on human activity and property. Boin (2005) has stated that in the long run disasters and crisis situations may become the agents of political and social change, they may very well function as policy windows (Kingdon, 1984), helping to reconstruct the policy or social agenda. The use of the RTI is proposed to bring about one such change to act as a catalyst for public services transformation.

The worst challenges often happen after the initial crisis has already occurred. Sometimes due to non-availability of records false claims are also passed post disaster. There are no ways of checking this information; however, the RTI Act can be useful to dig out such information or to cross-check the information. The RTI can be used in the field of disasters not only for the collection of information but also for cross-checking the validity of claims made and also to find out information about people or places affected by disasters. It is a handy tool for collecting data of those affected, surviving, compensation to be given and land records. Undoubtedly, government capacity to manage disaster risks is enhanced through RTI. The aim of using the right to information in disaster management is to strengthen the core competencies of local governments.

Also, in some countries particularly in authoritative regimes, the media coverage on purpose has denied the full information on disasters. This has happened in both the pre- and post-disaster phases. In the Chinese famine in 1958–1961 as a result of the Maoist mismanagement approx. 30,000,000 deaths took place. The government machinery including the top level bureaucrats and politicians denied information regarding the famine and kept the media in the dark. In fact collection of food from starving areas continued despite the huge famine conditions. The colonial British Raj imposed wartime censorship on the Bengal famine of 1943 to avoid pressure to divert resources from the war front. Around 2,000,000 died in the Bengal famine and the British remained in denial (Dreze & Sen, 1989)

Even greater secrecy is created in situations of mass suffering which is sometimes deliberately created by authoritarian regimes to control their people. This could be in the form of concentration camps, labour camps, political killings, death camps and so on. This is an avoidable situation which can be controlled through the widespread dissemination of information. Any regime is under check when barriers of authoritarianism are placed through measures such as freedom of information.

Great devastation was caused by Typhoon Haiyan, called Typhoon Yolanda in South East Asia, particularly in the Philippines in November 2013. The natural disaster that disrupted life and property in early November caused widespread death and destruction and caused over 6,000 deaths (BBC report, 22 November 2013). Dead bodies were still being found till January 2014. Joey Gabieta (9 January 2014). Asia News 21 January 2014. There was severe criticism of the lackadaisical response of the Philippines government (*Manila Standard Today*, 14 November 2013). The main reason was the lack of coordination between government agencies. This could have been improved had the record keeping been improved, and if the public authorities were duty bound to provide information to the seekers of such information be it other public bodies or the citizens themselves.

There are huge aftermaths of such displacements, not only in terms of lives lost but also lives disrupted. In 2009 after much pressure from civil society and international bodies the Government of the Philippines has enacted the 'Philippine Disaster Risk Reduction and Management Act of 2010'. The preamble of the act states that it is an act for strengthening the Philippine Disaster Risk Reduction and Management system, providing for the National Disaster Risk Reduction and Management Framework and institutionalizing the National Disaster Risk Reduction and management plan, appropriating the funds therefore and for other purposes.

Section 2(f) of the act provides for the adoption and implementation of a coherent, comprehensive, integrated, efficient and responsive disaster risk reduction program incorporated in the development plan at various levels of government adhering to the principles of good governance such as transparency and accountability within the context of poverty alleviation and environmental protection

Section 4 defines the scope of the act as follows:

> This Act provides for the development of policies and plans and the implementation of actions and measures pertaining to all aspects of disaster risk reduction and management, including good governance, risk assessment and early warning, knowledge building and awareness raising, reducing underlying risk factors, and preparedness for effective response and early recovery.

Section 5 of the act provides for the setting up of the National Disaster Risk Reduction and Management Council.

The Philippines government national disaster risk reduction and management plan (NDRRMP) 2011 to 2028 has enumerated four distinct but mutually reinforcing areas in this field. The first one is disaster prevention and mitigation, disaster preparedness, disaster response and lastly disaster recovery and rehabilitation (2011 www.prevention.net).

Amongst these, disaster response is an area which can be strengthened by using the freedom of information laws. The response of government agencies can be made stronger and efficient if there is access to information through the Freedom of Information laws. Even though the Philippines has had the Freedom of Information Act since three decades, it is not a watertight law in the real sense of the enactment. The law does not make it easier to access information; in fact many restrictions are put in retrieving information from public authorities.

The importance of record keeping with a view to furthering post-disaster measures is illustrated best with the example of a descriptive study conducted at the Thai Tsunami Repatriation Centre in Phangnga Province one year after the tsunami hit Thailand on the 26 December 2004. The objectives of the study were to determine the usefulness of dental records for victim identification following the Indian Ocean tsunami disaster in Thailand and to evaluate the dental identification system in Thailand, the homeland of a large number of the victims.

For this purpose, the dental records of 3,750 dead bodies and 3,547 missing persons in the Thai Tsunami Victim Identification (TTVI) database, updated on 12 December 2005, were analysed.

The findings showed that the identification rate of missing persons with dental records was significantly higher than that of those without ($P < 0.01$). Most victims identified by dental records were returned home within the first four months after the disaster. Dental records were the primary identifier in 46.2 per cent of those identified. However, among the Thai citizens reported missing, only 2.0 per cent used dental identification, 18.1 per cent had dental charts and 0.8 per cent had dental X-rays. In addition, only 7.4 per cent of Thai dental records could be used for dental identification and one-third of Thai victims remained the majority of those unidentified.

Moreover, the retrieval of these records post disaster was very difficult in the absence of a clear transparency policy of the Thai government. However, it is also true that crisis may not necessarily result in drastic change till there is a political and administrative will to bring about change in the system. This process of evaluation and assessment is political in nature and driven by various factors. It is in this phase that managerial challenges give way to political challenges, such as the 'framing' of the crisis impacts processes of accountability and blame allocation (Boin, 2005).

Conclusion

It is this context that the RTI has to be used effectively and efficiently towards disaster mitigation. The resilience towards disasters can be strengthened through the effective implementation of freedom of information. Mapping of water bodies, improving building bye-laws and record keeping can be properly done; claims can be efficiently and correctly settled; rehabilitation can be fairly carried out; and most importantly the marginalized sections of society can be heard and helped.

However, until and unless there is an actual will on the part of all workers, the whole exercise may fail. It appears that organizations often fail to learn (Sagan, 1993), refuse to learn (Perrow, 1999) and learn only in symbolic ways (Clarke, 1999) or in very slow ways. The challenge for crisis and disaster researchers is to identify conditions that facilitate effective learning that can improve future performance. The RTI provides one such tool in the hands of the public authorities through which the process of disaster management can benefit and resilience towards disasters can be augmented.

References

Alexander, D. (2005). 'The Meaning of Disaster, A Reply to Wolf Dombrowsky'. In Perry, R. W. & Quarentelli, E. L. (eds.) *What Is a Disaster? New Answers to Old Questions*. Bloomington, IN: Xlibris Corporation.

Alexander, D. (2008). 'What Is a Disaster; An Interpretation of Disaster in Terms of Change in Culture, Society and International Relations'. In Perry, R. W. & Quarentelli, E. L. (eds.) *What Is a Disaster? New Answers to Old Questions*. Bloomington, IN: Xlibris Corporation.

Alexander, D. E. (1993) Natural Disasters. London: UCL Press.

Anderson, M. B. (May 1990). Which Costs More: Prevention or Recovery? In Kreimer, A. & Munasinghe M. (eds.) *Managing Natural Disasters and the Environment*, pp. 17–27. Washington DC: World Bank.

Anderson, Mary B., & Woodrow, Peter J. (1989). *Rising from the Ashes: Development Strategies in Times of Disaster*. London: Westview Press.

Barton, A. H. (1969) Communities in Disaster. A Sociological Analysis of Collective Stress Situations. NY: Doubleday.

Boin, A. (2005). 'From Crisis to Disaster: Towards an Integrative Perspective'. In R. W. Perry & E. L. Quarentelli (eds.) *What Is a Disaster? New Answers to Old Questions*. Bloomington, IN: Xlibris Corporation.

Cannon, T. (April 2008). *Reducing People's Vulnerability to Natural Hazards: Communities and Resilience*. UNU-WIDER Research Paper No. 2008/34.

Dombrowsky, R. W. (2005). 'Not Every Move Is Step Forward: A Critique of David Alexander, Susan L. Cutter, Rohit Jigyasu and Neil Britton'. In R. W. Perry & E. L. Quarentelli (eds.) *What Is a Disaster? New Answers to Old Questions*. Bloomington, IN: Xlibris Corporation.

Ellemers, J. E. (2001) "Rampen in Nederland," Sociologische Gids 48: 231–252.

Erikson, K. T. (1994) A New Species of Trouble: Explorations in Disaster, Trauma and Community. NY: Norton.

Fothergill, Alice. (2000). Knowledge Transfer between Researchers and Practitioners. *Natural Hazards Review*, 1(2), 91–98.

Gusain, R. (30 May 2015). *Funds Down the Drain amid Uttarakhand Deluge*. Letter Vide Office Letter No. RTI/ZPHQ/42/2013/24286-87 dated 07 September 2013. Retrieved from www.dailymail.co.uk/indiahome

Jean Dreze and Amartya Sen. (1989) Hunger and Public Action, Oxford and New York: Oxford University Press.

Joshi, C. V. (7 June 2015). *Gurgaon's Disaster Fight Plan too Secretive to Share: RTI Reply*. Retrieved from www.timesofindia.com

Kashmir Susceptible to Major Quakes. (2011). 21 December. Retrieved from www.scidev.net/global/earth-science/news/kashmir

Khetrapal, A. (17 September 2014). *Where Is the Disaster Management Policy for Disabled in India?* Retrieved from www.indiaamericatoday.com

KingdonJohn W., (1984) Agendas, Alternatives, and Public Policies, Boston: Little, Brown, Journal of Public Policy, 5(2), 281–283.

Kroll-Smith, J. Stephen & Gunter, Valerie J. (1998). 'Legislators, Interpreters, and Disasters. The Importance of How as Well as'. In Enrico L. Quarantelli (ed.) *What Is A Disaster? Perspectives on the Question*. New York: Routledge.

Large Scale Tree Felling in Mangar Forest. (25 December 2013). Retrieved from www.rtiindia.org

Majumdar, S. (14 November 2014). *The Tsunami Hit Women of Chennai Who Fought for Their Rights*. Retrieved from www.thebetterindia.com

Oliver-Smith, Anthony & Hoffman, Susanna M. (2002). *Catastrophe & Culture: The Anthropology of Disaster*. Santa Fe, NM: School of American Research Press.

Perrow, C. (1999). Organizing to Reduce the Vulnerabilities of Complexity. *Journal of Contingencies and Crisis Management*, 7, 150–155.

Perry, Ronald E., Quarantelli EL, eds (2005) What Is a Disaster; New Answer to Old Questions; Bloomington: Xlibris

Philippines: The National Disaster Risk Reduction and Management Plan (NDRRMP). (2011). Retrieved from www.prevention.net

Quarantelli, E. L. (1993). Converting Disaster Scholarship into Effective Disaster Planning and Managing: Possibilities and Limitations. *International Journal of Mass Emergencies and Disasters,* 11(1), 15–39.

Quarantelli, E. L. 1993. The Environmental Disasters of the Future will be more and worse but the prospect is not hopeless, Disaster: Prevention and Management, 1: 11–25.

Quarantelli, E. L. (1998b) What is a Disaster? Perspectives on the Question. London: Routledge.

Rochlin, G. I. (1996) "Reliable organizations: Present research and future directions," Journal of Contingencies and Crisis Management. 4: 55–59.

RTI Reveals Lack of Disability – Inclusive Disaster Management in India. (30 January 2015). Retrieved from http://theenablist.blogspot.in

Sagan, S. (1993). *The Limits of Safety: Organizations, Accidents, and Nuclear Weapons*. Princeton: Princeton University Press.

Sebastian, D. (2 November 2007). *RTI Brings Tsunami Funds Irregularities to Light*. Retrieved from www.dnaindia.com

Selznick, Philip (1957) Leadership in Administration, New York: Harper and Row.

22 Can laws ensure disaster risk reduction? A study of Mandarmani Sea Beach in West Bengal

Rabindranath Bhattacharyya

Through the Hyogo Framework

Disaster is an overwhelmingly devastating event both in terms of massive loss/injury of human and cattle lives and huge destruction of infrastructure and essential commodities (like food, drinking water, shelter) of a community involving economic costs. It is not possible to stop the occurrence of disasters, especially natural disasters but their impact upon human and other life forms can be minimized through preparedness and local information dissemination. Reid Basher in his paper 'Disaster Impacts: Implications and Policy Responses' (2008, pp. 937–954) writes that 'a key characteristic of severe hazards is their relative uncommonness and uncertainty for most places or people, which often leads to lack of awareness and understanding and to complacency or denial of risks by individuals and policymakers alike'. For a large part, the impact of disaster can be reduced if the community remains informed and aware regarding healthy ecosystems, an effective warning and evacuation system. Hence one of the basic points of disaster risk reduction is to remove the ignorance of the community about the environmental hazards.

The World Conference on Disaster Reduction, held from 18 to 22 January 2005 in Kobe, Hyogo, Japan, which adopted the present *Hyogo Framework for Action 2005–2015: Building the Resilience of Nations and Communities to Disasters* held in its Preamble that

> Disaster risk arises when hazards interact with physical, social, economic and environmental vulnerabilities. Events of hydrometeorological origin constitute the large majority of disasters. Despite the growing understanding and acceptance of the importance of disaster risk reduction and increased disaster response capacities, disasters and in particular the management and reduction of risk continue to pose a global challenge. (p. 1)

So it is required from a policy perspective that the risk of disaster should be lessened by following environmental laws so that sustainable development of a country can be engendered. But there is always an inverse correlation between myopic developmental vision and long-term protection of environment for the purpose of sustainable development. In this inverse correlation money and muscle power always lay its hands on environmental governance so that profit making goes unbridled, ignoring the environmental laws with an utter arrogance that ultimately affect the public at large. In the light of this inverse correlation, this chapter attempts to focus on the lack of coordination among different government departments and other authorities in West Bengal that resulted in non-performance of duties and in the corrupt nexus between political authority, local administration and the promoter/developer/businessmen that leads to the increase in all sorts of environmental hazards that becomes evident from the study of Mandarmani, a village on the sea coast of East Midnapore in West Bengal.

Environmental conservation and the doctrine of Parens Patriae

Judicial action in environmental conservation is required for establishing, on the one hand, social regulation, which among other things includes the regulation of safety and, on the other hand, economic regulation in terms of regulating big business houses and the monopolies in misusing natural resources. The environmental conservation contestations in the courts generally follow five principles: sustainable development, intergenerational equity, 'polluter pays' principle, doctrine of public trust and precautionary principle. In India the development of an environmental jurisprudence basically started its meaningful journey after Stockholm Conference held on 5–16 June 1972. Out of 113 countries, India also had to play a significant role under the leadership of Indira Gandhi. Ultimately in the year 1974 the Indian government had first time promulgated Water (Prevention and Control of Pollution) Act, 1974, and thereafter in the year 1981 India had promulgated Air (Prevention and Control of Pollution) Act, 1981.

It will not be out of place to mention that sociologically and politically India was possibly not ready to assess the preventive measures, which it ought to have taken with reference to the climate scenario that enveloped the country as well as the consequence of the technological advancement of the civilization. Such a state was obviously a consequence of the obligation bestowed upon the parliament under

Article 253 of the constitution of India, the result being that whenever India becomes a part of international treaty, it is the obligation of the parliament to enforce such treaty by way of legislation. Thus India confronted with an effect of mindless cruelty, which was obviously an outbreak of not only trivial negligence on the part of an industry but also an indication of the inability of the government to stop the functioning of harmful industry like Exide, which was the cause of Bhopal gas leak tragedy. The country was virtually without any regulatory law and/or authority, which could prevent such genocide in the event of omission or commission of negligence. With Bhopal gas leak incident Indian Parliament came out with a law, namely Environment Protection Act 1986 – the first-time attempt to make an exhaustive code covering the field of environment. The Environment (Protection) Act, 1986 is the first all-embracing act that attempted 'to take measures to protect and improve environment' and to prevent, control and abate the environmental pollution. India also had reverted to promulgate a legislation mainly Bhopal Gas Leak Disaster (Processing of Claims) Act 1985 for securing the compensation towards the victims of Bhopal gas leak disaster. This principle is known as the doctrine of *Parens Patriae* that refers to the legitimate power of the state as a parent 'in providing care to its citizens who are unable to care for themselves'. Since then three decades have passed and people in all states of India have become more aware of the need for the protection of environment for the sake of their own existence and for the sake of their future generations. Despite this increasing awareness, implementation of environmental laws has become a real challenge in India.

Disasters therefore need strong environmental governance. Environmental governance therefore requires an integration of behavioural constituents from the social and economic processes related to the natural environment, human understanding of the processes in this natural environment and the changes impinging on natural ecosystems (Bandyopadhyay et al., 2013, p. 3). In an exceptional special article 'Social-Ecological Research in India: A "Status" Report', Ramachandra Guha (1997) identified

> three major and competing ideological trends in the environmental movement: Crusading Gandhians, who turn their back on modernisation altogether, looking towards a revival of a precolonial village-centred order; Ecological Marxists, who see social redistribution as logically prior to ecological sustainability; and Appropriate Technology, the most practice-oriented of the three, which seeks to develop and apply technical and institutional

> alternatives to the centralising, inequitous, and environmentally destructive process of development in independent India. (p. 346)

He also mentioned two other trends:

> Wildlife conservationists, who work with a more or less single-point agenda, the protection of wild species and wild habitats; and scientific conservationists, who seek to strengthen the state, in their view the only body capable of taking a rational, long-term view on what constitutes sustainable development. (p. 346)

Guha specified the development of such ideological trends in the context of 'fundamental opposition between two groups, termed omnivores and ecosystem people, respectively' (p. 348). As he viewed, omnivores include 'industrialists, rich farmers, state officials, and the growing middle class based in the cities' whereas ecosystem people 'would include roughly two-thirds of the rural population, say about 400 million people – (who) rely for the most part on the resources of their own vicinity, from a catchment of a few dozen square miles at best' (p. 348). He also identified the appearance of another segment of people, the 'ecological refugees', which has emerged due to the displacement of ecosystem people from their homes (p. 348). The major reasons of poverty, as Guha argues, are either channelizing the natural resources on the cost of state exchequer for the benefits of the omnivores with an untenable idea that relies on full market play for giving the opportunity to make every one omnivore or an unsustainable idea which claims that ecosystem people want to remain ecosystem people.

The three 'major and competing ideological trends' that Guha was speaking are basically ideal in nature in the sense that in reality these three ideological 'trends' often change their positions to accommodate development in favour of the omnivores in such a complex way that it looks like a development for the ecosystem people, by the ecosystem people and of the ecosystem people. In such a situation a total comprehensive account of 'development' explaining historical events and social and cultural phenomena based upon the appeal to universal value itself becomes a suspect. In reality the hazards, created by this sort of 'development' based on the unbridled greed of the 'omnivores', ultimately lead to increase in the risk of disaster. Who can challenge this frame of 'development'? Theoretically 'a systematic way of dealing with hazards and insecurities' in a risk society as an essential category of governance remains in the domain of 'pastoral power' of the state, which is actualized by the government. Hence this chapter focuses on the state responsibilities and legal remedies in dealing with risk reduction in West Bengal and utter failure of the government in dealing with that responsibility as evidenced in the study of Manadarmoni Beach.

Responsibility of the state authority and the legal remedies for environmental protection

Paul K. Freeman and Howard Kunreuther (April 2002, p. 197), in their paper 'Environmental Risk Management for Developing Countries', have identified three reasons that dictate the need for countries to consider risk management strategies for tackling natural events.

> First, if disaster impacts are not anticipated, the diversion of scarce financial resources to relief and reconstruction efforts causes high opportunity costs as other projects contributing to economic growth and the eradication of poverty cannot continue as planned. Second, the continuing and significant reallocation of resources post-disaster wreaks havoc on the budgetary planning process. . . . Third, poorer countries rely on international assistance to pay for a substantial portion of their losses. The resources available to the international development community are limited and have remained stagnant for nearly ten year.

So the responsibility of the state authority is to develop risk management strategies to cope with the environmental risk from natural hazard events. But the state responsibility is generally and more often dented with the issues of transparency and accountability. This puts them against people in most environmental and developmental projects.

Bhattacharyya (2015, p. 213) argues,

> In today's world, the responsibility of the government essentially focuses on the social wellbeing of population for organizing them as a political and civil collective. In case that responsibility is ignored by the government, then non-governmental organizations, even international organizations may creep in that place.

The responsibilities of the government for reducing the risk of disaster consist of a strong and committed Environmental Impact Assessment (EIA) involving the following:

i Assessing the hazards of a society that may increase the risk of destruction in case of a disaster

ii Building up of a legal framework to that end to prescribe certain standards of behaviour
iii Protecting the environment by regulating the behaviour of the citizens/groups/business organizations through penal measures, if the standards are not followed
iv Developing a harmonized system of response that can be operative during an emergency

If one focuses on the legal remedies that attempted to ensure the protection of environment since 1986, one should start with *Tarun Bharat Sangh, Alwar v. Union of India* (Sariska Case), where the Hon'ble Supreme Court of India had inter alia held that 'the issues of environment must and shall receive the highest attention' from the Supreme Court. In an article on 'Environmental Protection Vis-à-Vis Judicial Activism', Kanwar, Prashis, and Singla, Chandan (Manmohan Singh Gill et al., 2009, p. 253) cited some important verdicts in which the apex court of this country has expressed its clear and distinct views about the environment in the following decisions:

- every person enjoys the right to a wholesome environment, which is a facet of the Right to Life, guaranteed under Article 21 of the Constitution.

  [Case cited here: *Subhash Kumar v. State of Bihar*, AIR 1991 SC 420; *M C Mehta v. Union of India* (Delhi Crushing Case), 1992 (3) SCC 256 and *Virender Gaur v. State of Haryana*, 1995 (2) SCC 577]

- Enforcement agencies are under an obligation to strictly enforce environmental laws.

  [Case cited here: *Indian Council for Enviro-Legal Action v. Union of India* (CRZ Notification Case) 1996 (5) SCC 281, 294, 301].

- Government agencies may not plead non-availability of funds, inadequacy of staff or other insufficiencies to justify the non-performance of their obligations under environmental laws.

  [Case cited here: *Dr. B.L. Wadehra v. Union of India* (Delhi Garbage case) AIR 1996 SC, 2969].

- The 'Polluter Pays' principle which is a part of the basic environmental law of the land requires that a polluter bears the remedial or clean up costs as well as the amounts payable to compensate the victims of the pollution.

[Case cited here: Indian Council for Enviro-Legal Action v. Union of India (Bichhri case), AIR 1996, SC, 1446].

- The Precautionary Principle requires government authorities to anticipate, prevent and attack the cause of environmental pollution. This principle also imposes the onus of proof on the developer or industrialist to show his or her action is environmentally benign.

[Case cited here: Vellore Citizens' Welfare Forum v. Union of India, AIR1996 SC 2715].

- Government development agencies charged with decision making ought to give due regard to ecological factors including

a the environmental policy of the Central and State government;
b the sustainable development and utilization of natural resources; and
c the obligation of the present generation to preserve natural resources and pass on to future generations environment as intact as the one we inherited from the previous generation.

[Case cited here: State of Himachal Pradesh v. Ganesh Wood Products, AIR 1996 SC 149]

- Stringent action ought to be taken against contumacious defaulters and persons who carry on industrial or developmental activity for profit without regard to environmental laws.

[Case cited here: Indian Council for Enviro-Legal Action v. Union of India (Bichhri case), AIR 1996, SC, 1446].

- The power conferred under an environmental statute may be exercised only to advance environmental protection and not for a purpose that would defeat the object of the law.

[Case cited here: Bangalore Medical Trust v. B.S. Muddappa, AIR 1991 SC 1902]

- The State is the trustee of all natural resources, which are by nature meant for public use and enjoyment. The public at large is the beneficiary of the seashore, running waters, air, forests and ecologically fragile lands. These resources cannot be converted into private ownership.

[Case cited here: *M.C. Mehta v. Kamal Nath*, 1997 (1) SCC 388]

From these verdicts which set the environmental codes and norms in India, it is clear that environmental laws and the interpretation of laws as enunciated by the Supreme Court and high courts of the states cannot be treated as an incomplete attempt in order to keep pace with the need of this hour. The question therefore remains, as to why so little is done with the passage of time. Can it be said that an account of a lack of political will, callous executive inertia and tremendous influence of the business blinded with the myopic profit hunger and agonized mass consciousness in relation to environmental problem are the root causes for increasing environmental hazards in respect of water, air, fragile land, forests and other natural resources.

West Bengal scenario

Other than the central laws and the verdicts of the Supreme Court and high courts of the states, West Bengal state has enacted a plethora of laws dealing with the regulation of the environment. Nevertheless there exist many gaps and challenges in two major areas: (i) the implementation of laws preventing the misuse of natural resources and (ii) implementation of policies for a sustainable development. In West Bengal, *West Bengal Development Report* prepared by the Planning Commission, Government of India reports (2010, p. 145) that the forest occupies 13.8 per cent of land area. But the State of West Bengal ranks as the fourth most populous state in India, covering an area of 88,752 sq. km, and considering that the forestation in West Bengal appears insufficient. This insufficient quantity of forest again is facing challenge from illegal timber merchants. The report mentions that 'major threats to forest are reported from north Bengal and parts of Sundarbans. Organized illegal tree felling for timber has been reported from various parts of the state along with illegal poaching of wildlife' (p. 151).

As per river erosion is concerned, the said report mentions (p. 147):

> The Ganga and Padma have over the years and centuries inexorably nurtured and sustained human civilisation. The rivers are gnawing away land used for growing food and human habitation in two of the 19 districts of the state of West Bengal. In the district of Malda, till 2004, a report says it has taken away nearly 20,000 ha; during 1994–2004 and as many as 22 villages have disappeared. In the adjoining district of Murshidabad, it has taken away 359 sq. km of land belonging to Jalangi Ghosh Para Gram Panchayat, located in 14 mouzas. . . . Besides the problems of

> northern districts like Malda and Murshidabad, river erosion has also been reported from Bardhaman. In several blocks of the district, erosion and flooding is being evident.

Regarding the quality of river water, the said report has mentioned:

> In the state of West Bengal, the results of the water quality monitoring provides a differential profile in terms of some basic parameters, largely indicating that the Dissolved Oxygen (DO) level remain mostly higher than the permissible limit, as also the coliform bacteria count. Under such water quality scenario, preventive action at source becomes compulsive but the want of infrastructure for waste water treatment facilities continue to pose a major problem. (p. 149)

Besides River Ganga is used as lavatory by homeless people as well as by the people who live in homes without toilet and that increases the level of pollution of the water of Ganga. Regarding groundwater the report has expressed a great concern. The report mentions,

> The extent of groundwater development can be understood by the following data of groundwater withdrawal from Kolkata Municipal Corporation owned tube wells (Banerjee & Roy, 1992; Sikdar, 1999):
>
> 1956 – 55 million litres per day
> 1989 – 182 million litres per day
> 1992 – 219 million litres per day
> 1994 – 227 million litres per day
>
> As a result of this development, there has been a noticeable change in the hydrological regime. Obviously the situation must have changed further over last more than a decade. The over-abstraction of groundwater may not only cause serious concern for the future, but Kolkata being located in delta, the city can also face the problem of subsidence. (p. 150)

Besides withdrawal of a large quantity of groundwater, it also has led to the problem of arsenic pollution in the groundwater.

From the government report, thus it becomes evident that environmental governance is not going properly in West Bengal. Lack of coordination among different departments and other authorities resulted in non-performance of duties. But the report is silent about the corrupt nexus between political authority, local administration and the promoter/developer/businessmen that leads to the increase in all sorts of environmental hazards. Rampant construction on the seaside by the businessmen and hoteliers is taking place in violation of coastal regulations, in defiance of and/or an account of indifference on the inefficiency of coastal zone management authority. There is also an overt inability to draw a complete coastal zone management map covering the entire state. All these point to the inability to develop a harmonized system of response that can be operative during an emergency.

Increasing environmental hazards in the sea coasts of West Bengal

It has already been observed that *Hyogo Framework* views that 'events of hydrometeorological origin constitute the large majority of disasters'. Among these, floods and tropical cyclones hit the coastal areas most. Almost all the river basins and deltaic regions of West Bengal are flood prone due to the inadequate capacity of rivers to carry the extra water of heavy rainfall or the high flood discharge. Besides, high tidal waves due to cyclones also cause flood. Report on *Disaster Management in India* (Ministry of Home Affairs, Government of India, 2011, p. 21): 'Vulnerability to floods and other natural disasters is caused by the high population density, widespread poverty, unemployment, illiteracy, enormous pressure on rural land, and an economy traditionally dominated by agriculture.' Being the fourth populous state, West Bengal has a high density of population. All other causes of floods as mentioned also are present in West Bengal. The said report on *Disaster Management in India* also mentions that 'the major natural disaster that affects the coastal regions of India is cyclone and as India has a coastline of about 7516 kms, it is exposed to nearly 10 per cent of the world's tropical cyclones'. East Coast of India consists of 2,545 km within which West Bengal has 157 km of coastal length. That way coastal West Bengal is vulnerable to floods and cyclones.

In the pre-disaster phase, *West Bengal State Disaster Management Policy & Frame Work* (Department of Disaster Management Government of West Bengal, ND, p. 14) stipulates that West Bengal State Disaster Management Authority would

- Incorporate disaster reduction, prevention and mitigation in socio-economic development planning;

- Give recognition to and ensure that district administration and local authorities are able to enforce safety standards and rules and strengthen their institutional capacity to deal with disasters and implement disaster management plans;
- Facilitate in establishment of an enabling legislative and financial framework for disaster management, with due attention to the role of the different tiers of Government, the private sector and individuals.

But going by the sea beach in Mandarmani in East Midnapore district one may find the blatant violations of all sorts of CRZ notifications.

Mandarmani, a village on the sea coast of East Midnapore – with once abundance of red crabs and beach pines and with hard sand beach on which cars can be driven, is governed by panchayat at the local level. Since more than 15 years back, hotel business began to thrive in this village with the permission from panchayat authority showing utter disregard to CRZ notification. Initially it was some sort of ignorance on the part of panchayat to permit the hotel owners to establish hotels there. On 7 August 2006 West Bengal Pollution Control Board (WBPCB) imposed closure order on some hotels and directed OC of the Ramnagar Police Station to implement the order and directed the West Bengal State Electricity Board to take steps for immediate disconnection of electricity. Thereafter, not only the orders were not complied with but also the hotels continued to be constructed on the Mandarmani sea beach flouting all rules.

The *Telegraph Kolkata* reports on 25 October 2014 that 'during a visit to Mandarmani in January 2012, Mamata Banerjee [CM] had instructed the district administration to ensure that new hotels do not come up in the area. Local panchayats were stopped from giving permission for construction of hotels'. Even after that 'at least 19 hotels that have come up at the beach resort Mandarmani after January 2012, violating coastal regulations and flouting a directive by the chief minister against new constructions'.

So first it was the ignorance of the panchayat regarding CRZ notification dated 19 February 1991 that construction cannot be carried out in

> the coastal stretches of seas, bays, estuaries, creeks, rivers and backwaters which are influenced by tidal action (in the landward side) up to 500 metres from the High Tide Line (HTL) and the land between the Low Tide Line (LTL) and the HTL.

Then it was the arrogance of the hoteliers, administration and political leaders to vandalize the beach flouting all acts.

Priority of Environment Protection Act: Section 24(1) of E Protection Act:

> Subject to the provisions of sub section (2), the provisions of this Act and the rules or orders made there in shall have effect notwithstanding anything inconsistent therewith contained in any enactment other than this Act. On January 06, 2014, the Supreme Court has directed that 'under Section 3(3) of the Environment (Protection) Act, 1986, the Central Government should appoint a National Regulator for appraising projects, enforcing environmental conditions for approvals and to impose penalties on polluters.' [*T.N. Godavarman Thirumulpad v. Union of India & Ors.*]

Nevertheless, environmentalists in India often earn bad reputation as (i) obstructionists, who obstruct the development and thereby always pour water on the scope of employment for the poor people of India; and (ii) puppets in the hands of rival industrialists who blackmail in the name of ecosystem protection. The irony of the situation is that the problem of unemployment for the hapless poor and the burning desire for instant money by the filthy rich businessmen complement each other's need. Environmental concern here plays the role of a spoilsport from the notion of a monstrous social justice. So unless the basic concerns of poverty are dealt with, the hope for environmental sustainability will remain an elusive dream in the context of social justice.

Conclusion

The case of Mandarmani sea beach perfectly shows that just existence of laws cannot ensure the reduction of hazards interacting with physical, social and economic vulnerabilities of a community. Rampant violation of environmental laws on account of indifference or inefficiency of authority and an overt inability to draw a complete environmental management map covering the entire state are increasing the risk of disasters at every moment.

In 1972 in the plenary session of the United Nations Conference on Human Environment in Stockholm, the then prime minister of India, Smt. Indira Gandhi linked up lack of environmental awareness with poverty. In her convincing speech Mrs Gandhi observed:

> On the one hand the rich look askance at our continuing poverty, on the other they warn us against their own methods. We do not wish

to impoverish the environment any further and, yet, we cannot for a moment forget the grim poverty of large numbers of people. Are not poverty and need the greatest polluters? (Gandhi, 1972)

Crux of the politics of environmental governance lies in using poverty for systematic rampant violation of environmental laws with an utter arrogance. Here lies the real challenge of disaster risk reduction.

Acknowledgement

Author acknowledges the expertise of Mr Kallol Basu, an advocate of the Calcutta High Court in writing this chapter.

References

Bandyopadhyay, J., Chopra, K. & Ghosh, N. (2013). 'Environmental Governance: The Crucial Interface of Science, Economics and Policy' in J. Bandyopadhyay, K. Chopra & N. Ghosh (eds.) *Environmental Governance: Approaches, Imperatives and Methods*. New Delhi: INSEE.

Banerjee, I. & Sinha Roy, S. P. (1992). Management of Groundwater Resources in Calcutta Metropolitan District Area. *Proc. Sem. Calcutta Water Supply-Techno-Economic Options*.

Basher, R. (FALL 2008). 'Disaster Impacts: Implications and Policy Responses' in Social Research. *Disasters: Recipes and Remedies*, *75*(3), 937–954.

Bhattacharyya, R. (2015). Policy Interventions for Slum Improvement and Poverty Alleviation: A Case Study of Low Cost Housing under JNNURM in the Kolkata Municipal Corporation Area. *West Bengal Political Science Review*, *17*(1 & 2), ISSN 2230–8296, [Ed. Basu, Gautam Kumar], 210–230.

Dept. of Disaster Management, Govt. of West Bengal. *West Bengal State Disaster Management Policy & Frame Work*. Retrieved 7 August 2015 from http://wbdmd.gov.in/writereaddata/WEST_BENGAL_DISASTER_MANAGEMENT_POLICY.pdf

Freeman, P. K. & Kunreuther, H. (April 2002). Environmental Risk Management for Developing Countries. *The Geneva Papers on Risk and Insurance: Issues and Practice*, *27*(2), Special Issue on Risk Management, Palgrave Macmillan, 196–214.

Gandhi, I. (1972). What They Said – (Address of) Indira Gandhi. *What Happened in Stockholm, Science and Public Affairs – Bulletin of the Atomic Scientists*, *28*(7), Educational Foundation for Nuclear Science, 35–38 (36).

Government of India, Ministry of Home Affairs. (2011). *Disaster Management in India*. Retrieved 7 August 2015 from www.indiaenvironmentportal.org.in/files/file/disaster_management_india1.pdf

Guha, R. (15 February 1997). Social-Ecological Research in India: A 'Status' Report. *Economic and Political Weekly*, *32*(7), 345–352.

Kanwar, P. & Singla, C. (2009). 'Environmental Protection Vis-à-Vis Judicial Activism' in M. S. Gill & J. Kewlani (eds.) *Environmental Conscience: Socio-Legal and Judicial Paradigm*. New Delhi: Concept Publishers.
Planning Commission, Government of India. (2010). *West Bengal Development Report*. New Delhi: Academic Foundation.
Sikdar, P. K. (1999). Development Dynamics and Management of Groundwater in and around Calcutta, India. *Indian Journal of Geology*, *71*(3), 173–186.
The Telegraph Kolkata. (25 October 2014). Retrieved 7 August 2015 from www.telegraphindia.com/1141025/jsp/bengal/story_18960662.jsp#.VaJJj19Viko

23 Disaster risk reduction and city governance

P. K. Chaubey

Introduction

Much of the attention was earlier focused on disaster management which was then considered as post-disaster management activities and meant taking care of post-disaster problems and conducting operations which were better known as relief operations. They were identified as rescuing people affected by the event, clearing place of bodies and materials which could potentially cause diseases, providing relief for survival in terms of food, water, medicines, shelter and possibly feed for the animals, and, a little later, not so much as a part of disaster management, rehabilitation of people and reconstruction of place and attempts for restoring livelihood. There was a very little effort for the prevention of occurrence or mitigation for the severity of hazards or preparedness for meeting the challenges posed by disasters. It was perhaps not understood that human intervention could also mitigate the fury of disaster. It was least understood that too much of human intervention in natural processes could become an interference and be unwelcome by nature. However, as consciousness about climate change and its repercussions on frequency and amplitude of hazards increased, attention was also paid to climate resilience but its specifics have still to be adequately incorporated in disaster management approach.

Taking cognizance of rapidly rising human toll and economic losses due to natural disasters, the United Nations in its General Assembly in 1989 declared the last decade of the past century as the International Decade of Natural Disaster Reduction (IDNDR) and passed a resolution to make concerted international effort, especially in developing countries, to reduce the loss of life, damage to property and disruption of social and economic activities caused by natural disasters. The point, as noted by High Powered Committee (India), is that the focus of attention in disaster management shifted hereafter from rescue and relief to preparedness and mitigation. By 2005, in World Conference on Disaster Reduction (held in Kobe, Hyogo, Japan), a detailed framework of strategic goals, priority areas for action and tasks for stakeholders at operational levels, was evolved. A few years later, United Nations International Strategy for Disaster Reduction announced two years, 2010 and 2011, to be devoted to safer cities.

After facing quite a few disasters in the beginning of the past century, our parliament enacted National Disaster Management Act in December 2005 and the onus from Ministry of Agriculture except for drought to Ministry of Home Affairs for earthquakes, tsunami, floods and cyclones.[1] We also created Disaster Management Authorities at various levels with prime minister (PM), chief ministers (CM) and district magistrates (DM) as heads, organized disaster relief forces at different levels and strengthened institutions for carrying out training, doing documentation, preparing hazard maps, compiling city profiles and perhaps putting in place management information system coordinating several agencies and ministries.[2]

Yet there was little to suggest that human activities, particularly developmental activities, might be aggravating the risk of hazards and exacerbating the impact of disasters – specifically in the cities where development activities in terms of building infrastructure are carried out more intensively and extensively, which tend to make people more vulnerable and cause disruption in the people's sense of community.

Development activities have to be so carried out that they reduce the risk of hazards and make people less vulnerable but also improve communities' coping capacity. This will keep the scale of government operations not so high as to dislocate its other developmental and welfare activities. This aspect is yet to sink in the thinking and thought on disaster management discipline and practice. If our development activities keep in mind a long-term perspective, looking beyond nose, while planning and designing the complexion of physical infrastructure facilities for a locale well integrated with ethos of the people, we will do quite well. Paradigm of 'more' development engendering increased risk of disaster has to be replaced by 'better' development and reduced risk of disasters. Trade-off between doing positive activities and undoing negative activities for resources which we face today would then be less severe. We should not look for development opportunities occasioned by disasters, which unfortunately some scholars working in the area have pointed out in literature.

However, we focus in this chapter on the acts of commission and omission by governments and parastatal agencies whose employees, due to their attitude of indifference, coupled with their ignorance of consequences, cause problems of disastrous proportion, particularly in cities.

Disasters mostly human made

Disasters were accepted as natural phenomena or even supernatural phenomena; humans could do little about them but propitiate for community sins. Except drought, all disasters were seen as sudden occurrence of hazardous events. Floods, tsunamis, earthquakes, volcanic eruptions, landslides, hailstorms, cyclones, thunderstorms and forest fires were all seen as acts of God, which involved no human agency, and it was accepted that it is not realistically possible to guard against such occurrences and they occur directly and exclusively due to natural causes which have been classified in literature as geological, hydrological and meteorological in their origin. It was also accepted that their occurrences could not have been prevented by any amount of foresight, plan and care.

However, later on, it was recognized that disaster could be human made as well. Man could be responsible for immediate trigger, or he might have raised the risk of hazard by sheer negligence while planning the development. According to the Disaster Management Act (2005) of India

> disaster means a catastrophe, mishap, calamity or grave occurrence in any area, arising from natural or man-made causes, or by accident or negligence, which results in substantial loss of life or human suffering, or damage to, or degradation of, environment, and is of such a nature or magnitude as to be beyond the coping capacity of the community of the affected area

which defines a disaster with its possible causes and consequences. So does the UNDP which portrays it as 'a social crisis situation occurring when a physical phenomenon of natural, socio-natural or anthropogenic origin negatively impacts vulnerable populations causing intense, serious and widespread disruption of normal functioning of the affected social unit' (Western, 2007). These definitions do not provide an exhaustive list of the hazardous phenomena or events but seriously recognize the role of acts of man in the acts of God in disaster context. Normally, we recognize that disasters cause loss of life and/or property, as if taking cue from the duties of classical state, but the definition of the Indian Act includes damage to the environment. In fact, the triumvirate of environment, disaster and development took quite some time to hang together.

Scholars have counted dozens of hazards, and some of them cross-classified the hazards by two dichotomies of natural/human and sudden/over a period. Such scholars include within disasters even occurrences of pandemic influenza and civil strife. Famines and droughts are long term but natural, whereas weapons of mass destruction – chemical, radiological, nuclear or biological – are all human-made. They further characterize on the basis of frequency, magnitude of impact and geographical coverage. Floods are more frequent, while tornadoes are more violent.

To the list of fire by short circuit and road and rail transport accidents were added in the recent years stampedes, oil spills and nuclear radiation. Some do wish to add war, terrorism and deliberate attacks also, which are pretty old phenomena but not accepted as disasters. ILO classifies disasters into natural and technological categories and raises the level of practically all industrial accidents, compromising occupational health and safety to that of disasters (Bertazzi, 1996).

Most of the natural phenomena are not new. They were there perhaps before man came into existence. Man found nature bountiful and intervened extensively and called it civilizational triumph. Natural processes turned into disasters for us because of our follies. In fact, there is an assertion that 90 per cent of disasters happen due to human causes while hazards may be natural. Should we adjust with nature or should we overcome nature? There is no easy answer. Should we not build dams so that there is no breach which may cause disaster? Should we build dams so strong that they do not breach? In the former case, we live life less livable. In the latter, we do not know how strong a damn has to be and for how many years; and do we have technology to ward off all kinds of mishappenings and what is the cost? As an alternative, should we go for several small dams? A prudent principle in this context is to maximize net benefit over cost, keeping in reckoning probabilities of good happenings and bad happenings. It is a difficult proposition, yet that is what is adopted in principle and to a large extent in practice by man. There is limit to his clairvoyance, but there is no limit to his myopism. That is why we have so many philosophical discourses. The view that man could accidentally or by negligence be behind disasters is emerging quite dominant. It suggests that the laws dealing with negligence could be strengthened so that individuals and agencies, both private and public, could be identified and liability fixed.

Important point is that our development activities might also aggravate the risk of occurrence of certain disasters besides the fact such a development may not be sustainable in inter-generational terms. It was therefore reasoned that we ought to plan our development strategy in ways that the risk of disaster does not increase with our development activities. Though quite a few scholars do point out to the fact that disaster might provide development opportunities, it is not a correct attitude to look at the things. Now a global view is emerging that our developmental activities are causing climate change beyond raising global temperature by producing greenhouse gases.

There is also a view that we could reduce the risk of some of the disasters from taking place if we cannot prevent them altogether. Contemporary sober view holds that the risk of disaster could definitely be reduced in certain cases with better designing and planning by taking better care of environmental factors. If we cannot build disaster-proof places for human beings which should be our immediate concern, we can definitely reduce the disaster of risk or perhaps minimize it through stricter compliance of building bye-laws.

The issue is what do you do if, in quite a few cases, governments are themselves causing disasters either by accident or by negligence or by quarrel between them in the name of development or ignoring their duties towards regulations of private actions and activities despite the availability of framework? We have a bizarre kind of check-and-balance system in which executive wings of different levels of governments are at loggerheads. Chennai floods have exposed the manner in which the disaster was made by man in the manner in which natural drainage was constructed upon, natural waterways were blocked and the dam was irresponsibly managed.

Experts in disaster management express ‘disaster’ in terms of a formula in which the product of hazard and vulnerability is divided by capacity where they define ‘hazard’ as a rare or extreme event seriously threatening human life, property or activity (though not recession!). There are many things amiss in the formula, but it conveys the message. Disasters cause loss of life and/or property, but more importantly they hit people psychologically and may leave traumatized. A serious disruption of the functioning of a community, causing widespread human, material or environmental losses which exceed the ability of the affected people to cope using its own resources, is actually the disaster for that community. For a given intensity of hazard, two communities may not face the same level of disaster, because of either preparedness or capacity to cope. It has been pointed out that for earthquakes of the same Richter scale that hit two different countries (say Haiti and the US), the loss of life was widely different. For a given level of hazard, reduction of vulnerability and enhancement of capacity are the obvious answers for reducing disaster. So some scholars feel that proper development and deployment of science and technology is the answer. Vulnerability is thus reduced. Capacity of the community or government can be increased through equipping people better to face the disaster when it strikes. Thus, intensity of hazards can be reduced, vulnerability of people can be reduced and coping capacity can be raised.

Voracious city appetite and clueless villages

Cities have been shown to be a synonym of culture except by the likes of Edward Carpenter who considered them a kind of illness and actually wrote a book with the title *Civilisation: Its Cause and Cure* in 1889 where he proposes that civilization is a form of disease and all human societies pass through it. Civilization does not last for more than a thousand years, and no society has ever passed through it successfully. He proposes a life worth living, which is close to nature. Gandhi, who was in agreement with Carpenter, found 'agriculture civilization' or 'village civilization' to be the optimum civilization: note that he never argued man to move back to jungles and caves despite his belief in naturopathy. But surely he did not vote for cities in civilizational terms. He always thought that cities are parasites on villages and contribute very little in the well-being of the villages. His village civilization includes all that comes with agriculture, all crafts and handicrafts, all leisure and pastime activities. It was more symbiotic in its approach as a waste it produced in one process was a resource for another process. Most people argued that Indian civilization was village civilization but argued that a preponderant population of India lived in villages and India had hundreds of thousands of villages. In fact, we have quite a few oldest living cities in the world. If India is a village civilization it is because of ethos of its people, their value system and their activities, including those of pastime activities. Gandhi was not a status-quoist, and he wanted villages to develop and villagers to have more leisure time even with his fad for bread labour and dignity of labour. So what was his limit of development? Villages should develop but not into cities.

But here is Adam Smith who thought, reflecting on the early phase of industrialization in Europe, that 'manufacturing is the industry of the town as agriculture is the industry of the country'. This kind of spatial specialization seems to be natural extension of quid pro quo exchange that came to dominate in Europe. But later scholars did not accept it uncritically. For Gandhi, villages did not depend on cities while cities depended on villages. Then, how could cities survive? Most cities do not have enough agriculture of their own – not only for food but more importantly for raw material for industry. If there is nothing in the cities that villagers need why would they part with their surpluses to the city folk. The distinction between city/town and village is not the same as between industry and agriculture but, it seems, was not very different in Europe 200 years ago.

Villages look forward to get transformed into cities. Some of the districts in India are 100 per cent urbanized in terms of activities the people therein are pursuing. All union territories, barring two or three, and all small states in India have crossed the mark of 50 per cent. Tamil Nadu and Kerala are close to 50 per cent mark, while Maharashtra and Gujarat are well beyond 40 per cent mark. We already had 53 million-plus cities in India accounting for more than 40 per cent of urban population, which is itself more than 30 per cent of the total population of the country. In the first decade of the 21st century, the growth of urban population has been more than that of rural counterpart in absolute terms. In terms of the rate of growth, urban rate has been 2.5 times the rural rate (Census of India, 2011). In terms of absolute size urban population of India is more than the total population size of the US.

Cities are said to be not having the concentration of only population but also economic activities. They work as networks and have a lot of construction activity in terms of buildings and other infrastructure. Urban proponents are found to claim, with some exaggeration, that 31 per cent population (read 'labour force') is contributing 63 per cent of the GDP of the country (Ministry of Urban Development, 2015) and might contribute 70–75 per cent (Barclays, 2014). But what kind of cities we are building! Most scholars point out towards swelling slums, where we have all kinds of human problems, squalors, poverty, illiteracy and drug addiction and which are associated with all kinds of crimes. That criminal activities that are not unique to slum dwellers should not go unnoticed. But there is no doubt that there is a need for clear land use plan where all stakeholders are taken due care of.

Urban disasters and government

According to some accounts, urban disasters take place in the shape of collapse of structures like bridges and flyovers; bursting of pipelines carrying water or gases; incidents in mines, on roads and railway lines;

explosions in factory establishments; fires through short circuit, pollution of air and water and so on. They add to this list also terrorist activities, arson and loot, communal riots and civil strife, which are more city-oriented. Some of us have reservations on listing many such activities as disasters. We think human activities caused by accident and negligence, if they result in substantial loss of life or human suffering and/or damage to or substantial degradation of environment, could be called disasters. Neither a homicide nor cutting of a plant could be called a disaster. But a deliberate human mischief, which a terrorist activity is, could not be called disaster. Moreover, what we think is a mischief could be a mission for those who carry it out.

It is often pointed by scholars that urban growth puts pressure on physical infrastructure, socio-cultural fabric, natural environment and institutional systems. As analysed in a consultation report called 'India City Profile: Climate and Disaster Resilience' by a team of scholars from Kyoto University, National Institute of Disaster Management (NIDM) and Sustainable Environmental and Ecological Development Society (SEEDS), planned urban development in India was far less than needed to accommodate ad hoc urban population growth and thus forcing people to live in high-risk zones.

Urban disasters are not much different from non-urban disasters in terms of quality, nature or cause but by scale they become important. As urban areas are densely populated in residences and in workplaces, their vulnerability becomes higher and therefore the impact is also much larger. As there are economies in scale in putting in convenient infrastructure, we often resort to multi-storied offices and residences, elevators, electrical appliances and a lot of pipes and wires underground. But the same turns into a set of inferno when a hazard strikes. The same structures make evacuation impossible, despite a lot of safety provisions. Roads turn into streets and streets into lane for the level of traffic, compounded by a free vehicular choice, a city witnesses today. Cities are no more of Greek small in size and hardly marked by 'urbanity'.

What is the government supposed to be doing? A lot of activities of urban development are carried out by the government. Believing that the government is a benevolent despot, government is also entrusted, armed with statutory laws, to regulate private activities with the understanding that all persons in a given society are not equally enlightened or they have incentive in not pursuing the line in the larger societal interest. In fact, many of the governmental activities – at least of developmental nature – are carried out by private agencies whom the government outsources the activities. Government is supposed to be vigilant when activities are carried on its behalf and when they are carried out in private interests lest they should pose threat to other fellow being or the society at large. Urban locales have all the more reasons for extra caution. We as private persons are likely to have less access to scientific testing and do less scientific planning as these activities may cost huge sums. We as private persons are likely to cover some space around our building as we could afford larger space in better locality. Government has to keep tap.

We do recognize issues of regulations that are not well implemented whether it is about building plans or fixing of elevators or fire extinguishers and functioning of hydrants. We hear and read in newspapers about several accidents and several casualties. Governments do not take due cognisance of their non-performing officials, and of late they find it easy to pass on the buck for political reasons. The result is that our urban planning and urban planners are risk-insensitive.

The same is the case when it comes to development. Many years have passed when motorists were advised to keep the tyre pressure right rather than governments to maintain roads in good condition. Recently, higher courts have suggested governments to improve the speed breakers lest they break the vehicles and wreak the human bodies. Many persons just died as the speed breakers were bad and light had gone and rider could not notice to take care of. Kerosene lamps were dim but were at least timely lit. Streetlight might go anytime. Nocturnal civilization could not thrive in the absence of light. So what we argue out is that governments are at fault in many societies by creating 'holes' in the kind development which they promoted in the heads and minds of the people.

I am, however, going to raise an issue that is what if the government is itself to be blamed for much of disaster we witness! I am doing it by a particular hazard that has been entirely created by human agency by ill-conceived planning of roads and flyovers. And it is this dislocation in urban life, caused by not-so-heavy downpour in the absence of flood in rivers passing through/by the city.

Why blame nature? It's your government

Most cities in India suffer internal floods almost each rainy season. Recent Chennai flooding is a classic case as was Delhi and Mumbai in the past several times. Experts in disaster management and common people alike prefer to call it waterlogging. But one can see streets are waterlogged, leading to chaos in terms of huge traffic jams, breakdown of vehicles, out-of-order traffic signals, overflow of drains, people moving their sundry gadgets to safer places in knee-deep to waist-deep water. Trees get uprooted, and it is learnt that their roots had weakened not by age but because of poor municipal care. This is the scene witnessed in posh localities. Think of the poor colonies! At times sewage water gets mixed up with drains and water supply systems; in addition, with garbage littered on roads they lead to water-borne diseases. Sometimes, manholes remain open and live wire touch water claiming human and cattle lives. Water does enter many premises leading to what one can call 'internal flood'.

This all happens even when there is no flood in the rivers passing through the cities or by the city or there is no river around the city. Post-rain roads witness potholes, pavements are found broken and plastic material littered everywhere. Citizens are responsible for some of these troubles but, for others, government or say governments of several levels – in our context, state government and local government.

It happens in many urban areas, particularly metros whether it is Mumbai or Delhi or Kolkata or Chennai. Most of the cities have one or more rivers, big or small. All drains and sewages are emptying into the rivers. If rivers get flooded from upstream, open storm drains cannot be allowed to empty in the rivers as there is fear of back flow. Situation becomes worse. But when rivers do not get flood, the question is why should cities get drowned?

It was not happening say 40 years ago. Something must have gone wrong somewhere. It is not because of climate change. Rains have of course become more erratic, and the number of days of heavy downpour might have increased. It is claimed that the frequency and amplitude of temperature and rains have perceptibly changed. But I think highest precipitation has not gone higher on any given day.

The story is narrated thus. First all local depths were in competition, for construction by private parties who were permitted by governments and by governments which rarely seek permission. Then, roads are raised and broadened, making nearby areas and premises, including government ones, good ponds during the rainy reason. Governments make law for others, but they are the chief violators. Just witness police vehicles in Delhi! In their decision-making processes other stakeholders are rarely involved. Private parties are forbidden to carry out activities which create problems for others as two interests cannot be added. Simple Pareto principle does not allow interpersonal comparison of utilities. Then, there could be no development activities. To circumvent Pareto issue, compensation principle was evolved to compensate the parties suffering from development so that development works may be carried out and activities do not only prove to be zero-sum game or negative-sum game but ensure a positive-sum win-win game. Human societies have been using it since time immemorial. Pareto only gave a neat expression.

Metro operator in Delhi, formally known Delhi Metro Rail Corporation (DMRC), for example, has been adequately compensating the parties who had to suffer during construction activities. They took full care in their construction activities that people are least inconvenienced. Does the Public Works Departments (PWDs) do the same? Do they ever sit on their own with the parties likely to suffer from development? If nearby properties happen to be owned by a government, the day-sitters in those buildings are least likely to protest or approach the wrong-doing agencies unless they face an emergency situation. Private parties may not have enough strength to force the PWD to listen to them lest they are booked for obstructing the public servants to carry out their duty. The result is a peculiar scene. The cities have roads above the nearby built-up areas – having offices, residences, commercial complexes and streets. Highways in plain areas used to be above the level of fields around, but between fields and roads there were natural drains. Town roads used to be much below the plinth of houses. Are town-planning rules so bad that they permit inundation of neighbouring areas? Do we go by town-planning rules? Perhaps, not.

We cannot believe that our government engineers and officials do not understand the concept of externalities. In quite a few of our activities, there is a third party, not a direct beneficiary of the activity – neither as consumer, nor as producer – but gets affected either positively or negatively. One does not do much because one undertakes the activity in one's interest and it is the sweet will of the third party to become a second party or not. But if my activities are going to harm a third party, they have every right to stop me from undertaking it or seek adequate compensation. The principle is now well recognized in the case of, for instance, land acquisition proposals and legislation. In many other cases too, social impact assessment is now being carried out. But when it comes to city roads, it seems the detailed project report does not take this factor into account. This is the act of commission of wrong by the government whichever does it.

Excess road water is supposed to be carried away by proper drainage system. First, our drainage system is faulty which does not accept the excess rain water. Second, our drains remain chocked due to a lot of solid waste material, including thin plastic bags which either keep flying on streets or find way into drainage, thanks to our scavenging staff. Drains are not cleared in time. If they are cleaned at all, the slurry from the drains is kept by the side of the drains. It is left there deliberately to dry as, I am told, wet material cannot as per some archaic law be carried away on road. If this is the law it is pretty not bad because it pollutes the local air making difficult for pedestrians to breathe besides wet material gets dropped on way. Anyway, much before it dries, it gets carried back to the drains. Flood water and dirty drain water both fill the streets, lanes, bye lanes, premises and houses. People have to wade knee-deep through this dirty water. So not only roads and streets get flooded by rain but premises and houses also get flooded. People by and large have forgotten to enjoy rains by drenching in open; they worry about their health and property. This is the act of omission by the governments.

We have all read that a particular flyover was not properly designed for the traffic; it was likely to receive and it has to be widened. We may blame calculations. When a road is widened disproportionate to traffic requirement, we may blame short-sightedness. But a road is raised compared to other roads or neighbouring properties, there is every doubt that neighbouring areas will get inundated. If road-constructing agencies have no truck with drain maintaining agencies, the result is what we witness. Several such wrongs are committed. When hazards occur they become disasters simply because there was no adequate preparation for carrying away excess water. In fact, drains should never remain choked as they are breeding ground for injurious worms and insects. In any case, drains should not wait for rains to clean them! This is an act of omission.

We have tried to show here that many disasters are natural but they get aggravated because of our sins. We are not likely to avoid all environmental sins which are signs of civilizations, but we can perhaps moderate quite a few of them. Guided by our personal interests, we, the human beings, are likely to be frail. But we also create state and to run it, government and want them to act according to our aggregate social will. We do not want it to be despot in choosing to commit and omit. Unfortunately it does. Moreover if it has several levels they are not found to be scoring points not on good deeds but pointing fingers towards other governments for the misfortune. The public feels cheated.

If we go on creating hazards with so-called development, there is no way we can reduce the risk of disaster. There is a callous neglect on the part of governments, as far our experience in India goes, which keep blaming each other. It seems as if they were looking for such opportunities for blaming each other even if they are of the proportion of disaster dislocating life and livelihood. I would like to restrain myself from saying that bureaucrats were looking for making money through opportunities occasioned by disasters. It was once articulated that 'everybody loves drought'.

Government agencies are rarely found talking. We often read PWD telling newspaper and electronic media reporters that they had written two years ago to the railways for this, but there had been no response! They kept waiting for years together as though they do not have phone or phone numbers.

Conclusion

The chapter began with a discussion of hazards and disasters which are primarily natural, called acts of God, and anthropogenic – acts of man. Some of these hazards occur all of a sudden, some give out clear warnings and some of which develop in the course of time, but man cannot do much about them. The disasters become riskier when human mistakes get to combine with natural fiery. However, some of them are specific to urban habitations. Thus, urban habitations may suffer from general as well as urban-specific disasters. Urban style of living has been favourable for a few millennia and has come to stay, and therefore urban developments have to be resilient and sustainable. We choose to ignore the reasons for the disappearance of many urban civilizations in the antiquity. We pride in their marvels and tend not to analyse whether their decay and disappearance was also human-made.

In this chapter, my attempt was to highlight the acts of governments – both acts of commission and acts of omission, taking the case of frequent inundations during downpours, not necessarily very heavy, even in the absence of flood in the river(s) passing through or passing by the cities. This has been observed more frequently in metropolitan habitations in the recent decades. The blame has often been laid by disaster analysts on unplanned urban growth, with implications for migration of population, ignoring the fact of ill-planned developments. In fact, our urban planners have shown serious ignorance of negative externalities and gleefully highlighting positive externalities like enhancement of property value due to newly created park.

I choose to conclude with a larger concern. It is about sustainable development. It is not clear whether the kind of urban development we shall be pursuing is really sustainable. Economist Solow has allowed for some substitution between natural capital, physical capital and human capital, keeping the total intact. But there is so much focus on future generation that people tend to forget about the present generation in this discourse. Intra-generational discourses are deliberately kept away from inter-generational discourses as if they belong to two different worlds. Concern for children is so prominent in our breast that we tend to ignore and neglect our brethren's concerns. This is not good for humanity.

Notes

1 Biological, chemical, nuclear, air and railway disasters have their own nodal ministries. For air, railways and nuclear disasters, nodal ministries are Civil Aviation, Railways and Atomic Energy, respectively. For biological and chemical disasters, responsible ministries are Health & Family Welfare and Environment and Forests & Climate Change, respectively.

2 When we open, for example, the website of Central Water Commission (in existence since 1945, now an attached office of Ministry of Water Resources, River Development and Ganga Rejuvenation), we find several links, reports, information regarding its regular journal like *Bhagirath*, and current status of flood in several rivers – level and tendency. But when we open the link for the flood forecast site of Mathura (Prayag Ghat) for Basin Ganga of the River Yamuna, we find the division's name as Executive Engineer, Upper Yamuna Division, New Delhi, and when try to open this one we get to read 'no contact data recorded'.

References

Barclays. (2014). *Urban Population to Contribute 70–75% of India's GDP by 2020, Business Standard*, 20 March 2014. www.business-standard.com/article/news-cm/urban-population-to-contribute-70-75-of-india-s-gdp-by-2020-barclays-114032000273_1.html

Bertazzi, P. A. (1996). *Disasters and Major Accidents, in Chapter 39 on Disasters, Natural and Technological, Encyclopedia of Occupational Health and Safety*. www.ilo.org/. . ./part-vi/disasters-natural-and-technological

Census of India. (2011). *Provisional Population Totals Paper 2, Volume 1 of 2011, Rural-Urban Distribution, India Series 1*. www.censusindia.gov.in/2011-prov-results/paper2/data_files/india/paper2_1.pdf

Western, C. van. (2007). *Glossary of Terms Related to Risk Assessment and Management*. http://drm.cenn.org/Trainings/Multi%20Hazard%20Risk%20Assessment/Lectures_ENG/Session%2001%20Introduction%20to%20risk%20management/background/07%20Glossary%20of%20%20Risk%20Assessment%20terms.pdf

Part VI

Epilogue

24 Disaster laws in India

The way forward

Nivedita P. Haran

The Disaster Management (DM) Act was enacted in 2005 based on which the states (i.e. the provinces) notified their respective rules. The Disaster Management Authority was set up at the centre as the apex body for policy-making, advising and directing ministries, state governments and all other agencies on all matters pertaining to the management of disasters. The National Institute of Disaster Management was set up to build capacity within the government to prepare for and respond to disasters. Mirroring the set-up at the centre, each state established its State Disaster Management Authority headed by the respective chief ministers and the State Executive Committee headed by the chief secretary. Many districts in the country now have a well-equipped control room with reliable communication system and basic equipment to respond to a disaster situation. The National Disaster Response Force is a group of trained professionals with specialized training and equipment pre-positioned across the country in eight strategic locations with its own arrangement for quick mobility.

Achievements

The DM Act provides powers to the notified authority to requisition vehicles, equipment, premises and manpower to respond to a disaster. The act also requires the setting up of two separate funding heads: the National Disaster Response Fund and the National Disaster Mitigation Fund. The erstwhile Calamity Relief Fund is converted into the former that provides a budgeted amount to each state annually based on the recommendation of the finance commission. The Mitigation Fund is to consist of the amount released on an ad hoc basis by the centre to the states for meeting special calamities that may hit a state. Similar funds have been set up in the states, and the guidelines have been formulated on how to administer these funds.

In some states, the Hazard Vulnerability and Risk Assessment Cell is set up to prepare vulnerability maps of the state for the major disasters and to map the legacy data for the last 5–10 years. Riverbank mapping to ensure protection of riverbanks has been taken up in some states, and digitized maps have been prepared. Sensors have been placed upstream to monitor the flow of water on a real-time basis in order to be able to forecast floods downstream. Action is being taken to assess the damage caused by disasters more accurately and scientifically based on remote-sensing data with base maps prior to the disaster and real-time maps during and post disaster. There is also a system in place for ground-truthing such data to remove the possibility of manipulation as this often assumes political sensitiveness as a competition ensues between states to claim higher assistance from the centre.

The capacity to understand disasters and to communicate early warning wherever feasible is on the increase. This is especially true for cyclones, floods and tsunamis. INCOIS, the body set up to monitor tsunamis in the Indian Ocean, works in collaboration with the littoral states. It conducts mock drills on a regular basis to ensure the response network from the NDMA to the SDMA and down to the district and village level works like clockwork. The response time noted during the mock drills may not be the best, but it has definitely improved over time.

The result

The preparedness level when provided with adequate prior warning has seen some major successes: when Cyclone Phalin hit coastal Orissa in early 2014, less than 20 lives were lost; a cyclone of similar intensity in the same area 15 years ago had claimed over 10,000 lives. Similarly the post-disaster rehabilitation has also been better streamlined and made result-oriented: under the Tsunami Rehabilitation Programme, over 11,000 families living in vulnerable areas along the coast of Kerala were relocated to safer areas in disaster-resilient houses. Land was acquired for this purpose and the dwelling units were constructed in record time. However, the performance of some of the states remains largely indifferent. Thus, in spite of the positive cases mentioned earlier, we also have the tragic example of the huge loss of human lives and properties in the Himalayan State of Uttarakhand in the floods of 2013 where preparedness as well as reaching relief to those affected left much to be desired. More recently, the disastrous urban flooding in Chennai left the city inundated for weeks with huge loss of lives and properties.

One can, therefore, say with confidence that the disaster response is largely working in India, a country that is home to about one-fifth of the global population and one-third of the world's poor. But how can it work better and more uniformly in all the states of the country is the relevant question here. All over the world countries are waking up to the importance of preparing themselves better for disaster risk reduction (DRR) and climate change adaptation. While for DRR there is an agreed global framework on which member states can base their actions, the negotiations regarding climate change are yet to reach a final stage. Fortunately, many countries are wisely proceeding with their own priorities to make the lives of their people and their properties safer.

How to make it all work

As a career civil servant with the Government of India, working my way up from the bottom of the ladder, I have had the opportunity to be both at the front end of disasters and at the policy formulation top end. As a young sub-collector over 30 years ago and later as the district collector, it was my responsibility to deal with disasters, arrange rescue from flood-hit areas, relocate people in safe shelters with adequate provision for food and water and arrange return to their homes after the damaged houses were repaired or rebuilt. Disasters include natural disasters (primarily floods, sea erosion, landslide and an occasional tsunami) and anthropogenic ones (such as road accidents and chemical leakage). Two-and-a-half decades later as the professional head of the department, I had the privilege to guide and set up the State Disaster Management Authority in Kerala State and to manage and convene the State Executive Committee as required under the DM Act. Within the short span of three years, based on sound policy initiatives, the DM Training Centre was set up; the HVRA Cell (later converted into the State Emergency Operation Centre) became functional; the State Disaster Rescue Force came into existence; and the DM Policy and the DM Plans at the state, district and panchayat levels were readied and declared for the first time. At an operational level the post-tsunami reconstruction programme was implemented with alacrity and following the policy to Build Back Better. Creditable as these may seem, one has to admit that a lot remains to be done. Let us now focus on what more could have been done.

Priorities

In theory investing in disaster management makes sense as the cost of not investing is much too high.[1] There are now live examples where countries that have taken up disaster management on a serious note have been able to reduce the loss of human lives to almost nil and the loss of property to a fraction of what might otherwise have taken place. The World Bank Report 'Natural Hazards, Unnatural Disasters, The Economics of Effective Prevention' (2010) demonstrates with quantitative evidence that every dollar spent on the prevention of disasters is worth $7 in value of averted disasters.[2] It is also becoming clearer that even without climate change the cost of disasters can triple to USD 185 billion annually by the turn of the century. It may go up to hundreds of billions more if every climate change disaster cost from floods, landslides, storms, hurricanes, sea level rise and so on is added.

So countries, developed or developing, should be rushing to invest in disaster prevention. In developing countries, disasters cause bigger distraction from the growth path, often setting the economy behind by many years. Yet, as we have often seen in India, the danger posed by a potential disaster is unseen and therefore remains distant and does not get the priority it deserves. It is the fundamental economic dilemma of 'limited resources, unlimited needs'. In a developing country the priority would naturally and invariably be given to investment on basic developmental needs: health, education, infrastructure and employment. Policy-makers in developing countries may argue that Switzerland can afford to spend its resources in constructing a completely disaster-resilient additional wing in selected hospitals, which can withstand the severest of earthquakes, landslide or a nuclear disaster. Last year when I visited such a hospital wing near Davos I was both amazed and impressed to see that even the entrance to this underground structure is disaster safe, and it is fully equipped to handle any type of medical emergencies, has alternate power supply and has stored supply of dry food and potable water to last up to five days. This is a perfect example of disaster preparedness.

Yet, in many developing countries, there are many villages that still lack the basic infrastructure, and in such places creating a spare set-up seems a luxury. It is in this context that the statement that poverty is one of the biggest disasters carries added significance. It is high time the developing countries take up eradication of poverty on a mission mode, and while doing so they mainstream disaster prevention and mitigation into their developmental programmes. Developing countries need to learn their lessons from the developed countries and save a large amount of funds by not repeating the mistakes. It is the responsibility of the developed world to share technology, knowledge and resources to help their lesser-developed neighbours to pull themselves up to a minimum level of existence. For it lies in the interest of the developed countries too, indeed the entire global community, to help in the eradication of poverty as a world filled with inequalities makes life dangerous for everyone in each part of the world.

Academicians and administrators: an indispensable collaboration

Another crucial way to hasten the progress on disaster risk reduction is to reduce the gap between policy-makers and academicians. Disaster management is a subject that has attained focus over the last two decades, with countries bringing about suitable changes in their techno-legal framework as well as in enforcing them. It is during these two decades that disaster management has moved from being relief-centric to mitigation and prevention oriented. Earlier to this disaster management was a topic that fell within the domain of the international organizations. It is said that there are at least 50 conferences, seminars and workshops that are held every month globally on issues related to disaster management. Many of these are held within the closed doors of educational institutions. With disaster management now a discipline that provides degrees, there are graduates passing out with specialization on the subject. Also dissertations and theses are being written on topics based on disaster management. But, unfortunately, the result of most of these conferences, seminars and workshops remains confined within the four walls of the conference hall or in the bookshelves of libraries. Some excellent ideas may have been mooted in some of the papers, some technically sound solutions could have been proposed based on extensive field study, and some well-thought-out policy framework may have been strategized by some deep-thinking scholars. Yet these ideas, proposals and strategies remain stillborn. On the other side, administrators struggle to seek cost-effective solutions to tackling disasters and try to frame alternate policies, quite ignorant of the wealth of data gathering dust in our university libraries.

If disaster management is to become a discipline in its own right, the wide chasm that exists between academicians and researchers, on the one hand, and bureaucrats and policy-makers, on the other, has to be bridged. Organizations like the NAPSIPAG[3] have a crucial role to play in this effort. First, every research paper, thesis or article related to disaster management should be forwarded to the NDMA and the SDMA by the head of the institution with clear action points relevant to the government. Second, major universities and institutes having faculty to teach disaster management should hold at least two interactive workshops every year where research scholars and other academic experts should be invited to participate along with selected civil servants both from the field level (i.e. sub-collectors/SDMs and collectors) and from the policy-making level. The contents of these workshops should be a balanced combine of classroom discussions and field visits and activities. Government of India may consider assigning the work of preparing a detailed curriculum for such workshops to a group of experts. NAPSIPAG conferences in the past have already debated this issue and based on those discussions set up the NAPSIPAG Young Scholars and Administrators Forum (NYSAF). Such a forum is the need of the hour and should get activated without further delay.

Capacity building

I wish to briefly touch upon the importance of capacity building in disaster management. While the theoretical issues of hazard-mapping and climate change predictions can be well understood at the global and national levels, there is still a lack of adequate understanding on the topic at the local level. Let it be clear that at the end of the day when a disaster strikes, the first responders are the local authorities and the local people in general, hence the urgency and the need to generate awareness and train the local body officials and elected representatives. Local communities experience floods, droughts and landslides with fearful regularity. If made aware they will be the first to imbibe new ideas and techniques to handle and mitigate these as they will help to improve their own quality of life. In order to address this issue panchayat-level action groups had been set in about 100 panchayats in Kerala. These action groups consisted of volunteers who were trained in 'first-response', first aid, swimming and diving and were trained to act as the eyes and ears of the panchayat head. The result in these 100 panchayats now needs to be evaluated and their impact assessed in order to decide whether the project is worth replicating.

Techno-legal issues

There are also certain basic techno-legal issues that are crying for attention. In order to mainstream disaster resilience into our development programmes, it is necessary to make disaster-resilient construction mandatory for all public buildings. When a disaster takes place, it is the public buildings that act as temporary shelters. Hence government office buildings, educational and health institution buildings and other public premises should invariably be constructed using disaster-resilient technology. Similarly, public or private buildings where public gathers in large numbers, for example hotels, malls, auditorium and stadium, should mandatorily be constructed in a disaster-resilient manner. The cost of the construction will only be marginally higher, but the safety level it would provide would be many times more. In order to enforce this it is necessary to make suitable amendments in the building bye-laws of the state. When the government sets good examples, others are bound to follow.

Findings and conclusion

From the earlier discussion a few areas in disaster law have been identified for urgent attention:

- The institutional set-up as required under the DM Act should be set in all states without fail and the policy, DM Plan and the standard operating procedures (SOPs) should be clearly laid out.
- The DM Act itself is now a decade old and needs a revisit, especially with regard to engaging the local bodies, building capacity and so on.
- The State Disaster Mitigation Fund needs to be set up in every state with clear guidelines; funds need to be sourced from various agencies, corporates and so on and utilized for prevention, mitigation and resilience building.
- In spite of clear evidence, disaster management and adaptation to climate change are not linked either in the DM Act or in administrative functioning. This leads to duplication of efforts and needless wastage of funds which can be avoided.
- The use of renewable energy and mainstreaming disaster management into development projects is essential if efforts are to be effective.
- Disaster management is too important and overarching a subject to be left to the government alone: educational institutions, health institutions, the corporate sector and common citizens should all be engaged in this work.
- In order to strengthen the cutting-edge resilience and adaptability, local task force teams at the district and panchayat levels are a must. These teams act as the eyes and ears and as the foot soldiers for the district collectors and for the panchayat heads. The task force teams need to be adequately trained and provided with the basic resources to act as the first responders in case of a disaster.
- There is a need to introduce insurance against disasters for loss of or damage to property, crop loss and injury or loss of life especially for the economically weaker sections.

- Encroachment and illegal use of public lands, including commons and greens, encroachment on riverbanks and riverbeds, filling up of water bodies and their illegal use should be made into criminal offence invoking strong penal action against the encroachers, the public servants and the elected representatives responsible.

Disaster prevention activities are no doubt working. There have been major improvements in disaster management over the last few decades. Yet the climate clock is ticking and disasters have been occurring frequently. Hence close collaboration between all sections is the need of the hour. Ideas need to be shared, and policy-makers need to keep an open mind to consider new ideas. Academicians need to work towards implementing their proposals.

Notes

1 It is well established that the economic cost of disasters is very high. Many studies have been highlighting this in the last one decade: S. Hallegatte, and V. Przyluski (2010) and R. D. Guha-Sapir, S. Ponserre and F. Vos (2011).

2 The economic benefits of disaster risk reduction have even gone beyond the economic calculations of the World Bank studies. Dedeurwaerdere (1998) and Nepal Red Cross (2008) have taken into account that the benefits of ecosystem restoration of mangroves and rainforests lead to sustainable livelihoods which add to the economic benefits of DRR. Recently, Shreve and Kelman (2014) have studied the benefits of major DRR.

3 NAPSIPAG or Network of Asia Pacific Schools and Institutes of Public Administration and Governance is one of the largest academic networks of academic bodies and universities in the Asia Pacific with a membership of more than 75 institutions and government organizations such as INTAN (Malaysia), IIPA (India), NIPA (Indonesia) and SLIDA (SriLanka).

References

Hallegatte, S. & Przyluski, V. (2010). *The Economics of Natural Disasters: Concepts and Methods. Policy Research Working Paper 5507*. Washington D.C.: The World Bank.

Guha-Sapir, R. D., Ponserre, S. & Vos F. (2011). *Annual Disaster Statistical Review 2011: The Numbers and Trends*. Centre for Research on the Epidemiology of Disasters (CRED), p. 17.

Nepal Red Cross. (2008). *Cost Benefit Analysis of a Nepal Red Cross Society Disaster Risk Reduction Programme*. Kathmandu, Nepal.

Shreve, C. M. & Kelman, I. (2014). Does Mitigation Save? Reviewing Cost-Benefit Analyses of Disaster Risk Reduction. *International Journal of Disaster Risk Reduction*, *10*(Part A) (Dec.), 213–235.

Index